The Cambridge Companion to Victorian and Edwardian Theatre

This *Companion* is designed for readers interested in the creation, production, and interpretation of Victorian and Edwardian theatre, both in its own time and on the contemporary stage. The volume opens with a brief overview and introduction surveying the theatre of the time followed by an essay contextualizing the theatre within the frame of Victorian and Edwardian culture as a whole. Succeeding chapters examine specific aspects of performance, production, and theatre, including the music, the actors, stagecraft, and the audiences themselves; plays and playwriting and issues of class and gender that have developed in recent scholarship are also explored. Chapters also deal with comedy, farce, and melodrama, while other essays bring forward new topics and approaches that cross the boundaries of traditional investigation, including analysis of the economics of theatre and of the theatricality of personal identity.

THE CAMBRIDGE
COMPANION TO
VICTORIAN AND
EDWARDIAN THEATRE

EDITED BY
KERRY POWELL
Miami University, Oxford, Ohio

CAMBRIDGE
UNIVERSITY PRESS

PUBLISHED BY THE PRESS SYNDICATE OF THE UNIVERSITY OF CAMBRIDGE
The Pitt Building, Trumpington Street, Cambridge, United Kingdom

CAMBRIDGE UNIVERSITY PRESS
The Edinburgh Building, Cambridge, CB2 2RU, UK
40 West 20th Street, New York, NY 10011–4211, USA
477 Williamstown Road, Port Melbourne, VIC 3207, Australia
Ruiz de Alarcón 13, 28014 Madrid, Spain
Dock House, The Waterfront, Cape Town 8001, South Africa

http://www.cambridge.org

First published 2004

Printed in the United Kingdom at the University Press, Cambridge

Typeface Sabon 10/13 pt.   *System* LATEX 2$_\varepsilon$ [TB]

A catalogue record for this book is available from the British Library

Library of Congress cataloging in publication data
Cambridge companion to Victorian and Edwardian theatre / edited by Kerry Powell.
p.   cm. – (Cambridge companions to literature)
Includes bibliographical references and index.
ISBN 0 521 79157 X (hardback) – ISBN 0 521 79536 2 (paperback)
1. Theater – England – History – 20th century.   2. Theater – England – History – 19th
century.   3. English drama – 20th century – History and criticism.   4. English drama –
19th century – History and criticism.   I. Powell, Kerry.   II. Series.
PN2595.P663   2003
792'.0942'09034 – dc21   2002041552

ISBN 0 521 79157 X hardback
ISBN 0 521 79536 2 paperback

CONTENTS

Part 3. Text and context

ILLUSTRATIONS

NOTES ON CONTRIBUTORS

NINA AUERBACH is John Welsh Centennial Professor of English at the University of Pennsylvania. She is the author of seven books, of which the most theatrical are *Ellen Terry, Player in Her Time* and *Private Theatricals: The Lives of the Victorians*. She is currently writing about ghosts and those who see them.

MICHAEL R. BOOTH has retired from the Department of Theatre at the University of Victoria and now lives mostly in Greece. He has been a long-time editor of *Theatre Notebook*, and is the author or editor of *English Melodrama* (1965), *English Plays of the Nineteenth Century*, 4 vols. (1969–76), *Victorian Spectacular Theatre, 1850–1910* (London: Routledge, 1981), and *Theatre in the Victorian Age* (Cambridge: Cambridge University Press, 1991).

JACKY BRATTON is Professor of Theatre and Cultural History, Royal Holloway, University of London. Her edited publications include *Music Hall: Performance and Style* (Milton Keynes: Open University Press, 1986); *Melodrama: Stage, Picture, Screen* (joint editor with Jim Crook and Christine Gledhill) (British Film Institute, 1994); and *Four Plays by Arthur Wing Pinero* (Oxford: Oxford University Press, 1995). She is working on a revisionist historiography of the British stage.

SUSAN CARLSON is Professor of English and Associate Provost at Iowa State University. She is currently researching the relationships between suffrage theatre and the production of Shakespearean comedy in early twentieth-century London. She has published two books on women and comedy. She has recently published essays on Aphra Behn, Timberlake Wertenbaker, and Shakespearean production, as well as on suffrage theatre.

MARY JEAN CORBETT is Professor of English and Affiliate of the Women's Studies Program at Miami University. She is the author of *Representing Femininity: Middle-Class Subjectivity in Victorian and Edwardian Women's*

Autobiographies (Oxford: Oxford University Press, 1992) and *Allegories Of Union in Irish and English Writing, 1790–1870: Politics, History, and The Family from Edgeworth to Arnold* (Cambridge: Cambridge University Press, 2000).

JIM DAVIS is Associate Professor of Theatre at the University of New South Wales. He is the author of several books and many articles on nineteenth-century British theatre. His most recent book is *Reflecting the Audience: London Theatregoing 1840–1880* (University of Iowa Press, 2001), co-authored with Victor Emeljanow.

TRACY C. DAVIS is Barber Professor of the Performing Arts at Northwestern University. Her books include *Actresses as Working Women: Their Social Identity in Victorian Culture* (London, Routledge, 1991), *George Bernard Shaw and the Socialist Theatre* (Westport, CT: Greenwood Press, 1994), and *The Economics of the British Stage, 1800–1914* (Cambridge: Cambridge University Press, 2000). She is also co-editor (with Ellen Donkin) of the collections *Women and Playwriting in Nineteenth-Century Britain* (Cambridge: Cambridge University Press, 1999) and *Theories of Theatricality* (forthcoming).

JOSEPH DONOHUE, Professor of English at the University of Massachusetts Amherst, is a theatre historian with special interests in the Victorian and twentieth-century theatre and the plays of Oscar Wilde. He is the author of *Dramatic Character in the English Romantic Age* (Princeton, NJ: Princeton University Press, 1970) and primary editor of a reconstructive edition of the first performance text of *The Importance of Being Earnest* (Gerrards Cross: Colin Smythe, 1995).

SOS ELTIS is a Fellow and Tutor at Brasenose College, Oxford University. She is the author of *Revising Wilde: Society and Subversion in the Plays of Oscar Wilde* (Oxford: Oxford University Press, 1996), and of articles on Victorian theatre, and Bram Stoker's *Dracula*.

VICTOR EMELJANOW is Professor of Drama at the University of Newcastle, Australia. He is a professional theatre director as well as a theatre historian. His most recent work has been on nineteenth-century theatre audiences culminating in the award-winning book *Reflecting the Audience: London Theatregoing 1840–1880* (co-authored with Jim Davis). He is currently researching popular theatregoing in England in the period 1880–1918.

HEIDI J. HOLDER is Associate Professor of English at Central Michigan University. Her work on British, Irish, and Canadian theatre has appeared in such periodicals as the *Journal of Modern Literature*, *Essays in Theatre*, and the *University of Toronto Quarterly*. She has recently published chapters on women dramatists in London's East End (in Tracy C. Davis and Ellen Donkin (eds.), *Women and Playwriting in Nineteenth-Century Britain* (Cambridge University Press, 1999) and on the dramatic writings of Mary E. Braddon (in Marlene Tromp, Pamela Gilbert and Aeron Haynie (eds.), *Beyond Sensation: Mary Elizabeth Braddon in Context*: State University of New York Press, 2000). She is at work on a study of Victorian and Edwardian drama in London's East End.

RUSSELL JACKSON is Director of the Shakespeare Institute and Professor of Shakespeare Studies at the University of Birmingham. His publications include *Victorian Theatre, A New Mermaid Background Book* (London: A. & C. Black, 1989) and critical editions of plays by Oscar Wilde and Henry Arthur Jones.

DAVID MAYER is Emeritus Professor of Drama and Research Professor, University of Manchester. Books include *Harlequin in His Element: The English Pantomime, 1806–1836* (Cambridge, MA: Harvard University Press, 1964) and *Playing Out the Empire: Ben-Hur and other Toga-Plays and Films, 1883–1908* (Oxford: Clarendon Press, 1994). He has written numerous essays on melodrama and on links between the Victorian stage and early film, and is founder-director of the Victorian and Edwardian Stage on Film Project.

CARY M. MAZER is Associate Professor of Theatre Arts and English, and Chair of Theatre Arts, at the University of Pennsylvania, where he has directed plays by Euripides, Shakespeare, Webster, Strindberg, Shaw, Barrie, Beckett, and Pinter. At People's Light & Theatre Company he has dramaturged plays by Shakespeare, Wilde, and Shaw. He writes about Shakespeare performance history and Edwardian theatre.

MICHAEL PISANI is Associate Professor of Music at Vassar College. He has served on the music staff of the Houston Grand Opera, Seattle Opera, and other professional companies. His article on Prokofiev's *Love for Three Oranges* for the *Musical Quarterly* received the 1999 Kurt Weill Prize for distinguished scholarship in music theatre. His forthcoming book, *Recreating Native America: The Evolution of a Musical Stereotype*, will be published by Yale University Press. He is at work on a study of nineteenth-century Theatre music.

KERRY POWELL is Professor of English at Miami University, Oxford, Ohio. He is the author of *Oscar Wilde and the Theatre of the 1890s* (1990) and *Women and Victorian Theatre* (1997), both published by Cambridge

University Press. He contributed essays to *The Cambridge Companion to Oscar Wilde* (1997), *The Cambridge Companion to George Bernard Shaw* (1998), and *Critical Essays on Oscar Wilde* (with G. K. Hall). He is at work on the interaction of Oscar Wilde and Victorian feminism in the formation of new performativities of gender.

PETER RABY lectures in drama and theatre at the University of Cambridge. He is the editor of *The Cambridge Companion to Oscar Wilde* (1997) and the *Cambridge Companion to Harold Pinter* (2001), and has written extensively on Wilde. Among his recent books are *Bright Paradise* (London: Pimlico, 1997), a study of Victorian scientific travelers, and *Alfred Russel Wallace: A Life* (London: Chatto & Windus/Princeton, NJ: Princeton University Press, 2001).

PREFACE

The theatre of the Victorian and Edwardian period, once thought to be comparatively insignificant, even unworthy of attention, has today become one of the most fruitful areas of inquiry into the literature and culture of the age. At the same time that the importance of theatre to Victorian and Edwardian culture is increasingly evident, the theatricality of that culture itself has begun to be recognized, calling into question time-honored understandings of the period as having been defined by such ideals as sincerity, earnestness, and devotion to productive labor in the "real" world. As we learn more about Victorian and Edwardian theatre, we enrich not only our understanding of a previously undervalued phase of theatre history and theatrical literature, but also of the complexly textured social world which engendered this drama and was in turn informed and articulated by it.

The map of this emerging, rapidly developing field of study is far from complete, but *The Cambridge Companion to Victorian and Edwardian Theatre* provides some notable landmarks which allow an appreciation of its recent progress and current status. It incorporates the results of exciting archival investigations which have recovered lost or neglected plays that are already beginning to alter the landscape of the drama of this period, as we know it. These textual discoveries and re-readings are complemented by close analyses of dramatic genres and movements within the historical scope of this *Cambridge Companion*, not only surveying but revaluing the typology which defined the theatre of the period. A number of chapters give attention to theatrical production techniques, providing insight into a unique range and variety of Victorian and Edwardian stage effects – indeed, bringing some of these to our attention for the first time. Others bring to light the connections of theatre with the social world outside the playhouse, finding those linkages in the performance of gender, the operations of a market economy, and the dynamics of audience in relation to what transpired in the performing space behind the footlights. In this mixed approach to Victorian and Edwardian theatre the reader will find not only a guide to significant plays, dramatic movements, and acting and production techniques, but also a theoretical and critical framework that encourages thinking beyond stage texts and technologies toward a larger context of meaning that incorporates but is not bounded by the theatre.

The book begins with an introduction by Nina Auerbach, whose work, along with that of other contributors to this *Cambridge Companion*, has given new direction to the study of theatre, literature, and culture in the period. Auerbach makes large claims for the theatre of this time, finding in its diverse genres a magnet of entertainment which enthralled all classes of people, making it a kind of universal language despite the antitheatrical feeling that it always confronted, and still does. The theatre, Auerbach writes, was the prism through which Victorians and Edwardians saw themselves and their world. It exposed the artifice of this age of "sincerity," revealing the assumed truths of the time to be scripted performances themselves, enveloping this world, even its hallowed domestic scenes, in theatricality. Auerbach's overview is followed by a two-part division of the remaining chapters, the first group of which is entitled "Performance and context" because of its focus on acting, production, and the theatre as such, including the dynamics of theatre in relation to the world around it. This section is framed by an analysis of the "business" of Victorian and Edwardian theatre as a profit-seeking enterprise operating within a vigorous free-market economy, and thus frustrating the dreams of a nonprofit, aesthetically rich "national theatre." Subsequent chapters observe change as well as continuity in the styles and theories of acting in the Victorian and Edwardian periods, bring forward for the first time some important connections between specially written music and plays themselves, and trace a growing tension in the period between, on one hand, a realistic stagecraft that aimed at producing "an optical illusion through a huge hole in the wall," and on the other, a new scenography that offered a suggestion or a symbol instead of a detailed imitation of life. Another essay challenges some long-held assumptions about the audiences who attended Victorian and Edwardian plays, and this section of the book concludes with a consideration of the life and autobiography of Ibsen actress Elizabeth Robins as a key to understanding how gender was experienced and performed on and off the nineteenth- and early twentieth-century stage, finding a continuity in the "performative modes" of Hedda Gabler on stage and that of the "naïve ingénue" in life.

In the section of this *Companion* entitled "Text and context," contributors offer their analyses of the genres which dominated the Victorian and Edwardian theatre – comedy and farce, melodrama, and music-hall entertainment. Other essays chart the rise of a new and more consciously literary theatre in the 1890s, a period in which the horizons of drama were expanded to make room for the discussion of contemporary social issues. Oscar Wilde and Bernard Shaw, in particular during this period, "shook the drama into life." There followed the growth of a "new drama" for a "new theatre," originating with the Vedrenne–Barker management of the Court Theatre in the early years of the twentieth century and staging plays there and elsewhere that examined a range of social issues from class inequities to the "the woman question" and looked ahead to the formation of a National Theatre freed from the constraints of a profit-driven marketplace. Other chapters in this section deal with long-neglected, yet crucial aspects of Victorian and Edwardian drama – the role played by women playwrights in a male-dominated theatre, and the character and importance of the vital, but still little-known, working-class theatre of London's East End.

The chapters which form this *Companion* will improve our understanding of an important, emerging field of study, but one that remains underdeveloped from long neglect as well as difficulties inherent in the subject matter itself. What emerges from these pages, therefore, is not a complete or fully connected narrative of Victorian and Edwardian theatre, but necessarily a fragmentary one – a scholarly adventure in progress. Old assumptions about the theatre of this period are challenged, new views and new methods of inquiry put forward, and in the process the centrality of theatre and theatricality to Victorian and Edwardian culture is well-documented. But the subject matter is elusive, as Nina Auerbach points out in her introductory essay, made up as it is of many thousands of plays, most never published, and of performances long disappeared. One notable achievement of this *Cambridge Companion to Victorian and Edwardian Theatre* is that it restores so much about the drama of the period that has been inaccessible to us. Another, equally important, is that the map it provides, although still a sketchy one in many respects, will point out directions for those who come after, enabling further advances in our knowledge and appreciation of the theatre of this period, and of the period itself.

Kerry Powell

I

INTRODUCTION

NINA AUERBACH

Before the curtain

For many, the Victorian theatre is the scruffy orphan of high culture, somewhat redeemed by the cultivation of its Edwardian successors. Today's high-minded aficionados take their antitheatrical tone from the stuffiest Victorians: the stage was and is crude, embarrassing, primitive, compared to its sister arts, prose, poetry, and painting.[1] In any case, the medium is by definition ephemeral, and so impossible to study. Its scripts, when they exist at all, are not moored by weighty volumes as literature is, or heavy canvases like paintings; like most screenplays today, Victorian plays are sketches for productions and performances now vanished in the mists that engulfed the world before film preserved it.

Collaborative, messy, and lost, the theatre is generally, and wrongly, dismissed as sub-canonical, at least until the 1890s, when the self-conscious literacy of Wilde and Shaw elevated it to the verbal sophistication that would become Edwardian drama. But the theatre's elusive art can be retrieved and, in books like this, it is. Once we begin to piece this hybrid medium back together, we restore the prism through which *all* Victorian artists and audiences – and these were most Victorians – saw their world.

I like hybrid media because as far as theatre history goes, I am myself a hybrid, a literary scholar who learned nothing about the Victorian theatre except that like everything else, it pertained in some vague way to Dickens. When I began to write about the celebrated Victorian actress Ellen Terry, I realized that even for my fellow Victorianists, she was in another world than her literary contemporaries. This most famous of artists was abandoned to a field called "Theatre History," whose denizens read archives, not what I called texts, and had a clinging mistrust of the literature that was my livelihood. But literary critics were still more suspicious of the theatre. Most of my colleagues persisted in assuming that I was writing about Dickens's secret mistress Ellen *Ternan*, a sullen ingénue whose only sustained role was that of great man's lover.[2] Most natives of English departments ignored everything about the theatre that Dickens did not control. Like Dickens's own blusteringly English Podsnap, they did not want to know about things they did not know. But in nineteenth-century England, literature and the theatre were collaborative storytellers; they were the dominant media through which audiences understood the world. Had they continued to collaborate, both would be stronger today.

Admittedly, we cannot see or hear Victorian productions as readily as we can read Dickens or look at Turner, but with the help of the essays in this *Companion*, they come back to life in our mind's eye, and with them, the makers and recipients of a culture steeped in theatre. Michael Pisani's evocative "Music for the theatre" lets us hear with our inner ears the sorts of melodies that underlay Victorian productions and molded its actors, who, like opera singers, attuned their voices to musical accompaniment; Russell Jackson's "Victorian and Edwardian stagecraft" encourages us to see sophisticated and fluid visual effects as exquisite as painting and as overpowering, in their day, as today's thoroughly inhuman cinematic computer graphics; while Tracy C. Davis reminds us of who paid for all this, or, more important, of who refused to pay: since the theatre was a creature of pure capitalism, state subsidy was inconceivable. The theatre may have been raffish compared to arts we now define as canonical, but it drew expertly on those arts. Moreover, like an exemplary Victorian hero but unlike many actual Victorians, it was both sumptuous and self-supporting.

All the essays in this book insist on the centrality of the theatre in nineteenth-century culture; until the end of the century, its broad popularity gave its conventions the aura of universality. Many essayists make large claims that are absolutely true. Cary M. Mazer states baldly: "in the nineteenth century, theatre was – despite the prevailing antitheatricalism of official high culture – perhaps the most widespread arena of popular culture." David Mayer reminds us that the violent moral absolutes of theatrical melodrama were not just a sop to groundlings, for whom we may read the working class; in a society racked by seemingly meaningless and malevolent changes, changes melodrama's fascinating villains came to personify, absurd contrasts reflected common perceptions, for "the nineteenth century was the first era of mass theatre-going, with theatre attendance active in all parts of the British Isles." In the best and broadest sense, theatrical experience was common; until it became respectable, it was not limited to any coterie.

One of the greatest strengths of this book is its determination to disentangle theatre history from the class snobbery and exclusions – our own as well as the Victorians' – that initially limited the field. A few decades ago, the official story of the Victorian theatre, which several essays label "triumphalist," was that of progressive rise.[3] In the first half of the nineteenth century, the story goes, audiences were predominantly lower class, thus by definition drunk and raucous; in the 1860s, the Bancrofts and other canny managers appealed to a middle-class family audience who, by the Edwardian decade, evolved grandly into the cultivated – for which we may read wealthy and fashionable – classes. As the audiences "rose," so, like a Victorian hero, did the theatre, evolving out of association with vagabondage and prostitution to genteel, even titled, respectability.

Such a theatre, if there ever was such a theatre, is as fractured as the mutually antagonistic classes it served. To many observers, it was segregated by geography as well as time. A trip from London's West End to its East End was often described as an excursion into savagery. In 1877, *Household Words* presented a taxonomy of London audiences according to their class: there were "the purely society or fashionable audience; the fast fashionable audience; the domestic audience; the respectable audience; the mixed audience; the working-class audience," which itself fractured into "the transpontine, the extreme East-end, the flash, the decorous, the criminal, the honest, the drunken and the sober."[4] Presumably, the rising respectable Edwardian theatre saved the institution, if not England itself, from these working-class intrusions, couth or uncouth.

This paradigm of a rising theatre is itself Victorian in its snobbish complacency, and it is, like most snobbish paradigms, wrong – though I have obtusely used it in my own work. The *Cambridge Companion* shows that like the theatre itself, Victorian audiences were more capacious and diverse than divisive commentators, then or now, have wanted to see. In "Victorian and Edwardian audiences," Jim Davis and Victor Emeljanow insist that London's "multifaceted, variegated audiences have been generically and artificially constructed and often simplified by their contemporaries" – and by ourselves as well. In the same spirit, Heidi J. Holder's account of London's East-End theatre, generally defined as a ghetto of raffish roughs, argues for the capaciousness of the East End: while it gave something of a voice to women, criminals, blacks, and Jews, much of its repertoire also overlapped with that of the more refined West End. Jacky Bratton's account of the Victorian music hall similarly refuses to ghettoize its subject, stressing the congruence of this witty, impertinent, seemingly self-contained world with the so-called legitimate stage. Davis and Emeljanow reveal that even the so-called lower classes attended plays in the West End, though managers did their best to expel them by raising prices and gentrifying the house, replacing the pit with more expensive stalls.

These fascinating chapters reconstruct not a theatre fractured into class-segregated communities, shunned by each other, but a fluid mixture of genres that drew virtually all classes. The theatre may not quite do the work of the culture that Matthew Arnold fruitlessly tried to bring to his aesthetically brutish countrymen, a universal balm that consolidated warring and mutually ignorant social classes, but it came closer than any art, even the lovable but long Victorian novel, to becoming a universal language – as movies would claim to be before the coming of sound – providing a common audience with common visions. Outsiders constructed the divisions that were partially transcended in the theatre.

The theatre was not democratic (is anything?), but it did come as close as any art could to creating an experience that felt both topical and universal. For this reason, I am sorry that good as they are, almost half of the essays in this volume focus on the urbane theatre of the *fin de siècle* and its Edwardian descendants. It was in the 1890s that the theatre, like the novel, grew ashamed of mere popularity and aspired to high art. Now relying on smart talk in smaller theatres, late-Victorian and Edwardian plays were written for publication as well as performance, with elaborate (and, in Shaw's case, interminable) stage directions and commentary. As the characters' IQ rose, so did their social position. The idiom of the new theatre was reformist – its prophets were Ibsen, William Archer, and Shaw – but the more progressive it claimed to be, the more elitist it became. In short, theatre at the beginning of the twentieth century made itself up as the refined institution later historians claim it actually was.

The new Shavian theatre was never commercially self-sustaining, but because it published itself incessantly, it is what we have; scholars need not go to archives or forage for out-of-print anthologies to find plays and manifestos. But as the theatre aspired to literature, and literature itself became more rarefied, a unity was lost. I hope it does not seem obtusely nostalgic to suggest that the theatre that mattered in the nineteenth century was the theatre we no longer quite have.

Perhaps because the theatre had such a powerful imaginative hold, many of the most eminent Victorians shunned its compelling artificiality, its direct displays of emotion and fear, its unending music, its implicit deceit, its continual shape-changing. Charles Dickens has made himself known as Mr. Theatre, as well as Mr. Social Criticism and Mr. Jollity, but in fact he could not be farther from authentic theatricality. When he writes about the theatre, he does so with a moralistic fastidiousness that becomes, at times, revulsion. Several of the essays in this *Companion* take Dickens to task, rightly, for his condescending descriptions of East-End playhouses, as if this former child of the streets feels compelled to distance himself from a melee of workers cavorting around. But even those virtuoso self-displays, his novels, find it hard to treat the theatre without insulting it.

Jacky Bratton's essay on the music hall cleverly brings in a snippet of *Bleak House*. An officious coroner comes to the foul heart of London's slums to interrogate its crushed inhabitants about a pauper's death. A local song-and-dance man in a public house tries to lighten this gloomy visitation:

> In the zenith of the evening, Little Swills says, Gentlemen, if you'll permit me, I'll attempt a short description of a scene of real life that came off here to-day. Is much applauded and encouraged; goes out of the room as Swills; comes back as the Coroner (not the least in the world like him); describes the Inquest, with recreative intervals of piano-forte accompaniment to the refrain – With his (the Coroner's) tippy tol li doll, tippy tol lo doll, tippy tol li doll, Dee![5]

Not the least in the world like him – with this taunt, throughout his novels, Dickens banishes actors, claiming sole reality for himself and his visions. Never mind that his own subsequent description of the slums – "Come night, come darkness, for you cannot come too soon, or stay too long, by such a place as this!" (*Bleak House*, chap. 11) – sounds like Little Swills parodying East-End melodrama. For Dickens, who constituted a theatre in his person, the actual theatre was a meretricious snare.

Dickens's sourness toward the theatre stretches from the beginning of his career to the end. After the good-hearted protagonist of his third novel, *Nicholas Nickleby*, realizes that he can do nothing to earn a living, he becomes a popular actor without half trying. Vincent Crummles, the fraudulent company manager, asks suggestively, "You don't happen to be anything of an artist, do you?" "That is not one of my accomplishments," Nicholas answers, thereby assuring his theatrical future: to be an actor is to be an artist in no sense. With polite horror, he shares the bill with Crummles's daughter the infant phenomenon, a putative child star who is really a monster without an age:

> the infant phenomenon, though of short stature, had a comparatively aged countenance, and had moreover been precisely the same age – not perhaps to the full extent of the memory of the oldest inhabitant, but certainly for five good years. But she had been kept up late every night, and put upon an unlimited allowance of gin-and-water from infancy, to prevent her growing tall, and perhaps this system of training had produced in the infant phenomenon the additional phenomenon.[6]

A caricature of eerily versatile child actors like Master Betty and Jean Davenport, who were authentic stars in the early nineteenth century, the infant phenomenon is an embodied lie who turns performance into lies.

Great Expectations, written when Dickens was an established literary star, equates all expectations with theatre, and thus with deceit and self-deceit. Pip, an ambitious laborer, is given a mysterious gift that will make him a gentleman – which means, in practice, that he wears fancy clothes and idles about. Like the actors in *Nicholas Nickleby*, Pip is made a sham person, deferred to for being, and doing, nothing. Around the middle of the story, Mr. Wopsle, a repellent clergyman, repeats Pip's degrading transformation by becoming an actor. With no credentials but overweening vanity, he plays Hamlet. Wopsle's Hamlet is one of Dickens's renowned comic set pieces; it is also one of the most excoriating antitheatrical passages in the English novel.

The point is not that Wopsle is a terrible actor in an amateur production; he is damned, doomed, and mocked for being an actor at all. His embarrassing performance is an icon of artifice, from his appearance, on which Pip muses, "I could have wished that his curls and forehead had been more probable," to his elocution, which was "very unlike any way in which any man in any natural circumstances of life or death ever expressed himself about anything."[7] Somewhere, no doubt, there is a natural Hamlet with probable curls and real speech whom Pip, and Dickens, would approve, but this Hamlet would never see a stage. Like Pip himself, Wopsle's Hamlet is a creature of costume – his tyrannical dresser critiques his performance only because "when he see the ghost in the queen's apartment he might have made more of his stockings" – and thus a sham. Like poor Little Swills who does his impotent best to irradiate *Bleak House*, Wopsle's Hamlet is "not the least in the world like him."

For Dickens, the only authentic theatre was himself. His novels are performances of Dickens; he acted in his own plays; in the end, he shortened his life touring in blazing readings from his own novels. Like many non-actors, he loved to have everybody watching him enthralled as he pulled his world out of his head. His hostility to the actual theatre, his compulsion to expose its meretriciousness, was more than professional rivalry; it was a symptom of a typically Victorian, and perhaps particularly masculine, fear. In those innocent days before talk shows and television, the mark of a great man was sincerity. Thomas Carlyle's blueprint for would-be heroes boomed through the minds of all ambitious men: "I should say *sincerity*, a deep, great, genuine sincerity, is the first characteristic of all men in any way heroic."[8] A hero was unremittingly himself. If audiences turned from man to performer, from word to show, the commonwealth would lose itself in chaos.

For Dickens and other Victorian heroes, the theatre was suspect unless it was a testament to his own solitary sincerity. But stars, memorable though they were, were not the heart of the Victorian theatre; it was not so much Hamlet as home that was consecrated on the stage. From the domestic comedies and farces Michael Booth's essay describes to Tom Robertson's prestigious cup-and-saucer plays of the 1860s – staged by the Bancrofts in a dollhouse theatre that was a winning facsimile of a middle-class house – to Ibsen's, Shaw's, Pinero's, and Henry Arthur Jones's Edwardian problem plays, the theatre may have been run by men, but it dwelt on women's ostensible sphere, family and its simulations.[9] If the theatre was perilous to great men on heroic missions, it was still worse company for the good women who were supposed to wait for them at home.

Victorian novels, with their subtle elisions and divisions, have always drawn feminists to search out hidden protests against the tyrannical contradictions that governed women's lives. Though literary feminists endlessly dissect Dorothea Brooke's marriages or the "low, slow ha-ha" of the madwoman in the attic, they perpetually neglect the theatre. I have never understood this neglect, for in the theatre, even at its most pious, home is an arbitrary series of plays. Victorian novels about women's lives, and these are most of the novels we still read, have frozen into predictable ritual: we know what Dorothea will feel when. But women-centered plays are open to almost infinite suggestion.

The essays in this anthology illuminate women's role in the nineteenth-century theatre – both as troubling presence and speaking absence – from many vantage points. Joseph Donohue's stirring "Actors and acting" affirms the continuity of the theatrical grand style from the late seventeenth century to the present: despite the rhetorical changes in theatrical fashion, Donohue draws a firm line from Kemble's Shakespearean performances to Gielgud's, and after him to those of Ralph Fiennes. In Donohue's account, British actors forge a tradition as distinct and immutable as the great tradition that dignifies the British novel.

I love this vision of a tradition; I too believe that distinctive actors like Gielgud contain glimpses of distinctive actors like Kean. But Donohue's tradition has trouble containing women, for the actresses he describes all seem more eccentric than the men. Are actresses part of the same grand tradition as actors, or do they compose a tradition of their own? I find it harder to locate a tradition that would link Sarah Siddons, Ellen Terry, Peggy Ashcroft, and Judi Dench, and so, I suspect do many theatre historians. Donohue himself concludes cryptically: "All the same, the vitality and presence we find in actors and acting today, in this post-Gielgud era – Ralph Fiennes's Richard II and Coriolanus come happily to mind – have such clear affinities with performances of such roles by Kemble, Kean, Macready, Fechter, Tree, Martin-Harvey, their actress counterparts, and their illustrious or unsung predecessors, that the connections seem, finally, too close to challenge."

Who are "their actress counterparts" and what roles would they play? Not, probably, Richard II or Coriolanus or their female foils: to play Richard's queen or even Volumnia in the grand manner would unbalance these actor-centered plays. I suspect that I am not the only believer in Donohue's thesis who finds herself drawn by his essay to the anomaly of theatrical women.

Other essays address theatrical women more directly, but they emerge as scarcely less anomalous than Donohue's "actress counterparts." Sos Eltis finds one thread of tradition in the recurrent figure of the fallen woman, but proclaims that this figure disappeared after Noël Coward's unsuccessful use of a fallen woman in 1924. Mary Jean Corbett writes suggestively about the sly self-creation of actress autobiographies, as exemplified by the Edwardian feminist Elizabeth Robins. Susan Carlson and Kerry Powell continue to spotlight Robins in their exhilarating reconstruction of Edwardian women's theatre as the suffrage movement galvanized it. But all these essays highlight fragments of theatrical history, making me wonder what happened before and after. Are theatrical women today infused by the glamour of the fallen woman, the self-awareness of Elizabeth Robins, the communal power of suffrage theatre? Or do men transcend time, while women are lost in it?

Two of the strongest essays in the book emphasize the comprehensive degree to which women's issues, if not always women themselves, dominate the Victorian and Edwardian theatre. Michael R. Booth's "Comedy and farce" points to the fixation on marriage, family, and unruly women that fuel these apparently escapist genres. Booth reminds us that while, true to form, comedies end conservatively and in couples, the spur of much Victorian comedy involves trouble in the home.

In contrast to Booth's suavely descriptive account of plays that are predominantly mid-Victorian, Peter Raby's "Theatre of the 1890s" is a plangent evocation of domestic problem plays that implicitly denounce a dying class and a sick society. For Raby, male dramatists like Pinero, Shaw, Jones, and Wilde scrutinize marriage hopelessly and diagnostically, as a microcosm of terminal social decay. The urgency of *fin-de-siècle* plays may be tempered by conservative endings, but their lacerations are no longer comic.

If we knew how earlier Victorian comedy erupts into *fin-de-siècle* and Edwardian extremities of social despair, we might discern a tradition of theatrical domesticity, one focused on theatrical women, whose roots precede the nineteenth century and whose aftershocks are with us today. The most durable achievement of these essays should be to stimulate new ones, and books as well, giving sequence and substance to omissions, while restoring works this anthology necessarily omits.

What, for instance, happened to *East Lynne*? Many essays dwell on Pinero's sophisticated domestic melodrama, *The Second Mrs. Tanqueray* (1893), but all are silent about the earlier, phenomenally popular domestic melodrama *East Lynne*. Perhaps *East Lynne* still embarrasses us. It is such a sentimental cliché of a weeper – through the 1920s, a failing repertory company had only to post on its boards "Next Week – *East Lynne*!!" to bring back hungry audiences – that we still shun its Victorianness. Most scholars would rather think than weep, but *East Lynne* is not just tearful. Its play with women's being embodies Victorian theatricality before the theatre achieved smart Edwardian awareness.

Without the extravagance of *East Lynne* in the 1860s, *Mrs. Tanqueray* might never have achieved her polish in the 1890s. Based on Ellen Wood's 1861 best-selling novel, *East Lynne* exists in myriad patchy adaptations, of which T. A. Palmer's 1874 version was the most frequently staged in England. Pinero's *Mrs. Tanqueray*, literate and well-made, was not an echo of a well-known novel, but an original play that claimed the independent status of art. Pinero was eventually knighted, in part for the triumph of *Mrs. Tanqueray*; no one connected with any version of *East Lynne* could dream of a title. *Mrs. Tanqueray* launched the career of the legendary, uniquely abrasive actress Mrs. Patrick Campbell; it was assumed that any actress with tear ducts could play Lady Isabel Vane. *Mrs. Tanqueray* was a triumph of distinctive talents; *East Lynne* was intimately loved in so many versions that it achieved the anonymity of folk art. Yet these plays are theatrical kin in that both expose the artificiality of family life, especially the porousness of women's iconic essence as wife and mother.

East Lynne is a cautionary account of a runaway wife, but it is also a kaleidoscope of unstable domestic identities: the only permanent structure is the stately home East Lynne itself. At the outset, the death of her improvident father deprives Lady Isabel Vane of her status as protected daughter. Chivalrously, the middle-class barrister Mr. Carlyle buys East Lynne, restoring Isabel's security and her childhood home by making her his wife. Having fallen from aristocratic daughter to middle-class wife, Isabel is at once bored with her exemplary husband and jealous of his intimacy with Barbara Hare (both Isabel and Mr. Carlyle are rigid believers in their domestic roles, but emotionally, they are watery: either could at any point love somebody else). In a mad flight beyond East Lynne's boundaries, Isabel elopes with a scoundrel, Sir Francis Levison, only to creep back disguised as her own children's governess after Levison's abandonment and her own supposed death in a train wreck. In her final incarnation as a servant, Isabel performs in its extremity the dependent she has always been in essence. The story languishes to its end as the disguised Isabel watches in anguish the death of her son, then reveals herself to Mr. Carlyle (who is now married to Barbara Hare) and dies.

Like a female King Lear, the penitent Isabel falls because there is no longer anyone to tell her who she is: "My husband, my children! – Oh, never again to hear *him* say 'Isabel, my wife!' Never again to hear *their* infant tongues murmur the holy name of '*mother!*' Lost, degraded, friendless, abandoned, and alone!"[10] The climax is not her awkward reunion with her now-bigamous husband, but the perplexity of her dying son, whose mother remains a role without a face. Traditionally played by a woman, Little Willie, like the imaginary son in Edward Albee's *Who's Afraid of Virginia Woolf?*, personifies the theatricality of family life. Fading fretfully, he asks his supposed governess whether he will see in Heaven "my very own mama, she who is gone away . . . And shall I know her, I have quite forgotten what she was like, shall I know her?" Since there is no Heaven beyond East Lynne, he knows no one, expiring without recognizing the mother within the governess. Isabel's eulogy is less a eulogy for her son than for her own lost roles: "Oh, Willie, my child dead dead dead! and he never knew me, never called me mother!" (act III). Mother is a matter of class and clothes; when the accouterments vanish, so does the being.

Thirty years later, *The Second Mrs. Tanqueray* does not deign to make us weep. Like many plays of the 1890s, it makes us laugh uneasily. Yet later, more knowing audiences laughed with Paula Tanqueray in the same spirit in which their parents wept over Isabel Vane: her histrionics over her own supposed trespasses expose the fiction of family. East Lynne is a looming, symbolic presence, while Pinero's stage directions construct with minute precision the settings of *Mrs. Tanqueray*: "At back C., a fireplace, with fire burning brightly. A luxurious easy chair on each side of the fireplace. On the R. of fireplace, against the wall, a writing-desk and chair. On the writing-table, writing materials, a small cigar-cabinet and lighted spirit-lamp," and so on. But if we are reading the play, we are aware of who owns these rooms even before we see them: "The Scene of the First Act is laid at Mr. Tanqueray's rooms, No. 2x the Albany . . . the occurrences of the succeeding Acts take place at his house, 'Highercoombe,' near Willowmere, Surrey."[11] In these annexed rooms, Paula Tanqueray is always a trespasser, trying at her peril to preside.

Even before the play begins, the protagonist is at odds with the woman of the title. In the 1890s, Paula Tanqueray was discreetly categorized as "a woman with a past" – a mercurial past that, unlike Isabel's, was staged before the play began, effectively separating the past Paula from the floundering Paula we see, who has snatched respectability by marrying a well-intentioned widower, Aubrey Tanqueray. In the days when she was euphemistically called a "hostess," Paula Ray had gone by a series of names, Mrs. Dartry and Mrs. Jarman among them, but these identities are excised by a marriage that nullifies her, for "the second Mrs. Tanqueray" is the one being she cannot be.

Pinero's stage directions call her simply "Paula," a naked name with nothing attached to give it substance. The play revolves around the star's inability to play a wife.

Like Isabel, Paula craves ratification, not from her patriarchal husband, but from the next generation – in this case from her step-daughter Ellean, the prissily devout daughter of Aubrey's puritanical first wife. Little Willie could not recognize his fallen mother; Ellean will not recognize hers until the fateful final act. When Ellean's exemplary fiancé turns out to have been one of Paula's lovers in her hostess days, Ellean turns on her would-be mother with excoriating recognition: "I have always known what you were!" (act IV). For these simulated wives and mothers, it is equally lacerating not to be known and to be known. Like Isabel, Paula has nothing to do but die. Isabel, however, has been dying from one role into another throughout the play, while only suicide can extinguish Paula's vitality. By the 1890s, death is at least no longer inherent in women's performances; as it does for Shakespeare's heroes, death thumps down to shut their mouths and stop their play.

Willie did not know Isabel; Ellean does know Paula; both women evaporate when their domestic performances unravel. Actresses in roles Victorian moralists assumed were natural to women, these two compelling heroines implicated their ostensibly unfallen audiences, many of whom also played unplayable roles badly, tragically like Isabel or cynically like Paula. Even melodramas with conservative endings, like the broad *East Lynne* and the knowing *Mrs. Tanqueray*, call into question lies that look like truth. In Victorian novels, marriage and motherhood are the immutable ends of a heroine's destiny; they authenticate a life while ending the life of the novel. In the theatre, marriage and motherhood are snarled roles it is a lie to play and death to stop playing. Domesticity in novels is a charmed haven; on stage it is a contagious game.

No doubt my reading of these two plays is, from a theatre historian's perspective, hopelessly literary: I look at the scripts, but can only imagine how they would play in their original productions. In *East Lynne*, did the adult actresses who played Little Willie bring artifice or authority to the deathbed scene? In *Mrs. Tanqueray*, did Stella Campbell play the caustic Paula as a comic woman striking tragic attitudes, or as a tragic figure with satiric murmurs? What did the houses look like? What were the climactic scenes? Where were the music cues, what was the music, did it enhance the performances or add counterpoint to them? The essays in this volume begin to allow us to answer such questions about language that realizes itself only when it is spoken on a stage.

NOTES

1. Two encyclopedic books from the 1980s illuminate the range of the theatre, from the fears – ontological, political, spiritual – it has always aroused to its full aesthetic amplitude, especially in the nineteenth century. Jonas Barish's *The Antitheatrical Prejudice* (Berkeley and London: University of California Press, 1981) is a long compendium of diatribes against performance. Martin Meisel's *Realizations: Narrative, Pictorial, and Theatrical Arts in Nineenth-Century England* (Princeton and London: Princeton University Press, 1983) is the first and still the most ambitious demonstration of the centrality of the theatre in the spectrum of the Victorian arts.

2. Claire Tomalin, *The Invisible Woman: The Story of Nelly Ternan and Charles Dickens* (New York: Knopf, 1991) gives a full account of Ellen Ternan's strenuous but obscure career before she met Dickens.

3. Michael Baker, *The Rise of the Victorian Actor* (Totowa, NJ: Rowman & Little-field, 1978) is a particularly convincing example of a triumphalist narrative.

4. *Household Words*, 19 May 1877, quoted in Jim Davis and Victor Emeljanow, chap. 5, below.

5. Charles Dickens, *Bleak House* (1851) (rpt. New York: Norton Critical Editions, 1977), chap. 11.

6. Charles Dickens, *Nicholas Nickleby* (1838–39) (rpt. New York: Dutton, Every-man's Library, 1970), chap. 22.

7. Charles Dickens, *Great Expectations* (1860–61) (rpt. Baltimore: Penguin, 1965), chap. 31.

8. Thomas Carlyle, "The Hero as Prophet," *On Heroes, Hero-Worship and the Heroic in History* (1841) (rpt. Lincoln and London: University of Nebraska Press, 1966), p. 45.

9. The great American plays of the mid-twentieth century simulated domesticity as reassuringly as the mid-Victorian domestic theatre. Classics like Arthur Miller's *Death of a Salesman*, Eugene O'Neill's *Long Day's Journey Into Night*, and Edward Albee's *Who's Afraid of Virginia Woolf?* let audiences pretend they were coming home, not leaving it, when they went to the theatre. Only at the end of the twentieth century did Americans embrace, through the extravaganzas of Andrew Lloyd Webber and Stephen Sondheim, the fantasy and spectacle that were the more sensuous facet of the nineteenth-century British stage.

10. T. A. Palmer, *East Lynne: A Domestic Drama in a Prologue and Four Acts* (1874), act II.

11. Arthur Wing Pinero, *The Second Mrs. Tanqueray* (1893), act I and "Dramatis personae."

2

PERFORMANCE AND CONTEXT

I

JOSEPH DONOHUE

Actors and acting

In the preface to the second volume of *Plays Pleasant and Unpleasant* (1898), George Bernard Shaw specifies the sort of actor he requires for the new kind of play represented by his first public success, *Arms and the Man* (Avenue Theatre, London, 1894). Actors in his plays, Shaw explains, had to become participants in transforming a society mired in pernicious romantic illusion into one grounded in a "genuinely scientific natural history." The task was a demanding one. Actors in Shavian plays must comprehend mental states that "still seem cynically perverse to most people" and cultivate a goodhumored contempt for "ethical conventions" that had once seemed "validly heroic or venerable."[1] In his own sunny, arrogant way, Shaw is addressing actors who seldom if ever consider themselves the "abstract, and brief chronicles of the time," as Hamlet had insisted they were, but who in Shaw's view amount nevertheless to epitomizing presences, reifying on stage the assumptions, attitudes, and prejudices of their age. Mere imitation of this kind, he insists, is no longer acceptable.

From our century-long perspective we can perceive Shaw to be aligning himself with the programmatic dramaturgy embraced by Continental practitioners of naturalism like Zola and Brieux,[2] whose works reflected a "scientific" analysis of contemporary social conditions and their deleterious effects. Shaw's champion exemplar of this radical strategy was, of course, Ibsen, whose "terrible art of sharpshooting" at an audience was intended, as Shaw would argue in his 1913 revision of *The Quintessence of Ibsenism*, to make them so uncomfortable that they would become "guilty creatures sitting at a play" (again, the idea is Hamlet's) who might then rise up and reform society.[3] Evidently, Shaw intends to draw actors away from unthinking service to a society against whose *mores* he is in revolt; for it is actors, he realizes, who are the ultimate means of enlisting audiences in that arduous enterprise.

In advancing these ideals, Shaw is seemingly placing himself outside the mainstream of contemporary acting theory and practice, as an aberrant example of disaffection with the current state of society and theatre. The situation is more complex than this, however, and also more interesting. Paradoxically, Shaw's plan for the reformation of society remained completely consistent with his dependence, as a dramatist, on the style and practice of the traditional theatre and traditional acting, and on the genres of drama still familiar to playgoers.[4] As a reviewer of plays in the 1890s Shaw repeatedly acknowledged his unabashed love for the theatre. The advice about their craft that Shaw gave such willing listeners as Mrs. Patrick Campbell, Ellen Terry, and Harley Granville Barker indicates that, for all his unorthodox political agenda, Shaw knew what good acting really was and could describe it in vivid detail. Of Mrs. Campbell's Juliet in Forbes-Robertson's 1895 revival of Shakespeare's play, he said he approved of her "lively theatrical instinct" but deplored her performance for having "not a touch of tragedy, not a throb of love or fear, temper instead of passion."[5] Coaching Ellen Terry as Imogen in Henry Irving's Lyceum production of *Cymbeline* in 1896, he advised her, in playing the false recognition scene, to omit her line about the "headless man" to avoid anticlimax, so that she can "go tearing, screaming, raging mad and rave your way to the swoon" with complete conviction.[6] And while rehearsing Robert Lorraine as John Tanner in the Royal Court *Man and Superman* in 1907, Shaw praised Lorraine for acting "extremely well in the style of [Charles] Wyndham," the eminent West-End actor-manager. "He has got all the comedy side of the part capitally," Shaw explained to the actor-director Granville Barker, "and does it quite in my old-fashioned way, with a relish and not under protest, like you."[7]

What Shaw acknowledged as "old-fashioned" was a style of acting and an approach to characterization that had held the boards since the late seventeenth century, or even before, and showed little sign of dying out. A memorable example occurs in Shaw's admiring description of Barry Sullivan, "incomparably the greatest" of English-speaking stars,

> . . . a tall powerful man with a cultivated resonant voice: his stage walk was the perfection of grace and dignity; and his lightning swiftness of action, as when in the last scene of *Hamlet* he shot up the stage and stabbed the king four times before you could wink, provided a physical exhibition which attracted audiences quite independently of the play.
>
> (*Terry and Shaw: Correspondence*, p. xvii)

Sullivan's full-blown theatricality places him squarely in a long actorly tradition of boldly stated personification, still alive and thriving at the end of Victoria's reign after almost two-and-a-half centuries of uninterrupted activity since the Restoration of King Charles II in 1660. Sullivan was effectively a lineal descendant of Edmund Kean (to go no further back), as was the more controlled yet flamboyant Tommaso Salvini, Sullivan's contemporary, who could convince audiences he was "a volcano in eruption," Shaw observed, "when he was . . . hardly moving" (*Terry and Shaw: Correspondence*, p. xviii). As King Lear, Salvini's reply to Gloucester's inquiry "Is't not the king?" produced a "wonderfully bold piece of business," Henry James recalled approvingly: "he rushes to a neighbouring tree, tears off a great twig, grasps it as a sceptre, and, erecting himself for a moment in an attitude intended to be royal, launches his majestic answer: 'Ay, every inch a king!' "[8] Even such an understated realist as Barker ("Don't suppress your people too much," Shaw cautioned him; "remember the infernal accoustics of the theatre" [*Letters to Granville Barker*, p. 58]) had more in common with those actors than he had differences. Despite the enormous changes in the English theatre over the hundred years from Kean's London debut (as Shylock, at Drury Lane, in 1814) to the outbreak of the First World War – changes including the demise of a repertory system still the norm after Kean, William Charles Macready, Madame Vestris, Samuel Phelps, and Helen Faucit had all retired – an English actor's approach to the creation of a role remained so consistent that even the oldest of playgoers would have been hard pressed to describe any new departures in the enactment of character.

Two examples will serve to illustrate this remarkable continuity. First, Charles Lamb's loving description of the great comedian Joseph Munden as Old Dozey, the inebriated Greenwich pensioner in Thomas Dibdin's much-performed farce *Past Ten O'Clock, and a Rainy Night*. In his "determined attention to grog," Lamb recalled, he looked "fireproof." "He *steers* at a table," Lamb explained, "and the tide of grog now and then bears him off the point."[9] In much the same vein is the actor George Honey's long mimed sequence as old Eccles, Polly Eccles's irresponsible, seldom-sober father, in act III of Tom Robertson's comedy *Caste*, produced in 1867 by Squire Bancroft and Marie Wilton at the rehabilitated Prince of Wales's Theatre:

> ECCLES *takes out pipe from pocket, looks into it, then blows through it making a squeaking noise and finishes by tenderly placing it on the table. He then hunts in all his pockets for tobacco, finally finding a little paper packet . . . which he also places on table after turning up the corner of the tablecloth for the purpose of emptying the contents of his right-hand pocket of the few remnants of past screws of tobacco on to the bare table and mixing a little out of the packet with it and filling pipe . . .*[10]

Robertson has custom-tailored this business to Honey's own style, described by Percy Fitzgerald as "of the old broad, boisterous, exaggerated school"[11] – or he may simply have recorded Honey's own invention. Robertson had resisted casting this actor, a veteran of burlesque and extravaganza and an eminent portrayer of drunkards who had acted with Wilton at the Strand, because Honey's exaggerated manner ran at odds with the restrained ensemble acting Robertson had established at the Prince of Wales's. In the event, Honey triumphed in the role, perhaps because the character itself required an actor of the old school, versed in the techniques of calculated overstatement, to do it justice. Honey's Eccles would have been perfectly intelligible a half-century earlier to audiences that had relished Munden's memorable portrait of Old Dozey.

Despite Robertson's reluctance and Fitzgerald's disdain, the grand style did not die out in the 1880s and 1890s but continued to reinvent itself up through the twentieth century. Match Shaw on Sullivan against his predecessor George Henry Lewes on Kean, and the similarities are unmistakable. The last three acts of Kean's Othello were without peer, Lewes contended:

> In the successive unfolding of these great scenes he represented with incomparable effect the lion-like fury, the deep and haggard pathos, the forlorn sense of desolation, alternating with gusts of stormy cries for vengeance, the misgivings and sudden reassurances, the calm and deadly resolution of one not easily moved, but who, being moved, was stirred to the very depths.[12]

For all Kean's singularity, the grand style he embodied had avatars without number. One of these, Henry Irving, was a kind of Disraeli of the theatre, Max Beerbohm observed: "both men were romantic to the core, ever conceiving large and grandiose ideas, which they executed with a fond eye to pageantry."[13] Add such mid-twentieth-century exemplars as John Gielgud, Laurence Olivier, and Ralph Richardson, and we may conclude that a single, coherent English acting tradition over three centuries old remains intact.

What are we to make, then, of Robertson's innovations and, on a larger scale, the grand narrative still to be heard of the eventual triumph of a reformative "realism" in the twentieth century? A test case occurs in the most well-known advice to actors of the period, imparted by W. S. Gilbert to the performers of his "entirely original farcical comedy" Engaged (1877). Sometimes cited as evidence of the emergence of "realistic" acting (whatever that may be), Gilbert's caveats are better understood in the context of the long tradition of a homogeneous art extending from Betterton and Bracegirdle to Wyndham and Mary Moore. Here is Gilbert's advice:

> It is absolutely essential to the success of this piece that it should be played with the most perfect earnestness and gravity throughout. There should be no exaggeration in costume, make-up or demeanour; and the characters, one and all, should appear to believe, throughout, in the perfect sincerity of their words and actions. Directly the actors show that they are conscious of the absurdity of their utterances the piece begins to drag.[14]

Gilbert is not concerned with the degree of "realism" that should mark an actor's performance but, rather, with the need to maintain the illusion of virtual life on the stage – a different matter entirely. Why did Gilbert feel the need for such a warning? Because he knew so well how the actors of his time responded to the presence of an audience, namely, by intentionally breaching the aesthetic barriers of footlights and proscenium arch. Ever since the days of the thrust forestages of Restoration theatres, the actor's ways of acknowledging an appreciative audience in a constantly lighted auditorium had little or nothing to do with what we now call "realism." Plausibility of character was not based, as our twentieth-century bias misleads us into believing, on a verisimilitudinous illusion of "three-dimensional" personages inhabiting a fictional space sealed off behind a transparent fourth wall. Instead, it depended on something far more frank and open. Despite definable differences in the particularities of their styles, Betterton, Garrick, Macklin, Kemble, and Kean, and Bracegirdle, Woffington, Pritchard, Siddons, and Jordan all shared an ability, upon which Gilbert casts latter-day aspersions, of taking the audience in on the pleasures and delights of character (*their* character) in situation. These traditional representations of fictive personages, cheerfully acknowledged to be no more (nor less) than that, had a manifest *calculating* quality that persisted even through such innovations as the much touted "naturalistic" style of Garrick's Richard III in his astonishing debut in the role in 1741.[15] Placed in this long tradition of open engagement with an audience, Gilbert's advice to the players proves to be less radical and prescient than we might have thought. In advising his actors on their presentation of character, Gilbert is simply cautioning them to avoid blunting the sharp edges of their dialogue by telegraphing the punch lines in advance. He is not asking them to change the basic style of enactment. Robertson's emphasis, in mounting *Caste* and other Prince of Wales's plays in the previous decade, on a more faithful representation of contemporary life was later aptly (if heavy-handedly) described by Shaw as a "tiny theatrical revolution."[16] Too much should not be made of innovations that remained quite consistent with the effectiveness of actors comfortably clothed in the familiar "lines of business" of hero, confidant, heroine, soubrette, low comic, old man, and grande dame. Rutland Barrington's brilliant performance as Pooh-Bah, the corrupt, self-aggrandizing Lord High Everything Else in Gilbert and Sullivan's *The Mikado* (Savoy, 1885), testifies to Gilbert's understanding of how broadly conceived character can be rendered with complete conviction.

Although it anticipates the moderation of acting styles produced by the darkened auditoriums of the last two decades of Victoria's reign and the much better lighted, electricity-based illusion of reality on stage, Gilbert's advice to the players marks a significant way-station, not a sudden turn in a new direction. To grasp the persistence of acting style over the years from the Restoration to the end of Edward VII's reign in 1910, one has only to view the silent films of Edward's time, populated by actors trained not for the camera but for the stage. Herbert Beerbohm Tree's silent film of Shakespeare's *King John*, though quite brief, provides a convincing example (see Figure 1).[17] The "overacting" we associate with the films of the silent era appears as such to us because of an extravagant style that worked in spaces where the median distance from spectator to actor was far greater than that from camera lens to subject.[18]

An account of the history of acting from, say, Kean to Beerbohm Tree should therefore comprise a chronicle of near-seamless continuity, punctuated by gradual change, occasional innovation, and practical adjustments to new conditions and circumstances. Among them, the following appear especially significant: the advent of the railway train and more efficient ocean-going vessels, and the consequent increase of touring companies at home and abroad; the building of new theatres of varying sizes and configurations (notably, the shrinking and ultimate disappearance of the pit in favor of individual "stalls"); new means of lighting the stage and auditorium, with gaslight and limelight earlier in the century and then, in the 1880s, with electricity controlled by dimmers,[19] making possible the darkening of the auditorium and the selective brightening of the stage, thus altering the aesthetics of play production and the social milieu as well; the remarkable development of entrepreneurship, as in the careers of Augustus Harris, George Edwardes, J. Comyns Carr, and the American producer Charles Frohman, who ventured into London venues, and the theatrical agent, as in the case of the internationally influential American Elisabeth Marbury; the decline of the repertory company, the principal casualty of the ever more popular long run, from William Moncrieff's *Tom and Jerry; or, Life in London* (Adelphi, 1821) to Brandon Thomas's *Charley's Aunt* (Royalty, 1892) and Tanner, Greenbank, and Caryll's *Our Miss Gibbs* (Gaiety, 1909),[20] and consequent changes in the terms of actors' contracts; and the gradual return to the theatre, over the second half of the century, of a long-absent fashionable audience and the correlative improvement of the actor's social status.

That improvement may easily be overstated, however, skewed by the rise of a fortunate few. The first actor awarded a knighthood was Henry Irving, in 1895 (though he had declined the honor as early as 1883); others, like George Alexander and Charles Wyndham, followed within a few years. Their brilliant social success, a reflection of the tastes and pleasures of fashionable audiences as much as their distinction as actors, should not be taken to indicate that latter-day descendants of Elizabethan "rogues and vagabonds," the workaday actors and actresses who peopled the stages of the Victorian

Mr. Tree.

The Wrench Series, No. 995 Printed in Saxony. Photo Biograph Studio.

Figure 1 Herbert Beerbohm Tree as King John in the silent film of Shakespeare's play.

century and after, had suddenly become respectable. Clarice, the heroine of Gilbert's drama *Comedy and Tragedy* (Lyceum, 1884), describes the inveterate, painful prejudice against the woman who follows a stage career:

> While I live women gather their skirts about them as I pass; when I die I am to be buried, as dogs are buried, in unholy ground . . . In the mean time, I am the recognized prey of the spoiler – the traditional property of him who will best pay for me: an actress with a body, God help her! but without a soul: unrecognized by the State, abjured by the Church, and utterly despised of all![21]

Irving had separated from his wife on precisely this issue of social disapprobation. His long-time leading lady Ellen Terry had herself felt the icy disapproval of polite society more than once. After a childhood debut as the boy Mamillius in Charles Kean's production of *The Winter's Tale* (Princess's, 1856) and a brief, disastrous teenage marriage to the dour portrait-painter George Frederick Watts, she lived out of wedlock with the architect and designer Edward William Godwin until Godwin's death in 1886 – bearing him two children Edith Craig and the brilliant theatrical director and visionary Edward Gordon Craig – even while she pursued a distinguished career with Irving at the Lyceum. Of sufficient celebrity to pose for John Singer Sargent, American artist-in-residence to the English aristocracy, whose painting of Terry (1889) as a grand, statuesque, self-crowning Lady Macbeth is one of the greatest of theatrical portraits, she was recognized in the honors list, as Dame, only in 1925 and after a late marriage. For most other performers, professional recognition might come, as it did for Terry and Irving, as a result of talent, persistence, mutual support, and luck, whereas social acceptance, or its lack, was a sacrifice made for one's art.

All the same, the attractions of a stage career could overwhelm prudence and defeat solicitous concern. How else explain the willingness of uncounted young men and women, some hardly more than boys and girls, to endure long hours, burdensome memorization, fierce competition, drafty and often unsanitary working conditions, inadequate pay, uncertain and unsavory meals, lost sleep, tedious and uncomfortable travel, unscrupulous managers, self-aggrandizing stars, victimization by charlatans of various stripes, and the nearly palpable bias of society at large against their chosen profession? Little wonder that ambitious performers like the one who took over the lease and management of the St. James's Theatre in King Street, London, in 1890 had shortened his given name of George Alexander Gibb Samson, on the advice that it was "too biblical," to the more elegant "George Alexander."[22] Little wonder that Alexander went on to establish a house whose social ambience was unexceptionable, where plays were thoroughly well rehearsed and performed by actors with flawless diction ("Be distinct!"

was Alexander's thrice-repeated cardinal rule), where performers and staff alike were treated with the utmost favor and consideration, where men's and women's dressing rooms were located on opposite sides of the backstage area, and where strict decorum, on stage and off, remained the inviolable rule of professional life. Little wonder also that, as star actor and manager of a theatre astutely aimed at cultivating the tastes and preferences and tacitly endorsing the biases of the highest strata of London society, Alexander made sure the plays he mounted included a character in a central, sympathetic role who functioned as a surrogate for that audience, whether in the guise of a dashing eighteenth-century aristocrat or a crisply morning-suited man about town like Aubrey Tanqueray, the luckless hero of Arthur Wing Pinero's fashionably risky study of modern sexual *mores*, *The Second Mrs. Tanqueray* (St. James's, 1893). He was "romantic in modern clothes, and romantic in costume," said his biographer.[23]

The truth was that at the St. James's and everywhere else as well only superficial differences distinguished the flamboyant romantic hero of costume melodrama from the more restrained West-End gentleman of comedy-drama and problem play; the same actorly skills were required, regardless. Alexander had mastered those skills over eight years of advanced apprenticeship playing supporting roles of every stamp at Irving's Lyceum; Alexander's Macduff, for example, had complemented Irving's Macbeth in the Lyceum production of "that Scottish play" (so called by superstitious actors wary of its reputation for failure) in 1888. Among the valuable lessons Alexander learned was the quintessential one: style was comprised of the way the head was held and the chapeau worn, even when the hero was indoors and hatless. (Irving was famous for hats that conveyed his mood.) The faultless cut of evening dress went all for naught unless it announced its wearer as being to the manner born. As the eponymous Paula Tanqueray, Mrs. Patrick Campbell, perhaps Alexander's most soulful, empathetic leading lady, brought a similar set of conspicuous talents to her part as the demimondaine "Mrs. Jarman," who enjoys a short-lived season in the sun of respectability as the newly married wife of the widower Aubrey Tanqueray, but who is soon cruelly indicted by her checkered past and, in the end, driven to suicide over the hopelessness of her future. Together, they presented St. James's audiences with impersonations marked by tasteful flair and well-rehearsed exaggeration (see Figure 2). They did so within the sumptuous visual surroundings of a "box set" enclosed by an ornate, "picture frame" proscenium arch, the set constructed on a raked stage whose arrangement of furniture, frankly oriented toward the footlights, left the center unencumbered and available for star turns at opportune moments. St. James's audiences, while newly impressed by the splendors of electric light introduced by Alexander

Figure 2 Mrs. Patrick Campbell in *The Notorious Mrs. Ebbsmith* by Arthur Wing Pinero.

(the program called attention to them nightly), would have found the rigorously orchestrated performances of his ensemble gratifyingly familiar. They would have perceived no contradiction between the contemporaneity of the settings (Tanqueray's swank bachelor rooms in the Albany, Piccadilly, and his bucolic country house in Surrey) and the intense theatricality of the action they set off, as in the closing moments of the last act. Aubrey runs off, at his daughter Ellean's panicked insistence, to Paula's room, while Ellean describes to Aubrey's friend Cayle Drummle the terrible sight she has seen:

> ELLEAN. I – I went to her room – to tell her I was sorry for something I had said to her. And I *was* sorry – I *was* sorry. I heard the fall. I – I've seen her. It's horrible.
>
> DRUMMLE. She – she has – !
>
> ELLEAN. Killed – herself? Yes – yes. So, everybody will say. But I know – I helped to kill her. [*She beats her breast*] If I had only been merciful!
>
> *She faints upon the ottoman. He pauses for a moment irresolutely – then he goes to the door, opens it, and stands looking out.*   CURTAIN[24]

Behind the intense engagement of an audience's emotions invoked by such a scene, crafted by Pinero for maximum climactic effect, lies a tradition of effective acting method as old as the working habits of the strolling players who arrive in Shakespeare's Elsinore at a propitious moment. Beneficiaries of expert advice from that aficionado of acting, the Prince of Denmark, these fictive players understood no less well than did their actual Victorian and Edwardian counterparts the basic requirement of the craft: moderation and control in the service of memorable overstatement, safely this side of tearing a passion to tatters, yet boldly conceived and confidently executed.

The two scenes with the Prince and the players in *Hamlet* function together as a sort of *de facto* rehearsal, a precedent for more fully fledged rehearsal plays, along with plays about the theatre in general, that appear at frequent intervals thereafter. Three such plays, produced a century apart, establish a perspicuous pattern broadly definitive of the art and craft of the English actor. The Duke of Buckingham's aptly titled *The Rehearsal* (1671) contributes to the lore of acting by lampooning the heroic hero, here called Drawcansir, who boasts: "I drink, I huff, I strut, look big and stare; / And all this I can do, because I dare."[25] In the same vein, *The Critic; or, A Tragedy Rehearsed* (Drury Lane, 1779), Richard Brinsley Sheridan's consummate spoof of authorial, critical, and actorly excesses, endorses implied salutary standards by depicting gross departures from them. A century later still, in *Trelawny of the "Wells"* (Court, 1898), Pinero's nostalgic tribute to Robertson and the palmy days at the Prince of Wales's in the 1860s, the terms of actorly engagement with role and audience had changed hardly at all. Act III brings to a head the conflict between the haughty old Sir William Gower and his stage-struck grandson Arthur, who is being coached in a more circumspect style by Tom Wrench (Robertson's fictional counterpart). At the mere mention of Edmund Kean, Sir William reenacts the performance he once saw of Kean's Richard III: *"He paces the stage, growling and muttering, and walking with a limp and one shoulder hunched"* (Bratton [ed.], *Pinero*, p. 276). His attempt to revisit Kean's idiosyncratic style reconciles Sir William to the ambitions of his grandson. By analogy, Pinero reconciles the superficial differences in style between the old Drury Lane and the new Prince of Wales's by bathing them abundantly in the magic of the stage.

These examples of acting method and their underlying ethos illustrate a range of approaches to the task of rendering feeling and reifying action on stage. In the case of an actor possessed of extraordinary resources and the skill to marshall them effectively, accomplishment can rise to the level of high art. Fanny Kemble's description of the phenomenal Irish actress Eliza O'Neill may stand for numerous such responses to the challenge of expressing potent emotion; at the same time, it raises a profound, and perennial, issue about the art of acting. From the night of her Covent Garden debut as Juliet in October 1814 until she left the stage a few years later for a fashionable marriage, O'Neill was mentioned as a worthy successor to the sublime Sarah Siddons. Although Fanny Kemble did not inhabit the rarefied sphere dominated by her celebrated aunt (her father Charles Kemble's elder sister), like other members of that illustrious family she was a genuinely talented performer herself and able to recognize transcendent ability when she saw it. She did not see it in Eliza O'Neill. In her memoir *Records of a Girlhood* (1879) Kemble reveals what in her opinion lay behind O'Neill's remarkable ability – within the range of the much-besieged, lachrymose heroines that were her specialty – to cry "buckets full" of tears. O'Neill's copious weeping, Kemble points out, occurred unaccompanied by the grimaces or other facial distortion that usually highlights the travails of stage heroines. Such actresses "have fountains of lovely tears behind their lovely eyes, and their weeping, which is indescribably beautiful, is comparatively painless, and yet pathetic enough to challenge tender compassion." Kemble attributes this condition to "deficient rather than excessive feeling." To be sure, by her own account deficiency of feeling was something of which Fanny Kemble herself could never have been accused. In her first appearance as Juliet, she recalled, she developed a sympathetic identification with the character only gradually, but by the third scene, on the balcony, she had virtually become the character herself, "the passion I was uttering sending hot waves of blushes all over my neck and shoulders." For as long as she played Juliet, Kemble insisted, those same blushes were always present.[26]

The contrast between Eliza O'Neill's and Fanny Kemble's technique of portraying strong emotion points to an issue that has perplexed philosophers and theorists time out of mind. "What's Hecuba to him, or he to Hecuba, / That he should weep for her?" – Hamlet's troubled inquiry into the wellsprings of strong emotion – states the issue well. Denis Diderot first framed it systematically in his treatise *Paradoxe sur le comédien* (1773). A pair of concerns together captures its paradoxical quality. The first is: where does the actor begin, outside or inside? Is the outward expression of emotion (grief, anger, pity, scorn, and a host of other primary and less unitary feelings) an inevitable physiological consequence of feeling originating in the recesses of human consciousness, or does the outward representation of appropriate gesture, attitude, and facial expression spontaneously conjure up the intended emotion? The second question is a corollary of the first: once an actor has succeeded in registering the required emotion, from then on will the mere imitation of its outward expression serve to reify that emotion in an authentic way, or does the actor need to experience that emotion internally every time the role is performed?

Diderot came down squarely on the side of rationally managed technical facility. The actor "is not the person he represents," Diderot explained; he plays the emotion "so well that you think he is the person," but it is the audience, not the actor, that is deceived.[27] William Archer, reviewing the alternatives in his aptly entitled *Masks or Faces?* (1888), proposed to solve the problem by showing that "the real paradox of acting . . . resolves itself into the paradox of dual consciousness" (p. 184). A double mentality, partly "executant," partly "observant," is what guides the actor through the repetition of the role over succeeding nights – or years. The American actor Joseph Jefferson once pointed out that every actor desires inspiration but cannot depend on it and must therefore take care to regulate everything in advance, even, as Archer illustrated the point, "down to pulling off each finger of a glove at a given word of a given speech" (quoted p. 209).

Finally, it appears, the paradox of acting remains just that, a paradox, a conundrum; some would say, a non-issue. Audiences care nothing about theory, after all; what they prize is energy, presence, and conviction. They are willing consumers of lies like truth. Cibber, Garrick, Kean, Irving, and Forbes-Robertson were all consummate actors, though their individual styles were quite disparate. For all, success was a matter, first, of detailed preparation and, afterwards, sustained concentration. In no case did moving an audience to convulsions of laughter or paroxysms of fear exclude the representation of authentic character. Whether they kept up a sympathetic engagement with their character even while offstage, like Mrs. Siddons, or wrote letters and conducted playhouse business between scenes, like Garrick, has ultimately no bearing on the question of what they felt while performing. The Coleridgean "suspension of disbelief for the moment" that characterizes a sophisticated audience's attentiveness finds its actorly analogy in the ability of the seasoned performer to enter wholeheartedly into the imaginary reality of the dramatic action, moment by moment, while at the same time maintaining the sleight-of-mind that simultaneously makes for authenticity and control. Some actors find that a sudden, distanced awareness of themselves in the character they are performing can be death to concentration and can induce sudden, heart-stopping panic; others find it the ordinary condition of life onstage, and thrive on it.

The emergence and persistence of acting theory, from Hamlet's advice to the players to Gilbert's, and beyond that to Shaw's peremptory demands and Craig's architectonic visions, follow a course roughly parallel to acting and performance itself, from the rise of professional companies in Elizabethan London and their reconstitution after the Restoration to the appearances of Lynn Fontanne (1905), Gertrude Lawrence (1910), Noël Coward (1911), Edith Evans (1912), Cedric Hardwicke (1912), Eva LeGallienne (1914), and other preeminent British-born stylists of the English-speaking stage in the years just before the First World War. Together, theory and practice form a complex continuum embracing the development of the art and the craft of performance. Over this long period significant points of transition can of course be identified, points as preeminent as the debuts of Garrick and Kean and the later, decade-long pursuit of historicized verisimilitude by Kean's Eton-educated son Charles. Macready's intense characterizations of "classical" and Romantic roles, such as the eponymous character of Sheridan Knowles's tragedy of virtue besieged, *Virginius; or, the Liberation of Rome* (Covent Garden, 1820) and the Cardinal in Edward Bulwer Lytton's extravagant costume drama *Richelieu; or, The Conspiracy* (Covent Garden, 1839), both highly acclaimed by their first audiences, are less transitional works than conspicuous triumphs. They merit a place on the timeline of the history of acting largely because of the sheer competence of the relentlessly self-critical Macready.[28]

Similar distinction can be accorded to the deeply felt yet carefully restrained renderings of Shakespearean and other female characters of Macready's sometime leading lady Helen Faucit, whose Rosalind, first performed opposite his Orlando in 1839, became her brightest Shakespearean achievement, and whose Clara Douglas, in Bulwer Lytton's *Money* (Haymarket, 1840), provided prime opportunities for the hauteur and the melting sympathy for which her talents were equally strong.[29] Irving himself deserves a niche in that pantheon of actors who advanced and altered in some memorable way the style or substance of an actor's realization of character, yet without attaining the preeminent status of a Garrick or a Kean as an authentic transitional figure, one whose originality is of such pith and moment that, once it asserts itself, the discipline will never be the same.

As it happens, the most significant transition occurring in the late Victorian and Edwardian era cannot be fixed by pointing to the preeminence of any one actor, not even so singular a presence as Irving. The truly significant change in the quarter-century leading up to 1914 is one estimable not primarily in terms of influential personality or tellingly original performance but, on a larger scale, in terms of the cultural predicament of the actor – a development not attributable to any one individual or even to the theatre and drama of any one country but, rather, pan-European in origin and scope.

To view this transition clearly we should address several, seemingly unconnected developments that were surfacing at about the same time. The earliest of these, the impulse toward verisimilitude, actorly and scenic, noted in the Bancrofts' (and Robertson's) renovation of the Prince of Wales's and the rise of a more fully articulated *mise en scène*, continued to gain momentum as the Edwardian decade began. Beerbohm Tree's reorganization of Shakespeare's plays into seven acts so as to accommodate a series of spectacular full-stage settings is symptomatic of the trend. Meanwhile, in Russia in the last years of the century Constantin Stanislavsky was pursuing a new method of preparing a role and building a character, establishing a minutely detailed introspective process in which the actor plumbs the depths of his own experience and transmutes his psychic life into the stuff of art. And while this was happening, in England William Poel and, after him, Gordon Craig were attempting, each in his own way, to escape from what they saw as the dead end of scenic superrealism. Poel's retrograde strategy was to return to what he believed to be the unadorned stage of the Elizabethan theatre, attempting to uncover the true meanings of Shakespeare's plays by disencumbering them of their latter-day scenic accretions.[30] Craig, rebelling against what he viewed as the star performer's self-indulgent subordination of the work to his own magnetic personality, insisted that the play, not the actor, was the thing. To realize that goal, Craig called for a strong controlling intelligence bent on achieving complete consistency of style and tone; for without that, he believed, clarity of meaning was impossible. The means to that radical end was the subordination of the actor to the stylistic and thematic exigencies of the scene. Ideally, the actor would become a kind of human puppet – Craig's highfalutin term was "übermarionette" – whose every move was planned, willed, and executed by the *régisseur*.[31]

What these disparate initiatives held in common was their pursuit of the possibilities of *dimensionality*: mimetic, in Robertson's case; psychological, in Stanislavsky's; historical, in Poel's; and visual and tonal, in Craig's. In one way or another, their quest was to achieve a convincing representation of *depth*, variously construed; the means to that end was a necessary reinvention of the basic elements of the actor's art, *gesture* and *attitude*.

Whether classifiable as theory or not, a long series of books dating from the eighteeenth century (and before) had offered a systematic understanding of gesture and attitude comprising a "universal" language of the passions.[32] Henry Siddons's *Practical Illustrations of Rhetorical Gesture and Action, Adapted to the English Drama* (1807) may stand for a hundred others. Diderot and all who debated the paradox of the player's art or themselves employed those gestures on stage knew of them, and they still served as vehicle for the articulation of emotional states as silent film began to draw upon the experience of stage actors (Mayer, "Acting in Silent Film," pp. 16–23). The presence of a uniform, comprehensible means of non-vocal expression provided more continuity over the history of English acting than any other element of the actor's craft. Allowing for a certain range of difference and much variation in individual implementation, acting from Robertson to Craig maintained fundamental assumptions about audience and performance, even while the ethos of acting was responding to great cultural pressures from several quarters.

Observing the process of continuity and change in this period, we may wonder how to understand what some historians of nineteenth-century theatre and drama have identified as the dominant trend of acting over the years to the end of Victoria's reign and the subsequent death of Edward VII: namely, the bold simplification and flattening of character that occurred through the century-long ascendancy of melodrama. Certainly, a well-reputed actor like Charles Hawtrey (the original Lord Goring in Oscar Wilde's comedy-drama *An Ideal Husband* [Haymarket, 1895]) would have scoffed at the notion that his acting was in any sense "flat," or in any way based upon concepts of human nature and dramatic character that came to the fore in the age of Coleridge and Shelley. In the same breath he would have been careful to differentiate his suave impersonations from the well-advertised excesses of melodramatic heroes and villains. The remarkable range of acting that articulates itself in the late Victorian period, extending from the high-profile, blood-and-thunder absolutes of East-End melodrama to the nuanced, white-glove-and-crush-hat sophistication of the Haymarket and St. James's, is perhaps the most obtrusive fact about play production in that age.

For all that, despite the obvious divergence of styles and their uneasy coexistence during this long period, they were grounded, like the gestural basis on which they were built, on a unitary concept of effective acting – namely, that it required, as Hamlet profoundly phrased it, "the motive and the cue for passion." The assumptions underlying Hazlitt's descriptions of Kean's performances of Shylock and other characters[33] differ only in detail from James's empathetic picture of Salvini's Lear, from Shaw's tribute to Lorraine's John Tanner, and from Hawtrey's witty lord. They share an unquestioned acceptance of the confluence in an actor's performance of concepts of character, "Romantic" and "melodramatic," that together held sway from well before Victoria's accession in 1837 to well after her death in 1901. These were the paths traversed by English actors, intermittently signposted by English method and, to a much smaller extent, theory, from the age of Kean to the age of Irving and beyond. A century later, their performances, like the audiences that witnessed them, survive only as record or recollection. All the same, the vitality and presence we find in actors and acting today, in this post-Gielgud era – Ralph Fiennes's Richard II and Coriolanus come happily to mind[34] – have such clear affinities with performances of such roles by Kemble, Kean, Macready, Fechter, Tree, Martin-Harvey, their actress counterparts, and their illustrious and unsung predecessors that the connections seem, finally, too close to challenge.

NOTES

1. *The Bodley Head Bernard Shaw: Collected Plays with Their Prefaces*, ed. Dan H. Laurence, 7 vols. (London: Max Reinhardt, Bodley Head, 1970), 1: p. 381.

2. See Shaw's introduction to *Three Plays by Brieux* (New York: Brentano's, 1911), pp. vii–liv.

3. George Bernard Shaw, *The Quintessence of Ibsenism*, in J. L. Wisenthal (ed.), *Shaw and Ibsen: Bernard Shaw's "The Quintessence of Ibsenism" and Related Writings* (Toronto: University of Toronto Press, 1979), pp. 218, 219.

4. Martin Meisel, *Shaw and the Nineteenth Century Theater* (Princeton, NJ: Princeton University Press, 1963), pp. 94–118.

5. George Bernard Shaw, *Our Theatres in the Nineties* (London: Constable, 1932), 1: p. 203.

6. Christopher St. John (ed.), *Ellen Terry and Bernard Shaw: A Correspondence* (New York: G. P. Putnam's Sons, 1932), p. 39.

7. C. B. Purdom (ed.), *Bernard Shaw's Letters to Granville Barker* (New York: Theatre Arts Books, 1957), p. 84.

8. Henry James, "Tommaso Salvini," in Allan Wade (ed.), *The Scenic Art: Notes on Acting & the Drama: 1872–1901* (New Brunswick, NJ: Rutgers University Press, 1948), pp. 179–80.

9. "Munden's Farewell," *London Magazine*, July 1824.

10. William Tydeman (ed.), *Plays by Tom Robertson* (Cambridge: Cambridge University Press, 1982), p. 164.

11. Percy Fitzgerald, *Principles of Comedy and Dramatic Effect* (1870), quoted in Daniel Barrett, *T. W. Robertson and the Prince of Wales's Theatre* (New York: Peter Lang, 1995), p. 118.

12. George Henry Lewes, *On Actors and the Art of Acting* (New York: Grove, n.d.), p. 17.

13. Max Beerbohm, "Henry Irving," in *Around Theatres* (London: Rupert Hart-Davis, 1953), p. 401.

14. Reprinted in Michael R. Booth (ed.) *English Plays of the Nineteenth Century*, vol. iii: *Comedies* (Oxford: Clarendon Press, 1973), p. 330.

15. Kalman A. Burnim, *David Garrick Director* (Carbondale, IL: Southern Illinois University Press, 1973), pp. 57–58.

16. Shaw, *Our Theatres in the Nineties*, iii: p. 167.

17. *British Mutoscope and Biograph Company, 1899*, in *Silent Shakespeare* (New York: Milestone Film & Video, 2000).

18. See Nicholas A. Vardak, *Stage to Screen: Theatrical Method from Garrick to Griffith* (Cambridge, MA: Harvard University Press, 1949); and David Mayer, "Acting in Silent Film: Which Legacy of the Theatre?" in Alan Lovell and Peter Krämer (eds.), *Screen Acting* (London: Routledge, 1999), pp. 10–30.

19. See Terence Rees, *Theatre Lighting in the Age of Gas* (London: Society for Theatre Research, 1978); and Frederick Penzel, *Theatre Lighting Before Electricity* (Middletown, CT: Wesleyan University Press, 1978).

20. This last, for some 638 performances; see J. P. Wearing, *The London Stage 1900–1909: A Calendar of Plays and Players* (Metuchen, NJ: Scarecrow Press, 1981), p. 722.

21. W. S. Gilbert, *Comedy and Tragedy*, in *Original Plays*, 3rd series (London: Chatto & Windus, 1895), p. 5. See Tracy C. Davis, *Actresses as Working Women* (London: Routledge, 1991); and Joseph Donohue, "Women in the Victorian Theatre: Images, Illusions, Realities," in Laurence Senelick (ed.), *Gender in Performance: The Presentation of Difference in the Performing Arts* (Hanover, NH: University Press of New England), pp. 117–40.

22. A. E. W. Mason, *George Alexander & the St. James' Theatre* (London: Macmillan, 1935), pp. 8, 12, 16; J. B. Booth, *London Town* (London: T. Werner Laurie, 1929), p. 87.

23. See Mason, *Alexander*, pp. 105 and *passim*, and the résumé of Alexander's career and roles in Joseph Donohue (ed.) with Ruth Berggren, *Oscar Wilde's "The Importance of Being Earnest": A Reconstructive Critical Edition of the Text of the First Production, St. James's Theatre, London, 1895* (Gerrards Cross: Colin Smythe, 1995), pp. 53–55.

24. J. S. Bratton (ed.), *Arthur Wing Pinero, "Trelawny of the 'Wells'" and Other Plays* (Oxford: Oxford University Press, 1995), pp. 211–12.

25. In Simon Trussler (ed.), *Burlesque Plays of the Eighteenth Century* (London: Oxford University Press, 1969), p. 41.

26. Frances Ann Kemble, *Records of a Girlhood* (New York: Henry Holt, 1879), pp. 195–96, 220.

27. *The Paradox of Acting*, by Denis Diderot (trans. Walter Herries Pollock), and *Masks or Faces?*, by William Archer, with introduction by Lee Strasberg (New York: Hill and Wang, 1957), p. 20.

28. See Alan S. Downer, *The Eminent Tragedian: William Charles Macready* (Cambridge, MA: Harvard University Press, 1966); and Charles H. Shattuck (ed.), *Bulwer and Macready: A Chronicle of the Early Victorian Theatre* (Urbana, IL: University of Illinois Press, 1958).

29. Carol Jones Carlisle, *Helen Faucit: Fire and Ice on the Victorian Stage* (London: Society for Theatre Research, 2000), pp. 69, 82–83.

30. Robert Speaight, *William Poel and the Elizabethan Revival* (London: William Heinemann, 1954).

31. See Edward Gordon Craig, *The Art of the Theatre* (London: Heinemann, 1911); Christopher Innes, *Edward Gordon Craig* (Cambridge: Cambridge University Press, 1983); and Irène Eynat-Confino, *Beyond the Mask: Gordon Craig, Movement, and the Actor* (Carbondale, IL: Southern Illinois University Press, 1987).

32. Joseph R. Roach, *The Player's Passion: Studies in the Science of Acting* (Newark: University of Delaware Press, 1985).

33. See Joseph Donohue, *Dramatic Character in the English Romantic Age* (Princeton, NJ: Princeton University Press, 1970), pp. 323–43.

34. Almeida Theatre productions, Gainsborough Studios, Shoreditch, London, April–July 2000.

2

TRACY C. DAVIS

The show business economy, and its discontents

Economists, like all historians, make assumptions. One of their favorite assumptions concerns a hypothetical but ubiquitous entity called *homo economicus* ("economic man"), who makes rational choices to maximize his or her own profit within the organized chaos that is called a marketplace, buyers seeking to pay low prices and sellers trying to get high prices. When *homo economicus* is present, the degree of maneuverability on prices is determined by the scarcity of what is being sold. While this may be too reductive to encompass the entire range of human choices, economists nevertheless recommend that historians test the concept against the evidence.

Historians often balk at the abstraction of *homo economicus* motivated exclusively by material advantage. After all, we do not live by bread alone. True enough. But admit that most people devote a considerable proportion of their energies to seeking material gain, especially in the realm of activity that deals with producing, earning, buying, and selling, and you open the intellectual door to *homo economicus*. Let's temporarily ignore non-pecuniary motivations, construct a model featuring economic man, take it for a ride, and see whether the results (in terms of predictive power) justify such an extreme assumption. Furthermore, don't forget that economics makes no predictions about the uses to which *homo economicus* puts his wealth; grasping merchants may use their profits to support the church, to build monuments to themselves, or to endow homes for stray cats – the economist pays no heed.[1]

This chapter proposes just such an investigation, taking *homo economicus* "for a ride" to examine the limits of the concept's applicability to the theatre, the Victorian and Edwardian contours of the quest for material advantage on the part of producers and consumers, and the willingness to operate outside the confines of a marketplace predicated on material gain.

The theatre's operations are like all other branches of the economy, seeking an equilibrium of supply and demand. A diva's voice was the rarest of all performance commodities, and hence the prestige of opera and deep pockets of its connoisseurs. Star actors were also rare, hence their recognition through salaries. Most of the marketplace, however, was supplied by mediocrities who neither fetched extraordinary prices nor received unusual recompense. There was demand for this kind of entertainment too, and it was plentifully answered.

Theatre depends on teams of specialized laborers to produce performances – everyone from the leading lady to the call boy – and it often comes down to the efficiency of the team in producing an acceptable product and the proficiency of the manager in packaging the product that determines who will stay to supply the market again and who will "exit" the marketplace in penury. But leaving the market in penury does not always mean leaving it in obscurity, any more than staying in it meant acclaim. What is unusual about this thinking within theatre studies is that it provides a way of telling history according to the principles that describe the circumstances of participation rather than focusing mainly on the exceptions to common practice. Thus, presence (however fleeting), precariousness, and perhaps disappearance from the marketplace (whatever the circumstances) may be more important – and more telling – with regard to overall practices than extraordinary longevity, "impact," or notoriety. Likewise, the complete inability to enter the market when seeking to do so on unconventional terms also helps to reveal the informal laws that regulate commerce.

Too often, theatre history focuses on the idiosyncratic rather than the typical in identifying "success." The mid-Victorian industry was sustained, for example, not by Charles Kean's determination to produce historically informed scenography at the Princess's Theatre but rather by his competitors' decisions not to do so. This is not the way history is usually told: Kean's inability to make much profit at the Princess's is underplayed in favor of his exceptional decision to practice a different aesthetic. But while historians admire Kean the antiquarian, mid-Victorian *homo economicus* thought him a bore, so he never again managed a London theatre. He did much better as a touring star, without his scenery in tow. On the other hand, Augustus Harris was phenomenally successful at Drury Lane in the latter part of the century, producing annual pantomimes and spectacular melodramas long after West-End audiences were supposed to be too sophisticated for that sort of thing. Harris wrote that he owed his success to obeying "intelligently in the matter of dramatic entertainment the unerring law of supply and demand."[2] The long line of Drury Lane managers before him who lost fortunes and usually departed insolvent were the norm, yet who remembers them? Perhaps even more importantly, who remembers much about Harris? He consolidated rather than innovated. He sustained old genres and styles rather than created new ones. He became rich by pleasing *homo economicus*, but what does history care about that?

When in pursuit of profits, rational man, it seems, behaves very differently from how theatre historians would prefer. Even Henry Irving, a darling of historians, who for two decades spent lavishly on productions and brought the Lyceum Theatre to international fame for hosting his singular artistic vision in popular renderings of legitimate dramas, was not helped much by the variety of *homo economicus* indigenous to London. In twenty years of autonomous operations at the Lyceum, Irving had a net loss of approximately £20,000.[3] While Irving's products were admired, he had to pursue other means to remain in the London market. Thanks to his exertions on tour in the provinces, and the greater enthusiasm of out-of-town *homo economicus*, the balance turned in Irving's favor by less than £10,000. That represents £500 profit per year, a comfortable middle-class salary but nothing to trumpet in the history books. Only by touring in North America, repeatedly and strenuously, did Irving become wealthy. In effect, he traded on his London prestige to command favorable returns elsewhere. To accommodate these facts, theatre historians might have to acknowledge that American *homo economicus* better appreciated Irving's rationality, for only abroad did he find an advantageous price. While this explanation still allows London to be an arbiter of taste and center of culture, it makes Irving less an inspired artist and more a nomadic merchant, indefatigably seeking a favorable marketplace.

In the cases of Edmund Kean and Henry Irving, taking their wares to North America was extremely profitable. It is by precisely this tactic that the London theatre profits today exceed the British steel industry's trade surplus. And it is by virtue of this fact that understanding the nineteenth-century theatre's operations in the economy becomes significant for canny evaluation of what sustained live performance in the past and what might still do so today.

The working out of supply and demand is a Darwinian idea, the fittest entrants to the marketplace surviving by attracting the consumers who deftly weigh quality against price. In such an analogy, *homo economicus* is unchanging while the goods for sale adapt or propitiously mutate to ensure that the marketplace constantly evolves, however imperceptibly at times.

For theatre historians, always more attuned to the aesthetics of presentation than the mechanisms of price, and for literary historians, seeking respite from the long winter of Victorian drama and salvation from its legions of playwriting hacks, the advent of Realism is the evolutionary explanation par excellence. It serves as a chronological marker between the Victorian and Modern, a stylistic breach between populism and art, and a paradigm-shifting event in the unfolding story of dramatic improvement. While the enablers of the new style loom larger in theatre histories than they probably did in their contemporary scene, Realism is undeniably an important development in the English theatre. Ibsen is credited as its architect, with critics like William Archer and George Bernard Shaw its heralds, artists like Elizabeth Robins and Mrs. Theodore Wright its engineers, and dramatists like Arthur Wing Pinero and Henry Arthur Jones its beneficiaries. Adaptations of Ibsen could first be seen in London in 1880, though it was more than another decade before he was recognizably and consistently produced and another decade still before *bona fide* Realism took hold in a generation of British playwrights dedicated to the new aesthetic. Thus, at the brink of the *fin de siècle*, a contemptible mixture of excessive spectacle and miscellaneous genres gave way to a more enlightened and coherent alternative. This, as we all know, experienced its fullest flowering in the twentieth century, when a more mature modernism became evident in works by Shaw, John Galsworthy, and Granville Barker under progressive managements such as the Vedrenne–Barker seasons at the Royal Court.

What is missing from this triumphalist narrative, apart from fine attention to historical detail, is any account of how this was accomplished in economic terms. Yes, enough artists and intellectuals were persuaded to experiment, but how did they afford to do so? Yes, somehow they staged productions by renegade authors and artists, but what happened when they sought an audience? What did *homo economicus* make of what historians celebrate as an undeniable and inexorable improvement?

If Realism found a public airing – and it did, though haltingly, not without its share of setbacks, and never eclipsing all other styles – what of the crass commercialism that had prevailed in theatre business? It is possible that "rational man" – for so long unaware of his alienation by mass production, blissfully ignorant of his turbulent psychology, and so low-brow as to spend leisure hours in fantasies of respite from strife and woe – embraced modernism and made it as commercially viable, creating a sizeable new consumer bloc with a secure hold on the marketplace. But how was the advent of modernism possible when the majority of "rational" consumers clearly preferred irrational entertainments? William Archer, the Scot who championed bringing the international modernist movement to England, acknowledged by his "Law of the Hundred Thousand" that the mark of a play's success was a run of at least one hundred nights. At a theatre seating 1,000 this meant a minimum of 100,000 needed to see a play, yet "it is absurd to imagine that there are in London, at any one time, 100,000 playgoers of keen intelligence and delicate perception – capable, in short, of appreciating the highest order of drama."[4] What a more demanding repertoire required was a system whereby an "advanced" play (or an English classic) could be seen by only 25,000 people paying four shillings apiece, underwritten by an endowment or subsidy and operating as an artistic repertory theatre, perhaps with more than one stage. In other words, Archer wanted to operate outside of capitalism, and envisioned a theatre immune to the marketplace.

Modernism traded on the unpleasant: its themes, characters, plots, and *mores* all turned to the darker sides of human nature and the bleaker aspects of human experience. Modernism's preoccupation with being edifying rather than entertaining and difficult to understand rather than uplifting to the spirits depended on a reversal of the status quo: the less pleasure was valued, the more bleakness and pain rose in status. Modernism's champions strategically emphasized that Victorian theatre managers pandered to the public's low taste, portraying them as beings of the marketplace rather than the mind, pragmatists rather than visionaries, and servants to the masses rather than masters of an art. Archer is the pivotal figure in these narratives, for in his work and writings we see united the uncompromisingly critical view of Victorian theatrical practice with a practical solution in his 1904 proposal for a theatre devoted to higher goals, *A National Theatre: Scheme and Estimates*, written with Granville Barker.[5] In fact, however, what Archer proposed was neither workable nor novel. A comparable scheme predates the Victorian era, and nothing like it came into permanent existence in Britain until the National Theatre opened its doors on the South Bank in 1976.

Archer's first endorsement of "An Impossible Theatre" appeared in 1887. He casts his description as a Christmas story, a fantasy prompted by gastronomic over-indulgence.

> I dreamed that a certain number of wealthy and æsthetic persons had combined to found a theatre, with the express design of affording a home for plays, old and new, which are impossible at the ordinary commercial theatres . . . The theatre was built by twenty subscribers, each of whom contributed £2,500 – in a dream one has vague ideas of the value of money. This conferred a right to vote in the election of the committee of management, a board of five, not necessarily composed of subscribers alone. Each subscriber, too, was owner in perpetuity of one of the twenty boxes, which he could use himself, or give away, or sublet, just as he pleased.[6]

Permanent, *ad hoc*, domestic, and foreign play-producing societies would mount productions and rent, borrow, or share the space. Thus, the repertoire might range through ancient Greek classics, Calderon, Shakespeare's histories and the neglected Elizabethan and Jacobean masters, Restoration comedy, and nineteenth-century poetic dramatists like Tennyson, Shelley, Michael Field, and Swinburne, all for the sake of instruction and exploration rather than to create scintillating entertainment. Daring contemporary works would also have their place, encouraging indigenous writing as well as showcasing emerging Continental dramatists such as Ibsen. Obviously, this dream theatre superseded the needs of commercialism on every count:

> The object of the architect had been, not to seat as many people as the space would possibly contain, but to give everyone elbow room, knee room, and a perfect view of the whole stage . . . Every seat in the theatre was a roomy and substantial arm-chair, so that whoso listed could sleep as comfortably as at his club. This (I saw in my vision) was one of the chief attractions of the house. Doctors soon began to recommend sufferers from insomnia to take a stall on Browning nights.[7]

Though tongue in cheek, Archer's ideas had substance. He envisioned a theatre emancipated from its accountants through an enlightened and liberal donor class capable of endowing £50,000 toward a laboratory that even now more closely resembles university drama departments than the Royal National Theatre on the South Bank.

As Archer explained in a more earnest mood in 1891, the actor-manager system and especially the commercial pressures of the long run forced professionals to apply as their *sine qua non* whether a play had money in it rather than whether it had merit.

> We require a theatre which shall not be forced, as a condition of its existence, to pay large interest on the capital invested in it – a theatre at which a homogeneous company of artists shall play a varied repertory, and hundred-night runs shall neither be aimed at nor permitted. State aid being out of the question, private liberality and intelligence must come to the rescue.[8]

For this, Archer thought an "English [André] Antoine" who "happened himself to be a millionaire . . . would be the most convenient arrangement of all," for a mere £100,000 investment "in trying to make actors and plays" could bring as much fun to the benefactor as a yacht or racing stable. (Apparently, his ambitions and expense estimate had doubled in four years.) As long as it was not "an ordinary set of commercial adventurers, intent on getting the highest possible interest on their money" by reverting to hiring an actor-manager, then the scheme stood a chance. Archer recommended a company of shareholders bound to no more than 2 percent interest, with the excess going into an endowment fund that would eventually buy out the shareholders who could then serve as trustees.[9] This was truly philanthropic, for in a period when other investors in limited liability theatre and music-hall companies thought a 10 percent annual return low, it was extraordinary to expect founders to oversee a venture in which they no longer had any share whatsoever.

Archer's dream hinges on two aspects that mark a sharp contrast between nineteenth-century theatre and what followed. The first is that the nineteenth-century theatre was resolutely commercial, run by capitalists for gain. As Alfred Bunn wrote, theatres "are matters of private speculation," and it was incumbent upon managers to answer public opinion and taste "in a manner most calculated to repay such speculation."[10] The playgoer ruled, and as John Hollingshead, who brought the Gaiety Theatre and musical comedy to prominence, noted, the manager "must never attempt to make his taste their taste" or "commit the folly and impertinence of suggesting to a customer who asks for a baked potato the propriety of selecting a rose or a volume of poems." However diligent the manager is, it will be neither a fine aesthetic nor extensive experience that brings profit. As Hollingshead reflected, after years of work the manager "may probably hold his peace in the market-place; but in the privacy of his study he will admit that no particular training in literature and art is necessary for the good government of a theatre, but precisely those qualities that make a successful cheesemonger."[11] Instead, Archer envisioned a theatre liberated from the marketplace, and run by literati, not merchants.

Notably, Archer opted out of the status quo rather than attempting to challenge it. In the nineteenth century a government-subsidized theatre was unthinkable in Britain. Even Archer did not dare specify that the government should underwrite what he proposed. In 1879 Matthew Arnold called for an alternative, based on the Comédie-Française, seeing an "organized" theatre as inseparable from a literary theatre, and a well-trained company of actors arising only from a stable institution.[12] In the French tradition, from Napoleon's decree of 1807 until the removal of license restrictions in 1864, four Parisian theatres bearing a national title were subsidized out of the public purse.[13] In Britain, however, there was neither a sector receiving direct state grants nor, after 1843, theatres carrying meaningful symbolic responsibility of crown representation. While there was always the implied obligation of the theatre toward the state, no fiscal obligation was assumed in reverse. What Arnold does not account for is how such an institution would either supplement or replace the marketplace in which theatre operated. His idea was not popular with capitalists. Adding an institutionalized theatre – whatever its revenue sources – promises to create disequilibrium in the market, and sometimes even create substitutions for markets. At the very least, institutionalized theatres circumvent markets by their different repertoire and lesser reliance on box office.

What evolved in the latter part of the twentieth century was a subsidized sector in parallel to the commercial sector, with a less cost-intensive additional "fringe" sector that was subsidized sometimes and as commercial as it could be while catering to a less risk-averse public. The finances of civic and other not-for-profit theatres are routinely overseen by boards of directors who are neither theatre artists nor investors. At the beginning of the twenty-first century, the West End is sometimes inseparable from the subsidized theatres, as the commercial transfers of mega-hits attest. They may also embrace elements of the fringe by running second or third stages on a smaller scale, often with unconventional repertoire, trying out ideas, developing new playwrights, and honing artists' skills in a challenging environment. But in the Victorian era, none of this existed, and reciprocity between the commercial market and any other was unthinkable. While alternatives to this market were periodically envisioned, few were tried. The reasons for ideas' stagnation on the drawing board offer important clues to the operation of the theatre within its culture, and ways to challenge the assumptions that have pervaded study of this period.

There were fledgling efforts to create a not-for-profit sector at the beginning and end of the Victorian period. This does not include the legion of purely amateur theatre groups which existed to provide an outlet for performance amongst largely middle-class enthusiasts: by 1871, organized clubs of this nature numbered 308 in London alone, with 5,500 members.[14] But amongst professional theatres, not-for-profit schemes are with one exception limited to the latter part of the Victorian period and the Edwardian era.

Like the amateur theatres, an 1811 proposal for a professional theatre stipulates a plan on a private basis, which is to say one removed from the exigencies of the marketplace. The proposal outlines a plan to create a theatre in either Marylebone or St. George's parish, which were then the northern edge of London, catering to members three nights a week from November through June with a repertoire of "unexceptionable Comedies or Tragedies" as well as "Musical Entertainment." In contrast to the commercial theatres, where the lengthy bill of fare began early in the evening and could end after midnight, performances here would be contained between the hours of 8.00 and 11.00 pm, with rehearsals also open to the theatre's subscribers. Two forms of membership are conceived: 200 Proprietors paying 100 guineas each (£105), and 200 Life Subscribers at 50 guineas each (£52 10s. 0d.), comprising a total capital of £31,500. This would supply the capital costs – securing a building and needed equipment – but not necessarily create an endowment for annual operating funds. The operating budget would derive from admissions in various categories, including annual payments by the

Life Subscribers, annual subscriptions to boxes, and other tickets sold by the year, month, or week, altogether bringing in £19,950 a year.[15] To work, the plan required a high degree of consumer loyalty.

Though the burning of Drury Lane a few years before and momentary unlikelihood that it would be resurrected played some part in sparking the scheme, its proposers were more concerned with creating a commodious house for well-to-do audiences than an alternative to commercialism *per se*. This was to be a class-exclusive institution, governed by its endowers rather than by either actors or speculators. It was to be a private theatre in the sense that no money would be taken at the doors, though not in the sense that it was under the control of any one person, or that it could completely bar the public. In a way, it presaged the concept of the not-for-profit institution, though it did not come to fruition.

The 1866 Select Committee sparked a proposal for two subsidized theatres – one for original poetic and historic drama and another primarily for Shakespeare and classic drama – clearly in the mode of old school dramatic theory and the Royal Academy's priorities.[16] In 1877, the Dramatic Reform Association in Manchester mooted the idea of a subsidized theatre, and though a few meetings were held on the subject at the instigation of Lord Dufferin, nothing came of them.[17] George Godwin proposed to the Congress of the Social Science Association in 1878 that one hundred guarantors be found to establish a permanent theatre to produce quality drama. Henry Irving warned against seeking state subsidy, for "The institutions of this country are so absolutely free that it would be dangerous, – if not destructive, – to a certain form of liberty to meddle with them . . . an unscrupulous use might be made of the power of subsidy . . . such a scheme . . . must conform to the requirements of art, polity, and commerce."[18] So, Matthew Arnold's 1879 call to action, "The theatre is irresistible" so "organize the theatre," was mere polemic. The first concrete proposal for a national theatre was published circa 1885, almost two decades before Archer and Barker's *A National Theatre: Scheme and Estimates*. The 1885 document proposes a theatre to be modeled after the Comédie-Française, with one house for historical and poetical plays and a smaller venue for comedy and domestic drama.[19]

This prospective National Dramatic Institute was intended to improve the artistic standards of dramatic presentation as well as the dance: "Improved ballets in which the long vanished 'poetry of motion' shall, if possible, be revived, in place of the undress Terpsichorean athletics now in vogue."[20] It was a for-profit scheme, not dissimilar in organization to the theatres royal created under parliamentary aegis in the late eighteenth century but with the kinds of artistic goals associated with state theatres in the twentieth century. A so-called Donors' Fund created through contributions of £500 or more by trustees would bear interest at 5 percent. Smaller investors could reap dividends from the Directors' Fund and the Members' Fund. An Authors' Fund would also dispense profits in payment for selected plays and a Surplus Fund would allow for loans to be made to professionals at low interest rates. This is a "national theatre" only in name, commensurate with its artistic goals, and as such is an impractical panacea for a range of the industry's chief complaints in this period. While it resembles in some respects the not-for-profit proposals that followed, it was on a commercial plan.

When a not-for-profit sector actually emerged, it was on a much more modest scale than any of these plans foresaw. The model came from the Continental avant-garde, though adapted to local circumstances. On seeing *Ghosts* in Paris, George Moore wondered "Why have we not a Théâtre Libre? Surely there should be no difficulty in finding a thousand persons interested in art and letters willing to subscribe five pounds a year for twelve representations of twelve interesting plays."[21] Evidently, Moore was unaware that the entire financial operation of the Théâtre Libre hinged so crucially on Antoine's £72-a-year salary from the gas company that the first performances were timed to coincide with his pay days. Thus, neither London's Independent Theatre Society, founded in 1891, nor Antoine's venture came anywhere close to Moore's vision of a £5,000 budget, let alone the 1811 projection of £31,500 or Archer's 1891 estimate of £100,000. The Independent Theatre Society's chief promoter, J. T. Grein, recalled that

> Among our first members were George Meredith, Thomas Hardy, A. W. Pinero, H. A. Jones, Mrs. J. R. Green [sic], and many other people of distinction; but . . . the roll of our members never exceeded 100 and 75, and the income was barely £400 a years [sic] during the whole of its existence. In fact, so poorly was the theatre patronized that in October, 1891 [between its first production, *Ghosts*, and its second, *Thérèse Raquin*], we had only £88 in the bank, and it was due to the help of Frank Harris, Frank Danby, and a few others, that I obtained enough to give a second performance.[22]

This, like the 1811 scheme, was a subscription theatre. It charged £2 10s. 0d. to each subscriber for a projected season of five productions,[23] evading the Lord Chamberlain's censorship by taking no money at the doors. Its record fell far short of André Antoine's Théâtre Libre, which produced 111 plays by eighty-three authors, for the Independent Theatre Society produced only twenty-six plays in eighteen programs under its own mantle during its first four seasons, with three more programs in 1897–98.[24] This was achieved against great odds and through sheer will power. As Grein's biographer stated, his "financial optimism was more than godlike. If he picked a sixpenny piece from the gutter he would see in it the possibility of a perma-nent theatre in London."[25]

The Independent Theatre Society's uncommercialism was an anomaly in London, both with respect to its idealism in selecting repertoire and its com-plete disinterest in generating an endowment.[26] Beerbohm Tree's matinees and other experiments at the Haymarket came closest in spirit, though this was in the context of a fully functioning theatre company that already owned scenic, costume, and property stores from which to borrow the necessities for these eccentric productions. The Independent Theatre Society owned nothing, and in the best circumstances used scenery stored in the theatres it rented, probably relying on the performers' own wardrobes. No other es-tablished manager either emulated or supported the laboratory approach. They preferred to know the boundaries of their market through much more conservative means of consumer testing or to not test at all.

The theatre was by far the costliest art form, according to Dorothy Leighton's prospectus for incorporating the Independent Theatre Limited in 1896, for a minimum of 50,000 spectators (half of what Archer stipu-lated) were needed to make a play pay.[27] By contrast, the dress rehearsal and sole performance of *Ghosts* by the Independent Theatre Society in 1891 accommodated a maximum of 1,300 spectators. As an alternative to, but not a competitor with the theatrical establishment and the avant-garde, such as it existed in London, the Independent Theatre Society demonstrated that minor tastes in literature could be provided for at much less expense and risk. But coterie art theatres, Leighton argues, expand the range of the imaginable, with direct benefits to the mainstream venues. Thus, by having a healthy not-for-profit sector, the commercial sector is strengthened. This comes about not through competition, for the art theatre tries experiments that paradoxically the commercial theatres cannot afford. Yet "If the London managers were wise, they would be amongst the most ardent supporters of the Independent Theatre, through which they could feel the pulse of the public from time to time as to new departures in dramatic art and authorship much more eas-ily, cheaply, and irresponsibly than by formal productions under their own management."[28] There are more residual benefits than just dividends capa-ble of resulting from this activity, she argues. It is not just an assertion that virtue is its own reward, but that capitalists themselves benefit by keeping the marketplace as open as possible. History proved her right.

It was by eschewing the concept of a fully produced play that the greatest strides were taken in the not-for-profit sector. A Bank of England employee, Frederick Whelen, established one such organization, the Incorporated Stage Society, in 1899. It presented modern plays with simple costumes and no sets in large studios, rejecting both the star system and long runs. At first,

300 members were attracted through annual dues of one pound plus an entrance fee of the same amount, and the membership grew to between 1,200 and 1,500 in 1914.[29] By performing on Sunday evenings and Monday afternoons, the Stage Society, as it became known, could attract actors otherwise engaged in the West End, and thus more prominent and perhaps more proficient casts than the Independent Theatre Society, which presented on the same nights as regular theatres. While the Stage Society's record of producing unlicensable plays might bring a direct analogy into question, it shared similar goals with the municipal theatre movement championed by socialists such as Dan Irving and the Fabian Charles Charrington in the same period.[30] Such schemes were closer in spirit to the German civic, and formerly ducal, repertory theatres than the plethora of play-producing societies springing up in all regions of Britain by which amateurs or professionals promoted the principals of modernism.[31] Their shared purpose was to provide theatre that edified and improved the citizenry through art and/or politics, rather than being motivated foremost by commercial, capitalist, or competitive goals.

Archer believed that provincial municipalities were more likely to endow theatres than Parliament, and yet a truly national theatre demanded to be located in the capital. The ambitious scheme he outlined with Barker initially in 1904, with numerous revised versions in subsequent years, involved a self-supporting institution established through a scale of arts philanthropy still not seen from corporate or private sources in the British arena. He projected that a total of £330,000 was needed to set up the venture: £150,000 to endow a Guarantee Fund created by a hundred donors pledging £1,500 each to guard against deficits, £75,000 for a site, and £105,000 for a minimally ornamented building with state-of-the-art equipment. In all, just half the cost of a battleship.[32] Their projections of costs for a normal season, after initial high outlays for building up stocks of scenery, costumes, armour, and historical properties, come to £50,181 for wages including 235 staff and seventy performers, £14,050 for running and production expenses, and £6,859 for royalties. The total annual budget of £71,091 is just 6 percent higher than Tree's average expenditure at His Majesty's Theatre from 1903 to 1914, and 31 percent lower than what they claim to be the expenses of the Théâtre-Français in 1902.[33]

Though not solely an "advanced theatre," this repertory company would produce a range of British and foreign classics and contemporary works, avoiding long runs. It would operate rent-free and tax-free under the supervision of a board of trustees appointed by universities and the Royal Academy, who in turn would hire the professional managerial staff. With a capacity box office of around £345 (1,500 persons), they projected that a minimum nightly receipt of £178 (52 percent capacity) must be achieved fifty weeks in the year, or £196 (57 percent capacity) if the usual six-week vacation period is observed. At His Majesty's in 1904–05, when house receipts after a season of 309 performances were £71,912 – almost exactly what Archer and Barker called for at the national theatre – the average nightly take was £232. In other words, judging from His Majesty's Theatre, the national theatre scheme was viable in terms of the box office. Raising £330,000 to get it off the ground, a donated site, donated building, and municipal and state absolution of taxes is another matter entirely. Even if the Guarantee Fund was dispensed with, raising £180,000 was a pipe dream. Perhaps Archer and Barker sought to measure the distance between what David Belasco dichotomized as pragmatics versus prospectuses: "When the profession of theatre management is under discussion I would urge contemporary writers for the press to pause, reflect, consider; remember that . . . we who manage theatres, equally with those who direct affairs of state, 'are confronted by a condition, not a theory.' "[34]

Except on the most meager scale, there could be no not-for-profit sector in the British theatre, nor could there be a non-commercial "national theatre" showcasing the very highest of artists' aspirations. When George Rowell calls Irving's theatre, the Lyceum, "a National Theatre in all but name" he refers hyperbolically to its social recognition rather than any aspect of its fiscal operation.[35] Like its counterparts in the West End and throughout the island, the Lyceum was a strictly profit-seeking enterprise. Unlike the royal theatres of Scandinavia or the state theatres of France, the British "theatres royal" were strictly commercial concerns – if they received any monies from the aristocracy it was solely in exchange for shares or the privilege of box rental – and the Lyceum was not even nominally "royal." There might be collective public pride in the accomplishments of theatres and theatre artists, but apart from regulation of the marketplace and the considerable effect that had on operations, theatres were independent businesses.

The presence of state involvement in the British theatre – as subsidizer, patron, and even owner – sharply demarcates the post-Second World War scene from what preceded it, though not for Victorians' lack of trying. Part of the distinction they drew was between what Rocco Landesman, President of Jujamcyn Theatres, calls dedication to art rather than to the audience.[36] But what we can see with historical hindsight is the irony that dedication to the audience, as Landesman calls it, does not necessarily mean that the law of supply and demand applies. Archer initially theorized that supplying for a smaller demand could be viable under certain circumstances. The commercial managers, not surprisingly, resisted this kind of impetus, arguing that subsidy or endowment would undermine the health of what was indisputably not only a viable but a robust laissez-faire theatre marketplace.

They tolerated the small-scale experimental ventures because they could not stop them. No kind of mutuality was contemplated: if an art or modernist theatre was to develop, it had to be in overt opposition to – though not competition with – the status quo. What emerged in the latter part of the twentieth century, with considerable reciprocity between the commercial and not-for-profit sectors, and sometimes no distinction whatever between their products, was an utterly unforeseen consequence.

True, Victorian theatre managers resisted every innovation in the marketplace, from greater freedom to state inspections. They were consistently conservative in their outlook, trusting prices to regulate and profits to come if and only if new ideas in doing business were curtailed. In a sense, the economic category offered by *homo economicus*, that rational being who encompasses both supplier and consumer, comes down to human nature. Self-protectionism prevails in laissez-faire, and it is difficult for any capitalist to look an institution in the eye the same way that a fellow capitalist can be scrutinized, and know that it was a fair fight. Perhaps economists' characterization of *homo economicus* is imperfect, perhaps it is erroneous, but it is the human agency within capitalism and the human resistance to capitalism's alternatives. Decades later, with more extensive involvement of government in equalizing not only marketplaces but households' wealth, British theatre diversified in form and funding. It became a matter of civic pride to do so, as long as liberal values prevailed. *Homo economicus* grew to include the state as well as corporations securing prestige and advantage other than the purely monetary from their own versions of "homes for stray cats" in the non-commercial theatre sector, ensuring experimentation in a wide aesthetic base.[37]

NOTES

1. Thomas G. Rawski, *et al.*, *Economics and the Historian* (Berkeley: University of California Press, 1996), p. 246.
2. Augustus Harris, *The Fortnightly Review*, n.s. 38 (Nov. 1885), rpt. in Russell Jackson (ed.), *Victorian Theatre: The Theatre in its Time* (New York: New Amsterdam, 1989), p. 278.
3. Tracy C. Davis, *The Economics of the British Stage, 1800–1914* (Cambridge: Cambridge University Press, 2000), pp. 221–25. Based on data from the Theatre Museum (London), BTMA 1959/W/17 (C), Irving Archive, Box 52.
4. From William Archer's introduction to *The Theatrical "World" of 1896* (1897), rpt. in Jackson (ed.), *Theatre*, p. 289.
5. William Archer and H. Granville Barker, *A National Theatre: Scheme and Estimates* (1904) (rev. edn., New York: Duffield, 1908). This updated edition includes the authors' responses to skeptics.
6. William Archer, "An Impossible Theatre," *Theatre Annual* (1887), 31–32.

7. *Ibid.*, 32.

8. William Archer, "An Uncommercial Theatre," *Illustrated London News*, 7 February 1891, 187.

9. *Ibid.* Antoine was founder of the Théâtre Libre in Paris.

10. Alfred Bunn, *The Stage: Both Before and Behind the Curtain* (Philadelphia: Lea and Blanchard, 1850), 1: 207.

11. John Hollingshead, *Plain English* (1880), in Jackson (ed.), *Theatre*, p. 274.

12. This was originally published as "The French Play in London" in the *Nineteenth Century*, and later reprinted: Matthew Arnold, *Irish Essays* (London: Smith Elder, 1882).

13. John McCormick, *Popular Theatres of Nineteenth-Century France* (London: Routledge, 1993), pp. 13, 77.

14. The prospectus for the Amateur Theatre Company Limited of 1871, a plan which was not executed, was a for-profit venture designed to service these clubs. It proposed to raise £5,000 in share capital to equip an appropriate building to be available to the clubs on a nightly flat rental. Clubs taking fifty shares would have priority in choosing their nights. The promoters estimated that if open three nights a week at £10 per night, the company could yield 12.5 percent dividends (PRO LC1/247).

15. *Heads of a Plan for a Private Theatre* ([London]: W. Bulmer, 1811).

16. *Illustrated London News*, 26 July 1866; and PRO LC1/167.

17. George Godwin, *On the Desirability of Obtaining a National Theatre not Wholly Controlled by the Prevailing Popular Taste* (London: Wyman and Sons, 1878), p. 7; PRO LC1/326, Circular and letter from Dramatic Reform Association and Literary Society, 1877.

18. Godwin, *Desirability*, p. 28.

19. "Scheme for the Establishment of a National Theatre (Somewhat Similar to the 'Comédie-Française') by the Formation of a National Dramatic Institute from Amongst Real and Influential Patrons of Dramatic Art and Literature, and Eminent Artistes Earning Their Livelihood Thereby" ([London: 1885]).

20. *Ibid.*, p. 15.

21. George Moore, "Note on *Ghosts*," *Impressions and Opinions* (London: David Nutt, 1891), p. 226, rpt. in Michael Egan (ed.), *Ibsen: The Critical Heritage* (London: Routledge and Kegan Paul, 1972), p. 186.

22. J. T. Grein, *Stage Society News*, 25 January 1907, quoted in Miriam A. Franc, "Ibsen in England," Ph.D. thesis, University of Pennsylvania (1918), p. 87.

23. *The Independent Theatre of London (Théâtre Libre) Founder and Sole Manager – J. T. Grein* [Prospectus] [London, 1891]. See also "The Independent Theatre," *Stage*, 12 March 1891, 8.

24. Marvin A. Carlson, "The Théâtre-Libre, the Freie Bühne, the Independent Theatre: a Comparative Study," Ph.D. thesis, Cornell University (1961), pp. 120–24; N. H. G. Schoonderwoerd, *J. T. Grein, Ambassador of the Theatre, 1862–1935: A Study in Anglo-Continental Theatrical Relations* (Te Assen Bij: Van Gorcum, 1963), pp. 114–16.

25. Michael Orme, *J. T. Grein: The Story of a Pioneer* (London: John Murray, 1936), p. 11.

26. Tracy C. Davis, "The Independent Theatre Society's Revolutionary Scheme for an Uncommercial Theatre," *Theatre Journal* 42, 4 (December 1990), 447–54.

27. Dorothy Leighton, *Short Summary of the Position and Prospects of the Independent Theatre* [London: 1896], p. 3, provided courtesy of the Dan H. Laurence Collection, University of Guelph Library.

28. *Ibid.*, p. 8.

29. Anna Irene Miller, *The Independent Theatre in Europe: 1887 to the Present* (New York: Ray Long and Richard R. Smith, 1931), p. 178; Thomas H. Dickinson, *The Contemporary Drama of England* (Boston: Little, Brown, 1917), pp. 158–59.

30. Eight of the Stage Society's one hundred plays produced between 1899 and 1914 were banned (Edward Garnett's *The Breaking Point*, Granville Barker's *Waste*, S. Olivier's *Mrs. Maxwell's Marriage*, G. B. Shaw's *Mrs. Warren's Profession*, Eugène Brieux's *Les trois filles de M. Dupont*, *Maternité*, and *Les Hannetons*, and Maurice Maeterlinck's *Monna Vanna*) while Hermann Sudermann's *Midsummer Fires* and Leo Tolstoy's *Power of Darkness* were licensed only after some difficulties. Mary Jane Watson, "The Growth of an Independent Theatre Movement in London, 1891–1914," M.Litt. thesis, Bristol University (1970), p. 38; and Chris Waters, *British Socialists and the Politics of Popular Culture, 1884–1914* (Stanford: Stanford University Press, 1990), pp. 136–37.

31. Allardyce Nicoll, *English Drama 1900–1930: The Beginnings of the Modern Period* (Cambridge: Cambridge University Press, 1973), pp. 79–86.

32. Archer and Barker, *Schemes and Estimates*, pp. 8–9.

33. *Ibid.*, pp. 104–05; Bristol Theatre Collection, University of Bristol, His Majesty's Theatre (Tree Collection) Accounts. The bulk of Tree's financial information is located in profit-and-loss statements for 1904–09 and a simplified profit-and-loss statement for 1910; balance sheets for 1904–05, 1907, 1911–12, and 1914; trading account summaries 10 September to 23 December 1903, and for the fiscal years ending 1905–12 and 1914; and analyses of production expenses and/or running expenses pertaining to selected shows 1899–1914.

34. David Belasco, quoting Grover Cleveland, in "The Business of Theatrical Management," *Saturday Evening Post*, 7 June 1919, in New York Public Library, Robinson Locke Scrapbook, 53: 55.

35. George Rowell, *Theatre in the Age of Irving* (Oxford: Basil Blackwell, 1981), p. 1.

36. Rocco Landesman, "Broadway: Devil or Angel for Nonprofit Theatre?" *New York Times*, 4 June 2000; Robin Pogrebin, "Theatre for Fun or Profit: Producers' Two Camps Remain Uneasy Allies," *New York Times*, 15 June 2000, B1, 6.

37. Significantly, this does not include much foundation funding in Britain. Different tax laws in the USA make this sort of subvention much more common.

3

RUSSELL JACKSON

Victorian and Edwardian stagecraft: techniques and issues

When we think of the Victorian theatre's staging techniques, two complementary tendencies come to mind, which stand out in the requirements indicated by the stage directions in the acting editions of the scripts. One is spectacle, and in particular, the kind of effect described vividly in 1881 by Percy Fitzgerald in *The World Behind the Scenes*:

> All will recall in some elaborate transformation scene how quietly and gradually it is evolved. First the "gauzes" lift slowly one behind the other – perhaps the most pleasing of all scenic effects – giving glimpses of "the Realms of Bliss," seen beyond in a tantalizing fashion. Then is revealed a kind of half-glorified country, clouds and banks, evidently concealing much. Always a sort of pathetic and at the same time exultant strain rises, and is repeated as the changes go on. Now we hear the faint tinkle – signal to those aloft on "bridges" to open more glories. Now some of the banks begin to part slowly, showing realms of light, with a few divine beings – fairies – rising slowly here and there. More breaks beyond and fairies rising, with a pyramid of these ladies beginning to mount slowly in the centre. Thus it goes on, the lights streaming on full, in every colour and from every quarter, in the richest effulgence. In some of the more daring efforts, the *femmes suspendues* seem to float in the air or rest on the frail support of sprays or branches of trees. While, finally, perhaps, at the back of all, the most glorious paradise of all will open, revealing the pure empyrean itself, and some fair spirit aloft in a cloud among the stars, the apex of all. Then all motion ceases; the work is complete; the fumes of crimson, green, and blue fire begin to rise at the wings; the music bursts into a crash of exultation, and possibly to the general disenchantment, a burly man in a black frock steps out from the side and bows. Then to [a] shrill whistle the first scene of the harlequinade closes in, and shuts out the brilliant vision.[1]

Another aspect of spectacle was the depiction of natural and man-made disasters. Thus, at the conclusion of *The Miller and his Men* (Covent Garden, 1813), the mill is crowded with the *banditti* whose lair it has been, the hero and heroine are safe, and the famous order is given "Ravina, fire the train!"

RAVINA. *instantly sets fire to the fuse, the flash of which is seen to run down the side of the rock into the gully under the bridge, and the explosion immediately takes place.*

KELMAR. *rushing forward, catches* CLAUDINE *in his arms.* CURTAIN.[2]

The second tendency is towards an ever-increasing accuracy in the realistic depiction of everyday life, which is amply represented in the first third of the detailed opening stage direction of Tom Robertson's *Caste* (Prince of Wales's Theatre, 1867):

SCENE. *A plain set chamber, paper soiled. A window, centre [back] with practicable blind; street backing and iron railings. Door practicable [up right], when opened showing street door (practicable). Fire-place centre of left-hand piece; two-hinged gas burners on each side of mantelpiece. Sideboard cupboard in recess, left; tea-things, teapot, tea-caddy, tea-tray, &c., on it.[3]*

In addition to showing the picturesque but exploding hideouts of villains and the humble intimacy of domestic life, the theatre could make good the promises of its playbills and deliver such transformation scenes as those described by Fitzgerald and embellish *Macbeth*, as Charles Kean did in his 1853 production, with a "distant view of Iona by moonlight" to accompany the witches' appearance in act IV.[4]

Pantomime and melodrama often combined trick effects and spectacle, always musically supported, with large-scale landscape painting. The fairy-tale "opening" of a pantomime was followed by the transformation scene, which heralded the harlequinade – usually providing a series of contemporary and topical townscapes for the traditional characters to disport themselves in. In 1835 Henry Crabb Robinson went to Drury Lane for the third act of *The Red Mask*, despite having already been "sufficiently fatigued" by the spectacle, in order to see "the last splendid show of *King Arthur* of which the finest scene was a beautiful landscape of the Vale of St. John in Cumberland in which the magical rocks by means of a strong light put behind are made to become a *castle* with all its appurtenances."[5] This was also (although Crabb Robinson was not complaining) a show that included the equestrian element associated with such theatres as Astley's: scenery and action were displacing the "legitimate" spoken drama in the very theatres that were privileged by patent to perform it. Playbills commonly list the various scenic locations of any entertainment in bold, larger type, and often credit the scene-painters for each one.

The staging techniques current in the middle of the nineteenth century were a refinement of those developed in the preceding century, and shared the same basic elements. Scenery, painted in perspective, was set parallel to the front of the stage, and consisted either of cloths (painted canvas on rollers) suspended from the flies, or flats (painted canvas stretched on wooden frames) of various dimensions. Originally, in a continuation of eighteenth-century practice, these were supported in two sets of wooden grooves, one of which ran permanently across the stage floor while the other was lowered from above.[6] Later, as scenery set at an angle across the stage became common, it would be propped on the wooden stage floor and fixed with braces, held in position with weights or, more permanently, screws. Practicable doors and windows would be set into the flats as appropriate, and such elements as skirting boards and cornices would be painted rather than represented by mouldings. By the end of the century the increased use of electric lighting – at first criticized as being too bright for traditional scene-painting techniques – prompted an increase in the employment of "built-out" architectural features, and of three-dimensional scenery, on which light and shade could be created with the more easily manipulated and colored lighting.

Until the 1860s, most interiors would be depicted by flats painted in perspective and set at the usual intervals from front to back, and ceilings would be indicated by corresponding "borders" – framed or loose cloths hung above the stage: viewed from the center of the auditorium and seen in register, these would provide an acceptable illusion of solidity. From any other angle, the illusion was inadequate. From the 1860s "box sets" became the norm. The side walls would be set at an angle (but not usually at right angles to the backing) and a ceiling suspended above them. Much ingenuity was devoted to hiding the joins between wall sections, and softening the edges of such cut-out elements as foliage. For outdoor scenes, the representation of landscape in perspective could be achieved with wings set in diminishing perspective, supplemented by "cut cloths" to indicate rows of trees and "ground rows" to mask the join between the floor and the backdrop. Additional platforms, ramps and "built-up" units of scenery (for hillocks, etc.) supplemented these. In outdoor scenes the representation of sky above the stage was never satisfactory. The edges of the borders always showed, although framing the picture with such features as overarching boughs and foliage could do much. Figure 3, which shows the traditional wooden stage installed in the new Shakespeare Memorial Theatre at Stratford-upon-Avon in 1879, illustrates these limitations.[7] Seen under appropriate lighting conditions, and by audiences used to them, such scenes were adequate if not wholly convincing. By the time this stage was installed, however, expectations had been raised considerably. As with interiors, closing off the upper reaches of the stage space would have created problems in sourcing and directing light. The principal light sources were footlights, battens set in the wings or behind the borders, and follow spots generated by limelight or (from the mid-1850s) electric arcs.[8] At the end of the century the problem of achieving

Figure 3 The Shakespeare Memorial Theatre, Stratford-upon-Avon, *c*. 1912.

an expressive and convincing representation of the sky was solved by the introduction of the curving back wall and overarching cyclorama, together with appropriate electric lighting. These resources placed a great emphasis on the scene-painters' ability to render subtle and impressive lighting effects, to which the gas (and later, electric) lamps provided appropriate illumination. Percy Fitzgerald, writing in the early years of the new century, lamented the lost glories of the work of Clarkson Stanfield and William Telbin, whose "refined and mellow treatment" was suited to the gentler quality of gas but would have been lost in the "fierce light" of electricity.[9] Gas remained in use at the Lyceum for footlights and gas limelight until the end of Irving's tenure. Ellen Terry, in a heartfelt tribute, wrote of "the thick softness of gaslight, with the lovely specks and motes in it, so like natural light" which "gave illusion to many a scene which is now revealed in all its naked trashiness by electricity."[10]

The means used to achieve such transitions as sunrises included mechanical devices attached to lighting hardware and the manipulation of colored mediums placed in front of the light sources. The scenic artist Frederick Lloyds, in his *Practical Guide to Scene-Painting and Painting in Distemper* (1875) describes the complex process of priming, painting and lighting transparent and translucent cloths in order to achieve sunset (and, in reverse, sunrise) effects.[11] Gauzes were commonly used for transformation scenes (particularly in pantomimes) and were sometimes combined with long painted backcloths moving laterally ("panoramas") and vertically. The term diorama, often used for such moving backcloths, should in fact be reserved for the use of gauzes that showed different states of a scene according to the direction of lighting: large paintings of this kind were exhibited as entertainments in themselves.

In some cases, such as the forest scenes in Samuel Phelps's 1853 production of *A Midsummer Night's Dream* at Sadler's Wells, whole sequences might be played behind gauze, in order to create an effect of mysterious gloom. Henry Morley's enthusiastic review in the *Examiner* observed that there was "no ordinary scene-shifting; but, as in dreams, one scene [was] made to glide insensibly into another." The green gauze curtain "subdu[ed] the flesh and blood of the actors into something more nearly resembling dream-figures, and incorporate[d] more completely the actors with the scenes, throwing the same green fairy tinge, and the same mist over all."[12]

The directional lighting afforded by limelight could be combined with different colors of smoke for apparitions (for example, supernatural beings) and also for more general atmospheric effects. By the end of the century steam was being employed: it was less noxious than the chemicals formerly used, but had a tendency to make the theatre smell like a laundry. Other "special effects" included lantern-slide projections, mirrors (most famously, "Pepper's Ghost," in which a sheet of glass on stage was angled to reflect an off-stage figure), and traps. There was usually an oblong "grave trap" (named after its use in *Hamlet*) placed centrally upstage of the curtain line, and at least two counterweighted traps, which could be adapted with a set of hinged and sprung wooden segments as "star traps" for the sudden and athletic apparition of supernatural beings (such as demons in the pantomime).

The famous "Corsican" trap used a combination of counterweighted platform and slatted shutters to allow an actor to rise gradually through the floor while simultaneously traveling across it. The stage directions in Dion Boucicault's *The Corsican Brothers* (Princess's Theatre, 1852), for which the effect was devised, illustrate the result. In the second act Fabien dei Franchi receives an admonitory vision of his brother: "LOUIS DEI FRANCHI *has gradually appeared rising through the floor, in his shirt sleeves, with blood upon his breast; and as* FABIEN *is about to place his seal on the wax [of the letter he is sending]* LOUIS *touches him on the shoulder.*" He then reveals (through the rear wall of the room, which divides with a "rise and sink" mechanism) a vision representing his own death in a duel in a snow-covered glade in the forest of Fontainebleau. In the second act the incidents leading up to the duel take place, and at the end the same scene is repeated, this time with the forest in the foreground and the room and Louis revealed behind it. The final act ends in another climactic duel, in which Fabien is mortally wounded, and the ghost of his brother Louis appears once again "*rising gradually through the earth*" and places his hand on his shoulder with the words "Mourn not, my brother, we shall meet again."[13] The apparition was accompanied by a famous musical theme. The play thus combines trapwork, trick scenery, atmospheric music and a tour de force of acting – as the same actor played the two brothers.[14] A similar combination of ingredients can be found in another of the century's most famous melodramas, *The Bells*, in which Henry Irving achieved one of his greatest successes as the burgomaster Mathias, whose guilty secret – the murder of a rich Polish Jew and the disposal of the body in a lime kiln – is embodied in a vision seen through the back wall of the inn room. The jingling sleigh bells of the play's title accompany the apparition. Later Mathias dreams that he is being tried in a court of law, where under a mesmerist's influence he relives the events of the fateful night. This time Mathias, as if confessing in his dream, re-enacts the events of the night, and the visionary portion of the scene is restricted to the court. The pictorial effects thus support rather than replace the actor's formidable skills: Irving as Mathias seems to be dreaming that he is being hypnotized – until the final moments of the play reveal that he imagines himself hanged for his crime and he does indeed die. Typically for its period, the play hovers between the psychological and the supernatural, and the illustrative contribution of the visions anticipates similar devices in the cinema.[15]

Until the last decades of the nineteenth century the auditorium might be darkened during scenes using such effects, but as a rule it remained evenly lighted throughout the play. Among the innovations credited to Henry Irving is the dimming of the auditorium lights throughout performances as general practice, although this was already among the requirements imposed by Richard Wagner on the festival theatre at Bayreuth, which opened in 1876. Wagner's other innovations included hiding the orchestra and the light sources, and constructing the auditorium in a single sweep without side boxes or gallery supports, so that the audience would look directly and with an uninterrupted view at the stage picture. Although existing houses could not be remodeled along these lines, some elements of this scheme were finding their way into the contemporary commercial theatre. In 1880 Sir Squire Bancroft altered the Haymarket Theatre in London, placing a gilded picture frame round the proscenium opening. The orchestra was hidden, giving stalls spectators an uninterrupted view of the stage, and the footlights were modified. "My intention," wrote Bancroft, "was to contrive hidden footlights, which, when the curtain fell, and was within a few feet of them, would descend to make room for the heavy roller, and which would, when the curtain was raised, follow it immediately, so that the stage should never perceptibly be darkened in either case." [16]

Refinements of the technology of illusion continued into the twentieth century, and may be said to have their inheritors in the cinema and in modern achievements in computer-generated virtual reality. Many of the devices developed in the late nineteenth century, such as the turntable (generally credited to the "machinist" of the Munich Court Theatre, Karl Lautenschläger) and the sliding stage, were essentially means of shifting the scenic pictures efficiently while concealing the machinery. This was a theatre whose ways and means were not normally to be enjoyed in themselves, and only in pantomime and burlesque was there any self-conscious reference to them, from within the entertainment. The ingenuity of the transformation scenes, and the splendors of fairy grottos, fountains and such extravagant devices, was applauded – sometimes (as the description by Fitzgerald quoted at the beginning of this chapter shows) the machinist or the manager might even take a curtain call after the scene – but this was by and large an art devoted to its own concealment, a feat of legerdemain operated by many hands in a labor-intensive business.

Throughout the century, technical innovations refined the theatre's ability to provide convincing representations of spectacular action and historically authentic settings and costumes. William Charles Macready, who did much to further the cause of artistic unity and appropriate and correct design in Shakespearean and other "period" plays, extended his enthusiasm to contemporary life in staging Edward Bulwer Lytton's comedy *Money* (Haymarket, 1840), particularly in the scene set in a Pall Mall club. However, the most influential productions of modern plays were those of the Bancrofts and their principal dramatist, Tom Robertson, at the refurbished Prince of Wales's Theatre in the 1860s. The relationship between the theatre's social priorities, the intimacy of the auditorium, and what was shown on stage, was reflected in a retrospective article in *The Era* in 1885. This was "a tiny theatre, where the stalls, boxes and balcony were the paying portions of the audience, where the pit and the gallery were small, and somewhat higher priced than at ordinary theatres. But what fascinated the public most was the perfect harmony of the whole entertainment. Never had been such delicacy and dainty staging, such photographic reproduction of familiar types" (*The Era*, 24 January 1885). By the end of the century the West-End "society drama" was expected not merely to reflect, but to embody fashions in dress and interior decoration. The actor-managers George Alexander, and Charles Wyndham at the Criterion, were leading exponents of a drama in which couturiers and gentlemen's outfitters furnished the clothes of the protagonists, while such establishments as Heal's provided the furniture – all, of course, fulsomely credited. George Bernard Shaw remarked in 1897 that this kind of drama consisted of "a tailor's advertisement making sentimental remarks to a milliner's advertisement in the middle of an upholsterer's and decorator's advertisement."[17]

Most critics and many of its direct inheritors viewed the Robertson/Bancroft legacy with great affection. Tom Wrench, the playwright in Pinero's *Trelawny of the "Wells"* (Court Theatre, 1898) is a tribute to Robertson's energy and good-heartedness. But these achievements also entailed limitations. There was much hankering after a broader, simpler style of performance and writing. *Punch*'s obituary verses (22 July 1882) on the veteran actor and manager Benjamin Webster represent the "venerable sage" as turning his back on "coat-and-trouser pieces and a milk and water stage" and despising "a decorated drama and an Art of bric-a-brac." Eight years later a correspondent in *Truth* (2 January 1890) even blamed Robertson and the Bancrofts for the state of pantomime: now it had become "the pantomime of panoply rather than the pantomime of fun" because "years ago the Bancrofts started the era of stage extravagance." Pantomime, of course, was an institution in a constant state of being reinvented, and just as constantly subject to head-shaking editorials complaining that fun was not what it had been. However remote from domestic realism the "stage extravagance" of its fairylands and exotic processions and transformations may seem (Figure 4), the complaint was that audiences had been taught to demand what might be called a higher degree of definition in stage pictures. Contemporaries sometimes drew comparisons with (or apportioned blame to) the rapid spread of photography and the Pre-Raphaelite painters' quest for minute detail.

As the new means of building and – more important – shifting scenes permitted yet greater variety and grandeur of effect, reviewers hankered after a golden age in which melodrama had included but not been dominated by spectacle. Drury Lane and the Adelphi had become the most celebrated producers of these equivalents of the late twentieth century's blockbuster movies. *Pluck; a Story of £50,000* (Drury Lane, 1882), by Henry Pettitt and the theatre's manager, Sir Augustus Harris ("Druriolanus"), was a fair representative of its class. Its incidents included a double train crash; the interruption of a wedding breakfast (with the arrest of the bridegroom); the murder of a banker and the hiding of the corpse in a Chatwood safe; Piccadilly Circus and the Criterion restaurant in a snowstorm; and the destruction of a three-storey slum (containing the villain) in a fire. *Vanity Fair* observed: "nothing that the mechanist's or scene-painter's art can manage has been unsampled; the supper of horrors (in seven courses) is full and complete. But what of the play and the characters? Do they interest? Are they real? Not a bit of it. In the mad hunger after 'effect' the authors [. . .] have

Figure 4 Pantomimes in London, 1872: figures from fairy tales and mythology, trick effects of scale, and romantic landscapes. The figure on the left represents a masked performer. Illustration from the *Graphic*.

crushed all semblance of humanity out of their puppets" (12 August 1884). The spectacular melodrama persisted well into the twentieth century. Such entertainments as *The Whip* (Drury Lane, 1909), whose sensation scenes included a train crash (Figure 5) and the running of the Two Thousand Guineas, were recalled by Noël Coward's *Cavalcade* (Drury Lane, 1931), with its blend of family drama and historical occasions.

If pantomime and melodrama were endangered by the new possibilities for realism, what hope was there for the "poetic drama," that holy grail of Victorian theatrical culture? For many commentators, the age was ultimately to be judged by its ability to reproduce the glories of the Shakespearean heritage, which meant that the antagonism between realism and the poetic ideal had somehow to be overcome. During his management of the Princess's Theatre, from 1851 to 1859, Charles Kean had endeavored to stage literary drama – and Shakespeare in particular – with as much authentic historical detail and lavishness of stage effect as he could muster. His three-leaf playbills, with a "flyleaf" setting out his archaeological authorities, are remarkable documents of diligence combined with educational fervor:

> In the production of Lord Byron's tragedy of *Sardanapalus* [staged in 1853] I have availed myself of the wonderful discoveries made within the last few years by Layard, Botta, and others, on the site of the ancient Nineveh . . . To render visible to the eye, in connection with Lord Byron's drama, the costume, architecture, and domestic manners of the ancient Assyrian people, verified by the bas-reliefs, which, after having been buried for nearly 3,000 years, have in our own day been brought to light, was an object that might well inspire the enthusiasm of one who has learnt that scenic illustration, if it have the weight of authority, may adorn and add dignity to the noblest works of genius.[18]

Unfortunately, many found his attention to detail (he prided himself on his fellowship of the Society of Antiquaries) stiflingly pedantic. There were times, however, where history itself, and the playwright's treatment of it, seemed to demand such effects. His *Henry VIII* (1857) featured the triumphal coronation procession of Anne Bullen, the vision of the dying Katherine, the citizens progressing in barges of state to Greenwich (a moving panorama effect), and the christening of the infant Elizabeth. The German author Theodor Fontane, an enthusiast for history, observed that this expressed the taste of the age, "an inclination towards the balletic and operatic," but insisted that such pageantry was not in itself reprehensible: "What matters is whether one presents a series of disconnected illustrations or a historical picture."[19] In other productions, Kean's work might seem labored, and to work against the "poetic" by an excess of fussy detail. Here, it seemed appropriate.

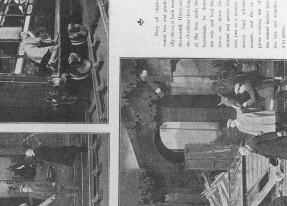
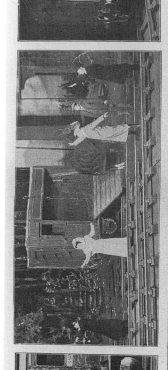
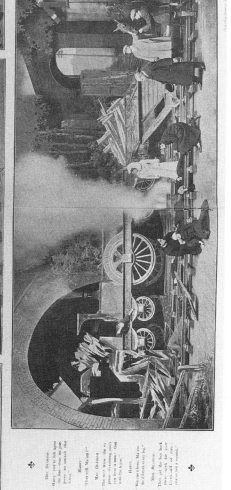

Figure 5 The train crash sequence in *The Whip*, Drury Lane 1909. Illustration from *Play Pictorial*.

In 1884 the *Athenaeum* reviewed the publication of Tennyson's plays, including *The Cup*, which Henry Irving had staged at the Lyceum in 1881. The critic reflected gloomily that stage realism, already an almost insurmountable obstacle to the poetic drama, had now been given added weight by technical refinements of illusionist scene-building. It was now an accepted fact "that literary beauties seem positively out of place in an acted play, whether tragic or comic, being destructive of that realism which the dramatist is obliged to make his one quest" (8 March 1884). Sometimes a production converted the poetic drama into spectacle, and there was no shortage of critics ready to point out the losses, however impressive the gains.

A case in point was Irving's *Faust*, with a script by William Gorman Wills, some way after Goethe. It was first seen at the Lyceum in 1885 and revived in 1894 in an enhanced version with the scene in the witches' kitchen, as well as the more spectacular *Walpurgisnacht* on the Brocken mountain. The whole production was in every respect a triumph of lavish scene design, supported by splendid music, diligent research (some of the properties had been obtained in Nuremberg) and ingenious stage machinery. The Brocken scene began with a view of the summit:

> A simple broad effect of rock and tree and cloud, it might have been expected to pass for what it is – the mere foundation of the great sensation act of the play. But the audience, affected by its calm true spirit, welcomed it with applause. Illuminated with a cold effect of stormy moonlight, the scene is singularly impressive. It is a study in black and white and grey. A mass of time-worn rock on one hand, two weather-beaten pines on the other, between them a snowy valley, the distance a mystery of vaporous cloud. But how deftly laid for the purposes of the stage-manager! . . . Presently the luminous shadow of the red Mephistopheles shows a cleft in the mountain, whence he appears leading Faust to the summit. The devil is accompanied by thunder and lightning. There is a big hazy moon with a watery halo. A sudden flock of witches on broomsticks crosses its yellow disc. A flock of owls flap their solemn wings through the stormy night.

This, of course, is only the beginning of a scene soon filled by some 250 dancing, gesticulating extras. Mephistopheles exercises his power by making the revellers vanish, then summons them again until the scene becomes transformed:

> Mephistopheles, with laughing approval, reclines upon a rock which gives forth flashes of electric light, a pair of apes fondling him, until once again he leaps into the centre of the throng, and the world of the Hartz [sic] is ablaze. Earth and air are enveloped in a burning mass. Then rocks seem to melt like

lava. A furnace of molten metal has broken loose. The clouds shower down fiery rain, the thunder rolls away into distant valleys.[20]

With such resources as Irving's, the stage directions for the cataclysmic finale of Wagner's Ring cycle, with Valhalla in flames and the Rhine overflowing its banks, should have held no fears. (In fact at Bayreuth in 1876, the critic Eduard Hanslick complained, the scene painting was exquisite, but the effects very poor: the mighty river had wobbled its "badly daubed and visibly sewn-up waves - like the Red Sea in a provincial production of Rossini's *Moses*."[21])

In a speech delivered at Harvard in 1887, Irving had made one of his many statements of the theatre's pictorial priorities:

> It is most important that an actor should learn that he is a figure in a picture, and that the least exaggeration destroys the harmony of a composition. All the members of a company should work towards a common end, with the nicest subordination of their individuality to the general purpose.

The actor "who is devoted to his profession" should study painting, music and sculpture, for he is "susceptible to every harmony of colour, form and sound." As if to deflect the habitual objections to realism, Irving insisted that "an absolute realism is not always desirable in [art], any more than the photographic reproduction of Nature can claim to rank with the highest art."[22] Irving's foremost admirer among the critics, Clement Scott, described his Mephistopheles in terms of silent – but somehow poetic – effect by invoking a combination of poets and painters:

> He has nothing to say, only to look. His words are immaterial – but in that face there is a world of meaning. No one but an imaginative actor could have conceived such a picture, or overmastered it with such a commanding presence. All the preconceived visions of Manfred and Sardanapalus and Balthasar pale before this extraordinary scene. In it we detect the weird fancy of Gustave Doré, the splendid daring and invention of John Martin.
>
> (*Illustrated London News*, 26 December 1885)

Irving and his advisers (including his business manager and biographer Bram Stoker) were expert at placing newspaper items and articles in support of the Lyceum and its productions. *Faust* was well served by the journalist Joseph Hatton, whose article in the *Art-Journal*, reprinted in part in an illustrated souvenir brochure, has been quoted above, as well as by such associates as Clement Scott. But there were notable dissenters. Henry James had been expected to write in praise of *Faust*, and his article on the acting in the play followed a more or less laudatory piece on its stage pictures in the *Century Magazine*. Unfortunately, James was far from impressed: the acting was for the most part mediocre or worse, and the witches' Sabbath was "a horror cheaply conceived, and executed with more zeal than discretion." Even less welcome were his strictures, in passing, on the very stagecraft that Irving took so much pride in: "the importunate limelight . . . is perpetually projected upon somebody or something."[23]

Whatever their relation to the original poetic vision they claimed to convey, such spectacles required a degree of artistry in their coordination and execution, as well as in the component elements of music, scenic art, and engineering. Irving frequently alluded – sometimes through his faithful supporters in the press – to the extent of his own supervisory efforts. The figure of Mephistopheles, presiding over the Brocken, was elided with that of the actor-manager himself, orchestrating the grand design. Increasingly, managements that employed experts to arrange processions and ballets, or to advise them on scenic matters, found that they were allowing these skilled helpers to take over what was usually referred to (in days before the "director") as stage-management. There is some evidence that the architect Edward William Godwin, engaged to advise on "archaeology" (that is, matters of historical authenticity) by a number of managers, effectively directed portions of the productions. Godwin also published articles and reviews outlining a series of reforms to the outmoded customs and conventions of scenic art, proposing, for example, that scenes set in a large church should never attempt to represent the whole of the building, but simply show a portion of it full-scale, leaving the rest to the audience's imagination.[24] Godwin, for some time lover of Ellen Terry, had little to do with the Lyceum, but their son, Edward Gordon Craig, acted there. From his father's example and writings, and from his experience of Irving's absolutist stagecraft, Craig developed some of the ideas that were to form the basis of his own more abstract methods.

In terms of fully realized productions, Craig's practice was relatively limited, but his ideas were enormously influential. In some respects, their rejection of the values of Victorian theatre was bold and uncompromising. "The theatre," he wrote, "must not forever rely upon having a play to perform, but must in time perform pieces of its own art."[25] He sought to diminish the actor as representing the supremacy of ego, hoping for a theatre in which the "super-puppet" (he coined the term *übermarionette*, redolent of Nietzsche) would replace the actor as currently trained with a figure more responsive to the artist's (Craig's) unifying vision. At the same time, he venerated Irving, and his own productions, with their careful management of limited scenic resources in patterns of light, mass and color, consistently provided a new version of the grandeur achieved at the Lyceum with acres of painted canvas, papier-mâché moldings and trick effects. One of Craig's supporters, the critic Arthur Symons, joined the attack on the "costly and inartistic aim at reality . . . the vice of the modern stage" and described the new methods:

What Mr. Craig does is to provide a plain, conventional, or darkened background for life, as life works out its own ordered lines on the stage; he gives us a suggestion instead of reality, a symbol instead of an imitation; and he relies, for his effects, on a new system of lighting from above, not below, and on a new kind of drill, as I may call it, by which he uses his characters as masses and patterns, teaching them to move altogether, with identical gestures. The eye is carried right through or beyond these horizons of canvas, and the imagination with it; instead of stopping entangled among real stalks and painted gables.[26]

The impetus towards the emergence of the independent director – the supervisor of stage effect who is not a performer in the production – came primarily from the world of ballet, extravaganza and pantomime. C. Wilhelm (the professional name of William Pitcher) was best known for the fantastic costumes he created for ballets at the grand music halls of London – the Alhambra and the Empire. His co-ordination of color effects gave him a say in what would now be regarded as the work of choreographers and scene designers. At the Empire he effectively supplanted the choreographer Kati Lanner, in pursuit of "a completeness of ensemble and pictorial effect," and his costume designs were notable for their extraordinary attention to detail. However fantastic the concept (disguising dancers as butterflies, for example) everything had to be true to the original on which it was based, "and had to be perfect at close quarters down to the finest embroidery and the last button."[27] In an article in the *Magazine of Art,* he declared that the designer was "certainly the most important factor in a theatrical production of artistic pictorial pretensions," and laid down his ground rules for success: "It cannot . . . be too distinctly set on record that the success of the stage picture – grouping and background – depends on its initial conception as a whole, and this must undoubtedly emanate from one brain." Wilhelm objected to crude and excessive use of light, with its production of contradictory shadows and failure to support delicate gradations of color. As an example of excellence he picked out William Telbin's scenery for Hades in *Orfeo ed Euridice* (Empire, 1892): "the effective counterbalancing of the tender blues and bronzes, and the gold-and-white harmonized with pale apple-green in the Arcadian scene, with the more severe and gloomy colouring of the kingdom of Pluto."[28]

The scenography of romantic realism, which in the Victorian and Edwardian theatre counted as "modern," continued into the new century, reaching its apogee in the work of Herbert Beerbohm Tree, a staunch defender of its values against would-be reformers such as Edward Gordon Craig or the "Elizabethanist" William Poel. But it was Craig's promise of extravagant effects by simplified means, and Poel's polemics and productions on behalf of new configurations of the theatre space that eventually prevailed. Much that is now recognized (and rebelled against) as "traditional," especially in staging Shakespeare's plays, derives from these sources.

George Bernard Shaw's comment on a production of *Twelfth Night* in "Elizabethan" conditions by Poel's Elizabethan Stage Society sums up the opposition between the theatres of scenic display and that of the restored primacy of acting and speech: "I am convinced that if Burbage were to rise from the dead and accept an invitation from Sir Henry Irving to appear at the Lyceum, he would recoil beaten the moment he realized that he was to be looked at as part of an optical illusion through a huge hole in the wall, instead of being practically in the middle of the theatre."[29]

In demonstrating the viability of earlier methods of staging, and asserting that they allowed the performance of Shakespeare's plays without the cuts and transpositions required in the theatre of scenic illusion, Poel provided the basis for many more adventurous innovators in the century that followed. Even so, many elements of the pictorial method survived in popular theatre. On a somewhat diminished scale, traditional Christmas pantomime is still associated with transformations, if only to get Cinderella from her dreary kitchen hearth to the splendors of the Prince's grand ball. Some nineteenth-century ballets, still in the international repertoire, demand scenic contrivances such as the "panorama" that brings the Prince to the enchanted castle in Tchaikovsky's *Sleeping Beauty* or the miraculous change of scale that reduces Clara to mouse-size and raises the Christmas tree to towering heights in the *Nutcracker*. (The music has even the gradual build to a "crash of exultation" described by Fitzgerald.) By the end of the twentieth century the vogue for spectacular theatre also survived in lavish popular musicals. To stage one of the most successful of these, *The Phantom of the Opera*, the producers had to refit Her Majesty's. This was the house Beerbohm Tree proudly referred to as "my beautiful theatre," and substantial remnants of the old technology, preserved there, had to be removed in order to accommodate the hydraulics and electrical devices required. With its elaborate rise-and-sink effects, transformations and apparitions, this stage version of a famous (and often remade) film testified to the romantic appeal of the magic and mysteries of nineteenth-century stagecraft.[30]

NOTES

1. Percy Fitzgerald, *The World behind the Scenes* (London: Chatto & Windus, 1881), pp. 89–90.
2. Michael R. Booth (ed.), *"The Magistrate" and other Nineteenth-Century Plays* (Oxford: Oxford University Press, 1974), p. 120.
3. William Tydeman (ed.), *Plays by Tom Robertson* (Cambridge: Cambridge University Press, 1982), p. 137.

4. Playbill for *Macbeth*, Princess's Theatre, London: 14 February 1853 (The Theatre Museum).

5. Eluned Brown (ed.), *The London Theatre, 1811–1866. Selections from the Diary of Henry Crabb Robinson* (London: Society for Theatre Research, 1966), p. 147.

6. A comprehensive account of the workings of stage scenery during the period will be found in Richard Southern, *Changeable Scenery* (London: Faber & Faber, 1952).

7. The stage and the setting shown in Figure 3, destroyed in a fire in 1926, are visible on film. See Russell Jackson, "Staging and Storytelling, Theatre and Film: *Richard III* at Stratford, 1911," *New Theatre Quarterly* 16, 2 (May 2000), 107, 121.

8. The fullest account of this subject is Terence Rees's *Theatre Lighting in the Age of Gas* (London: Society for Theatre Research, 1978), which also includes much information on stage effects in general. J. P. Moynet's invaluable and lavishly illustrated compendium *L'envers du Théâtre* (Paris, 1873) has been translated and augmented by Allan S. Jackson and M. Glen Wilson under the title *French Theatrical Production in the Nineteenth Century* (Binghamton, New York: Max Reinhardt Foundation, 1976).

9. Percy Fitzgerald, *Shakespearean Representation. Its Laws and Limits* (London: Stock, 1908), pp. 119–20.

10. Ellen Terry, *The Story of My Life* (London: Hutchinson, 1908), p. 173.

11. Lloyds's description of the effect is reprinted in Russell Jackson (ed.), *Victorian Theatre* (London: A. & C. Black, 1989), pp. 82–84. See also Rees, *Theatre Lighting*, pp. 35–37, where Lloyds's diagrams are reproduced.

12. Henry Morley, *Journal of a London Playgoer*, edited with an introduction by Michael R. Booth (Leicester: University of Leicester Press, 1974), p. 57. Rees (*Theatre Lighting*, pp. 137–39) quotes the account of this effect by the scene painter Frederick Fenton.

13. Booth (ed.), "*The Magistrate*," stage directions on pp. 216–17; 230–31; 240.

14. See George Taylor, *Players and Performances in the Victorian Theatre* (Manchester: University of Manchester Press, 1989), chap. 2, for a discussion of the play's effectiveness as an acting piece.

15. A comprehensive account of the play's staging, acting and history, together with a transcript of Irving's personal script, is given by David Mayer (ed.), *Henry Irving and "The Bells"* (Manchester: Manchester, University Press, 1980).

16. Sir Squire and Lady Bancroft, *The Bancrofts, Recollections of Sixty Years* (New York: Dutton, 1909), p. 247.

17. Quoted by Joel Kaplan and Sheila Stowell, *Theatre and Fashion. Oscar Wilde to the Suffragettes* (Cambridge: Cambridge University Press, 1994), p. 11.

18. Quoted by John William Cole, *The Life and Theatrical Times of Charles Kean, FSA* (2 vols., London: Bentley, 1859), II: 57.

19. Theodor Fontane, *Shakespeare in the London Theatre 1855–58*, translated with an introduction and notes by Russell Jackson (London: Society for Theatre Research, 1999). A thorough and perceptive study of Kean's methods and their intellectual background is Richard W. Schoch, *Shakespeare's Victorian Stage: Performing History in the Theatre of Charles Kean* (Cambridge: Cambridge University Press, 1998).

20. Joseph Hatton, *The Lyceum "Faust"* (London: Virtue, 1894), p. 23. See Michael R. Booth, *Victorian Spectacular Theatre, 1850–1910* (London: Routledge, 1981), chap. 4.
21. Eduard Hanslick, *Music Criticisms, 1846–99*, translated by Henry Pleasants (Harmondsworth: Penguin, 1963), p. 155.
22. Henry Irving, "The Art of Acting," reprinted in *The Drama: Addresses by Henry Irving* (London: 1893), pp. 35–82.
23. Henry James, "The Acting in Mr. Irving's *Faust*," *Century Magazine* (December 1887), rpt. in Allan Wade (ed.), *The Scenic Art: Notes on Acting and the Drama* (New York: Hill and Wang, 1957), pp. 219–25. James's article appeared anonymously.
24. On Godwin, see John Stokes, *Resistible Theatres* (London: Elek, 1971) and the first two chapters of Christopher Innes's *Edward Gordon Craig* (Cambridge: Cambridge University Press, 1983).
25. Edward Gordon Craig, *On the Art of the Theatre* (London: Heinemann, 1911), p. 144.
26. Arthur Symons, *Plays, Acting and Music* (London: Duckworth, 1903), p. 164.
27. Ivor Guest, *Adeline Genée. A Lifetime in Ballet under Six Reigns* (London: Black, 1958), p. 32.
28. C. Wilhelm, "Art in the Theatre: Art in the Ballet (2)," *The Magazine of Art* (1895), 48–52.
29. *Our Theatres in the Nineties* (3 vols., London: Constable, 1932), 1: 190: review of *Twelfth Night*, Burlington Hall, 21 June 1895.
30. David Wilmore, "The Substage Equipment at Her Majesty's Theatre, London," *Theatre Notebook* 52 (1998), 38–45.

4

MICHAEL PISANI

Music for the theatre: style and function in incidental music

In an 1845 issue of the London *Musical World*, editor Henry Lunn criticized the use of music in the contemporary theatre. He objected first of all to managements' abuse of audiences by requiring them to endure continuous and apparently irrelevant entr'acte music during the intervals. Secondly, he offered a sharp criticism of the pervasive style of "incidental" music designed to accompany the standard melodrama:

> Tender strains usher in the "acknowledged heroine" and grim discords announce the villain; "hurries" are got ready for the combats and struggles and a comic song for the faithful countryman. As the principal female character has, of course, been inveigled from her native village, the overture must contain a reminiscence of her happy home, which reminiscence will probably be repeated during the final tableau.[1]

For this, Lunn alleged, the theatre management wasted the services of a small orchestra each night. Moreover, the theatre's music director (usually also a composer), was obliged to choose and lead such music, a procedure that Lunn called "a mere mechanical matter."

Similarly, George Bernard Shaw described incidental music as principally a "mechanical part" of a play, "the music man at the theatre seldom count[ing] for more than a useful colleague of the gas man."[2] This essay attempts to illustrate that the music emanating from nineteenth-century pit orchestras often served purposes other than merely to highlight ideas and emotions already present in the text. The use of the term "mechanical" provides a key starting point. At a time when the study of nineteenth-century theatre largely meant drama as literature, the role of music could be marginalized, even ignored. This is no longer the case now that drama is more often analyzed as a theatrical process, and the "mechanics" of production, including music, loom as important as dialogue, acting style, and scenic design.

No comprehensive study exists for nineteenth-century British theatrical music (unlike Roger Fiske's monumental *English Theatre Music in the*

Eighteenth Century). This essay must therefore provide in part a concise overview of the normative practice in professional theatres during the Victorian and Edwardian years (including not only those of Great Britain but also New York City, where plays, managers, actors, and technical staff were often imported from London). I have based this study principally on an examination of source documents: surviving music, theatrical records, playbills and programs, periodicals, rehearsal promptbooks, reviews, and actors' and managers' published accounts.

Theatre music and the problem of genre, *c.* 1800–1837

Before the mid-nineteenth century, theatrical music was called simply "music" or "appropriate music." The term "incidental music" was not used with any consistency until later. (*Webster's* places its entrance into the English language in 1864.) An 1855 publication of John Liptrot Hatton lists "Overture and Music incidental to Shakespeare's play *Henry VIII*" (written for Charles Kean). Shaw used the term "incidental music" in his 1892 review. Yet in 1911 Norman O'Neill found it necessary to put the term in quotes – as I have done above – adding that it could only correctly be applied to marches, dances, and songs which are "incidental" to the action of the play. For music "which accompanies the dialogue and reflects the feeling and emotion of the spoken lines," O'Neill – an experienced theatrical composer who led the orchestra at the Haymarket Theatre for over ten years – preferred the original French term *mélodrame*.[3] In this sense, *mélodrame* as a musical procedure takes on a separate meaning from the theatrical genre. It describes music used to underscore any dialogue, as, for example, Weber's four melodramas for the Covent Garden production of *Oberon* (1826) or Mendelssohn's melodramas scattered throughout *Antigone* (also Covent Garden, 1844). "Appropriate," "distinctive," "characteristic," "incidental," and "melodramatic" are descriptions of roughly the same process: music used to assist the actors in establishing and sustaining the emotional pitch at any given moment of a play. That is its principal function, though clearly not its only one. Such music may also create mood and atmosphere, convey time and place, or suggest status, ethnicity, or class. Even truly "incidental" music for routine functions – such as taking up the curtain or bringing on a character – may serve doubly as an indicator of mood or characterization. Music may also work at a subconscious level to make audiences more susceptible to extraordinary situations onstage. Perhaps the most striking form of theatrical music was used to work *against* the action or dialogue onstage, as an editor writing for *The Stage* recognized in 1887:

> One very charming effect, more than half made by music . . . is the result of pathetic dialogue – a tender parting for example – while some light-hearted character is supposed to be in an adjoining room innocently playing the cheeriest and brightest of music. This is a serio-comic effect of the highest order.[4]

Nearly all forms of drama in the nineteenth century, at least in the French, British, and American traditions, incorporated incidental music of some kind, whether this consisted of songs and dances, curtain or scene-changing music, overtures and entr'actes, or dialogue and action underscoring. A comparison of sources ranging from published scores for early nineteenth-century melodramas, such as Thomas Busby's music to Matthew Lewis's *Rugantino, or The Bravo of Venice* (Covent Garden, 1805) or Charles Horn's music to Samuel Arnold's *The Woodman's Hut* (Drury Lane, 1814)[5], to Georges Jacobi's music for Henry Irving's 1889 production of *The Dead Heart* or Raymond Roze's 1898 music to Herbert Beerbohm Tree's *Julius Caesar* reveals that there remained a demand for music throughout the century, despite changing tastes toward more realism. (An 1898 published text of the French version of Pierre Decourcelle's *The Two Vagrants* includes a list of sixty-eight separate music cues, although twenty to forty was more typical of late nineteenth-century British productions.[6])

Musical language also varied considerably. Actor-managers and their bandleaders at Covent Garden, Drury Lane, and the early decades of the Adelphi adapted a style of music that had been developed in concert and operatic melodrama by composers such as Jean-Jacques Rousseau, Georg Benda, Mozart, Beethoven, and Luigi Cherubini. This music featured accompanimental devices derived from the *recitativo accompagnato* of Italian opera and the various instrumental Austro-Germanic "topics" of late eighteenth-century music. (The latter, as identified by Leonard Ratner, include military and hunt music, musette and pastorale, marches, and stylized dances.[7]) Music for plays later in the nineteenth century sometimes shows stylistic influences of Weber, Mendelssohn, Verdi, Liszt, Massenet, or Grieg, particularly in the use of reminiscence themes, national or exotic characteristics, and occasional vivid harmonic effects.

In the early decades of the nineteenth century, music served a prominent role in the production of nearly every dramatic genre, whether for tragedy, comedy, burlesque, English opera, ballet, melodrama, pantomime, hippodrama, or spectacle.[8] Productions from about 1800 to 1820, with music by composers such as Michael Kelly or Henry Bishop, appear to us today as somewhat confusing genres, proto-operettas, perhaps – not exactly plays with a consistent use of music throughout, nor operas with some spoken text.[9] Both Great Britain's "legitimate" royal houses and the "illegitimate" theatres produced such works under the rubrics of opera, pantomime, spectacle, ballet, and farce.

The non-patent theatres (at least until the Theatre Act revisions of 1843) largely staged "burletta," which usually featured a number of songs for the major characters as well as choruses and dances.[10] (Edward Fitzball's *The Flying Dutchman*, produced in 1826 at the Adelphi with music by George Rodwell, is one example.) Burletta's strong pantomimic component, acted without text but against music, led to the emergence of the distinctive musico-dramatic style of British melodrama. A significant number of published piano scores survive in the British Library for late eighteenth- and early nineteenth-century pantomime scenes. These pieces, sometimes called "comic tunes," were generally short and could be inserted for a bit of commedia-style business into a dramatic work.[11] William Moncrieff recalled the inclusion of pantomime in "the early minor theatres." They used not only musical accompaniment – sometimes only a piano – but also placards or "scrolls" of text which the actors brought in from the wings to clarify the action (as in spectacles at Astley's Pavillion in 1812, for example).[12] These forms of pantomime with "title cards" are important from the standpoint of early melodrama and connections between character type, the character of the music, and dramatic gesture.

One example of early burletta with pantomime is H. B. Code's *The Patriot, or the Hermit of Saxellan* (first performed Dublin, Royal Hibernian Theatre, 1811). John Stevenson's music was published in London and reveals the work to be operatic in the inclusion of songs and vocal ensembles. Each of the melodramatic cues (unnumbered) is given verbal descriptors, some of them resembling texts like those that might have appeared on the placards or scrolls onstage.

Maestoso	The Landamman commanding Emma's obedience
Allegro	Gristler and Jacqueline: Expressive of anger and termagency
Playful	Emma arrives at the Confederate camp
[no tempo]	Landamman reproaches Conrad for not preventing Emma's flight
[no tempo]	Emma having eloped from her father – *melos* expresses timidity and irresolution
Furioso	Expressive of the Character of Ulric, the old bachelor

Most of these descriptors characterize the action by nature of a strong active verb or illustrative noun – "commanding," "anger," "reproach," "irresolution" – and suggest postures similar to those that the actor might assume. Such "stock gestures" were also outlined in manuals, the most important perhaps being Johann Jacob Engel's *Ideen zu einer Mimik* (1785), translated in the early nineteenth century by Henry Siddons as *Practical Illustrations of Rhetorical Gesture and Action, Adapted to the English Drama*.[13] Here we might apply Roland Barthes's concept of "anchorage" to early melodrama, for such descriptors help to anchor or root non-texted music in specific characterization. In other words, the music must seem to be appropriate to the physical gestures displayed by "a commanding father," or suggestive enough to convey such things as "Emma's timidity." Such gestures – in place of textual anchors – assist the viewer/listener in choosing the "correct level of perception" for the music.[14] Musical gesturing did not, of course, originate with early nineteenth-century British melodrama. Such manifestations represent an ongoing interest in the specific "affects" of music, in terms not unlike how many eighteenth-century theorists of music might have identified them.

James Kenny's *The Blind Boy* (Covent Garden, 1807) was not a burletta and had no songs and choruses. Yet John Davy's music similarly used textual anchors to connect the musical cues to specific actions and emotions. The information in columns one to three below are from Davy's published score and are clearly cues to the pianist. (No known orchestrations survive, though the music must originally have been performed by an orchestra.) Descriptors in the fourth column are those in Kenny's published version of the play.

The Blind Boy, act 1, nos. 1–5

No. 1	Andantino allegretto	When the curtain rises	Soft musick, expressive of the harmony of a fine summer morn
No. 2	Allegretto	When Oberto appears	Musick expressive of joy
No. 3	Largo espressivo	When Edmond appears on the bridge	Musick expressive of fear
No. 4	Andante affetuoso	When Edmond is off the bridge	Musick expressive of affection
No. 5	Affetuoso	When Edmond deplores his situation	Soft musick, expressive of love

The practice here, as it would continue to be throughout the nineteenth century, is to use the descriptors as cues in the stage action as well as indicators of emotion. As in the pantomime tradition, each number is also given a sight cue, rather than a text cue as was more common later. Musically, each cue consists of balanced eight-bar melodic phrases, which lend the accompaniment an almost relentless lyricism. The Greek word *melos*, used in the *Patriot* cue above, means song or lyrical phrase and was a standard nineteenth-century term for music cues. It signifies the musical component of *mélodrame*. The root of the word reveals its fundamental connection to melody.

Davy's score also includes one unnumbered cue, a simple dominant-seventh chord to be played "When the ring is discovered":

$$\mathit{ff}\ (\,\flat \,|\,\overset{\frown}{\circ}\,)$$

The descriptor for this in Kenny's published text is merely a "pause of astonishment." The "chord" – as managers liked to label it in the margins of their promptbooks – was most often a dominant-seventh for surprise and a diminished-seventh for shock. It would remain a popular musical device to anchor key revelatory moments throughout the melodramatic tradition.

Such scores serve to illustrate that a collection of musical cues for a play consisted of several but clearly distinguishing types of *melos*. They might include somewhat more extended "storm music" or "battle music." They could signify "appropriate" music characteristics of specific stage action. Or they could serve to anchor music to emotions (made specific through gestural acting), as in these unnumbered music cues from Thomas Busby's published piano score to Thomas Holcroft's *Tale of Mystery* (1802)[15]:

– Selina laments the unfortunate situation of Francisco.
– Bonamo hands a chair to Francisco with an air of friendship and conciliation.
– Francisco being ask'd who made him dumb, gives signs of horrible recollection.
– Romaldi being announced, Francisco starts up, struck with alarm.

These relatively early traditions of British melodrama are indebted, of course, to the practice of German and French theatres, where such plays as those of Kotzebue and Pixérécourt, with their fashionable musical accompaniments, were adapted to the British theatres. Melodrama developed in Britain across lines of genre and was eventually established as a common feature in nearly all styles of popular theatre at minor houses such as the Adelphi and the Surrey theatres in the 1820s and 30s. In Fitzball's manuscript of *The Flying Dutchman*, his instructions throughout for non-vocal music ("<u>Music –</u> <u>agony, rage</u>, *despair*") make it very clear that specific music is required to underscore a specific emotional display.[16] By the time of the premieres of John Buckstone's *Luke the Labourer* (Adelphi, 1826) or Moncrieff's *Eugene Aram* (Surrey, 1832), however, music to underscore spoken text also was taking on an increased importance. The 1843 legal revisions removed the song requirement, but music continued to remain an essential ingredient. As the practice of text and action underscoring became normalized at the minor theatres, publishers ceased to make this music available in print (as they had for the works of Henry Bishop). Perhaps only the royal theatres could afford the expense of having theatre music engraved. As a result of this, none of J. M. Jolly's "new music" for *Eugene Aram*, for example (or any other music from Adelphi or Surrey productions) survives.[17]

Music and style in the Victorian theatre

Scores for plays in the Victorian period can be grouped into three types: (1) a re-used (and perhaps adapted) score from an earlier production; (2) a score "compiled" from various sources, often from the manager's notes; and (3) a newly composed score. Some managers did not feel constricted by using an existing score, particularly for Shakespeare's plays. Matthew Locke's late-seventeenth-century music for *Macbeth* was continually republished throughout the nineteenth century and was used in several major productions, among them, at the Olympic Theatre in March 1848 and the Strand Theatre in 1853, each playbill announcing "the whole of Locke's music."[18] Also popular was Mendelssohn's music to *A Midsummer Night's Dream*. The extensive music was included in many productions, among them, by Kean at the Princess's (1856) and in America by E. A. Marshall at the Broadway Theatre (1854).[19] For revivals of more recent works, however, newer and more fashionable music was necessary. For Kean's production of *Pizarro* (Princess's, 1856), John Liptrot Hatton arranged and composed a new score, rather than incorporating any of Michael Kelly's music from the first British productions of Sheridan's play.

Another method was to recycle music from well-known plays, operas, or classical symphonic repertoire. Parts for an unknown production of Boucicault's *The Old Guard* are essentially compiled bits from Verdi's *Rigoletto* and other Italian operas.[20] Such quoting from well-known pieces was not necessarily the result of hasty last-minute work, however. For an 1887 production of Mary Russell Mitford's *Rienzi* in Washington, DC, actor-manager Lawrence Barrett quoted music from Verdi's *Don Carlos* (entrance music for Philip II) to lend specific dramatic emphasis to the line: "Ushered with music like a king."[21] This stringing together of pre-existing music – and largely music known by the audience – to underscore and highlight moments in the play resembles what scholars of early twentieth-century silent-film music have called a "compilation score."[22] A pure example can be found in a list of musical cues that Tree prepared for his 1895 production of *Fedora* at the Haymarket.[23]

Cue #	Music and Notes
1. Opening	"Non più andrai" from <u>Nozze di Figaro</u>
2.	Boccherini's minuet
3.	Gounod's "Meditation" – onstage
4.	Letter reading music from act 3 of <u>La Traviata</u> etc.

Tree also relied heavily on some combination of original music, classical works, and popular melodies. For his production of Paul M. Potter's *Trilby* (Haymarket Theatre, 1895), Tree's list of musical cues to Raymond Roze requests that the play should begin with Schubert's "Rosamunde" overture, so that "Schubert's 'Adieu' " could be used thematically in act I and again in act IV during the death scene. He also requested that, in addition to the classical excerpts by Berlioz and Rubinstein interwoven throughout the evening to accompany certain scenes of the hypnotist Svengali, the popular mid-century tune "Ben Bolt" be used to bring up the curtain in act I (Nelson Kneass's setting having been cited as Trilby's "operatic" piece in George Du Maurier's original novel) and that it be used again as the source for a "fantasia" between acts II and III to set up Trilby's on-stage singing of the song in act III. For later in that scene, Tree requested the use of an on-stage band to strike up a cheerful *Au clair de la lune* to heighten the tension during the riot at the close of the act. Tree's notes on music exhibit not only stylistic diversity, but show an intent to establish maximum contrast between the serious classical works for Svengali with the folk-like simplicity of the popular songs.[24]

Compilations using known classical music, however, seem to have been a late development. The overwhelming majority of evidence from playbills suggests that, during most of the nineteenth century, actor-managers required new music for a new play and that the music became the property of the manager, to be retained with the promptbook and actors' sides. Much of this music was in manuscript, was continually re-used and heavily marked by the musicians, and therefore simply deteriorated. Scores even by such eminent British composers as Arthur Sullivan or Edward German were not published until later and circulated in manuscript between several theatres. Such reworkings knew no national or linguistic boundaries. For his version of *Le juif polonais* as *The Bells* (Lyceum, 1871), Irving brought Etienne Singla from France to adapt his original music, written in 1869 for the Théâtre Cluny.[25] Tree brought Saint-Saëns to His Majesty's Theatre in 1909 for *False Gods* to supervise the adaptation of the composer's original music for Brieux's *La Foi*, performed at Monte Carlo, 1909.

Orchestras and music directors in Victorian theatres

While playwrights and actor-managers may have had specific ideas for the type of music they wanted, the music's effectiveness in performance depended upon the skills of their resident orchestra leaders. In his autobiography, Edward Fitzball lists the musicians with whom he specifically worked in his career. His roster includes many of England's most important composers and conductors from about 1810 to 1850.[26] Although trained largely in the classical traditions of German, French, and British conservatoires, British and American theatrical music directors worked in an essentially popular medium. They had to be skilled musicians themselves and would even lead the band – like dancing masters of earlier generations had done – with violin and bow in hand. Orchestra leaders required the personal skills to motivate other musicians around them; they needed to possess innate dramatic sensibilities; and they required an enormous knowledge of music repertoire consisting of classical works, current and older popular songs and dances, and traditional folk music (or music thought to be characteristic of a given country or region, whether in any degree authentic or not).

Most music directors' contracts obligated them to provide all required music, which could be extensive. A typical evening in the Victorian theatre might consist of: (1) an overture that showcased the orchestra and sometimes even set the tone for the play to follow; (2) the principal theatrical attraction (a multi-act play which may or may not have been accompanied in sections by the orchestra with melodramatic music); (3) some short musical pieces that featured the orchestra during each entr'acte (usually of light fare – quadrilles, polkas, and opera potpourris were common favorites); and (4) one or more relatively short afterpieces. If the afterpieces were not "divertissements" but comedies or farces, musicians might be released after the last entr'acte. For most of the early Victorian period there was no established consistency in theatrical billing. An evening at the Olympic Theatre on 11 December 1843 began with an unspecified overture, and featured Blanchard's *Road of Life* (with music by the Olympic's music director John F. Calcott), a "musical farce" entitled *My Spouse and I*, and then concluded with Fitzball's "musical romantic drama" *Paul Clifford* (with music by George Rodwell – of the Adelphi – and James Blewitt).[27]

Some leaders maintained a close association with one theatre or manager, among them Alfred Mellon (Adelphi) or John Crook (Duke of Yorks). Particularly popular and successful leaders sometimes juggled positions, such as Edward Mollenhauer in America (Winter Garden, Niblo's Garden, Daly's), even on both sides of the Atlantic, such as Robert Stoepel (Princess's, Wallack's, Daly's, Lyceum). The life of a theatrical orchestra leader involved long evenings in the pit and many days in rehearsal. As composers and arrangers, they were as productive as many concert composers. Yet the lives of the theatre musicians have never been documented, nor can information about them be found in musical or theatrical reference works.[28] Robert Stoepel, for example, began his career in Paris in the orchestra of Dumas *fils*'s Théâtre Historique. He soon became a leader at the Théâtre de la Porte St. Martin, where he befriended Dion Boucicault and followed him first to London, then America. Together they produced *The Vampire* and *The Corsican Brothers* and other French-style melodramas with extensive musical accompaniment. With the exception of an overture to Boucicualt's *The O'Dowd* (which Boucicault kept in his personal collection), none of Stoepel's theatre music was saved. Dramatic music was often unsigned, or signed by the manager of the theatre. With the exceptions of Henry Bishop, much of whose published theatre music exists in the British Library, and Oscar Barrett, whose manuscripts resided in storage in the Drury Lane Theatre until the mid-1980s (and are also now at the British Library) no single collection of any theatre composer survives. Presumably much of their work remained with the theatre and either went up in smoke in the various theatre fires or else was liquidated with old copies of actors' sides and other outdated material. Odd that a composer like Edwin Ellis, for example, should be so highly praised for his work, yet no one thought to preserve his music.[29]

Most of the composers for theatre music in England and America from about 1820 to 1880 have publication lists that consist primarily of adaptations of operas and operettas, songs, and many titles of instrumental "characteristic pieces" of the type popular during these decades: waltzes, polkas, marches, quadrilles, schottisches, galops, mazurkas, varsovianas, and, occasionally, "danses caractéristiques." The connection between the theatre and popular music had long been established as a successful authenticating device, whether it be the use of (real or fabricated) Scottish folk tunes, as in Isaac Pocock's *Rob Roy Macgregor* (Coburg, 1818), "Dibdin's naval airs" for Douglas Jerrold's *Black Ey'd Susan* (Surrey, 1829), or American popular "folk songs" (actually songs with words and music by Stephen Foster) for *Uncle Tom's Cabin* (Adelphi, 1853).[30] Such known music stimulated a sense of pleasure in recognition. For a production of Boucicault's *The Streets of London* (Princess's, 1864), Charles Hall provided an overture that incorporated "the street tunes of the time" and therefore "early obtained the goodwill of the audience."[31]

Furthermore, music directors were required to have skills in adapting larger symphonic works for smaller pit bands as well as the ability to coax a convincing performance from a chamber-sized group of musicians. In the early decades of the nineteenth century, large London theatres such as Covent Garden and the King's Theatre needed substantial orchestras for the production of opera. Contracts for the Covent Garden orchestra in 1818 indicate thirty-one paid musicians, nineteen of them string players.[32] In the early years of the Adelphi, when burletta was still fashionable, the orchestra was often larger. On a playbill for an 1824 "romantic burletta spectacle" (*Valmondi*, 18 October), forty musicians are identified by name, though their instruments are not specified. The standard size of the orchestra in the early Victorian professional theatres seems to have been between eighteen and thirty. The model was no doubt that of the French theatres, where in 1828, orchestras ranged from twenty-four at the Théâtre du L'Ambigue Comique to twenty-eight at the Théâtre de la Porte St. Martin.[33]

For productions of operas at the Princess's in the late 1840s, conductor Edward Loder had about thirty musicians. When Charles Kean took over in 1851 and converted the repertoire to historical drama and "gentlemanly melodrama," he maintained roughly this size of an ensemble. For *The Corsican Brothers* (1852), Stoepel led twenty-four musicians (fourteen strings). For Kean's production of Byron's *Sardanapalus* (1853), John Liptrot Hatton expanded the size of the orchestra to include not only a larger percussion section but also six harps for Sardanapalus's entry into the Assyrian court. The Lyceum Theatre under Irving in the 1870s also had between twenty-six and thirty musicians (about nineteen strings), although Irving expanded the orchestra for such productions as *Faust* (1885) and *Robespierre* (1899).[34] By mid-century, nearly every professional theatre kept a permanent orchestra, although many were of chamber dimensions. By the 1870s, the Adelphi orchestra under Ellis consisted of only about fifteen musicians. The City of London Theatre in the 1860s under Alfred Cooper had only about eleven to twelve musicians (seven strings) and this was roughly the standard size for smaller houses and provincial theatres.[35]

In America, even the best theatres maintained orchestras on the chamber model. In the 1860s Wallack's had a regular orchestra under Stoepel of about nineteen musicians (eight strings).[36] The female manager and actress Laura Keene sustained an orchestra under Thomas Baker of sixteen musicians (eight strings), Niblo's Garden under Harvey Dodworth had sixteen (seven strings), and the Winter Garden under Edward Mollenhauer had thirteen (six strings). While such small groups might today seem inadequate to take on the operatic overtures of Halévy and Auber (popular curtain-raisers in the American theatres), some saw an artistic advantage in this size. A correspondent for *Dwight's Journal of Music* in 1863 noted the unusual power of the three first violins at Wallack's and praised the character of the orchestra under Stoepel's leadership:

In some respects, the performances of his orchestra are more compact and complete than those of the large concert-rooms, since, in the first place, a small body of musicians can always be wielded with more precision, and in the next, regular and repeated performances under the same direction give a smoothness and evenness which cannot be attained when frequent changes are made.[37]

At London's larger theatres, however, orchestras of twenty-five to thirty musicians remained standard well into the twentieth century. In their proposal for a National Theatre in 1907, William Archer and Harley Granville Barker included twenty-four permanent orchestral musicians in their budget.[38] It was apparently only once theatre musicians began to take on cinema jobs that this number dwindled. In the 1930s, according to Eric Jones-Evans, theatre orchestras were even reduced to a trio of piano, violin, and cello.[39] (Although piano accompaniment was common in the early part of the nineteenth century,[40] I have found no evidence that a piano formed a part of the professional Victorian theatre orchestra. Allardyce Nicoll noted "the tinkling of a piano," although he didn't specify his sources. Later in the century there are piano reductions for some of Irving's productions at the Lyceum, Tree's at Her Majesty's, and Belasco's in New York. But these were presumably used only in rehearsal as these three directors tended to use, if anything, larger orchestras.[41])

The practice and technique of music in the theatre

Given the lack of surviving theatre music, the reconstruction of a play by even the most popular of nineteenth-century playwrights – such as Edward Fitzball, Dion Boucicault, or Tom Taylor – poses a difficult problem.[42] The most mechanical use of music was simply to accompany the movement of the curtain or entrance of a character. French's published copy of Tom Robertson's *Play* specifies "enter the Chevalier Browne, smoking cigarette, on last bars of music." Before an actor actually delivered his or her first line, music functioned to focus the audience's attention on the scene, engaging the "listening" mode, rather than simply the "viewing" mode, and then lead directly into the actor's line. For these purposes, it would seem that music was rarely necessary once the dialogue began.

But the practice of *mélodrame* continued throughout the nineteenth century, suggesting that its importance to the audience's involvement in a scene, as well as the actor's delivery of a line, remained an essential part of Victorian theatre. Music played an accompanimental role to the speaking voice, but sometimes one as important as the piano part to a German or French art song. Louis Calvert has related how Irving decided in a rehearsal of Byron's *Werner* (1887) that he wanted to deliver a speech to music and asked the (unnamed) music director to come up with something.[43] At the following rehearsal, however, the music director became increasingly distressed as Irving pared away at the cue, removing instrument after instrument, until only the second violins, violas, cellos, and bass remained – essentially preserving a kind of mellow sound-cushion for the already musical delivery of his lines. Irving's ear told him that any melodic activity, particularly that which might interfere with the natural range of his voice, would provide too much distracting counterpoint. Yet his desire for underlying accompaniment suggests that he thought of his voice as a musical instrument equivalent to that of a singer's.

Only with the spoken "voice parts" restored, then, is this music complete, and, conversely, only with the music restored is the play complete. George Taylor notes that this practice, what Eric Jones-Evans called V-O-M ("voice over music"), exerted a crucial effect on acting in the nineteenth century and "led to a heightened, deliberate, and passionate mode of delivery."[44] The actor's need to have music to support the voice appears to have formed the substance of Shaw's criticism that "the old-fashioned actor . . . will tell you that certain speeches are easy to speak 'through music' and frightfully hard without it."[45] The perfect combination of dialogue and music was not easy to achieve. The Irving incident illustrates one case where a director took control to find the right balance, in lieu of a music director who did not sufficiently grasp the difference between leading and accompanying. Frederick Corder, a Liszt pupil who composed for solo recitations of poetry in the 1890s, observed that music from the pit was not always subordinated, and actors, especially male actors, had to raise the pitch of their voice to be heard. He counseled against any "sing-song" or "chanting" of the text in order to make it more musical.[46] It was the composer's job to weave the music in such a way as to leave the natural speaking voice unobscured. Writing in the 1890s, Corder is responding to a movement toward more naturalistic style of vocal projection, away from the more heightened delivery of a Macready or Kean, whose styles of elocution against music must have seemed quite operatic in comparison.

Given the importance of music in the conception of their roles, many actor-managers worked with music from the earliest rehearsals. Jerome K. Jerome observed that "scenery and props were not being used at this, the first, rehearsal, the chief object of which was merely to arrange music, entrances and exits, and general business." Jerome's memoirs "of a would-be-actor" include a line drawing of a rehearsal, the stage manager instructing two actors to "cower down," and the music director seated on a stool before them playing his "fiddle" in lieu of the orchestra. Jerome noted that the stage manager asked for "hurried music through all that Mr. P."[47] A surviving fragment of a rehearsal schedule in Dion Boucicault's hand, undated, indicates that he asked for the full instrumental ensemble ("full band") to be present at many staging rehearsals[48]:

Thursday	Read Phantom at 1
Friday	Phantom at 11, Dot at 12 1/2; music of Dot and Phantom at 2
Saturday	Full band
*	Dot, 1st scene at 11
*	Phantom, 1st act at 1
Wednesday	Dot without parts at 11 1/2 full band etc.

Not all music could necessarily be worked out so carefully in advance. Jimmy Glover tells the story, perhaps embellished for effect, of his first experience arriving at a Birmingham theatre at three in the afternoon, being handed a list of forty cues and told he would be leading the music for the evening's performance. Apparently, even these were not enough. At a tense moment, as an actor twisted in the throes of death by poisoning, the manager hurriedly called down to Glover to play something: "Give us four bars of agit."[49]

"Agit," of course, refers to "agitato." By the later nineteenth century, it seemed common that many music directors kept a storehouse of appropriate passages (*melos*) to underscore action and dialogue. (Some theatres also held libraries of music for this purpose, as one of Augustin Daly's stage managers notes in his unpublished memoirs.[50]) The private *melos* collection of Alfred Cooper, who began his career at the City of London Theatre in the 1860s, contained fifty-three *melos*, scored in parts for an orchestra of twelve musicians.[51] His folio included andantes, agitatos, moderatos, furiosos, prestos and others, which continued the same gestural traditions as "characteristic music" of earlier melodrama. Oscar Barrett, music director for Augustus Harris, kept a handwritten list of some eighty items, many with graphically descriptive titles such as "energetico pomposo" and "allegro: Chinese character," along with his collection of orchestra parts that he used as *melos* in pantomimes at Drury Lane and at the Grecian Theatre in the 1870s and 80s and at the Gaiety in Manchester in the early 1900s. In addition to many hurries and misteriosos, there are also such useful items as "three chords of exclamation" and "eight bars and chord for entrance." Barrett followed each description with the cue number from the pantomime in which it was presumably first used: the "storm" was no. $8\frac{1}{2}$ in *Esmeralda*. Barrett then probably recycled these cues into his other theatrical music as they seemed appropriate.

A large collection of similar *melos* was actually published for "amateur theatrical companies" by J. R. Lafleur and Sons in London in 1873. *The Theatrical Leader's Vade-Mecum* – 138 numbers in fifteen separate fascicles – was compiled by five international theatre musicians, E. Audibert, Edmund Reyloff, Charles Barthmann, Adolphe Lindheim, and L. von der Finck. Lafleur made individual fascicles available in parts either for full orchestra or for "octuor" (four strings, three winds, and piano). Information on the back of a bass trombone part indicates that the numbers have been "adapted for every possible situation or requirement in drama, burlesque, comic ballet, or pantomime." The individual numbers range in size from two measures (no. 28) to a full-length "transformation scene" (no. 138). Some cues have descriptive titles: "storm and calm" (no. 26), "comic rally" (no. 17), "air de ballet" (no. 21), "flourish" (no. 6), "combat" (no. 12), a "gavotte de Louis XIV" (no. 134). As late as the early twentieth century, music-hall performer Bransby Williams was still using two Reyloff "misteriosos" to underscore his popular Fagin sketch from Dickens's *Oliver Twist*.[52]

In the latter half of the nineteenth century, however, playbills for such professional theatres as the Adelphi, the Royal Court, the Lyceum, and the Haymarket continued to advertise "new and original" music for each play. Even an extremely popular and often revived work such as John Buckstone's *The Green Bushes* (Adelphi, 1845) had specific music associated with it for every major revival, and for which nothing remains but a short three-page published piano excerpt. The situation might be put into better perspective through the examination of source materials that do survive. John Brougham's *The Duke's Motto* (an adaptation of a French play by Anicet-Bourgeois after Dumas) was first produced by Charles Fechter at the Lyceum Theatre on 10 January 1863 and enjoyed well over twenty revivals in various British and American cities during the next thirty years. Neither the published original edition of the French play nor Brougham and Fechter's acting edition mentions much music, except for a gypsy song and dance and a ballet at the Regent's palace.[53] Later published versions of the French play do indicate music, most notably for the opening and closing of scenes. The only other evidence for music used was William Henry Montgomery's name on the Lyceum playbill and the publication of Montgomery's "Duke's Motto Waltz" that same year. (A promptbook from the Lyceum production would, of course, have logged musical cues along with other stage business, but this has not been found.) Given the play's popularity, the American actor Lawrence Barrett – who succeeded Fechter as Legardère in the New York revival at Niblo's Garden in 1870 – took *The Duke's Motto* on several American tours between 1870 and 1879. Fortunately, the manuscript orchestra parts used for these touring productions survive among the Barrett materials at the Harvard Theatre Library. The parts reveal an extraordinary amount of musical underscoring of almost cinematic continuity. With the exception of Montgomery's waltz, none of the music has been found from the British original. It seems plausible, however, that Barrett's music was the same (or nearly the same) as that used for the Lyceum production. Barrett retained two sets of orchestral parts (in different hands, but with identical music). The older of the two is signed by T. E. Morris and dated "New York, 1864." (Morris was an actor in the New York production and John Brougham's manager.) Moreover, the music at the Regent's ball in these scores exactly matches that of Montgomery's "Duke's Motto Waltz." It is therefore likely that the rest of the score, having belonged originally to Morris, is probably that of the London production and also that used for the 1863 premiere at Niblo's and the revival the following year.

The situation briefly outlined above captures in miniature a problem which plagues much of the nineteenth-century British and American theatrical repertoire. What little music that has survived has done so by chance and offers perhaps only an unrepresentative sampling. *The Green Bushes* was considerably more popular than *The Duke's Motto*. Yet virtually nothing of Alfred Mellon's music, though still in use at the Adelphi for revivals in the 1860s (as playbills announce), has managed to survive. Extensive music survives for Irving's 1889 reworking of *The Dead Heart*, although that was not one of his more important productions. The music for this play is again almost cinematic in scope, although the first through-composed score for a film would not appear until nearly twenty years later with Saint-Saëns's *L'Assassinat du Duc de Guise* (1908). To date, only two original scores for Victorian stage productions have been made available for study: Kean's *Corsican Brothers* (transcribed in a dissertation by Barry Yzereef as noted above) and O'Neill's *Monte Cristo* (edited by Anne Dhu Shapiro [McLucas] for Garland's series *Nineteenth-Century American Musical Theatre*).[54]

Boucicault's *The Colleen Bawn*

An example of the important connections between specially composed music and the play itself can be illustrated with a short excerpt from act 1 of Boucicault's *The Colleen Bawn*. The play was first performed in March 1860 at Laura Keene's Theatre in New York and opened six months later at the Adelphi in London. Music survives in two locations, fragments of a first-violin book in Boucicault's own collection, and a complete set of clean orchestral parts – apparently unused or archival copies – in the Drury Lane collection. The anonymous orchestral parts are signed "property of James Weaver, June 4, 1876" and are embossed with the address: "Orchestral band office, 45 Howland Street, Fitzroy Square W." (This may have been a loan office for theatre music, although I have not been able to find a listing for any such agency.) The first-violin part of this set matches that in Boucicualt's copy. A printed set of parts to *The Colleen Bawn* Overture by Thomas Baker (published by Lafleur in Paris) are included with the Drury Lane manuscripts. Baker trained as a violinist at the Royal Academy of Music in London and toured with the orchestra of the French-born director of the Drury Lane Theatre, Louis-Antoine Jullien (known simply as Jullien), to the United States where he settled in New York, first as a conductor of English opera at Niblo's Garden, then as music director for Laura Keene.[55] The Keene playbills for *The Colleen Bawn* announce Baker as the composer of "entirely new music . . . expressly to illustrate this drama." Baker is also listed as composer for the music in the Adelphi playbills.[56]

The first scene of the play establishes the situation: Hardress Cregan has secretly married the peasant girl Eily O'Connor. His mother is in debt to the farmers of her estate and assures her attorney, Mr. Corrigan, that her son's marriage to Anne Chute, the daughter of a wealthy landowner, will settle the matter. But Anne is already in love with Hardress's college friend Kyrle Daly, who she suspects may love her in return. Through a conversation with Danny, a boatman, Anne is misled to believe that it is Kyrle (instead of Hardress) who sails across the Killarney river each midnight to meet Eily. The musical cues for scene 1 are as follows:

1. Opening (Andante) – Music begins (7 bars before curtain)
2. Anne: "Stuck together with glue" (Allegro)
3. Corrigan: "These fifteen years" (Allegro agitato)
4. Corrigan: "Good evening kindly" (no tempo) – melody: "The Last Rose of Summer"
5. Mrs. Cregan: "Good night, my son" (Andante) – same melody
6. Hardress: "We will cross to Muckross Head" (Andante)
7. Danny: "Here comes the signal" (Andante con moto) – extended melodramatic music with several text cues

The page from Boucicault's prompt copy of the play shows cues relevant to music underlined in pen. In the following example, the text is aligned with the music for cue 7 (the orchestra parts here reduced to a piano score). At Anne's reply "the signal?" the strings play an eight-bar *melo*, here orchestrated with shimmering strings. But at Danny's "his honour jumps from the parlour windy into the garden behind," the strings reach a sustained tremolo (the augmented triad being a rare chord for this purpose). What follows are four agitato measures carefully composed (if performed correctly) to be timed to Eily's three signals. Each time her light appears in the cottage window, the

effect is punctuated by a sforzando chord in the woodwinds. The descending chromatic thirds in the strings suggest the light fading, as Eily moves her lamp from the window. The strings pause to tremolo for a moment of suspense on the more-typical diminished-seventh chord as Danny says "wait now, and ye'll see the answer." When the light goes out in Hardress's room above, Danny comments "that's my gentleman," and the strings resolve to a delicate rendition of "Last Rose of Summer," the melody taken by the flute. The traditional Irish folk song had earlier in the scene been linked with Hardress's love for Eily, but since Hardress's entry is delayed, the use of the tune now seems ironic against Anne's momentary flashback of her last conversation with Kyrle: "I was not deceived; he meant me to understand that he loved me!" The scene ends with Anne hiding to observe Hardress – camouflaged by his large cloak – emerge from the house and set off in the boat. The tune fades away gently, but hardly pausing before an immediate "segue" into the opening music for the next scene (necessitating an almost instantaneous scene change).

I chose this among many possible examples because of the music's important interweaving with the stage action. While the obvious use of *melos* continues to play an important role in these plays, so did action- and dialogue-specific music. It was such music that partly contributed to the play's success, which is probably why Baker's music was associated with both the New York and London productions. Over twenty years later, Samuel French still loaned out the music to *The Colleen Bawn*, along with music to over 200 other "burlesques, operas, and dramas."[57] Such a finely crafted theatrical score as this one leads one to hope that we will eventually come to understand better the strong connection between music and drama in the nineteenth-century theatre, especially in circumstances when it was at its best and most theatrically compelling.

NOTES

1. Henry Lunn, "Musings of a Musician: Theatrical Music," *The Musical World* (1845), p. 365.
2. George Bernard Shaw, review of Henschel's music for *Hamlet* at the Haymarket Theatre, 27 January 1892, rpt. in *Music in London, 1890–94*, vol. II (London: Constable and Co., 1932), p. 11.
3. Norman O'Neill, "Music to Stage Plays," *Proceedings for the Royal Musical Association, 1910–11* (21 March 1911), p. 88, rpt. in Derek Hudson, *Norman O'Neill, A Life in Music* (London: Quality Press, 1945).
4. Reprinted in Russell Jackson (ed.), *Victorian Theatre* (London: A. & C. Black, 1989), p. 205. This effect of dramatic irony, perhaps developed as early as the 1850s by Verdi, for example in *La Traviata*, has also been used effectively by film composers and was labeled "anempathetic music" by film theorist Michel Chion, *Audio-Vision: Sound on Screen*, ed. and trans. Claudia Gorbman (New York: Columbia University Press, 1994).
5. For more on early British melodrama see Aubrey S. Garlington, " 'Gothic' Literature and Dramatic Music in England," *Journal of the American Musicological Society* 15, 1 (Spring 1962), 48–64; Bruce Carr, "Theatre Music: 1800–1834," chap. 13 in Nicholas Temperley (ed.), *The Athlone History of Music in Britain*, vol. V, *The Romantic Age: 1800–1914* (London: Athlone Press, 1981),

pp. 288–306; and Anne Dhu Shapiro (McLucas), "Nineteenth-Century Melodrama: From *A Tale of Mystery* to *Monte Cristo*," ed. Lowell Lindgren, in *Harvard Library Bulletin: Bits and Pieces, Music for Theatre*, new series 2, 2 (Winter 1991), 57–73.

6. Pierre Decourcelle, *Les Deux gosses* (Paris: P.-V. Stock, 1898).
7. Leonard Ratner, *Classic Music: Expression, Form, and Style* (New York: Schirmer Books, 1980), pp. 9–30.
8. The genres here were each represented by characters in James Robinson Planché's "Camp of the Combined British Dramatic Forces," in *The Camp at the Olympic* (Olympic, 1853). Cited in Michael R. Booth, *Theatre in the Victorian Age* (Cambridge: Cambridge University Press, 1991), p. 196.
9. For a discussion of Bishop's music in *Miller and his Men* (Covent Garden, 1813), see David Mayer, "Nineteenth-Century Theatre Music." *Theatre Notebook: A Journal of the History and Technique of the British Theatre* 30, 3 (1976), 115–23.
10. The "burletta restrictions" apparently required some five songs to an act, although in practice this often applied only to the first act. On music in the "burletta" see Allardyce Nicoll, *Early Nineteenth-Century Drama*, vol. IV of *History of English Drama* (Cambridge: Cambridge University Press, 1961–5), pp. 101 and 138–89. The scores of many burlettas were published and copies exist in the British Library.
11. On the traditions of pantomimic music see Anne Dhu Shapiro (McLucas), "Action Music in American Pantomime and Melodrama, 1730–1913," *American Music* 1, 4 (Winter 1984), 49–92.
12. John Donahue, "Burletta and the Early Nineteenth-Century English Stage," *Nineteenth-Century Theatre Research* 1, 1 (Spring 1973), 29. Donahue cites examples by William Moncrieff and by Charles Kemble, including the latter's *The Black Castle* (1801). According to Simon Trussler, this practice began in 1782 at the Royal Circus where, because of the Licensing Act, gothic dramas had to be staged in mime to musical accompaniment and the practice continued throughout the 1800s. See Simon Trussler, "A Chronology of Early Melodrama," *Theatre Quarterly* 1, 4 (1971), 19–21.
13. London, 2nd edn., 1822.
14. Roland Barthes, *Image, Music, Text* (1964), trans. Stephen Heath (New York: Hill and Wang, 1977), p. 39.
15. Copy in the British Library.
16. Copy in the Lord Chamberlain's collection of plays, British Library.
17. Music for an unspecified production of *Black-Ey'd Susan* at the Theatre Museum, London.
18. A copy of the score (1840) is found in the Kean Collection at the Folger Library; it was used to supplement Hatton's music for performances at the Princess's in the 1850s, perhaps in an effort to evoke a more "historical" atmosphere.
19. Many nineteenth-century playbills of *A Midsummer Night's Dream* seem to feature Mendelssohn's music as a principal attraction.
20. Set of twelve orchestra parts at the Folger Library, Washington, DC. From the collection of Charles B. Hanford.
21. Cue no. 13 in *Rienzi* promptbook and orchestra parts. Promptbook signed "Washington, DC, 1887." Lawrence Barrett Collection, Harvard Theatre Library.

22. Martin Miller Marks, *Music and the Silent Film: Contexts and Case Studies, 1895–1924* (Oxford: Oxford University Press, 1997). See my review in *Journal of Musicological Research* 19, 2 (2000), 182–89.

23. Herbert Beerbohm Tree collection, University of Bristol Theatre Collection.

24. Tree collection. Typed cue sheet entitled "Music of 'Trilby.'"

25. See David Mayer, *Henry Irving and "The Bells"* (Manchester: Manchester University Press, 1980).

26. Edward Fitzball, *Thirty-Five Years of a Dramatic Author's Life* (London, 1859), II: 374. Among those in his list are Michael Balfe, William Vincent Wallace, George Macfarren, and Ferdinand Ries. Balfe, Wallace, and Macfarren were listed among "the five main composers [of English opera] of the day" (mid-nineteenth-century) by Michael Hurd in "Opera: 1834–1865," chap. 14 in Temperley (ed.), *The Athlone History of Music: The Romantic Age*, p. 341.

27. After Garlington's essay, noted above, the first historian to deal seriously with music in the Victorian theatre is David Mayer. Several of his essays are cited throughout these notes. Similarly, musicologist Anne Dhu Shapiro (McLucas)'s writings are also noted here. The fullest published study of nineteenth-century theatrical music in all of its manifestations is Deane L. Root, *American Popular Stage Music: 1860–1880* (Ann Arbor: UMI Research Press, 1981).

28. The brief entry on Edward Mollenhauer in *Baker's Biographical Dictionary of Musicians* does not even mention his theatre career. I have compiled an extensive amount of information on Stoepel's life and work in my unpublished manuscript "Robert Stoepel: A Musical Life in the Nineteenth-Century Theatre."

29. Charles Reade wrote a moving obituary for Edwin Ellis: "To the Editors of the *Era*: A Dramatic Musician" (1878), rpt. in Charles Reade, *Readiana: Comments on Current Events* (London, 1881), pp. 28–31. So far, only a single theatrical score of Ellis's has been located (music to Watts Phillips, *Lost in London*, Drury Lane Collection, Box 13). The "Drury Lane collection" (largely the personal collection of Oscar Barrett) is so called because it resided in the basement of that theatre until it was removed to the British Library in the 1980s.

30. Music for *Uncle Tom's Cabin* by Alfred Mellon. Overture published in piano score (London: Jeffreys, 1853). Copy at the British Library.

31. Review in *The Era* 26, 1350 (7 August 1864), 10.

32. "Covent Garden: Memoranda of Agreements, 1818." Manuscript ledger book at the British Library.

33. Dispensation of French theatre orchestras are specified in *L'Almanach des spectacles: 1828*. A superb and richly detailed overview of theatre orchestras in both Britain and America in the early nineteenth century can be found in Susan Porter, *With an Air Debonair: Musical Theatre in America, 1785–1815* (Washington and London: Smithsonian Institution Press, 1991), pp. 361–405.

34. Advertisement in *The Times*, 30 Dec. 1878, cited in Alan Hughes, "The Lyceum Staff: A Victorian Theatrical Organization," *Theatre Notebook* 18, 1 (1974), 14.

35. Information on Cooper in David Mayer, *Four Bars of "Agit": Incidental Music for Victorian and Edwardian Melodrama* (London: Theatre Museum, 1983), p. 2.

36. "Theatre Orchestras" in *Dwight's Journal of Music* [Boston] 28, 18 (31 Jan. 1863), 345–47. [Originally published in the *New York Tribune*. Author and date of original unknown.]

37. *Ibid.*, 346.

38. William Archer and H. Granville Barker, *A National Theatre: Schemes and Estimates* (London: Duckworth, 1907).

39. From Eric Jones-Evans's BBC radio broadcast "The Music of Melodrama," program no. 3. Copies of the series are on tape in the Jones-Evans collection, University of Bristol Theatre Collection.

40. Reference in Nicoll, *Early Nineteenth-Century Drama*, pp. 138–39.

41. Music manuscripts for nearly a hundred of Belasco's plays are at the New York Public Library, Research Division.

42. One dissertation is devoted to such a reconstruction: Barry Yzereef, "The Art of Gentlemanly Melodrama: Charles Kean's Production of *The Corsican Brothers*," Ph.D. diss., University of Victoria, 1995.

43. Louis Calvert, *Problems of the Actor* (New York: Henry Holt and Co., 1918), pp. 222–24.

44. George Taylor, *Players and Performances in the Victorian Theatre* (Manchester: Manchester University Press, 1989), p. 125. Jones-Evans, BBC radio broadcast "The Music of Melodrama," program no. 1.

45. Shaw, *Music in London*, p. 12.

46. Cited by George Taylor in *Players and Performances*, p. 126.

47. Jerome K. Jerome, *On the Stage and Off: The Brief Career of a Would-Be Actor* (1885) (rpt. London: Leadenhall Press; New York: Scribners [1891]), p. 54.

48. Boucicault papers, Special Collections, Tampa Campus Library, University of South Florida.

49. From *Jimmy Glover: His Book* (1911), pp. 240–41, cited in Mayer, *Four Bars of "Agit"*, p. 1.

50. George Parsons Lathrop, "Inner Life of a Great Theater," unpublished manuscript (*c.* 1895), Folger Shakespeare Library, Washington, DC.

51. See David Mayer, *Four Bars of "Agit"*.

52. According to Eric Jones-Evans, "The Music of Melodrama," program no. 1.

53. Auguste Anicet-Bourgeois and Paul Féval, *Le bossu, drame en cinq actes et douze tableaux* (Paris: Michel Lévy Freres, 1863) and Charles Fechter, adapted, *The Duke's Motto, "A Romantic Drama"* (London: C. Whiting, Beaufort House, 1870). (Copies at Carl A. Kroch Library, Cornell University and the British Library.)

54. Yzereef, "The Art of Gentlemanly Melodrama," and Anne Dhu Shapiro (McLucas), *Later Melodrama in America: Monte Cristo (c. 1883)*, vol. IV in Deane L. Root (ed.), *Nineteenth-Century American Musical Theatre* (New York: Garland, 1994). While this book was in production, a set of orchestral parts for *The Green Bushes* was found in the Drury Lane Collection, British Library. The music is indicated as that of Alfred Mellon.

55. Biographical information on Thomas Baker from T. Allston Brown, *History of the American Stage* (New York, 1871).

56. Herein lies the problem. Whereas Baker is listed as composer for both the New York and London productions, the set of parts found in the Drury Lane Collection are unsigned and cannot be proven conclusively to be copies of Baker's music. Given the exceptionally dramatic effectiveness of this music, however, I believe that it is indeed by Baker. It compares favorably with the other known Baker score, that of *Under the Palms* in the Oscar Barrett collection. See Anne Dhu Shapiro (McLucas), "Melodrama" in *New Grove Dictionary of American Music*,

ed. H. Wiley Hitchcock and Stanley Sadie (New York: Macmillan, 1986), III: 202–04.

57. List included in Wentworth Hogg, *Guide to Selecting Plays; or, Managers' Companion* (London: Samuel French, 1882), pp. 79–80. Among other orchestra parts for loan were those to *Black Ey'd Susan, Cricket on the Hearth, Guy Mannering, Luke the Labourer, The Sentinel, Pizarro*, and *The Vampire*. In subsequent editions, 1899 and 1910, this list is dropped and no items of this collection have so far been located.

5

JIM DAVIS AND VICTOR EMELJANOW

Victorian and Edwardian audiences

Victorian and Edwardian theatre audiences were so diverse that it is impossible to consider a generic audience for this period. Audiences varied from theatre to theatre and even within theatres to such an extent that any essentializing description is bound to be flawed. Consequently, Michael Booth's call for a more precise investigation of such audiences must be heeded, if we wish to understand the contexts in which Victorian and Edwardian playgoing took place. Booth laments that:

> Never, or hardly ever, are we told anything about audiences: what kind of audiences went to what theatres, what their class was, what jobs they did, how much they got paid, what their non-theatrical tastes were, how often they went to the theatre, where they lived and under what conditions. Such information, however, is essential if we are fully to understand the repertory or style of a particular theatre at a particular time in history, and ultimately the character and content of the drama itself.

Booth asserts that the social and cultural implications of a play will vary, according to the audience for whom it is performed, which in itself will change "theatre by theatre, district by district, decade by decade." Therefore, in order to understand a specific audience, one needs to know "something of its social and cultural habits, jobs, wages, cost of living, places of residence, class status, means of transportation, patterns of migration and settlement, moral and political outlook – anything that goes to make up complete human beings living at a chosen moment in history who came together for the collective but usually incidental purpose of seeing a play."[1]

Beyond Booth's concerns we should also consider issues of ideology and reception and the theoretical framework in which we place them. For some time Victorian studies have been dominated by the Foucauldian paradigm of containment and control. Yet Victorian and Edwardian theatre has generally eluded the shadow of Foucault, perhaps because the theatrical event is never totally containable. Nor, on the other hand, is it entirely susceptible to the Bakhtinian excess that critics sometimes invoke as the antidote to Foucauldian interpretation. Audiences were certainly not entirely contained or controlled in our period, despite the increasing efforts of the authorities to regulate the theatres, but neither were they the rowdy, rebellious masses of popular mythology. Complex negotiations took place in many theatrical performances in this period, both formulating and shifting the ideologies and outlooks of audience members, for theatre was one of the most omnivorous of public events. J. S. Bratton has suggested, for instance, that the popular genre of nautical melodrama "offered the ordinary individual a stirring and satisfying sense of national identity . . . because [it] implicated him inescapably in British imperialism, while at the same time accommodating doubts and tensions created by that role."[2] We must also allow for ironic or even ambivalent responses amongst a play's spectators as well as variable reactions according to location. For example, the moral implications of Lady Audley's bigamy in the many adaptations of Mary Braddon's *Lady Audley's Secret* may have been taken seriously at the St. James's Theatre in London's West End, but at the Britannia or Victoria theatres popular audiences may well have justified the choices made by Lady Audley on economic grounds even if they condemned her morally.

The orthodox history of English theatre audiences from 1843 to 1910 is often presented as an evolutionary and triumphalist narrative. Theatrical reform, improved conditions within the auditorium and the re-emergence of a respectable upper- and middle-class audience, attracted back after the absorption of disreputable and unruly elements by the music hall, apparently paved the way for a theatre and a drama that could once again be taken seriously. Yet the evidence militates against so simplistic a narrative. Admittedly, in the West End, new theatres opened to meet a greater demand for entertainment by an increasingly mobile population from the 1860s onwards. Neighborhood theatres, however, did not decline immediately nor did popular dramatic genres go out of fashion. The impact of Charles Kean's management of the Princess's Theatre in the 1850s and of the Bancrofts' management at the Prince of Wales's Theatre (1865–80) and subsequently at the Haymarket brought about changes in stage management and presentation and (in the case of the Bancrofts) in accommodation and pricing, which broadened and yet socially limited the appeal of their own theatres within the community. At the Princess's, Kean's combination of historical research and spectacle highlighted the educative function of theatre as well as its potential to promote a sense of national identity through its representation of history – particularly English medieval history. At the Prince of Wales's the dramatist Tom Robertson's simple but detailed portraits of contemporary life initiated new standards in stage realism. Yet the notion that a social and artistic revolution occurred within the English theatre during this period is nonsensical. Certainly, the Prince of Wales's Theatre achieved the sorts of changes in accommodation and repertoire which the Examiner of Plays, W. B. Donne, had long hoped would attract a more respectable class of people to the theatre and elevate the quality of the drama itself.[3] The Prince of Wales's Theatre did eventually draw largely middle- and upper-class audiences, but despite the Bancrofts' subsequent assertions, this was not its original intention. Initially, its pricing policy attempted to keep the options open and a mixed rather than socially self-selecting audience attended its programs. It has been asserted that the working-class sector of the audience at this theatre was drawn off to the music halls, yet many music halls were themselves catering for a middle- and upper-class market. Indeed, many audience members attended both theatre and music hall. Thomas Wright, the "journeyman engineer," indicates that an evening in a theatre gallery was much cheaper for a working man than an evening at the music hall, where you could not take your own provisions to eat and drink and were expected to tip heavily.[4] Although theatre audiences declined in some areas later in the century, better communications and demographic changes, as well as increasing poverty in previously prosperous neighborhoods, may have been more direct causes than the music hall itself.

The assumption that popular audiences were rowdy and unmanageable is also flawed. Drunkenness, for instance, was rarely a major problem in the theatres: even when beer and spirits were available, the theatres did not turn into surrogate public houses. Offensive behavior was usually condemned by the audience itself and troublemakers ejected by the theatres' own officers. Police were in attendance at most theatres, complaints were dealt with by the Lord Chamberlain's Office (if the theatre in question came under its jurisdiction) and renewal of licenses depended on a reasonable standard of behavior both within the theatre and immediately outside it. Indeed, records of affrays or of riotous behavior are relatively scarce, although they tend to color many accounts of nineteenth-century theatre audiences. Since the auditorium was generally lit up until the 1880s, the social aspects of playgoing were enhanced and a certain degree of noise was inevitable and even customary, as on the first night of the annual pantomime on Boxing Day. Noise, however, does not constitute rowdiness. In fact, the tendency to disapprove of such audiences has a lot to do with Victorian views of class and respectability and with the appropriation of the theatre as both mirror and propaganda vehicle by the bourgeoisie as the century progressed.

Much of the primary evidence on which we base our assumptions about nineteenth-century audiences derives from journal and newspaper articles and from police reports filed in the Lord Chamberlain's Office. Since, in so

Figure 6 The gallery on Boxing Night at the Drury Lane Theatre.

brief a space, we cannot do justice to the range of issues raised by an investigation of Victorian and Edwardian theatre audiences, we propose to look at some representative documentation and the assumptions that underlie it. Again, for reasons of space, our comments will be confined largely to London theatres. In so doing, we hope to show how these multi-faceted, variegated audiences have been generically and artificially constructed and often simplified by their contemporaries.

The regulation of the theatres in 1843, bringing all London theatres under the control of the Lord Chamberlain's Office, generated many reports which attempted to describe the composition of specific audiences at London's minor theatres. Early police reports indicated for example that in east London the City of London Theatre drew "persons in the neighborhood, many weavers," while the neighboring Standard Theatre drew tradesmen, mechanics, their children and silk weavers from Spitalfields. Further south the Garrick Theatre also drew a neighborhood audience, including tradespeople and mechanics, while the Pavilion Theatre in Whitechapel attracted a local audience, "many from the docks, many sailors." The audiences at the Effingham Saloon,[5] not far from the Pavilion, were characterized as "tradesmen and their children from the neighborhood of St. George's parish, Whitechapel, Stepney; sailors when the river is full of shipping. Families 2 or 3 times a week." A report on the Grecian Saloon described its audiences as "respectable tradesmen, clerks from the city, mechanics, neighbors." Not far away "tradespeople in the neighborhood, brickmakers, mechanics, watch-makers" patronized Sadler's Wells Theatre. South of the Thames the Surrey Theatre was attended by "sometimes nobility and gentry, tradespeople, me-chanics . . . 4 women to 1 man in the pit, the husbands and brothers being in the gallery to save expense," whereas the nearby Victoria Theatre drew "principally mechanics in the neighborhood." (Despite the popularity of nautical melodrama at the Surrey Theatre, the report does not refer to a preponderance of sailors or watermen in the audiences, although such asser-tions occur in subsequent accounts. A search of local census returns also fails to establish a maritime presence in the vicinity of the Surrey Theatre). Of the two theatres immediately north of London's West End the Queen's Theatre (later the Prince of Wales's Theatre) attracted "persons in the neighborhood, of an inferior class to the persons at the City of London (theatre)," whereas the nearby Princess's Theatre's audience was detailed as "fashionable, better class of tradespeople, housekeepers etc., not confined to the neighborhood." Further west the Marylebone Theatre drew "families from Bryanstone and Montague Squares, schools in winter, respectable tradesmen, mechanics &c, all from the locality," whilst the Yorkshire Stingo Tavern and Theatre not only catered for omnibus drivers, low mechanics, servants, boatmen, navi-gators and street sweepers, but also for "a great number of the lowest class of boys between 10 to 14 years of age."[6]

That individual theatres attracted audiences largely commensurate with the local population is unsurprising, although we should not forget that contemporaries thought nothing of walking long distances to the theatre and that transport facilities were constantly improving. As a boy of fourteen the playgoer P. P. Hanley recounts walking several miles from his north London home of Camden Town to see melodramas at the Surrey Theatre across the Thames in south London. A youthful John Coleman, after he had completed his daily office job and been home for supper, was prepared to walk up to eight miles to such theatres as Drury Lane in the West End, the Queen's in Tottenham Street or the Stingo in Paddington.[7] Accessibility by public transport is highlighted by the example of Astley's Amphitheatre, which drew an audience from across London to witness its equestrian and military spectacles. A playbill c. 1848 advertises "steamboats and omnibuses from all parts of town to Westminster Bridge," draws attention to the newly opened South-Western Railway Terminus five minutes' walk from the theatre and notes the scheduling of omnibuses to Paddington and Greenwich at the end of the performance.

While access to theatres on foot or by public transport is unproblematic, difficulties are raised by the way in which individual audiences were de-scribed. Youthful audiences, such as that noted at the Stingo Tavern, were continually categorized as thieves or potential thieves. "The Theatre appears to be detrimental to the morals of youths of the lowest order, who get in the company of thieves and young Prostitutes," wrote Superintendent Hughes of the Stingo, "and Boys are no doubt in many instances tempted to steal in order to secure admission." Another police report of 1844 asserted that prostitutes and thieves resorted to the Britannia and Albert Saloons in east London. A report on the City of London Theatre's gallery in the same year alleged the presence of "several males, the associates of thieves" and between "40 and 50 young prostitutes, some apparently not more than 14 or 15 years of age." Yet a report on the equivalent audience a year later could find no evidence that would give "any reason to say the least thing against them" (LC 7/6). The assumption that any young person in the gallery of a theatre in a working-class theatre must be either a thief or a prostitute seems a matter of prejudice rather than fact. Indeed, the *East London Observer* (13 November 1858) asserted that "the East-end population is not entirely composed of sailors and prostitutes," but also consisted of "respectable people seeking intelligent amusements." Bracebridge Hemyng, one of Henry Mayhew's reporters, "commented that it was high time the west-end prejudice that east-end theatres were filled with 'a rough, noisy set of thieves and prostitutes' was exploded."[8]

Nevertheless such prejudices remained explicit in much contemporary journalism. Ironically, Mayhew himself asserted that thieves living in East-End lodging houses went to the Britannia and Albert Saloons and the City of London and Standard Theatres in the east and the Surrey and Victoria Theatres south of the Thames.[9] The prejudice is also implicit in Charles Dickens's two famous accounts of the audiences of the Britannia Theatre, Hoxton and of the Victoria. In his first account of the Britannia in 1850 Dickens refers rather squeamishly to "a great many very young girls grown into bold women before they had ceased to be children," while ten years later he includes "prowlers and idlers" among the audience members he identifies, and draws attention to the pleasure of the younger males in the audience at a comic police chase, "as though it were a delicate reference to something they had heard of before." At the Victoria Theatre in 1850 he claims to have recognized "some young pickpockets of our acquaintance."[10] Dickens had a reason for perpetuating such a view of the audience. In both his novels and his journalism he argued that popular amusements were important for the common people not only because they kept them out of mischief, but also stimulated the imagination and often inculcated a moral. It was therefore essential that he (and those journalists such as Horne and Sala, who worked for him) constructed an audience that evidently required the stimulus of popular amusement. In so doing he tended not only to mytholo-gize nineteenth-century audiences, but also to establish the formula by which audiences were represented by journalists into the early twentieth century. This was certainly the case with Dickens's own journal, *All the Year Round*, in a series of articles in 1866. In "Mr. Whelks over the Water" (30 June 1866) the need for the civilizing presence of the theatre is emphasized: "We need not go all the way to Central Africa, or the wilds of South America, to study the conditions and habits of savages, when the New Cut, Lambeth, is within ten minutes' walk of the Houses of Parliament." The Victoria Theatre is moreover in an area inhabited by "swarms of creeping, crawling, mangy-looking people who constantly throng the thoroughfare" and "are suggestive rather of vermin than of human beings." Eleven years later the same journal (19 May 1877) revisited London audiences, dividing them into "the purely society or fashionable audience; the fast fashionable audience; the domestic audience; the respectable audience; the mixed audience; the working-class audience," the last of which are subdivided into "the transpon-tine, the extreme East-end, the flash, the decorous, the criminal, the honest, the drunken and the sober." A visit to the Surrey Theatre revealed "an en-thusiastic, nay, a noisy, but . . . well-behaved . . . audience," while at the Britannia the consumption of "Brobdignagian sandwiches" and "foaming pots of porter" did not "prevent the audience from diligently noting all that is said and done on the stage. Nothing could be more orderly, nothing more decent."

A good example of the construction of a Victorian audience through journalism occurs in Dickens and R. H. Horne's account of Samuel Phelps's management at Sadler's Wells Theatre. In many ways the success of Phelps at Sadler's Wells, a suburban theatre immediately to the north of the City of London and the Smithfield Markets, was a godsend for Dickens. It appeared to vindicate his view that an audience as well as a whole neighborhood could be reclaimed by the provision of rational amusement. Writing in 1851 in *Household Words* (4 October) under the title "Shakespeare and Newgate", Dickens and Horne retrospectively describe the old Sadler's Wells Theatre as having been located in an area dominated by petty criminals whose uncouth behavior in the theatre was exacerbated by the provision of free drinks in the pit and the low calibre of the repertoire. Dickens pointed to ways in which the drama "with its noble lessons of tenderness and virtue" had con-tributed to the reclamation of the inhabitants of Lambeth. The possibility of a similar transformation had occurred in Islington when Samuel Phelps became the manager of Sadler's Wells in 1844 and opened a summer sea-son with *Macbeth*. Prior to the advent of Phelps, according to Dickens's reconstruction, Sadler's Wells had been "a bear garden, resounding with foul language, oaths . . . [and] . . . obscenity." Phelps "conceived of the desperate idea of changing the character of the dramatic entertainments presented at this den, from the lowest to the highest, and of utterly changing with it the character of the audience." During his opening season, which also included performances of *Hamlet*, *King John*, *The Merchant of Venice*, *Othello* and *Richard III*, Phelps removed the "costermonger-scum" who congregated round the doors of the theatre and stopped performances to eject users of bad language. On occasions he "went into the gallery, with a cloak over his theatrical dress" to point out offenders to the police. Realising the error of their ways and "sensible of the pains bestowed on everything presented to them," the audiences by 1851 "[had] really come to the Theatre for their intellectual pursuit." The result, concluded Dickens, was a gallery "as orderly as a lecture room" and a pit "filled with respectable family visitors" sitting decorously as though in their own homes: "The place which was a Nuisance is become quite a household word."

Such was the authority of *Household Words*, both in its depiction of the exotically distant colonies and the exotic reaches of east and south London, that Dickens and Horne's account of Sadler's Wells was subsequently accepted as a narrative of social reclamation. Writing, for example, in 1916, J. R. Towse recalled his childhood in London and the one occasion that he visited Sadler's Wells as a very young boy to see Phelps's production of *A Midsummer Night's Dream*. He remembered nothing of it and confesses that his memories of Phelps date from the late 1860s, when Phelps was a starring actor at Drury Lane. Nevertheless, he felt able to write:

> The old Prince of Wales's Theater, before the occupation of it by the Bancrofts, was not so disreputable a hole as "The Wells" . . . Islington, indeed, was densely populous, but exceedingly poor and shabby. It abounded in small shops, taverns, cheap lodging-houses and slums, and small tradesmen, mechanics, the commoner kind of clerks, peddlers, innumerable wage-earners of different kinds, with a plentiful sprinkling of degraded "sports," constituted the great bulk of the inhabitants. "The Wells" had been devoted to what would now be described as vaudeville, to tenth-rate boxing matches, comic concerts, acrobatic shows, and so on. It was one of the dingiest, dirtiest, and in every way most objectionable resorts imaginable.[11]

The aftermath of Phelps's intervention, which succeeded in converting the "illiterate denizens of Islington," demonstrated that "there has never been a more striking instance of the educational power of the theatre or of the natural capacity of the masses to comprehend . . . what is noblest and best in the drama" (Towse, *Sixty Years*, p. 35). Michael Williams, writing about Sadler's Wells from the perspective of 1883, described it before Phelps as offering:

> Melodrama of the coarsest type . . . to a class of frequenters, in themselves so utterly vicious, that no respectable tradesman would dream of taking his wife or daughters to the place. The lessees [Phelps and Greenwood] had not only to purify the nature of the performances, they also had to unmake, as well as to create, their audience.[12]

A similar construction of Sadler's Wells also occurs in Shirley Allen's 1971 account of Phelps, in which she characterizes the theatre before him as reflecting "the tastes and attitudes of the relatively uneducated lower middle class typical of suburban London in 1840."[13] Thus Dickens and Horne's original narrative is transformed into a myth in which the theatre is established as an agency of social change. Yet Phelps's early attempts to control the audience as described by Dickens were discounted as inaccurate by Phelps himself, according to his nephew W. May Phelps,[14] and neither the *Athenaeum* nor the *Theatrical Journal*, which reviewed the occasion, saw fit to mention Phelps's personal intervention. Indeed, when Dickens addressed the Royal General Theatrical Fund dinner, held at Drury Lane on 6 April 1857, and attempted to characterize the Sadler's Wells audience as low and very bad, his words received a hostile reception from the floor. He was forced to modify his comments and describe the audience as a mostly "vagabond" one (May Phelps and Forbes-Robertson, *Life*, p. 251).

Moreover, such comments about Islington audiences and their disreputable environment were strangely at odds with the respectability of Sadler's Wells audiences which was noted by the *Theatrical Journal* when it visited Sadler's Wells in 1841, or the description in the same year by James Cook in *The Actor's Notebook* that the theatre was set within a "neighborhood . . . vastly picturesque."[15] In fact, the census returns show that when Phelps moved his family in 1844 from Chelsea to Canonbury, located north of the theatre, he moved into an area whose populations reflected both change and respectability. Certainly the presence of the main arterial road which connected York and the City inevitably meant that blacksmiths, carriers, carters and wagoners, coachmen, coach guards, and postboys lived in the area. Just as important, however, was the presence of a large professional and skilled artisan class. The area was already noted for its jewellery, gold- and silversmiths, as well as its watch-, clock-, and instrument-makers and had the second largest population in London of attorneys, solicitors, and law students, as well as of clerks and government civil servants, and the largest population of surgeons, apothecaries, and stock and insurance brokers of all kinds.

Such evidence seems to throw doubt on at least one element of the myth of Sadler's Wells: that the area in the early 1840s was a degraded one, characterized by blackguards and dominated by a culturally unappreciative working class. When Phelps undertook the management of Sadler's Wells in 1844, it may well have been the case that a respected Drury Lane actor found himself supported by audiences looking for a theatre whose repertoire would affirm their own self-conscious respectability. The evidence of Dickens and Horne therefore looks increasingly suspect.

When Dickens described the results of Phelps's "reformation" of Sadler's Wells, he pointed to the two areas which, in his opinion, best demonstrated the efficacy of Phelps's actions: the pit and the galleries. The pit in particular, traditionally regarded as the habitat of the true theatrical enthusiast, became at Sadler's Wells the domain of the respectable middle-class family: according to Dickens, "a father sits there with his wife and daughters, as quietly, as easily, as in his own house." (*Household Words*, 4 October 1851, 27) The pit in all theatres occupied the best vantage point from which to view the stage, and performers took the responsiveness of the pit patrons very seriously. The pits of most theatres were large and their bench seating could not be booked in advance. West-End theatre managers, who had become since the 1850s increasingly dependent upon the patronage of visitors, quickly saw the advantages of transforming this space into a fashionable and expensive part of the theatre. Loath to displace regular theatregoers in case they were needed when the fashion-conscious failed to attend, they began a process of encroachment whereby stall seats, which could be booked in advance, progressively replaced the front rows of the pit. In so doing West-End managers inevitably affected the composition and disposition of their audiences. Yet the evidence which supposedly documents these audiences is not necessarily reliable. Indeed it might be argued that the construction of a monolithic West-End audience is at least in part an invention of a consortium of managers and journalists. Even West-End theatres could continue to be sites of contestation much to the discomfort of those who sought to identify the image of the West-End audiences as the culmination of refinement and uncontested elegance.

Two "Symposia" took place in the pages of the *Theatre* in 1880 based around events which had recently occurred in the pits of two prominent West-End theatres. On 31 January 1880 the Bancrofts opened their management of the Theatre Royal, Haymarket with a performance of Bulwer Lytton's comedy *Money*. The performance was greeted with a protest at the abolition of the pit in a theatre identified as the traditional home of English comedy. Prior to the beginning of the season, the Bancrofts had issued a press statement in which they justified their innovation on the grounds that rising production and management costs had made the change inevitable. They also pointed out that for many years theatres had progressively introduced orchestra stalls, the effect of which had resulted in pushing the pit further back. The first discussion appeared in the *Theatre* in March 1880.[16] This drew attention to the Bancrofts' introduction of the practice whereby the encroachment of the stalls had transformed the pit area into the most expensive part of the house other than the private boxes. Yet, as the contributors noted, newer West-End theatres like the Opera Comique and the Charing Cross had been built without a pit, so that the Bancrofts' action was not in itself a revolution. Moreover, the costs of theatre management in the West End could not allow the best parts of the theatre to be given over to a chance aggregation of devoted playgoers. Financial considerations demanded long runs and an assurance that patrons paying the higher prices attended productions. The long runs depended not upon regular theatregoers but on visitors to the West End. Consequently the relegation of the pit patrons to an area euphemistically called the second circle meant that the acting and reception of a play lay in the hands of stall patrons, who often came late and were generally unresponsive. The old sense of engagement and interactivity between stage and auditorium was inevitably lost. Nevertheless the symposium, though airing a nostalgia for the passing of a popular theatrical institution, came down on the side of the Bancrofts. The discussion suggests that, despite the protests of traditionalists, West-End theatregoing reflected the patronage of those who came from elsewhere. From this perspective the Bancrofts' innovations in 1880 simply removed a limb whose usefulness to the financial wellbeing of the theatrical body had long been questioned, at least in the West End.

In August 1880 a second "Symposium" attempted to answer the question "The Police in the Pit – can such a system be justified?"[17] This was in response to the expulsion from the pit of a number of young men who had occupied the first row at the Vaudeville theatre on 29 May to see James Albery's *Jacks and Jills*. They had found little to please them in either the play or the performances and had tried to force the management to abandon the performance. The management with the help of the police ejected them. This second Symposium discussed the issue in terms of appropriate behavior. While vigorously defending the right of audiences to respond as they thought fit and deriding Albery's assertion that he had been the victim of an organized claque on the night, the symposium noted that appropriate behavior would obviate the necessity for police intervention. By implication it supported a code of behavior whereby an audience's reactions should appear only at intervals in the action or at the end of the play, and came to the conclusion that these reactions should manifest fairness, restraint and due deference for the performers' efforts and the manager's financial outlay.

There are two issues that need to be considered here. Firstly, in so far as it is conducting a debate about the nature of West-End theatregoing, the *Theatre* might seem to offer some of the best evidence available about problems in the early 1880s. However, the journal had commenced publication in 1878 under the editorship of Clement Scott, at the time a respected theatre critic, and until December 1879 had been owned by Henry Irving, already one of the West End's most distinguished actor-managers.[18] Given the leadership of Scott and Irving, the journal's policies reflected a self-conscious seriousness. Both men wished to emphasize the theatre's position as an art form, which was most highly developed in its West-End manifestations. The pages of the *Theatre* were there to inform the serious theatregoer and to explore issues which might affect theatregoing. Yet they might equally be accused of "constructing" the theatregoer in the image that was most appropriate for the agenda of both the *Theatre* itself and that of the West-End managers. The encroachment of the stalls could be seen as an inevitable consequence of necessary "progress," and equally the debates in the pages of the *Theatre* could be seen as essentially manufactured in order to mask economic rationalist decisions. Secondly, there is evidence to suggest that there was considerable resistance to the forcible reconstitution of the West-End audience. The veteran playgoer, P. P. Hanley, for example, complained:

> It would seem that anything is good enough for the pit and gallery folk, who are obliged to arrive early, for since stalls were introduced, a poor place at the best can only be obtained in the pit; in many theatres it consists almost entirely of seats under the boxes, in a most oppressive atmosphere. One theatre has done away with the pit entirely, and in the galleries of most houses several seats are fenced off and converted into amphitheatre stalls; so that the gallery visitor, who pays one shilling for his admission, is relegated to a position, where, if it is a large theatre, the actors look like pigmies. Going to the play is now a very expensive luxury and, unless you book seats beforehand, there is really no comfort, and it is not everyone who can afford to do so. For myself, I must say, if the present system had been adopted in my young days, fond as I was (and am) of the theatre, my visits would have been very few and far between.[19]

Though the supposed evidence of the *Theatre* implies that the displacement of the pit audience may have been an economic and social necessity in the eyes of the West-End theatre establishment, it would be wrong to regard this displacement as an uncontentious factor in the evolutionary progression towards the sort of dramas and audiences for which W. B. Donne had been yearning. Walter Besant, writing a few years after the symposia in the *Theatre*, commented:

> The people of London have in great measure lost their taste for the theatres, because they have gone to live in the suburbs. Who, for instance, that lives in Hampstead and wishes to get up in good time in the morning can take his wife often to the theatre? It takes an hour to drive into town, the hour after dinner. The play is over a little after eleven; if he takes a cab. The driver is sulky at the thought of going up the hill and getting back again without another fare; if he goes and returns in a brougham, it doubles the expense. Formerly, when everybody lived in town, they could walk. Again, the price of seats has enormously gone up. Where there were two rows of stalls at the same price as the dress circle – namely, four shillings – there are now a dozen at the price of half a guinea. And it is very much more the fashion to take the best places, so that the dress circle is no longer the same highly respectable part of the house, while the upper boxes are now "out of it" altogether, and, as for the pit, no man knoweth whether there be any pit still.[20]

Such remarks draw attention to the fact that West End "reforms" were now tending to exclude even the respectable fathers and their families whose return to the theatre Dickens had noted with satisfaction and questions the assumptions upon which the two symposia had rested.

The Bancrofts' actions at the Haymarket had effectively created an economic zone of exclusion, a policy eventually followed by all West-End managers. It cocooned the more affluent from contact with the "vulgar herd." The replacement of the pit by stalls had displaced one audience and replaced it by another on largely economic grounds. By the end of the century the subdivisions of the middle classes were themselves being reflected in the differing economic zones of the West-End theatres. Thus in 1897, when Her Majesty's Theatre was built for Beerbohm Tree in the Haymarket, "the theatre was designed for an audience divided into five separate classes" each of whom had "two distinct ways out, opening into different streets."[21] The Bancrofts' advocacy of the stalls and the rather contrived debates printed in the *Theatre* not only constructed a new audience; in this instance, they may have created it as well. In the course of the first symposium, Squire Bancroft was quoted as stating:

> The public for which I cater consists almost entirely of persons willing to pay more than five shillings for their seats, and they would not like to come into contact with the vulgar herd who pay less; therefore, following the example of those East-End theatres which cater for a public the majority of whom will not pay more than a shilling for their seat, I devote the greater part of my house to the majority of my patrons.   (*Theatre*, 1 March 1880, 130)

It was an admission that West-End theatres had divided their audiences into classes demarcated by their ability to pay. It was also an indication that, in the minds of the Bancrofts and their contemporaries, audiences were best categorized by class, affluence and neighborhood.

Even in the early 1900s the tendency to stereotype audiences by class and geography, often within long-established journalistic formulae, continued. Thus St. John Adcock characterizes East-End and West-End audiences in 1901 as two very distinct entities, the west as center, the east as periphery and other. In the West End the emptying of the theatres becomes a splendid spectacle in its own right, a veritable "flood" in fact:

> Men and women – and a sprinkling of children – aristocrats and plebeians mingling are now pouring steadily out of the Gaiety, the Lyceum, the Tivoli, Criterion, Her Majesty's, Charing Cross Road, and thereabouts, the swelling tide in the main thoroughfares being fed by narrower but more plenteous streams that gush into it out of the side channels from pit and gallery doors, till the surge and rush of foot-passengers everywhere, of cabs and carriages and 'buses, are denser and swifter than even at mid-day.[22]

Outside of the West End theatres tend to be solitary rather than clustered. The exodus from the Pavilion Theatre in Whitechapel Road on a Saturday night was on a smaller scale, shabbier and more disorderly with "batches of rampant, hooting boys" bursting from the gallery. Adcock also stresses that the East End is inhabited by a simpler, less sophisticated audience, the general inclination of which, especially among women, "is to discuss the play as if it had been sheer reality, and to pour scorn and loathing on the villain, a tearful pity on the distressed heroine, and unlimited admiration on the hero . . ." The disgorged audience, in search of transport, food and drink, is absorbed into the large crowd moving up and down Whitechapel Road. Here there are no carriages and no demand for cabs. The refreshment-rooms, restaurants and oyster bars frequented by the west-enders are replaced by the baked-potato can, the whelk stall, the fried fish shop and the public house. As in so many earlier accounts popular audiences are defined through difference, through deliberately contrasting them with the fashionable West-End theatregoers. Energy contends with potential disorder, glamor with shabbiness. East is east and West is west.

Yet, some East-End theatregoers also visited the West End and were well informed about practices there, as Charles Booth attested in 1889. By the early 1900s London was ringed by suburban theatres: touring productions and try-outs now visited these theatres as well as the provinces. While theatre certainly declined in some neighborhoods, it grew in others and attracted a diversified and mobile public. The new Edwardian audience is redefined by the Italian commentator Mario Borsa, whose contempt for popular fare leads him to refer to:

> the shop-girls, milliners, dressmakers, typists, stenographers, cashiers of large and small houses of business, telegraph and telephone girls, and the thousands of other girls whose place in the social scale is hard to guess or to define; who avail themselves of the liberty allowed by custom, and the coldness of the English masculine temperament, to wander alone at night from one end of London to the other, spending all their money on gadding about, on sixpenny novels, on magazines, and, above all, on the theatre.

Of course, Borsa is equally guilty of constructing and essentializing his audience, even if the tone is very different from that of Adcock and his predecessors. While the audiences described above were best appeased, according to Borsa, by the "wicked women" melodramas of the Melville brothers at the Standard Theatre, there was another, quite separate audience, attending the innovative Barker–Vedrenne seasons at the Court Theatre. The "great British public, artless, coarse-minded and dull-witted – does not frequent the Court . . . The Court audiences are composed of persons of culture and students, with a goodly percentage of society people."[23] Borsa's two audiences – the simple-minded working girls on the one hand and the "coterie" audience on the other (also largely female, according to Granville Barker) – set up an opposition determined by intellect rather than by class or neighborhood. In contrast A. E. Wilson, also drawing on his own recollections, suggests that men predominated over women as audience members in this period and that melodrama, which continued to be popular, drew a large and specifically working-class audience. Yet, filtered through the subjective nostalgia of W. Macqueen Pope, Edwardian audiences also reflect the world of high society, affluence, good manners and "carriages at eleven."[24] In all these examples the audience is once again being constructed; but in so many different ways that we can only be sure of one factor: that it continued to maintain the range and diversity, noted throughout this chapter, right up until the end of our period.

NOTES

1. Michael R. Booth, "East End and West End: Class and Audience in Victorian London," *Theatre Research International* 2, 2 (1977), 98–103.
2. Jacky S. Bratton, *Acts of Supremacy: The British Empire and the Stage, 1790–1930* (Manchester: Manchester University Press, 1991), p. 59.
3. Lord Chamberlain's Papers, Public Record Office, LC1/70.
4. Thomas Wright, *Some Habits and Customs of the Working Classes* (London, 1867), pp. 198–99.

5. Saloons differed from theatres in that the auditorium was accessible via the bar area rather than via separate entrances.

6. Lord Chamberlain's Papers, Public Record Office, Memoranda and Petitions, 1843, LC7/5, 1844, LC7/6.

7. P. P. Hanley, *Some Recollections of the Stage by an Old Playgoer* (London: privately printed, 1883), p. 6; John Coleman, *Fifty Years of an Actor's Life* (London: Hutchinson & Co, 1904), I: 94–96.

8. Henry Mayhew, *London Labour and the London Poor* (London, 1861–2) (rpt. New York: Dover, 1976), IV: 227.

9. Cited in Booth, "East End and West End", p. 102.

10. "The Amusements of the People," *Household Words*, 30 March and 13 April 1850; "Two Views of a Cheap Theatre," *All the Year Round*, 25 February 1860.

11. J. R. Towse, *Sixty years of Theater* (New York: Funk and Wagnall, 1916), p. 33.

12. Michael Williams, *Some London Theatres Past and Present* (London: Sampson Low 1883), p. 18.

13. Shirley S. Allen, *Samuel Phelps and Sadler's Wells Theatre* (Middletown, CT: Wesleyan University Press, 1971), p. 80.

14. W. May Phelps and J. Forbes-Robertson, *Life and Works of Samuel Phelps* (London: Sampson Low, 1886), p. 17.

15. *Theatrical Journal*, December 1841 and Cook quoted by Allen, *Samuel Phelps*, p. 79.

16. "Is the pit an institution or an excrescence," *Theatre* (1 March 1880), 129–142.

17. *Theatre* (1 August 1880), 63–76.

18. Laurence Irving, *Henry Irving: The Actor and His World* (London: Faber, 1951), pp. 349–50.

19. P. P. Hanley, *A Jubilee of Playgoing* (London: Tinkler & Hillhouse, 1887), p. 113.

20. Walter Besant, *Fifty Years Ago* (London: Chatto & Windus, 1888), p. 126.

21. *The Builder* (8 May 1897), 421.

22. St. John Adcock, "Leaving the London Theatres," in G. R. Sims (ed.), *Living London* (London: Knight, 1901), 11–12. All references to Adcock refer to this work.

23. Mario Borsa, *The English Stage of To-day* (New York: J. Lane, 1908), pp. 112–13.

24. See A. E. Wilson, *Edwardian Theatre* (London: Arthur Barker, 1951), and W. Macqueen Pope, *Carriages at Eleven: The Story of the Edwardian Theatre* (London: Hutchinson, 1947).

6

MARY JEAN CORBETT

Performing identities: actresses and autobiography

Among contemporary feminist theorists and critics, and particularly in discussions of identity, performance has become a central term. Scholars across a range of disciplines, inspired largely by the groundbreaking work of Judith Butler, now regard identity not as a stable construct, but rather as constituted by and through the performative acts that bring an "I" into being. Regarded in this light, performative acts generate rather than undermine the cultural fiction of the stable self, soliciting our assent to it, in Butler's words, as "a compelling illusion, an object of *belief*."[1] Extending the point to textual production, Sidonie Smith argues that "there is no essential, original, coherent autobiographical self before the moment of self-narrating": the textual "I" achieves subject status by "the inclusion of certain identity contents and the exclusion of others; the incorporation of certain narrative itineraries and intentionalities, the silencing of others; the adoption of certain autobiographical voices, the muting of others."[2] By contrast with Elizabeth Robins's view of stage performance, "where your business is not to be your real self," the poststructuralist discourse on identity seems to contend there is no "real self" not to be.[3]

All this may be taken as a challenge to the working assumptions of some theatre historians. If all identity is performative, then what is distinctive about theatrical performance, often explicitly positioned, as by Robins, in opposition to the "real life" that happens offstage and the "real self" who lives it? If, as Butler argues, "the acts by which gender is constituted bear similarities to performative acts within theatrical contexts" (Butler, "Performative," p. 272), how do we differentiate among the multiple sites of performance that comprise the Victorian or Edwardian actress for her publics? Where does performance-as-identity-construction leave off and performance-as-theatrical-work begin? And how do we assess those theatrical and textual performances that have been taken as contesting normative constructions of gender, such as the Ibsen roles that inspired actresses in the New Drama of the 1890s? If "actors are always already on the stage, within the terms of the performance" (Butler, "Performative," p. 277), then what about those representations that putatively contest and disrupt those terms? Many and various are the implications of performance theory for historical analysis of the feminist political and theatrical movements in which actresses at the turn of the last century took part. First and foremost, however, postmodern theory provides a useful lever for dislodging the too-rigid dichotomy between "real life" and theatrical representation, compelling us to rethink that relation in new ways. Theories of identity-as-performance can help us to recognize, for example, that feminist consciousness is something made – or performed – both in and out of the theatre, and so to conceive a more fluid relationship between theatre and politics, rather than assigning a wholly determining power to one or the other. For example, in *Ibsen and the Actress* (1928), Elizabeth Robins asserts that "the general bearing of Hedda's story . . . so little concerned" her and Marion Lea "when we were producing Ibsen that we never so much as spoke about it": "if we had been thinking politically, concerning ourselves about the emancipation of women, we would not have given the Ibsen plays the particular kind of whole-hearted, enchanted devotion we did give."[4] Taking her at her word, we might say that for Robins, "thinking politically" arises not from a feminist consciousness constituted in advance ("offstage," or in "real life"), but from theatrical performance itself: and not only from the experience of playing Ibsen parts, but also from the difficulties she elsewhere records of getting those parts on stage in a milieu largely dominated by actor-managers who sought to secure attractive leading roles for themselves.

To get the chance to perform Ibsen, moreover, meant very definitely to put in question the conventional womanly part of "the leading lady," one that Robins herself had first coveted on her arrival in London, which required "a sheer unconscious absorption in the other person's manifestations, in *his* point of view, his projects"; "not even actresses who by some fluke had proved their powers – had any choice as to what they should act."[5] Tracing a continuity here between theatre and "real life," Robins claims that "what was wanted of the women of the stage was, first and mainly, what was wanted of women outside – a knack of pleasing" (Robins, *Both Sides*, p. 242). So if producing *Hedda Gabler* was not an explicitly political act, aimed directly at furthering "the emancipation of women," we can still say that it was inspired in part by the gender politics of the contemporary theatre and contributed in turn to the political education of Englishwomen in the 1890s.

At the same time, attaining the power of choice was not merely a matter of imitating the doings of the actor-manager by persuading backers, amassing capital, finding the right play, and gaining access to a house to perform in – though all these material matters certainly mattered. For those

Victorian women unused to choice itself, and all too aware of the repercussions that some choices could entail, there was yet something more invidious than the male-dominated system to be encountered, as Robins's use of the phrase "unconscious absorption" suggests. In the contemporary diary she consulted in writing her first theatrical memoir, *Both Sides of the Curtain*, the young Robins remarks on "the difficulty of the modern woman of education doing powerful emotional or tragic acting. *That* requires capacity for *abandon* – of letting yourself go, which comes to be impossible to the well-bred" (*Both Sides*, p. 262). Being schooled in modesty, self-control, or repression to perform a lady's part offstage, Robins implies, may disable the "well-bred" actress from exercising the power to choose or stunt her very "capacity for *abandon*." But repudiating one's internalized performance of ladylike behaviors, so much a facet of how gender has operated historically to constitute intelligible female subjects, is not so simple as casting aside one part in favor of another. Those everyday performances, to return to Butler, that help to compose one's identity as a lady also exclude or abject that which does not fit, those "othered" non-identities one cannot be without ceasing to be, or to be intelligible as, a lady.[6] In this light, "not to be your real self" might well have meant something very different to Robins than it means to us.

Robins's narration of her own first encounters with Ibsen, whose work arrived on the London stage around the same moment as she did, provides a useful if conflicted site for analyzing how the "real self" is constructed through performative conventions of respectable femininity such as the one cited above. A chapter of *Both Sides of the Curtain* entitled "First Rift in the Lute – Ibsen" reports Robins's "enthusiasm for [*A*] *Doll's House*" (p. 195), in which she saw Janet Achurch perform in June 1889, an event she recollects in some detail in *Ibsen and the Actress*. But in expressing her excitement to Genevieve Ward – among the well-established women of the theatre who most interested herself on Robins's behalf – she was dealt a sharp check by this eminent actress of the old school. "If I hadn't read *Ghosts*, so much the better," according to Ward; "*Ghosts* wasn't a play, it was 'a piece of moral vivisection,' " "fit only for an audience of doctors and *prostitutes*" – "a word," Robins adds, "that took Miss Ward's courage to pronounce in those days" (*Both Sides*, p. 198). Ignoring the warning to steer clear, Robins did read *Ghosts* for herself, and "received full in my face the piercing blast . . . shrank, and shuddered. I found it terrible and revolting" and "turned from [his masterpiece] with horror" (pp. 208, 209). While the *Pillars of Society*, one of "his least unconventional plays" in which she played her first Ibsen part in 1889, "had stirred and pleased me" (p. 209), *Ghosts* only repelled, presumably for something of the same reasons that it horrified Ward: it produced and conveyed a knowledge suited only to medical professionals and sex workers, a knowledge that New Women were increasingly to appropriate and promulgate for their own purposes. Once more perplexed when offered the leading part of Mrs. Alving in the same play the following summer, Robins consults her friends: "as strongly as a year ago," Ward "disapproves of having anything to do with *Ghosts*"; George Alexander says "'Don't touch him.'" And "the only thing I was clear about was that when I read the play last Summer I had been awed and revolted" (p. 258).

Given the reputation Robins later achieved for both her Ibsen productions and her feminist activism, her hesitation, even "horror," seems to require explanation. Subsequently trying to account for her reluctance and disgust, Robins takes herself to task:

> With all my perorating on the theme, *No* Great parts for Women – when the great chance came my way I could not recognize it. *Ghosts* gives me the outstanding, if not sole instance, in my personal experience of the power of evil inuendo [*sic*] to corrupt the imagination. Whether the horror excited in other minds lead [*sic*] me to find in the play a horror greater than Ibsen gave warrant for, on second reading I found the play 'too dreadful for words – far worse than memory painted. I could never play *Ghosts*' – but the pretty confection in blank verse, that Dr. Dabbs had written for me – yes I will p[l]ay Nina in *Punchinello*. (*Both Sides*, p. 258)

Further negotiations later that summer notwithstanding, Robins never did play this particular Ibsen part, revealing just how deeply ingrained the conventions of ladyhood were. *Ghosts* was indeed strong stuff, "dangerous ground" (*Both Sides*, p. 263), as William Archer said – but Robins's adherence to respectability and convention, as much as any failure to recognize "the great chance," surely shaped her ambivalence about the play. Would acting Mrs. Alving lead to being tarred with the brush of syphilis and incest, the play's controversial, overtly sexual subject matter? Performing a less fraught part, Stella Campbell anticipated a similar response – "She could not play 'Mrs. Tanqueray' as she does if she did not know something of that kind of life" – and suffered "for a long time a queer reputation."[7] If an actress could become so identified in the minds of others with the roles she played, would not such a part have a dampening effect on her career? Choosing a costume play like *Punchinello* over the risky waters of *Ghosts* must have seemed the safe if tame option. But it is a choice easier to understand once we contextualize Robins's power to choose within the relatively narrow parameters of what constituted the performative dimension of feminine appropriateness. Whatever the difficulties she would have faced in mounting *Ghosts* – and there would have been many – part of what stood in Robins's way was her own visceral resistance to taking it on, a resistance we may attribute to the "real self," who shared the conventional horror at the play's unseemliness and who balked at performing a knowledge no real lady could or should possess.

The actress's performances on either side of the curtain may thus be understood as mutually determining: if being "well-bred" impedes the representation of passionate abandon, then representing passionate abandon may also imperil one's reputation for (or experience of oneself as) being "well-bred." Considering this historical and discursive construction of womanhood through the theoretical lens of performance, especially as negotiated at the level of the individual subject, we can see that avant-garde theatrical performances invited critical reflection on the gendered practices of everyday life, just as those mundane performances of gender conventions conditioned one's responses to the avant-garde. In this respect, the actress of the New Drama experienced and performed, in highly concrete ways, the contradictory imperatives attendant on the very concept of "the New Woman."

Moreover, reading for contradictions within "the new" may lead us to see the postmodern discourse on identity-as-performance not as a decided break with a confident "Victorian" belief in the authenticity of natural gender roles, but as a logical extension of the gender trouble and sexual anarchy that pervaded late Victorian culture. Among other restagings of gender as act rather than essence, the complex cultural work undertaken by women of the theatre, instantiated in Robins's mixed fascination and disgust at the prospect of playing *Ghosts*, invites us to deconstruct what may, after all, be a false dichotomy between the stable selves of a stable past and the more fluid or fractured identities of our own uncertain times. An historical and theoretical perspective that situates the dramatic contexts of the 1890s within the discourse of gender, and especially in relation to the "ideological contradictions of 1890s gender debates," may instead newly regard actresses of the period as putting normative femininity on display for the purpose of exploring and exploiting, without necessarily resolving, the fissures within it.[8] Turning to autobiography, which enacts the performative gestures that constitute a "real self" for writers and readers alike, we can understand better the multifarious effects that arise in the contest between dominant and emergent discourses about femininity, as well as observe the continuity between them. So, too, can we gauge more clearly the extent to which actresses participated in remaking the norms of performativity for the New Women of the new century through their theatrical and textual self-representations.

"The autobiographical 'act' of the actress differs significantly from other women's accession to that form," in that "in her professional life, she can already 'command an audience,' has already a place in 'the public arena.' "[9] Through their theatrical performances and other public acts, successful actresses establish a set of commodified images by which they are "known" such that the contemporary audience for their self-writing, as for their theatrical work, "comes to expect a certain kind of performativity that conforms relatively comfortably to criteria of intelligibility" (Smith, "Performativity," p. 110). When, for example, Eva Moore's publishers advertised her *Exits and Entrances* (1928) as "a light, witty, merry volume of reminiscence by one of the most fascinating and popular actresses the stage has ever known," the blurb captured precisely both the tone of the book and the signature keynotes of the actress's career. A different repertoire, composed of different parts, would no doubt have issued in another sort of book.

While the entry into self-writing activates the aura of the actress's public image – comedian or tragedian, New Woman or *femme fatale* – autobiography, too, invokes its own conventions for performance. J. M. Barrie exhorted Irene Vanbrugh as she drafted her memoirs, *To Tell My Story* (1948), to take up the writing of her life as if it were a part to play, a role to study: "If you were to act a woman writing memoirs how superbly you could do it – the pen nib getting so sharp at once. Well, concentrate on this chapter as if you were acting it."[10] Beyond the impact that her popular profile may have on the way she represents herself, then, the professional experience of preparing a part may be understood to have a determining effect on the "I" that autobiography brings into textual being. But Barrie's advice helps to frame the issue still more precisely: the actress's autobiography not only tells the story of her theatrical performances, but requires her to enact a role given in advance, a role she has not herself created – that of "a woman writing memoirs."

Whatever roles it may recount, an autobiography or memoir is less an originary act of self-expression than another formally constrained or determined mode of performance. And since all representation operates by reference to prior signifying acts, when the generic criteria for textually performing femininity alter, new criteria will arise in relation to the old. Moreover, we can see this process at work in as well as out of the theatre. The acting career of someone as innovative as Robins – who "spanned the paradigm shift from eighties ingenue to Ibsen heroine" and whose "mutability and power to metamorphose" (Marshall, *Actresses*, pp. 140, 141) became the hallmark of her style – provides an important site in this respect. Along with Janet Achurch and Marion Lea, Robins is generally credited with helping to initiate the new dramatic vocabulary for womanhood by figuring the performative conventions

of the unconventional woman; somewhat paradoxically, however, she instantiated a new norm for unconventional performance that became so recognizable as to inspire almost instant imitation of it. Indeed, as early as 1891,
with what Clement Scott called "the kindliest spirit," Irene Vanbrugh herself
successfully parodied in the very first part she ever created on stage both "the
timid, shrinking manner" of Marion Lea's Thea and Robins's "cynical[,] defiant" Hedda in Barrie's burlesque *Ibsen's Ghost*, produced just a few short
weeks after the Lea–Robins Joint Management had premiered its sensational
Hedda Gabler.[11] The new parts and performance styles – and along with
them, the paradigm for New Womanhood that Ibsenism helped to promote –
thus readily and rapidly achieved a certain currency, became reiterable as
parody, as part of a public conversation about femininity. In Vanbrugh's
discussion of her "creation" of these imitative parts, we can see an important convergence of theatrical and autobiographical discourse around the
question of performance.

Although Vanbrugh describes her creation of this composite role as different from her previous experiences of playing "characters [that] had all passed
through other hands before I had the fingering of them," which she depicts
as something like being "dressed up . . . in old garments" (*To Tell*, p. 24), this
first "creation" of hers differs only slightly from the well-worn roles she had
not originated during her first three years on the stage. Despite a professed
distaste for imitation in acting, she learns from her theatrical training that
no part is really her own: "what was expected of me was to reproduce the
style of my predecessors, to be so like them . . . that if their parents were in
front they could still think they were gazing on their child" (*To Tell*, p. 24).
And, according to the reviewers of *Ibsen's Ghost*, her achievement lay in her
ability to imitate Robins playing Hedda and Lea as Thea; the very nature of
the play mandated mimicry, not only of Ibsen's characters, but of the acting
style of the women who performed them.

Having at first misconceived the nature of the parts she was to play in
Ibsen's Ghost, Vanbrugh represents her youthful self imagining her first
"original" role in the stereotypical terms of stock drama: "here then was
a great emotional part – tears – sorrow – recrimination – the misunderstood
wife beating her hands together, sobbing into a cushion as she lay on the
sofa" (*To Tell*, p. 27). Refining that melodramatic conception once rehearsals
began, Vanbrugh not only "watched [*Hedda Gabler*] once or twice" to pre-
pare for the dual role, but also talked with Robins "to see if I could catch
something more of her personality in this way" (p. 23). Performing Robins
performing Hedda, but in a comic context, Vanbrugh's first created part, like
her role as "a woman writing memoirs," depends both on recognizing the
conventions of representation – even as they differ from Ibsen to Barrie – and

on adapting or reproducing them as the part requires, taking Robins as her model.

More than most, Vanbrugh's memoir self-consciously plays on how the genius of imitation, rather than originality, presides over both the creation of a part and the writing of a memoir. She asks archly, for instance, "am I writing [this book], or am I only playing the part of a writer?" and engages in a good deal of reflection on the "double life" (*To Tell*, p. 102) the actress supposedly leads, a rhetorical device recommended by both her literary advisors, J. M. Barrie and G. B. Shaw.[12] In her autobiographical performance, Vanbrugh demonstrates a thorough awareness of the conventional array of topics for theatrical autobiography: she discusses the famous people she has known, advises potential actors of pitfalls to avoid and practices to emulate, and retells anecdotes that illustrate the vagaries of theatrical fame and fortune. In this light, she performs the role of "a woman writing memoirs" with self-conscious regard for the typical parameters of her part, working within an established Victorian tradition of actress memoirs that had taken shape in volumes by Marie Bancroft and Madge Kendal. Among the published memoirs of actresses of her own generation – those who came of age in the last decade of the old century and the first of the new, most of whom came to the stage through the new training schools rather than by family connections – a certain array of topics does indeed appear with regularity: the influence of the New Drama, whether for good or ill; the power of the actor-manager system and its subsequent displacement by a producer-centered regime; the widespread involvement of actresses in the suffrage movement; and, of course, the contributions made by theatre people during the First World War.

By contrast, Robins is a good deal less inclined to follow the trajectory Vanbrugh and some of their other contemporaries trace, the narrative in which actresses "present their lives . . . as a series of necessary stages they had to pass on their journey to full professional status."[13] *Both Sides of the Curtain* covers only the period from the autumn of 1888 to the autumn of 1890, concluding before she had established her mark in the New Drama, and depends in good part for its source materials on the diaries Robins kept during these first two years in London, the years that immediately preceded and perhaps precipitated her full involvement with Ibsen theatre. The brief time span of this relatively long text as well as its rhetorical emphases sharply distinguishes it from other actress memoirs. And the framing of the memoir, in terms of both images and text, also differs in important ways from the "life and career" format that *To Tell My Story* exemplifies.

Unlike *To Tell My Story*, which includes ten or twelve photographs of Vanbrugh onstage in the most celebrated roles of her career, *Both Sides of*

ELIZABETH ROBINS

aged about 20, as heroine in the New York production of
James Albery's *Forgiven*

The only photograph of mine to achieve the distinction of being a
cigarette card. Bernard Shaw caught sight of it on my writing table at
Palace Gate among a heap of papers and other things discarded. I heard
his chuckle as he seized on the absurdity. "Here," he said, with some
gibe I have unfortunately forgotten, "here is your frontispiece."

Figure 7 Frontispiece from *Both Sides of the Curtain* by Elizabeth Robins.

Figure 8 Elizabeth Robins as Hedda Gabler, 1891.

the Curtain presents only one visual image (Figure 7). Its frontispiece depicts Robins in ingénue guise from the 1880s – a shot taken well before her move to London at a moment when, one supposes, "the distinction of being a cigarette card," as the photo caption conveys, may not have seemed "the absurdity" to her that it did at the time of writing more than fifty years later. The letters between Robins and Shaw that preface the memoir indicate that he recommended using this photo as front matter because it serves as visible shorthand for the point at which she begins. "I am not sure that you will not have to tell more about yourself," Shaw commented upon reading some early chapters of the manuscript, "unless you think it better to leave the reader guessing, which I rather incline to advise, just giving the reader that old portrait you showed me to start with" (pp. vi–vii). Robins replies with a defense of her autobiographical method: "if you blame me for not patronising that E.R. of 1888, for not making her out something less limited and sentimental, you miss the purpose. The book is really, I hope, going to be an attempt to show how, starting as she did, the creature little by little learned and grew" (p. vii).

Robins's "purpose," as it emerges from these lines, is to represent a discrete episode in a history of development, something along the lines of a coming-of-age narrative. Although her use of the third person to refer to her former self suggests distance in both time and sensibility from the "creature," her claim that she is "not patronising that E.R." by falsifying her – by making her seem more savvy than she was – constitutes the experiences Robins narrates in the text as formative of who and what she became, but without assigning any particular intention of becoming someone different from the "creature" she represents. In fact, she takes some pains to depict herself as decidedly unknowing, even artless, "as unconscious of the nature of my rescue" (p. 208) by Ibsen from a career of "being 'sweet' " (p. 249) "as a blind swimmer who has been picked up by a battleship" (p. 209), remarking, too, that "I have wondered much more in writing these chapters than I did in living them" (p. 74). That she portrays the contours of that "sweet" self by including a photograph, rather than generating an explicit textual description, may suggest a consciousness that the portrait of the ingénue *en role* adequately represents both the actress and the woman, each performing a pose according to a conventional script. "Think of the chasm between that early picture and the Hedda photographs" (p. vii), she writes to Shaw (Figure 8): whereas the text goes on to narrate the process of how she became someone altogether different by filling in the experiential gap between being a commodified portrait on a cigarette card and an anti-commercial, proto-feminist purveyor of "the Theatre of the Future," yet it attributes no particular project or political consciousness to that former self. The memoir instead rhetorically performs a prior self deeply invested in and attached to the norms of femininity that the photograph puts on display, norms on which the writer critically reflects even as she represents that former self enacting them.

In this regard, the distinctiveness of *Both Sides of the Curtain* is that it draws on a past that had already been constituted by Robins as a textual product: unlike the autobiographical texts produced by most actresses – who were not, of course, professional writers as Robins was – the memoir primarily reassesses the life not as it is recollected, but as it was constituted by and through the diary-writing of 1888 to 1890. Examining the past already constructed once in writing – that is, through and for who she was as she was then, keeping a daily record rather than shaping a retrospective account – Robins encounters the past primarily as text, as she states in the memoir proper:

> I write about those days at a great distance – not only in terms of time. I cannot feel very close to that young woman who went about with my name so long ago . . . She is often strange to me, sometimes antipathetic, now and then incredible, but for the self-conviction that stares me in the face from the scribbled page. There, too, I am often at odds with her. She records scenes and feelings I have clean forgotten; she leaves out some that in my memory stand fast forever. And the omissions, that I have now in mind, are not those prompted by discretion. They are mere failure to recognise values.
>
> (*Both Sides*, p. 18)

This judgment on that former self, for its "failure to recognise values," explicitly disavows "discretion" as a major structuring principle in the diary or, by extension, in the memoir. By contrast with such actresses as Ellen Terry or Stella Campbell, who do not narrate life events that would compromise their respectability, Robins approaches her own textualized past as if it were indeed another country, but not so as to maintain a feminized decorum about private life. As in her retrospective comments on her diary responses to the kind of plays she then enjoyed, in which she represents herself as at that time "just the sort of audience" (p. 33) for whom Haddon Chambers or Frances Hodgson Burnett had written, she emphasizes the strangeness of that person largely on the basis of difference and distance. Such a stance takes the rhetorical construction of a past self as its object of analysis, makes it an artifact, assesses it in terms other than the ones it once embraced or enacted: "from a new standpoint you will see the same thing so differently as to make it not the same," as Robins writes much further on, "but as new as the different standpoint is" (p. 242). Like almost all autobiography, then, Robins's text produces a past from a position very much rooted in the present.

From the standpoint of the time of writing, the central narrative construction of Robins's text emerges most distinctly as something other than the "deep" psychological subject, which has been assigned a privileged place within the modern history of western autobiography, or the divided, melodramatic self she came to play on stage as Hedda Gabler or Hilda Wangel. *Both Sides of the Curtain* instead obliquely narrates the feminist subjectivity that emerges from the experience of performing femininity onstage and off, the contradictions that arise from Robins's entry into a world in which the naïveté of the ingénue alternately does and does not enable her safely to negotiate a male-dominated metropolitan culture. It enacts via retrospect the process by which its young protagonist came to understand that accepting the feminine roles assigned to her by men would consign her, at best, to the life of a leading lady and, at worst, to actual physical danger.

Her candidacy for the leading lady role is, the older Robins implies, a function of a certain stereotype imposed upon her by those she met: an American abroad, mistakenly presumed to possess the necessary capital to fund a London debut. "The question of money bulked large with every theatrical enterprise," as Robins would come to know in a more immediate way when she went into management herself; and so, too, "the fact of my being of that nation supposed to be above all things astute in money matters . . . may have lent my profession of having no capital an air of mere cannyness [*sic*]" (p. 74). Adding to the presumption of her being a rich American, however, is the twenty-six-year-old Robins's adherence to the conventional costume for mourning: "from neck to heel, a widow must wear lustreless black," along with a bonnet to which was "pinned firm" an "unbelievably heavy, voluminous (and expensive!) crepe veil" (p. 77). In this "lugubrious" attire, "a face dead white, except under excitement, did I suppose arrest attention and a desire to do something about it" (p. 77) on the part of those men and women she met.

Swathed in mourning, Robins might be said to appear, then, as something on the order of a melodramatic heroine or a woman with a past. With an American stage career behind her that included tours with James O'Neill and Edwin Booth, her suitability for the companies assembled by such actor-managers of the 1890s as Herbert Beerbohm Tree and George Alexander might have been assessed, however, on what her demure, ladylike demeanor would have indicated: an ability to play demure, ladylike parts. And indeed, Robins remarks of her concern with appearances at that moment that "perhaps the greatest concern in my life, on this score, was not to have my mourning wrong" (p. 76). Adhering to the "rigid carrying out of the code I had brought from home" (p. 161), Robins's investment in observing the proprieties of mourning her dead husband – whose sensational suicide was no secret – not only prescribes her costume and constrains her behavior, but also visibly conveys her status and something of her situation to those she meets. The disparity between how she appeared to others and the aims she sought to achieve creates an important tension in the text, one that emerges gradually as a central site for Robins's retrospective analysis of her assault on the London stage.

Having secured an introduction to Beerbohm Tree, Robins describes their meeting between the acts of the play he was performing, Haddon Chambers's *Captain Swift*; on what was to have been her last day in London, Tree "spoke of a play that was being written for him" by Henry Arthur Jones, *Judah*, with "a woman's part that he had foreseen would be difficult to cast," "an unconventional part" (p. 27) she craves. But when Tree offers her the "part in the new piece to come," she replies that "it was too long to wait" (p. 37). When he urges giving a matinee in the meantime, she casts about in vain for a suitable play. When he rejects her choice of *Man and Wife* over *Adrienne*, she endures both an "ominous silence" (p. 41) and "a depressed interval" (p. 42): more meetings, more waiting, then nine days passing without further word from Tree as to what would or could be done. Re-examining via her diary the conversation in which Tree had announced that "he had definitely decided not to do Jones's play" (p. 51) for some sign that he had been "offended by something I said" (p. 70), Robins finds that "[I had] never let myself go once, except on the safe ground, as I thought, of the kind of parts I wanted to play" (p. 70). But by her narration of this portion of their interview from her vantage point in the present, Robins the memoirist seems to indicate that letting go on that ground is indeed the younger diarist's mistake, an error of the very worst sort. "I had laughed at his look when I cut short the kind assurance that he could imagine I would be delightful as Adrienne. Oh, but being delightful wouldn't be enough! . . . Nothing less than being terrific would content me." Asked to explain herself, the artless aspirant narrates the theatrical lore concerning the American actress Charlotte Cushman's performance as Meg Merrilees. "No one who saw it could forget the effect when that incredible hag made a flying leap from the wings to the middle of the stage with a cry that set blood thrilling, nerves twanging": hardly the sort of thing, one imagines, that Tree would have expected from the decorous lady in mourning – or that we might expect, for that matter, from a soon-to-be Ibsenite. Even when she "relapsed into the conversational," "Tree appeared uneasy at this prospect," not "as reassured as I expected" (p. 70). When he finally does return to her lodgings to discuss her debut once more, protesting that he cannot "constitute [him]self your champion," the perpetually hopeful Robins begins to see the chance of "my Matinee receding" (p. 72).

This event marks an important instance of showing, rather than telling, how "the creature little by little learned and grew": "in all this," Robins writes, "I have let my lack of direction speak for itself" (p. 118). Thus it is not at the moment in the text when she loses her chance at Tree's "unconventional part," but over one hundred pages later, after the narration of many further disappointments, that the memoirist directly affirms the upshot of her protracted negotiations with Tree:

> Hadn't I called him to account? Had I not scared stiff the lissom figure of the young Beerbohm by explaining clearly the kind of parts I wanted, the only kind that would content me – an unknown young foreigner without a backer presuming to demand of the Theatre, the *London* Theatre, precisely what the established actor-manager demanded of it: a chance to explore his talent to its farthest limit – at other people's cost. (pp. 185–86)

The memoirist's ability in the present to draw this conclusion depends in part, I suggest, on the creature's increasing ability in the past to recognize a pattern of sexism in her experiences that enables her to generalize. Regarding the impact of the rivalry between Tree and George Alexander on her career, the memoirist represents the younger-but-ever-wiser self as very clearly getting "the point": "neither of those Actor-Managers had any real use for me in their companies. Why should they? I had done nothing in their line that a hundred others couldn't do as well, or better. Worse, I showed no signs of genuinely *wanting* to do the kind of thing they required" (p. 272). One might say that it's only through the experience of frustration – not just with the parts she played onstage, but with what was required simply to get onstage – that the autobiographical subject comes to redefine "an unconventional part" as one which contests the prevailing patriarchal structure of the theatre.

While such a redefinition implies the younger self's movement away from many of her own more conventional attitudes and practices, it also coincides with the memoirist's far more ambivalent reflections on the substance of the orthodox "code I had brought from home."[14] Around the same time as she impatiently awaits word from Tree, the diarist notes "a terrible experience" at her boarding house in Duchess Street, what the narrative proper terms a "midnight shock" (*Both Sides*, p. 71). The memoir reveals the substance of the incident only gradually, as a particular instance of "a certain order of disagreeables" (p. 164) that all "unprotected" females had to face: "on the frugally-lit staircase, some transient guest would . . . attempt to bar the way"; "a foot from outside the corridor would be thrust between the jamb and an inhospitable door" (p. 164); so, too, such things might and did happen in "the open street in broad day" or during "Divine Service in church" (p. 167).

These incidents of harassment and attempted sexual assault, Robins suggests, were so common as to be almost unremarkable; while "the details" of the particular experience "are completely forgotten now," "that fact of itself most women will recognise as significant of how far the occurrence was from being without precedent" (p. 164). Juxtaposed with the other story she tells – of attempting in vain to get her footing on the stage by pleading her case to men with power – Robins's reflections on this ordinary experience offer a counterpoint to the critique of the conventional, reframing the performance of the ladylike norms that had put her at a disadvantage in professional life as serving an important function in the performative venues of everyday life.

"Though a woman's first business in life" – as on the stage – "was to please," Robins remarks, "she had to live out her youth in fear of the results of pleasing" (p. 167): identifying this contradiction at the heart of the womanly code, Robins focuses on how it translates psychologically, producing the threat of male violence that, as many feminist theorists have argued, keeps all women perpetually on guard. Providing one of the tried and true rationales for keeping women in their place, a patriarchal social structure implicitly legitimates men's power over women on two fronts: by creating a zone of protection in the heterosexual family home where women are presumed (in theory, though not in fact) to be safe in their secure possession by men; and by creating a zone of danger on the streets, where any lone woman is presumed to have given up her right to protection and is thus understood as "available" to others. Robins articulates her comprehension of this point specifically in terms of choosing a theatrical career, with all the lurid associations that entailed for the pious, but frames it somewhat differently: "having myself accepted all that was implied to the mind of that day . . . I had done a thing that must range me among those who set no limits to their liberty and thereby had no acknowledged right to set limits to the liberties others might take" (pp. 169–70). Understood as an individual choice, leaving one's father's house in pursuit of "liberty" deprives her not only of the protection that a more circumscribed sphere purportedly ensures, but even of the "right" to lay claim to protection from men. Presenting her case as "the problem of the woman bred under the old order who abandons that order, but does not for a moment intend to abandon its more valued advantages" (p. 169), Robins deploys the conventional performance of what she calls "the Lady-Barrier" (p. 175) – summed up in the Dickensian phrase "prunes and prism" (p. 168) – as her most effective means of protecting herself.

In *Ibsen and the Actress*, Robins advises her readers that the fictive Hedda Gabler and "a good many women . . . f[i]nd it possible to get through life by help of the knowledge that they have power to end it rather than accept certain slaveries," adding that "the particular humiliations and enslavements that threaten women do not threaten men. Such enslavements may seem so unreal to decent men as to appear as melodrama" (*Ibsen*, p. 30). By reading a woman's perception of sexual threat or conjugal "enslavements" as "unreal" or histrionic, a man may fail to recognize the full context for the everyday experience of being culturally situated as a woman that Hedda enacts and Robins sketches in *Both Sides of the Curtain*. But by implying that context in her memoir, Robins suggests both an alternative way of reading the performative dimension of femininity and a means of reading her own movement from ingénue to Ibsenite. For "the Lady-Barrier" is itself at once "unreal" in its artificial or conventional aspect and all too real in being part of a repertoire of protective devices that Robins "learned to impose . . . on myself" (*Both Sides*, p. 168) as a matter of necessity. Viewed in this light, any claims we might want to make about what constitutes the "real self" must take into account the effects of social and political inequalities on how gender – along with class, sexuality, and race – is both experienced and performed both on and off the stage. And so, too, "the chasm between that early picture and the Hedda photographs" may be re-read as signifying not only an experiential gap that Robins's circumstances propelled her across, as I characterized it above, but also a certain continuity among the seemingly diverse performative modes that compose late Victorian femininity, in which the actress who enacts a melodramatic Hedda perforce enacts, at the same time, something of the naïve ingénue as well.

NOTES

1. Judith Butler, "Performative Acts and Gender Constitution: An Essay in Phenomenology and Feminist Theory," in Sue-Ellen Case (ed.), *Performing Feminisms: Feminist Critical Theory and Theatre* (Baltimore, MD, and London: Johns Hopkins University Press, 1990), p. 271.
2. Sidonie Smith, "Performativity, Autobiographical Practice, Resistance," rpt. in Sidonie Smith and Julia Watson (eds.), *Women, Autobiography, Theory: A Reader* (Madison, WI: University of Wisconsin Press, 1998), pp. 108, 110.
3. Elizabeth Robins, "Oscar Wilde: an Appreciation," ed. Kerry Powell, *Nineteenth Century Theatre* 21, 2 (Winter 1993), 108.
4. Elizabeth Robins, *Ibsen and the Actress* (1928; rpt. New York: Haskell House Publishers, Ltd., 1973), p. 31.
5. Elizabeth Robins, *Both Sides of the Curtain* (London: William Heinemann Ltd., 1940), pp. 88, 250.
6. See Judith Butler, *Bodies That Matter: On the Discursive Limits of "Sex"* (New York and London: Routledge, 1993), pp. 2–4.
7. Mrs. Patrick Campbell [Beatrice Stella Cornwallis-West], *My Life and Some Letters* (1922; rpt. New York: Benjamin Blom, 1969), pp. 107, 118.

8. Susan Carlson, "Conflicted Politics and Circumspect Comedy: Women's Comic Playwriting in the 1890s," in Tracy C. Davis and Ellen Donkin (eds.), *Women and Playwriting in Nineteenth-Century Britain* (Cambridge: Cambridge University Press, 1999), p. 256.
9. Gail Marshall, *Actresses on the Victorian Stage: Feminine Performance and the Galatea Myth* (Cambridge: Cambridge University Press, 1998), p. 173.
10. J. M. Barrie quoted in Irene Vanbrugh, *To Tell My Story* (London: Hutchinson and Co., 1948), p. 27.
11. Quoted in J. M. Barrie, *Ibsen's Ghost*, ed. Penelope Griffin (London: Cecil Woolf, 1975), pp. 66, 70, 69.
12. See Mary Jean Corbett, *Representing Femininity: Middle-Class Subjectivity in Victorian and Edwardian Women's Autobiographies* (New York and Oxford: Oxford University Press, 1992), pp. 145–49, for further discussion of this aspect of Vanbrugh's autobiography.
13. Sandra Richards, *The Rise of the English Actress* (New York: St. Martin's Press, 1993), p. 64.
14. For another view of Robins's representation of "the code," see Iveta Jusova, "Elizabeth Robins: Women's Self-Determination vs. State Control," chap. 3 in "*Fin-de-Siecle* Feminisms: the Development of Feminist Narratives within the Discourses of British Imperialism and Czech Nationalism," Ph.D. dissertation, Miami University, 2000.

3
TEXT AND CONTEXT

7

MICHAEL R. BOOTH

Comedy and farce

The great social changes occurring in the early and mid-Victorian period affected the comedy and farce of the time as much as they did the more serious forms of drama, or any kind of artistic expression; this is equally true of the late Victorian and Edwardian periods. Chief among these changes was the vast expansion of urban populations and a substantial growth in audience numbers; the development of a railway system that brought audiences to London and actors and companies to the provinces; the growing sophistication and developing taste of a middle-class audience co-existing with a huge demand for regular entertainment from a much larger working- and lower-middle-class audience. All this contributed to a considerable increase, especially from the 1860s, in the number of theatres in London; the growth of theatres built for touring companies and neighborhood theatres and music halls catering to local populations and local class taste; the extinction by law of the monopoly on "legitimate" drama held by Drury Lane and Covent Garden and the consequent loss of their traditional primacy and importance for the drama and for actors.

Tragedy, melodrama, comedy, farce, pantomime, musical comedy, burletta, burlesque, extravaganza, opera, operetta, a mixture of one form with another, original creation and wholesale adaptation from the French and German stage – there is almost no such thing in this veritable maelstrom of dramatic writing as purity of form and singleness of genre. The problem of definition – if we are concerned about definition at all – is acute in a theatrical age in which potentially tragic and pathetic material is so often mingled in the same play with low and eccentric comedy, serious characters with comic ones, and a constantly changing dramatic tone.

This is just as true of comedy and farce as it is of melodrama and the "drama," and extends over the whole period. A wide range of comedy is illustrative of this mixture. One of the best-known Victorian comedies, Edward Bulwer Lytton's *Money* (1840), is comically satirical of greed and social arrogance, as represented by the grasping Sir John Vesey and his daughter

Georgina, and the scene in which the will of the late Mr. Mordaunt is read out to the squabbling legatees and almost all his large fortune is left to the poor and embittered dependent Alfred Evelyn. However, the play also carries a considerable weight of sentiment and romantic emotion in the scenes between Evelyn and his beloved Clara. A later but equally well-known comedy, Tom Robertson's *Caste* (1867), is similarly divided between the low comedy of the drunken Eccles, the social aspirations of Sam Gerridge, gas man and plumber, the snobbery of the Marquise de St. Maur – all comic in tone – and tender and serious love scenes between George and Esther. Other Robertson comedies, such as *Society* (1865) and *M.P.* (1870) contain similar opposites in tone and subject matter. The Victorians saw no incongruity in this, for such a blend followed established patterns of comedy, and it was only early in the next century that critics began to complain of disunity.

Indeed, it is often difficult to know what *was* a comedy, so much had the old separation of genres broken down. The themes of Dion Boucicault's comedy *The School for Scheming* (1847) are those of financial speculation, business intrigue, deception, and cheating – the sort of material that found its way readily into "drama" and melodrama: the main character deserts his loved one in a frantic pursuit of wealth. Likewise, the hero of George Henry Lewes's *The Game of Speculation* (1852), Affable Hawk, is a manic speculator in shares who schemes desperately to stave off his creditors and trick a supposedly wealthy suitor into marrying his daughter. Again, the themes – guile, fraud, manipulation, bankruptcy, extortion, the sacrifice of a daughter for money – seem hardly to be those of comedy, but the pace of the play, the wit and charm of Hawk, and the foolish gullibility of the creditors properly belong to comedy.

Affable Hawk was played by Charles Mathews, and in trying to determine the kind or type of play under consideration one must always take into account the actors who played in it. Mathews was the star light comedian of the English stage for over three decades, although he said that he did not belong to any particular category of acting. In the traditional Victorian stock company "lines of business," a light comedian was essential: a gentleman lover of immense energy, dash, vivacity, rapidity of precisely enunciated speech, and a great deal of charm. In this sort of acting Mathews was supreme. It was he who enlivened Boucicault's great success, *London Assurance* (1841), as Dazzle (a fitting name for his performance), and it was he who gave wit and style to the ruthless Affable Hawk. Such acting made heavy thematic material less weighty, emotionally lighter, more acceptable to the realm of comedy.

Other serious themes expansively treated in the Victorian novel also characterize Victorian comedy. Both use common material: rural virtue; social ambition; the sacred bonds of marriage; the idealization of the sweetheart, the wife, and the mother; the intense domesticity of home and hearth; and class conflict, especially in comedy the clash between the representatives of new wealth – often vulgar and tasteless – and the older gentry. The Liverpool merchant of Tom Taylor's *New Men and Old Acres* (1869) – a title encapsulating a major social theme in Victorian comedy – is Samuel Brown, a man who rejects the Bunters, comic parvenus whose costly and flashy new house with its up-to-the-minute furnishings and pictures ("modern hopulence with modern elegance") contrasts with decayed Cleve Abbey, the home of the ancient but financially hard-pressed Vavasours. Although the Vavasour way of life is preferable to the Bunter way, it is not Brown's either; for him, a forward-looking businessman, life "belongs more to those whose brains and hands shape the world about them, than to those who stand on the dignity of old names."[1] His engagement to the Vavasour daughter exemplifies the perfect union of decent and intelligent commercialism with the old values of beauty, stability, and tradition. The comedies of Tom Robertson likewise contain an eccentric assortment of the vulgar and upthrusting *nouveau riche*, such as Chodd Jr. in *Society* and Bodmin Todder of Todder's Original Patent Starch in *Play* (1868). Chodd's belief in the power of his own money is absolute: "The best house – cheque-book. The best turn out – cheque-book. The best friends, the best wife, the best-trained children – cheque-book, cheque-book, and cheque-book."[2] Such men as Chodd and Todder comprise a popular character type that indicates the essentially conservative attitudes of comedy.

These attitudes also comprehended the treatment of women and the glowing presentation of the domestic ideal. The importance of domestic life in comedy can hardly be overstressed; and it bulks as large in farce as it does in domestic melodrama after that genre shifted its emphasis in the 1830s and 1840s from Gothic and nautical subject matter to the life of the village, the country cottage, and the urban streets. The ideal itself may be stated in a few words. The happy home consists of a kindly uxorious husband (rather than a *paterfamilias*, since comedy is thinly populated by children) and a loving wife who dutifully submits herself to her husband's authority in all matters except for those of housekeeping trivia. Many plays deal with romantic love, concluding in marriage, but during the mid-Victorian period an increasing number focus on marriage and its problems rather than courtship. These problems may include the disaffection of the wife or an assumption on her part of domestic superiority. Eventually she sees the error of her ways and humbly begs forgiveness of her husband at the final curtain. The husband may be restless, neglectful of his wife, jealous of her attainments – as a painter or writer, for instance – or financially imprudent. A certain amount of henpecking and eccentric masculine behavior is acceptably within bounds, provided it does not go too far. (It was not until the Edwardian period that an important body of new drama, including some comedies, was written by women dramatists with a feminist point of view.)

Examples of such attitudes abound. The newly married Ormonde of J. S. Coyne's *My Wife's Daughter* (1850), having forsaken his man-about-town bachelor existence, has difficulty in adapting to a quiet domestic life. His overfond, jealous, and short-tempered wife at last acknowledges her faults (he has none), and kneels before him, humble and penitent; the curtain falls. The witty and charming actress Peg Woffington in Tom Taylor and Charles Reade's *Masks and Faces* (1852) is ultimately rejected by the previously enamoured Mr. Vane, who takes into his arms his timid, domesticated, and loving wife ("Angel of truth and goodness"). Mrs. Eddystone, the brilliant and ambitious heroine of the first act of Coyne's *The Woman of the World* (1868) is transmogrified into the gentle and charitable Mrs. Eddystone of the last, who finds her greatest pleasure in adoring a baby in a cradle. On the other hand, the idle Fitzherbert of Taylor's *Victims* (1857), who has literary aspirations, is redeemed by the love of his hard-working wife, who makes dresses to pay for his pleasures. She is balanced by the pretentious blue-stocking Mrs. Merryweather, who keeps a salon and completely neglects her amiable husband. Also in the play is the nasty Mrs. Crane, a supporter of Female Emancipation.

The happy ending was another idealistic and audience-pleasing feature of comedy. The treatment of courtship and romantic love demanded it, as did the treatment of marital problems. No matter what the difficulties between husband and wife, conventions and audience taste required that they be resolved – or evaded. This frequently means the frittering away of promising and serious thematic material so that the happy ending can be attained. Such plays as Tom Robertson's *Progress* (1869) and *Birth* (1870), *The School for Scheming*, Douglas Jerrold's *Retired from Business* (1851) – about a retired grocer with a socially ambitious wife – and two or three of H. J. Byron's comedies about unhappy marriages, such as *Cyril's Success* (1868) and *Married in Haste* (1876), illustrate what to us seems a crippling limitation upon the serious development in comic form of the themes of money, love, and social and marital relationships. Clearly, however, audiences did not see it that way, and the hunger for romantic illusions rather than domestic truths shaped the plotting and content of comedy.

A notable exception to the prevailing domestic coziness and rosy sentimentalism of comedy was W. S. Gilbert's *Engaged* (1877). Gilbert was the only true revolutionary of the mid-Victorian stage, and speaks more harshly in his comedies than in the Savoy operas. In a "fairy" comedy, *The Palace of Truth* (1870), a royal court is compelled, without being aware of it, to speak the truth within the walls of an enchanted palace. In *The Wicked World* (1873), another fairy comedy set in a world of clouds, human love is a destructive force. Here there is pathos and sentiment; in *Engaged*, an utterly subversive play, there is none, unless it is patently false. The main character, Cheviot Hill, possesses the unfortunate compulsion to propose to every woman he meets. His sinister companion, Belvawney, is paid to keep him out of these entanglements, but despite his endeavors Hill becomes simultaneously engaged to two women, after having purchased for two pounds the sweetheart of a Scottish peasant who wrecks trains so that the survivors can purchase refreshments from his mother's cottage. The male characters are completely selfish and mercenary, the women – and this was far worse for some angry critics – even more debased: fickle, disobedient, obsessed with money. All characters engage in wonderfully rhetorical protestations of love, friendship, and loyalty; all profess the deepest sentiments of tender heartfelt devotion. It is all lies and humbug. "I love you madly, passionately," Belinda Treherne tells her adoring Belvawney, "I care to live but in your heart; I breathe but for your love; yet before I actually consent to take the irrevocable step that will place me on the pinnacle of my fondest hopes, you must give me some idea of your pecuniary position" (Booth, *English Plays*, III: 335).

Thus *Engaged* deliberately violated all the ideals of the Victorian stage, which in turn were the dramatic images of the publicly professed ideals of domestic life. Despite the considerable critical protest that greeted *Engaged*, audiences were amused by its cleverness, and it ran for 110 performances, with revivals in 1878, 1881, and 1886. Obviously a minority audience did then exist for satire of this kind; it is unlikely that such a play could have been staged twenty years earlier. A much larger audience existed for Gilbert's satire in the later Savoy operas, but here the appeal was also that of Sullivan's music, which – sprightly or witty or pathetic as it may be – softened and sentimentalized the satire of the libretti. The stage would have to wait another generation for its next great iconoclast, Shaw.

By the 1880s the signs of sophistication evidenced by the presence of an audience for *Engaged* were multiplying, even though *Engaged*'s contemporary, Byron's *Our Boys* (1875), ran for nearly five years, a comedy with such standard characters and plot devices as a retired commercial man, a snobbish aristocratic father, their sons, the inevitable class hostility, and romance resulting in engagements between the sons and two young ladies that solve all thematic difficulties. However, the shadow of Ibsen loomed ever larger over the English stage, and there is no doubt that the drama of the 1880s took on a more serious tinge and became weightier, if still timid.

In the 1890s comedy was beginning to assume its Edwardian dress. It moved upmarket, both in setting and *dramatis personae*, and right into the heart of Mayfair. Characterization became less eccentric, dialogue less rhetorical and occasionally, as in the case of Pinero, ponderous. Under French influence plotting was more skillful and situations more credible. There was still a strong color of male domestic idealism in the views expressed on the role of women and the sanctity of marriage. Dramatists continued to develop the theme of the unhappy marriage, as Pinero does in his bitter comedy of the failure of not one, but two marriages, *The Benefit of the Doubt* (1895), and Henry Arthur Jones in his strongly anti-feminist *The Case of Rebellious Susan* (1894) and the superbly plotted *The Liars* (1897). As was his wont, Jones fudges the issue by patching up the miserable marriages in the last act. Both plays deal significantly with the Mayfair dread of social exposure, disgrace and ostracism that also informs Wilde's plays and other dramatic writing in the 1890s and the following decade.

A more charming side to late Victorian comedy is apparent in Pinero's nostalgic *Trelawny of the "Wells"* (1898), about a stock company of the 1860s and the relationship between its leading ingénue and the son of an aristocratic but rigid and tedious family. An earlier Pinero comedy, the sentimental *Sweet Lavender* (1888), concerns a love affair between a laundress's daughter and a young barrister. The dean of London dramatic critics, Clement Scott, praised it and declared that no matter how sad life is "let us sometimes, even in a despised theatre, dream how happy and ideal and beautiful it *might* be."[3] For a large part of the audience, *this* was the true purpose of theatre. It is not surprising that Scott loathed Ibsen.

The theme of marital discord is continued in *The Tyranny of Tears* (1899) by Haddon Chambers, a play that demonstrates many of the virtues of late Victorian comedy. Its subject is a contretemps between Parbury, a writer, and his wife. She constantly interrupts his work and is so jealous of his attractive young secretary that she demands her dismissal. Parbury refuses, whereupon she departs for the shelter of her father's roof. The problems of domestic strife and of the position of the lonely and dependent secretary are serious ones – *The Times* said of the play that "occasionally it becomes too serious for comedy"[4] – but they are not trivially resolved or evaded. The play shows a quiet domestic middle-class reality, a careful control of plot, an economy of characterization, and, in spite of the gravity of the themes, an admirable delicacy and lightness of touch.

In order to show the distance comedy had travelled from its mid-Victorian progenitors, it is instructive to compare *The Tyranny of Tears* with Taylor's *Still Waters Run Deep* (1855). Both plays are called comedies. Both contain serious matter; both have a realistic middle-class setting. In both the husband, after domestic conflict, emerges the wise master. But in a characteristically early and mid-Victorian manner, Taylor's play is strongly melodramatic. The aptly named Mildmay, ignored by his petulant wife and ferociously henpecked by her virago aunt, exposes the blustering Captain Hawksley's fraudulent business dealings which touch his own family, forces Hawksley to return sexually incriminating letters from the aunt, protects his wife from Hawksley's attempted seduction, and proves to be his superior in strength and courage. *The Tyranny of Tears* is on a much smaller emotional scale and more domestically restrained. Both comedies are of their time.

The part of Clement Parbury was played by Charles Wyndham, the suave actor-manager who was shortly to move into a glittering new West-End theatre named after him. It is important to remember that late Victorian and Edwardian comedy, as well as the heavier drama, was dominated by the West-End actor-manager. Comedy was especially the province of Wyndham, Cyril Maude at the Haymarket, and Charles Hawtrey at the Comedy, each of whom had his own style as a leading actor.

The sophistication of acting and production style at these managements was essentially a creation of audience taste and audience demographics. The growing affluence and social polish of the London upper classes and their growing number in the fashionable districts west of Piccadilly meant that audiences were either familiar with the rich and elegant domestic environments presented on stage, or, stimulated especially by newspaper and magazine coverage of this circle, admired and aspired after them as a satisfying social fantasy.

Certainly the drama and staging of the West End offered little to the lower classes. Rare indeed were excursions outside the drawing-rooms of Mayfair or the well-appointed country house. Forgetting about a hundred years of melodrama, Pinero told William Archer that "nothing of considerable merit, but low comedy, has ever come from the study of low life."[5] Archer, who objected to Pinero's narrow social range, was told emphatically that he would find, if he tried to write plays,

> ... not only that wealth and leisure are more productive of dramatic complications than poverty and hard work, but that if you want to get a certain order of ideas expressed or questions discussed, you must go pretty well up in the social scale ... You must take into account the inarticulateness, the inexpressiveness, of the English lower middle and lower classes – the reluctance to analyse, to generalise, to give vivid utterance to their thoughts and emotions.[6]

Even J. T. Grein, the founder of the radical and socially conscious Independent Theatre Society, criticized Somerset Maugham's popular *Smith* because "the fact that his central figure is a servant somewhat lowers the standard of

its comedy."[7] The late Victorian and Edwardian age produced the first audience "glitterati" since the Regency. They were undoubtedly more at home
with the nine titled characters of Wilde's *Lady Windermere's Fan* than with
Elizabeth Baker's shop assistants, servants, and secretaries, and at home,
at least imaginatively, in Lady Grayston's country-house drawing-room in
Maugham's *Our Betters*: "*It is a sumptuous double room, of the period of
George II, decorated in green and gold, with a coromandel screen and lac-
quer cabinets; but the coverings of the chairs, the sofas, and cushions show
the influence of Bakst and the Russian Ballet; they offer an agreeable mixture of rich plum, emerald green, canary, and ultra-marine. On the floor is a
Chinese carpet, and here and there are pieces of Ming pottery.*"[8]

If this luxurious setting was typical of the Edwardian stage, so was the
blurring of the lines between comedy and more serious drama, a blurring
familiar from the previous century. For example, *Our Betters* (1923, written
1915) is a vicious piece about snobbery, betrayal, adultery, and conspicuous
consumption. The characters are principally unhappily married or divorced
women and their unpleasant male hangers-on. The humor is ironic or cynical in Maugham's nastiest vein. But the play is called "a comedy", as is
Smith (1910), which is equally devoid of the comic. So is Hubert Henry
Davies's *Mrs. Gorringe's Necklace* (1903) – "A Comedy in Four Acts" –
which has only one comic character, the dithering Mrs. Gorringe, and ends
in the suicide of the juvenile lead. The main character of St. John Hankin's
The Return of the Prodigal (1905), "a comedy for fathers," as the author
puts it, is the appealing but sad Eustace Jackson, an utter failure in life who
eventually wangles a yearly allowance out of his unwilling father and goes
off to London, leaving behind him his unhappy sister and the girl with whom
he is falling in love.

Both *Our Betters* and *Smith* contain a character type well-known on the
Edwardian stage: the outsider, often a colonial, who regards the doings of
Mayfair society or the dysfunctional country-house family with distaste and
even horror. There are two such commentators in *Our Betters*, a young
man and woman newly arrived from America, the latter intending to stay
in England and make a good marriage. The former is completely alienated
by the twisted *mores* of the society in which he finds himself; by the end of
the play both are in flight to New York. Another such commentator – the
device was not only used in comedy – is Tom Freeman of *Smith*, who visits
from Rhodesia to take back a wife and is disgusted by the selfish and shallow
friends of his sister Rose ("flippant, frivolous, and inane"). The only good
woman he can find is Rose's housemaid Smith, who accepts him after some
hesitation.

By no means is all Edwardian comedy so dark. There are many light, romantic plays like Maugham's *Jack Straw* (1908), in which the eponymous and stylish hero impersonates the missing Archduke of Pomerania in a plot to revenge Lady Wanley upon the *nouveau-riche* Mrs. Parker Jennings, who has mortally insulted her. Of course he *is* the Archduke of Pomerania, and marries Mrs. Parker Jennings's daughter. Similarly, Maugham's *Mrs. Dot* (1908) shows the lively, charming, and very rich widow Mrs. Dot Worthley scheming and manipulating all around her to marry her true love. There are no problems here. However, even aside from Shaw, comedies were more intelligent and more daring in theme than a generation before; many were anti-romantic. Yet a last-act engagement could still solve difficulties only lightly touched upon. Hankin complained about critics who praised this type of ending: "To them all engagements are satisfactory, and all marriages are made in Heaven, and at the mere thought of wedding bells they dodder like romantic old women in an almshouse. No wonder they have reduced our drama to the last stage of intellectual decrepitude."[9] Even the romantically tinged last act of Cicely Hamilton's feminist comedy *Diana of Dobson's* (1908) throws its fiercely independent-minded but now unemployed and starving draper's assistant into the arms of her previously rejected £600 a year ex-Guards officer suitor. Nevertheless, the marriage is virtually dictated by Diana's circumstances; she has no other economic choice.

The conservative view of the theatre, that it should not concern itself with life's problems and unpleasantnesses, that it should be entertaining, that comedies should be romantic and end happily, persisted well beyond the Edwardian era. Comedies for the commercial West End were also conservative in the social and political sense, on the side of the established order against the parvenu, firm upholders of social distinction. Such attitudes were a legacy from Victorian comedy. The lower classes – when these appeared, mostly as domestic servants – were objects of laughter or indifference. Maugham's Smith is an exception, as is the brave bootmaker Stubbs in Jones's *The Heroic Stubbs* (1906), who saves his "ideal," Lady Hermione Cavendish, from the clutches of a rich cad with a private yacht. If they were vulgar or ambitious, they were objects of satire. In Hankin's *The Cassilis Engagement* (1907) the clever Mrs. Cassilis breaks her son's engagement to the common Ethel Borridge (who is accompanied by her fearsomely unrefined mother) by smothering her with kindness, extending her stay at Deynham Abbey, and insisting that the newlyweds shall live next door in the country – knowing that the flashy Ethel cannot stand the boredom of country life. There is a great deal of snobbery in the play – "a comedy for mothers" – and contempt for the unfortunate Borridges that was obviously acceptable to the audience.

In terms of class and the hierarchical ordering of society, honored as it was on the West-End stage, James Barrie's *The Admirable Crichton* (1902) is by far the most subversive of Edwardian comedies. Crichton, Lord Loam's impeccable butler in act 1, who detests the slightest slippage of distinction between master and servant in a well-ordered Mayfair household, becomes through sheer power of ingenuity and superiority of character the benevolent dictator of the tropical island on which the Loam family has been shipwrecked: master mechanic, electrician, metal worker, unchallenged ruler of all he surveys, very close to the heart of Lord Loam's daughter, almost a god. After an untimely rescue, and back in the rigid and sterile society of Mayfair, he resumes his role as the perfect butler without complaint, although shortly to leave service.

Barrie and Maugham dominated West-End comedy. Barrie never enjoyed anything like the success of Maugham in having four plays running simultaneously between 1907 and 1909, for a total of 1,261 performances: *Lady Frederick*, *Mrs. Dot*, *Jack Straw*, and *Penelope*. However, he was, even apart from *Peter Pan* (1904, and revived every year until 1938) popular enough. *The Admirable Crichton* ran for 328 performances, the often revived *Quality Street* (1902) for 459. This play tells the pretty story of Phoebe who, with her sister, is reduced to teaching school because of bad investment advice from Valentine Brown, who should have proposed to her in act 1 and did not. Keeping her straitened circumstances a secret from Brown, who returns from the army in 1815, ten years later, Phoebe disguises herself as an imaginary young niece, dazzling and captivating Brown, who finally confesses to the "niece" that he loved only Phoebe all along. All ends happily. *Quality Street* is both lively and charming, with a wonderful part for Phoebe and a warm humanity common to Barrie but mostly absent in Maugham, which makes the former the more attractive playwright. This humanity is much evident in one of Barrie's best plays, *What Every Woman Knows* (1908), the story of how the plain, loving, and determined Maggie masterminds the political rise of her indifferent, difficult, and unsuspecting husband and at last wins her way into his heart.

In *Quality Street* Phoebe, by disguising herself as a younger woman, turns time backwards by ten years. The stopping or retarding of time is a favorite device with Barrie: light and appealing in *Quality Street* (though there *is* a quiet desperation about Phoebe as she pursues her ruse), it darkens in *Peter Pan*, whose principal character refuses to grow up and lives in the dangerous fantasy world of Neverland, the polar opposite of the Darlings' Bloomsbury house of the first act. *Peter Pan* is the most autobiographical of the plays of Barrie, whose lost dead brother could *not* grow up, and the idea of time stopped or turned back recurs repeatedly. The one-act *Rosalind*

(1912) shows us a middle-aged Beatrice Page visited by Charles, an adoring admirer of a beautiful young stage Rosalind whom he assumes is Beatrice's daughter. But Beatrice undeceives him: it is *she* who is Rosalind. In a striking *coup-de-théâtre* she leaves the stage for her bedroom as a sloppy frump and re-emerges as Rosalind, "*a tall, slim young creature*" off to attend rehearsals of a suddenly revived *As You Like It*. The theme of time stopped is eerily suggestive of the supernatural in the post-Edwardian *Dear Brutus* (1917) and *Mary Rose* (1920), the first with its mysterious country-house host Lob and his even more mysterious wood that has the power not only to reverse time but change human circumstance, and the second with its strange island on which Mary Rose disappears and remains frozen in time. In his best plays the sometimes over-whimsical Barrie was a keen observer of the material world and also of another: lovely, tempting, extraordinary, and frightening.

Turning from comedy to farce, we find that features of the former also distinguish the latter, such as the necessity for domestic peace and harmony, often grievously absent until the final curtain, and the ultimate assertion of the authority of a wearied and battle-torn husband. From the point of view of the playbill, it is easy to say what farce was for the first thirty or forty years of Victoria's reign: a one-act or two-act afterpiece usually – but not always – of a pronounced low-comedy character and with a distinct – usually but not always – lower-middle-class tone. The low-comedy aspect was significant. Every stock company had its First Low Comedian and often a Second Low Comedian as well, for farce or Shakespeare or anything in between. Farce and a great deal of comedy as well was unimaginable without the low comedian, as important in his line of business as was the light comedian in his. The two kinds of acting were quite different from each other, as were the characters that fell into the two categories.

Farce was always domestic in nature; there are no Gothic or nautical farces. By the 1840s it was anything but the relatively refined farce of the eighteenth and early nineteenth centuries with its subject matter of romantic complications involving scheming lovers and servants and duped rivals, parents, or guardians, set in a world of comfortable gentry and fashionable residences. The new farce adjusted to the age it inhabited and the new mass audience to which it catered; it moved down the social ladder in setting and characterization, bustling with stage business and replete with eccentric behavior, addressing its audience directly in frequent asides and explanatory monologues.

For example: the extraordinary inventor Dr. Bang in John Maddison Morton's *An Englishman's House is His Castle* (1857) torments Perkins Pocock, the owner of a lodging-house in Bloomsbury, by walking around "*producing a number of explosions.*" Another lodger plays a piercing bosun's whistle; a third relentlessly practices "God Save the Queen" on a flageolet. The principal characters of Andrew Halliday's *The Area Belle* (1864), whose single act is set in a kitchen, are a kitchen maid, a milkman, a soldier, and a policeman; the three men engage in comic rivalry for the servant and a great deal of physical business. The funniest scenes in Coyne's *How to Settle Accounts with Your Laundress* (1847), Charles Selby's *Hotel Charges* (1853), and Mark Lemon's *The Railway Belle* (1854) concern comic misunderstandings and a great deal of business arising from the serving of elaborate meals on stage. In his terrified flight from an inexorable pursuer (whom he has never met), Triptolemus Brown of Morton's *Drawing Room, Second Floor, and Attics* (1864), a chemist's assistant, descends from his hiding-place on the roof, a chimney pot, to the drawing-room of the same house. In his progress he is blackened with soot, drops through the chimney onto a fire burning in the grate below, knocks over a servant carrying a tray of food, plates, and glasses, pulls a cloth off a table groaning with cakes, pastries, decanters and more glasses, dresses as a woman, and falls backward through a window "*with great smash of glass.*"

By the 1870s, under French influence, farce was changing. The one-act or two-act afterpiece grew to three acts and became the only item on the bill, now usually called "A Farcical Comedy." The lustful bourgeoisie and sexual imbroglios of French farce were thoroughly sanitized for the English stage, since neither the audience nor the Examiner of Plays could be offended, even though some critics *were* offended, as much by alleged triviality and meretriciousness as by the supposed sullying of domestic life. French farce planted the seeds of sexual adventure and adultery in a first act set in a solidly respectable middle-class home and matured them in a physically frantic and complex second act located in a shady hotel or restaurant in which predatory men and sometimes not unwilling women fail to achieve their sexual objectives because of an amazing series of mishaps and coincidences. The third act, back in the home once more, is devoted to sorting out the mess and to the desperate efforts of all concerned to hide the truth of their nocturnal misadventures and avoid exposure and disgrace.

The effort to avoid discovery carries over to English farce, although it is not the discovery of attempted adultery but rather that of a harmless but forbidden night out in suspect surroundings. James Albery's *Pink Dominos* (1877) and Dion Boucicault's *Forbidden Fruit* (1880) were two early adaptations of this kind of French farce, the English versions of which flourished especially at the Court Theatre in the hands of Pinero, the author of *The Magistrate* (1885) and *Dandy Dick* (1887). Such farce has a philosophical dimension in that the hero – or anti-hero, in this case – comes under increasingly unbearable pressure to conceal the truth, find a way out of his growing difficulties, and once more inhabit the state of domestic quietude which he had earlier so foolishly abandoned or from which he had been abruptly removed by capricious chance. So great is this pressure that as his world – it is always a he – is collapsing around him he can soon doubt his own identity, as does the hero in Gilbert's *Tom Cobb* (1875), who cries out wildly to a woman he has never met, "You say I'm engaged to you. I dare say I am. If you said I was engaged to your mother, I'd dare say it too. I've no idea who I am, or where I am, or what I am saying or doing" (Booth, *English Plays*, IV: 287). Dr. Jedd, the utterly respectable rural dean of *Dandy Dick*, falls ever deeper into trouble when he becomes mired in a seedy world of racing, betting, and doping horses. He finds himself in a village lockup, his identity still unknown, arrested for administering a stimulant to his sister's horse Dandy Dick so that it will win the Durnstone Handicap and a large bet for Jedd that will restore the church steeple. Bruised and besmirched, but extricated from his dreadful position (though with surprises still to come), the dean apostrophizes his restored domestic bliss: "Home! What sonorous music is in the word! Home, with the secret of my sad misfortune buried in the bosoms of a faithful few. Home, with my family influence intact! Home, with the sceptre of my dignity still tight in my grasp!"[10] For the totally humorless Jedd the situation is appalling; for the audience it is uproariously funny. That is precisely how this kind of farce creates its effects.

The difference between early and late Victorian farce is well illustrated by a comparison of Morton's *Box and Cox* (1847) with Pinero's *The Magistrate*, both classical farces of their time. The former is in one act, the latter in three. Box is a printer who works at night, Cox a hatter who works by day, and unknown to each other they share a bed and a room in the house of their greedy landlady Mrs. Bouncer. In Pinero's play the chief characters are socially more elevated: Posket is a respected magistrate, as is his friend Bullivant; two other men involved are Colonel Lukyn, a retired Indian Army officer and his friend Captain Vale. The setting of *Box and Cox* is merely "*A Room decently furnished . . . a few common ornaments on chimney piece*" (Booth, *English Plays*, IV: 211). The first act and the second scene of the third act of *The Magistrate* are set in Posket's comfortable drawing-room. Box and Cox cook bacon and a mutton chop; the meal of the Hôtel des Princes where Posket find himself in act II includes devilled oysters, sole, and champagne.

The literary style of *Box and Cox* is elegant, even ornate, that of *The Magistrate* simpler though hardly conversational. Box and Cox confront the audience with their predicament; *The Magistrate* is fairly well contained behind the proscenium arch. Cox twice addresses the audience with explanatory monologues, Box and Mrs. Bouncer with one each, and there are

Figure 9 The farce hero *in extremis*: Arthur Cecil as Posket in *The Magistrate* (III, 1).

numerous asides. In Pinero, Posket has one such monologue when he arrives exhausted and dishevelled at his court after fleeing the Hôtel des Princes and the police. The comedy of *Box and Cox* is initially derived from the surprise discovery on the part of each man that he is sharing his room with another, and then from their frantic efforts to rid themselves of their fearsome off-stage "intended," Penelope Ann – they are both, it turns out, engaged to the same woman – and their increasing panic at her approach. The characters of both plays are under that inexorable pressure essential to farce. In *The Magistrate*, in a typically late-Victorian fashion, the comedy arises from the fevered efforts of Posket, a man of the law after all (as Jedd is a man of the church) to avoid exposure for his inadvertent escapade in the private dining-room of a restaurant of ill repute. It also arises from the extreme contrast between this awful plight and his pitiable condition in his own court, and his former tranquil and esteemed existence. The difference between these two farces is not only one of changing patterns of social class, comedy, and dramatic technique but also, in the first instance, of a changing audience.

By the Edwardian period farce was in decline. The ubiquitous musical comedy had conquered the province of light entertainment; it was the charm and glitter of the Gaiety Girls rather than the homely and avuncular jollity of the low comedian – a vanishing race – that now drew the public. With its rigid social taboos the Edwardian age should have been fruitful soil for a great farceur like Feydeau in Paris. Or were audiences tired of and upset, as Shaw was, by what he believed was the sadism of farce and the cruelty of its spectators? "To laugh without sympathy is a ruinous abuse of a noble function," he said; audiences shout with laughter at "the deliberate indulgence of that horrible, derisive joy in humiliation and suffering which is the beastliest element in human nature."[11] Yet there is friendliness, naïveté, and a defense of domestic ideals in English farce, not present in Feydeau, that Shaw missed. In this sense farce is of a piece with its close relation, comedy.

NOTES

1. Michael R. Booth (ed.), *English Plays of the Nineteenth Century*, 4 vols. (Oxford: Clarendon Press, 1969–76), III: 263.
2. William Tydeman (ed.), *Plays by Tom Robertson* (Cambridge: Cambridge University Press, 1982), p. 44.
3. Clement Scott, *The Drama of Yesterday and To-day* (London: Macmillan, 1899), II: 17.
4. *The Times*, 7 April 1899.
5. J. P. Wearing (ed.), *The Collected Letters of Sir Arthur Pinero* (Minneapolis: University of Minneapolis Press, 1974), p. 182.
6. William Archer, *Real Conversations* (London: Heinemann, 1904), p. 21.
7. Quoted in A. E. Wilson, *Edwardian Theatre* (London: Barker, 1951), p. 15.

8. W. Somerset Maugham, *Selected Plays* (London: Penguin, 1963), p. 355.
9. "A Note on Happy Endings," *The Dramatic Works of St. John Hankin* (London: Martin Secker, 1912), III: 127.
10. A. W. Pinero, *Dandy Dick* (London: Heinemann, 1959), p. 73.
11. George Bernard Shaw, *Our Theatres in the Nineties* (London: Constable, 1932), II: 118 (UMI Research Press, 1986).

8

DAVID MAYER

Encountering melodrama

One of the earliest descriptions of melodrama – only it wasn't called melodrama but tragi-comedy – partly explains melodrama's ambiguous reputation. Writing in 1611, the English dramatist John Fletcher stated:

> A tragi-comedy is not so-called in respect of mirth and killing, but in respect it wants deaths, which is enough to make it no tragedy, yet brings some near it, which is enough to make it no comedy, which must be a representation of familiar people, with such kind of trouble as no life be questioned; so that a god is as lawful in this as in a tragedy, and mean people in a comedy.[1]

It was this deformed hybrid – this state of being neither one thing nor another, which refused to equate disaster and tragic excess with death, which acknowledged and celebrated common folk, and which did, despite Fletcher's denial, inject moments of mirth into serious business – which brought onto the English stage a theatrical genre previously found in the ironic "tragedies" of Euripides and in the "pastoral" plays of Renaissance Europe. Although Fletcher sought to link "tragi-comedy" with the Athenian satyr play, his plea for respectability and critical status was ignored.

This is the problem which I and others who write about melodrama inherit. Accordingly, in offering this brief essay, which cannot pretend to offer either a comprehensive history or full analysis of this intricate theatrical genre, I have set myself several tasks. These include presenting the various ways in which nineteenth- and twentieth-century critics and scholars have viewed melodrama, offering less a definition than a workable description which allows the reader to recognize and analyze the basic form and to anticipate variants to this form. I am concerned to show how melodrama functions as an essential social and cultural instrument and to encourage discussion of this crucial function. Because much criticism of "Victorian melodrama" tends to take the entire nineteenth and early twentieth century as a single entity – a huge confused clot of time in which political, social, cultural, and theatrical events are inextricably fused – I argue that melodrama is subtle and has often been responsive to immediate social circumstances and concerns. In being responsive, the form as well as the content of melodrama has regularly changed, and these transformations must be accounted for

Although some of the analyses of melodrama which I offer are contradictory, these interpretations must be read in terms of the scholar or critic's position when viewing the wide body of melodrama scripts, performances, performers, and other sources available. Moreover, rather than contradictory, these apparently discrepant approaches may be viewed, more helpfully, as complementary, each explicating another facet of, or response to, this variegated entertainment. There is no such thing as a "last word" about melodrama; its fascination and its vitality lie partly in the fact that, mutating as it goes and only provisionally defined, it confidently continues to this very day in motion pictures, indifferent to criticism and objection.

Underlying this essay is my conviction that melodrama, like all theatrical activity, is an essential social process, even if its vital function is not immediately recognized. People attend theatre because, as well as offering entertainment and relaxation (and melodrama offers both), the playhouse is a place to confront issues and to mediate social values, where plays themselves intervene in and obliquely or directly critique matters of daily concern. If a drama does not speak to what interests and concerns us, we are bored and indifferent to what is happening on the stage. Other plays hold our attention because the action touches on issues in which we have a vested, if sometimes undeclared, interest. Melodramas, however much they would seem to be offering a narrative distant from our daily lives, however much they might be labeled "escapist," are always about something far more immediate, even if we fail to recognize what that *something* is. Because most of the melodramas that have attracted critical scrutiny are at least a century old, we have to devise strategies which enable us to recognize and to foreground the sources of stress and anxiety which energize the play.

Theatre – and melodrama in particular – does not happen in isolation but is intimately related to the historical and cultural circumstances in which it appears, so anyone studying this form or considering a particular melodrama must ask certain key questions about its context. Moreover, as the nineteenth century was the first era of mass theatregoing, with theatre attendance active in all parts of the British Isles, it is useful for us to remember that there are numerous permutations in the possible answers to these queries: (1) When was this drama first performed? That is, what was happening in the world outside the theatre, and what understandings of these events were early audiences bringing to performances? (2) At which theatre was this drama performed? That is, what was the location of the theatre, and to which classes, occupations, and other constituencies did it cater? How consistent were the allegiances of this audience? (3) Which actors were performing the leading roles, and were they playing within their usual "line-of-business?" Knowing the identities of these actors and the kinds of roles (e.g. villain, hero, heroine, comic support, soubrette, etc.) they recurrently performed enables us to anticipate and understand audience expectations and readings of the new roles. (4) To what degree was the subject-matter curtailed or otherwise affected by censorship? A British stage censor was in place throughout the period in question, but the vigilance of the Lord Chamberlain's reader was inconsistent. Some dramas performed at the minor theatres appear to have been tolerated by local magistrates who were unaware of or indifferent to their contents. As the drama was circulated and performed at subsequent dates and at additional theatres by new casts, the same questions must again be asked because there is the expectation that the play retained some elements of its original relevance or was freshly appropriate to new circumstances.

We may not immediately recognize such connections. Melodrama enables the immediate concern, the cause of stress, to appear before us in partial disguise. It offers a brief, palatable, non-threatening metaphor which enables an audience to approach and contemplate at close range matters which are otherwise disturbing to discuss. The decades immediately preceding the nineteenth century, the century itself, and the first two decades of the twentieth century, we must invariably remember as we consider melodrama, constitute a period of rapid and profound change. Concomitant with these changes is intense stress. As we study a melodrama, we must factor-in the growth of a vast overseas empire, urbanization, industrialization, agricultural crises, emancipation and suffrage, the rise of new social classes and the enlargement or endangering of earlier ones. In North America and on the European continents there were revolutions and civil wars; in Britain revolution was narrowly averted by last-minute compromise, but the threat of a mass-uprising of an oppressed and exploited working class was a frequent murmured subtext. Along with more immediate concerns, British melodramas frequently explored the major fault-line of class and status and the anxieties which these subjects engendered; American melodramas similarly approached or investigated questions of race and national origin. In some melodramas these events and problems and resulting stresses are overt. In other dramas the underlying issues are concealed, but the metaphor may be recognized, read, and understood nonetheless.

There are further problems in approaching melodrama. For all its longevity, melodrama, and by this I mean nineteenth-century melodrama, has been subject to change, and the possibilities of these changes require additional – if optional – questions to be asked. It is helpful, therefore, to query a play in terms of its approach to its subject matter, to its very structure, that is, to the position of this drama on the theatre's bill for the evening's entertainment, to the duration of the piece and number of acts which are to be performed, to the way in which characters are depicted by dramatists and rendered by the actors, and, no less crucially, how melodrama as a *genre* is received by audiences. Is it billed as a "melodrama," or has the management attempted to disguise it as a "drama" or "military" or "naval drama" or as an "autumn drama" or by some other euphemism which tells us that at this date and at this theatre, audiences were put off by the term *melodrama*?

Before I identify how scholars have approached the study of melodrama, thereby providing us with many useful avenues for investigating this subject historically, culturally, and critically, I offer a brief working description of melodrama, acknowledging, first of all, that there is no description or definition which fully covers all examples or answers all questions. The numerous exceptions to my working definition are as important as any melodramas which lie within the perimeter of my broad generalization.

Melodrama, then, is a theatrical or literary response to a world where things are seen to go wrong, where ideas of secular and divine justice and recompense are not always met, where suffering is not always acknowledged, and where the explanations for wrong, injustice, and suffering are not altogether understandable. Melodrama tries to respond with emotional, rather than intellectual, answers to a world where explanations of why there is pain and chaos and discord are flawed or deeply and logically inconsistent, where there are all-too-visible discrepancies between readily observed calamities and palliative answers. Melodrama provides an emotionally intelligible picture of the world to deracinated western cultures, severed by science and technology from former religious and spiritual "truths." Melodrama also addresses, more simply, people who in Martha Vicinus's terms are "helpless and unfriended,"[2] finding their way in a rapidly changing, increasingly urban world. It offers them emotional satisfactions and emotionally validates the factual world as they have experienced it. For such spectators it is helpful and reassuring to depict a world which may be explained in comparatively simple terms of good and evil. Melodrama depicts such a world – *manichean* is the philosophic term frequently present in discussion of melodrama – where forces of wickedness and goodness are in constant contention and where there is no place for characters who are tainted, but not wholly good or altogether bad.

Such sharp divisions give rise to melodrama's principal characters – although it is essential to insist that the acute distinctions which I describe are chiefly associated with melodrama's early years and had largely vanished by the 1860s. These clear-cut characters are the villain, the hero, the heroine – the first unambiguously wicked, the latter two morally incorrupt and incorruptible. Villains are supported in their endeavors by henchmen and women of dubious virtue; the hero and heroine are aided by a range of servants, friends, family members, and associates who are largely virtuous. In all, there are roles for a standard stock or repertory company of a dozen to fifteen actors, many of these actors appearing in roles which are similar in characterization and dramatic function from melodrama to melodrama. Indeed, so stereotypical and morally defined are roles within the melodrama company that they can be burlesqued.[3] Melodrama depends upon our abilities to recognize evil and to distinguish it from good, and, lest we not possess this ability, the conventions of this genre are there to assist us. It is usually characteristic of melodrama that serious trouble comes from two separate sources. The first is the circumstance which may affect all that drama's characters and may be recognizable as the current social problem (*the contemporary source of stress and anxiety* which lies behind the choice of subject matter): war, military or naval service and the harsh regulations which govern lower ranks, economic depression, agricultural blight, disruptive industrialization and attendant unemployment or poverty, the vicissitudes of life in foreign lands. But none of these genuine, historic sources of difficulty is sufficient to drive the plot. The plots of melodrama have a further propelling force which takes precedence over the historic circumstances.

This is villainy. The villain, for reasons which are personal to him and altogether reprehensible, must instigate an action which destabilizes the hero and heroine and places their lives, fortunes, livelihoods, good names, social relationships, and romantic intentions in grave jeopardy. Having been abruptly extruded from stability and comfort by the villain – whose machinations the hero and heroine initially fail to recognize – these leading characters must endeavor to reclaim lost ground. Abetted by their friends and associates, often comic and of a lower social status, the heroine and heroine discover the nature of their peril, recognize that they are the victims of some combination of malice, avarice, lust, envy, and cruelty, and identify and expel the villain from his place of power.

Herein melodrama differs from tragedy, where regaining one's mental, emotional, moral, and physical environment exacts a severe price, often the hero's death. Melodrama, by contrast, exacts no toll. The good characters emerge unscathed; they have grown wiser in the ways of the world – wiser, but not cynical. Further, as they had only naïveté to lose, they are still innocent, not guilty of any crime, and rarely have cause for shame. They have briefly suffered physical and emotional hardships and may have been threatened with permanent social ostracism, poverty, ill-health, and even death, but, in comparison to tragedy, their fresh accumulation of wisdom has cost little. Although this aspect of characterization contributes to the moral clarity which was initially considered essential to melodrama, the wholly virtuous hero is theatrically boring and, not surprisingly, the role was destined to change and to bring in its place the morally fallible hero. Initially, and through much of the nineteenth century, the fallible hero is found in what is labeled "temperance" melodrama, plays in which the "good" and "bad" characteristics of the hero contend as he is first seduced by strong drink and must thereafter overcome his addiction to alcohol or lose health, livelihood, family, and social position. Here the self is polarized between sobriety and inebriation, but there is little moral ambiguity. We know that this is a good man unwittingly led astray, and suspense is limited to whether and how his better self will conquer his drink-sodden self. A hero who is tainted with crime, even if he is innocent of the crime of which he stands accused, is more interesting. We see such a development in Tom Taylor's *The Ticket-of-Leave Man* (1863) where the protagonist is a Lancashire bumpkin framed by hardened criminals and sentenced to prison. Paroled from prison and still suspect, he is shadowed by a plain-clothes detective who may be on the side of the law or, given the public's mistrust of the police at that date, may be an *agent provocateur* or engaged in activities which will further incriminate – not exonerate – the baffled, out-of-his-depth hero, whose taint of guilt will hang over him until the final act.[4] Such changes bringing ambiguous moral status were rarely visited upon the heroine because her innocence and purity could not be compromised for long. If her goodness were to appear impaired by an elopement without marriage – as in Henry Arthur Jones's *The Middleman* (1885) or in Arthur Shirley and Benjamin Landeck's *Tommy Atkins* (1895), it almost inevitably transpires that the heroine, mourned and shunned as a "lost" daughter, has not only confounded expectations by marrying, but she has acted bravely and resourcefully in adversity or genuine peril.

The way to make melodrama compellingly interesting was to create a villain almost too skillful for the hero and his friends to detect, for melodrama is villain-driven, and it is in the malign character of the villain that the best and most interesting roles lie. Indeed, melodrama becomes deeply interesting when the hero and villain are fused into one character, when the very self of a role is sharply and deeply divided. Moreover, the villain has a further function which helps to explain why it is that audiences continue to find melodrama a continuous source of pleasure. He helps to dispel or disguise unresolvable contradictions and conspicuous incongruities.

Contradictions abounded in Victorian England. Experience of work told the English that earning a living in the new machine-based industries was fraught with uncertainty, that employers were arbitrary in their decisions, that wages and jobs might end abruptly, but they also knew that a few people became wealthy beyond imagination. Urban life brought unsanitary conditions, contagion, and disease threatening the stealthy onset of sickness; crime and the unreliability of police and fire protection added physical peril and anxiety to their lives, but they also saw the splendor of new buildings, experienced the ease of leisure, observed people enjoying comforts and luxuries in the new metropolises. They were aware of the rigid structures of the traditional Victorian paternalistic family, but they were covertly aware that women were creating fresh careers and altering traditional domestic roles. Alcoholic beverages provided stimulation, relaxation, and inner warmth, but they saw daily examples of families impoverished and destroyed by alcoholism. They proudly basked in the grandeur of an expanding empire, seeing themselves military, naval, and commercial conquerors and the just recipients of the world's bounty, but they knew the cost in lives and occasionally shamefully sensed the spurious morality justifying the maintenance and expansion of this empire. Because melodramas are set within exciting, threatening, and disturbing environments – such as a rising capitalist economy, new cities, distant countries explored or fought-over in imperial or colonial enterprises, and changing family structures – the villain becomes closely identified with each hostile environment. The villain is not just a wicked individual but is also the bigger problem. When the villain is recognized, caught, expelled, or otherwise punished, the threatening circumstances with which he has become conflated are also reduced and made less threatening. Melodrama, providing a metaphor through which to approach disturbing subjects temporarily – throughout the melodrama and perhaps for a few hours thereafter – tames those subjects, offering relief as the problem recedes or, at the very least, becomes emotionally intelligible, congruous, and less menacing. The world can be viewed with sudden optimism.

Illustrations of melodramatic performance[5] are largely alike in depicting actors making large expressive gestures. These illustrations of actors and melodramatic scenes, often with actors standing with legs apart, arms flung wide from their bodies, and fingers spread, strike us as exaggerated, maintaining the fiction that performances were excessive, unsubtle, overblown, and clamorous. But there is no "typical" Victorian acting. Victorian actors were conscious that acting styles were changing within the century and that approaches to acting were continually adapted over time to meet the circumstances in which the melodrama was viewed. The "size" of melodramatic performances could be affected by such variables as the interior dimensions of theatres, the actors' distance from the audience, theatre lighting, orchestral size (affecting hearing of spoken lines), the rowdy or attentive behavior of spectators, whether the piece was performed in London or in the provinces or within a theatre or provincial fairground booth. Victorian acting becomes far more individualized and intimate – but not necessarily "realistic" or naturalistic – as the decades pass.

Stance and gesture were used by actors to illustrate and heighten the emotional subtext of the drama and to express feelings which cannot be stated in words.[6] Actors' gestures could travel far from the body, extending, elaborating, holding a movement, because they were supported by incidental music which gave tempo and sustaining duration to the gesture. Music variously assisted the fluidity and emotion of the actors' gestures, allowing performers to create meaning as their gestures extended, withdrew, hesitated, collapsed, as a stage wife would have reached, first with one hand, then an arm, then with both arms toward an obdurate magistrate, pleading vainly for her condemned husband's life. Music added force to a contemptuous toss of the villain's head or pathos to the bowed heads of the deserted heroine, the submissive widow, or the grieving child.

Speech, gesture, and music were closely integrated. Different national cultures and different theatrical managements imposed their preferences and priorities in terms of how gesture and speech, constantly abetted by music, might be employed. Percy Fitzgerald[7] wrote of the actor's gesture, drawing a distinction between the French and English stage:

> Gesture . . . is nearly as potent a medium of expression as the voice itself; in many cases it is more subtle, swift, and comprehensive. There is a language in gesture, with innumerable shades of meaning. It will convey everything – doubt, hesitation, eagerness, anger, joy, sorrow; with many more delicate emotions for which words are too formal, and too slow. There is one method of great force, and which is used to enrich the dramatic expression. It is, indeed, quite a common form on the French boards, but almost unknown to us. This is the anticipation of the utterance by the gesture. As an accomplished [English] actress has truly said, "With us it is more art than nature; with the French it is more nature than art." The body seems to run eagerly forward, in advance of the mind, as a sort of *avant-courier*. The dramatic result, which has extraordinary effect in the way of riveting attention, seems to work in this fashion. The anticipatory gesture is made. Then arises in the spectator's mind a sort of speculation as to whether the utterance to follow will correspond. Then a second or two of suspense follows; all is finally satisfied by the utterance itself . . . "On her first speech," she says, "her hands and tongue never set out together, but the one prepares us for the other. She sometimes begins with a mute, eloquent attitude; but never goes forward all at once, with hands, eyes, head, and voice. By this simple beginning is given a power of rising in the passion of the scene." This is an invaluable technical lesson for an actor; and what a light it throws, and how scientific is the device! . . . A French professor . . . has gone to the

root of the matter when he lays it down that gesture is a language to express ideas that are not written, that is, those delicate, almost impalpable thoughts and shadows of thoughts, for which words are too coarse and inefficient.[8]

According to Fitzgerald, the English actor, giving utterance to thought, spoke first, and the gesture followed to add emphasis and clarity to his words; the French actor led with the emotional impulse, which gave rise to the gesture, and finally to the word. In both instances music was present to provide a further layer of emotional meaning.

It is fortunate for the investigation of melodrama that valuable studies exist to discuss the characteristics and appeal and effects of melodrama. I identify from this extensive list a number of important texts which anyone contemplating a larger or more detailed investigation of melodrama will benefit from consulting. Inevitably, there is some overlap between these texts, also contradiction and dissent. My response to these authors is neither to contradict nor rationalize the various interpretations of and approaches to melodrama but to see each text as a facet of a large and complicated problem: all must be recognized and acknowledged if we are to understand the intricacies and appeal of melodrama.

The most lauded critical study, Peter Brooks's *The Melodramatic Imagination*,[9] is only marginally concerned with theatrical performance and even less concerned to describe or analyze melodrama from the English stage. Brooks, however, locates the origins of modern melodrama in the climate of the French Enlightenment which, over decades, had gradually substituted rationalism and logic for religious faith, creating in the 1790s what Brooks describes as a post-sacred vacuum in which traditional sources of morality and ethics and religious teaching have lost their authority. A function of the melodramatic stage is to offer clarity to dramatic action in such a fashion that audiences, who may have lost moral teaching through the absence or diminution of the Church, once again find a means of determining who, in the simplest terms, is good and who is evil. Their new faith in the inherent goodness of man – despite the lingering presence of evil – and in the value of good individual actions is recompensed with secular salvation and earthly rewards. Of melodrama, says Brooks in his most telling words,

No shadow dwells, and the universe bathes in the full bright lighting of moral manicheanism. Hence the psychic bravado of virtue, its expressive breakthrough, serves to assure us, again and again, that the universe is in fact morally legible, that it possesses an ethical identity and significance. This assurance must be a central function of melodrama in the post-sacred universe: it relocates and rearticulates the most basic moral sentiments and celebrates the sign of the right. From its very inception during the Revolution – the moment when ethical symbols were patently, convulsively thrown into question – melodrama addressed itself to this relocation and rearticulation of an occulted morality.[10]

Brooks may be read for his analyses of early melodrama. As melodrama begins to alter in the late 1820s, the accuracy of his descriptions is less sure, and his authority recedes.

The earliest critical approach to melodrama is a response to what its author, Sir Walter Scott, saw as the subverted values of class occasioned by the French Revolution. Attacking melodrama as a subversive genre for failing to show proper deference to class hierarchies, Scott insists that,

> The most obvious fault of this species of composition is the demoralizing falsehood of the pictures it offers us. The vicious are frequently presented as objects less of censure than of sympathy; sometimes they are selected as objects of imitation and praise. There is an affectation of attributing noble and virtuous sentiments to the persons least qualified by habit or education to entertain them; and of describing the higher and better educated classes as uniformly deficient in those feelings of liberality, generosity, and honour, which may be considered as proper to their situation in life. [Melodrama is] . . . "the groundwork of a sort of moral jacobinism."[11]

Scott's view – that melodrama, by presenting as villains the aristocracy and those who, by virtue of wealth and privilege, continued to exercise and abuse power – has an echo in modern writings on this genre. The most significant and articulate of these is Simon Shepherd and Peter Womack's essay on melodrama.[12] These two argue that melodrama retains its power because it infallibly attacks misplaced authority, irrespective of who holds authority and the nature and structure of the society in which authority is wielded. The hero is, therefore, someone whose actions challenge authority and abusive power.

Some other recent studies of melodrama also raise questions about the circumstances in which melodrama is created and enjoyed and how effectively melodrama is positioned to take sides in matters of current concern. Elaine Hadley in *Melodramatic Tactics*, similar to Peter Brooks, sees melodrama as a mode of rhetoric, expression, and, equally, of transaction which is invoked as various social groupings respond to the stresses of Victorian capitalism. In her description, melodrama permeates not only the theatre and narrative literature, but also numerous cultural and political transactions. Because the rhetoric of melodrama is used equally by both sides in social conflicts, such as in debating legislation aimed at ameliorating poverty, it is inaccurate to insist only upon melodrama's radical or adversarial stance. Hadley argues that melodrama is both palliative and subversive. As much as confronting and opposing the established power-structures of the Victorian era, melodrama and melodramatic practice identify and ultimately uphold these structures as well as restating social-class division and tolerating class privilege. Daniel Gerould,[13] while acknowledging a subversive streak in melodrama which provides frissons of excited delight to those spectators who see themselves oppressed, identifies a tendency for melodramatic villains to be most effectively opposed by virtuous members of their own class. For Gerould, change is in the moral climate, not in the drama's social environment.

In contrast to analyses of melodrama as a genre which intervenes in our cultural lives and social events to enlighten and confront – or which fails to do either – Michael Booth's major study, *English Melodrama*, looks at melodrama both as a theatrical form and in terms of the subgenres or categories of melodrama which the Victorian theatre itself recognized. By definition of its breadth and detailed descriptions of the numerous varieties of melodrama, this is an invaluable text and, although somewhat dated in approach, not to be overlooked. However, because I insist that melodrama does intervene and attempt, albeit briefly, to clarify and critique contemporary issues, I am uncomfortable with Booth's oft-quoted description of melodrama:

> Essentially, melodrama is a dream world inhabited by dream people and dream justice, offering audiences the fulfilment and satisfactions found only in dreams. An idealization and simplification of the world of reality, it is, in fact, a world its audiences want and cannot get.[14]

Nevertheless, for all his attempts to distance melodrama from "the world of reality," Booth's investigations of the various kinds of melodrama – domestic, military, nautical, Gothic, eastern, sensation – on offer to Georgian, Victorian, and Edwardian audiences show melodramatic authors both aware of and concerned with current events and issues and dedicated to placing their troubled heroes at the centres of such problems

An important contextual essay by Thomas Postlewait[15] is obligatory reading for every new student of melodrama. Postlewait's "From Melodrama to Realism: The Suspect History of American Drama," explains in detail how, in the closing years of the nineteenth century and the early years of the twentieth, melodrama was disparaged by the advocates of an emergent naturalism. The consequent acceptance of naturalism as an avant-garde and, subsequently, as an established theatrical language and aesthetic stance, distorted later perceptions of melodrama as excessive, inferior, and obsolete.

Because my essay is chiefly focused on *English* melodrama of the nineteenth century, I conclude with a brief, necessarily impressionistic, chronology of Victorian melodrama on the English stage. This chronology is not definitive but, rather, a decade-by-decade guide to some of the dramatists, theatrical and structural approaches to melodrama, influential developments from abroad, and other events and practices which had some modifying effect. This chronology is neither an account of progress nor improvement; neither is it a condemnation or allegation of deterioration. It merely documents change.

Acknowledging the focus of this volume, I begin with the late-1820s. Melodramas which survive from the first quarter of the century are chiefly spectacles in which the imagined opulence of a fantasized East give rise to dramas in which oriental despotism has to be met by virtuous rebellion. European nations breed merchants, millers, and squires who are also predatory bandits. Campaigns from the land and sea war with France are refought with British heroes and French villains. Spectacles shared the evening's program with other entertainments, and, as a consequence, melodramas rarely exceeded three acts in length and could be performed – combats, processions, and all – in somewhat less than an hour's duration.

A turning-point is the introduction, largely at the "minor" theatres, of proletarian characters who become melodrama's chief protagonists. The most-reproduced dramas from this period are John Baldwin Buckstone's *Luke the Labourer* (1826) in which both villain and oppressed hero are from the rural working-class and Douglas Jerrold's *Black-Ey'd Susan* (1829) in which the hero-victim is a naval seaman court-martialled for defending his wife's virtue when she is assaulted by his commanding officer. From this date and for the next two decades, melodrama flourishes at the minor theatres rather than at the patent theatres. We may identify tacit theatrical support for political change[16] in the shift from the Theatres Royal to the minor theatres and in the large number of dramas which are set in the working world – manufacturing, agricultural, and military and naval service – as well as in the emerging urban culture of proletarian characters. Jerrold leads a cluster of dramatists – Frederic Reynolds, H. M. Milner, George Dibdin-Pitt, T[homas] P[roclus] Taylor, George Almar, James Sheridan Knowles, William Moncrieff, John Thomas Haines, John Walker and, outstandingly, Edward Fitzball, and John Baldwin Buckstone – whose melodramas illuminate anxieties and pressures occasioned by agitation for the First and Second Reform Bills (1832 and 1848) and which are largely addressed to working-class and lower-middle-class audiences who frequented the minor theatres. Of this constellation of dramatists, only John Walker's *The Factory Lad* (1832), Jerrold's *The Rent-Day* (1832), and Haines's *My Poll and My Partner Joe* (1835) are found in modern anthologies, each prefaced by introductions which locate the drama in the social and economic contexts which contribute to their immediacy and theatrical power as they intervene in current disputes. Despite a paucity of printed texts, it is worth the time to read, at the very least, George Almar's

The Fire Raiser (1831) which, mounted as an historical drama set in Puritan England, illuminates agricultural distress and the fear of the "rick (or hay-stack and barn)-burners" who contributed to Reform agitation; Fitzball's *Jonathan Bradford* (1833), a narrative of murder, and a rural entrepreneur falsely accused; Dibdin-Pitt's *The String of Pearls; or, The Fiend of Fleet Street* (1847), the original Sweeny Todd drama which catches the fear of life in the expanding city; and Buckstone's *Vidocq* (1828) which, set against recent French political intrigue, explores English working-class fear of hidden surveillance and the *agent provocateur*; *The Green Bushes* (1845), a drama set in the American colonies which poses, in the New World, questions of class and race; and *The Flowers of the Forest* (1847), which also explores this material, now in a Scottish and gypsy environment. Buckstone and his contemporaries, aware that females and children were now regularly competing with men for factory jobs, also produced melodramas known in their time as "she-dramas" which foreground women and their fraught domestic lives. William Burton's *Ellen Wareham; or, The Wife of Two Husbands* (1834) is such a piece.[17] It is surprising that these plays and others from such a pressured and disrupted period of British life have never been gathered, introduced, and republished.

Not all melodramas explore the pressures of working-class life. As the populations of British cities, not all of them industrial and manufacturing centers, expanded, there was a corresponding growth of a new social class: the middle-class bourgeoisie. Entertainment for this new citizenry became a priority for some dramatists and theatrical managements. Consequently, there was an effort, towards the end of the 1830s, to make melodrama sufficiently respectable to be performed before middle-class audiences. Influenced by the success of the French "historical drama," especially the plays of Victor Hugo, dramatists clothed their melodramas in period settings, but these pieces, too, explore issues of class division, misused authority, and political rights. James Sheridan Knowles's *Virginius* (1837), hugely popular from the outset, differs from the proletarian plays of the minor theatres in several particulars: it is a costume-piece set in republican Rome, it is a five-act verse drama, its characters – virtuous and evil – are patricians, and it was first-performed at the patent-holding Covent Garden. This melodrama uses the freedom of a distant historical period to speak in the popular voice against hereditary privilege and to advocate political liberty and greater suffrage. The melodramas of Edward Bulwer Lytton – as with *Virginius*, written for and performed by William Charles Macready at Covent Garden – are period costume-pieces which intervene in contemporary issues. The most accessible of these to the student is Lytton's *Richelieu* (1839) which depicts the great cardinal as the voice for civil and political freedom in seventeenth-century

France and casts the sovereign, Louis XIII, and his nobles as the despotic abusers of personal and political rights. The language of Lytton's melodramas is elevated, meant for more educated audiences; the plays are five acts in length and so begin to displace the medley of shorter entertainments from the evening's program.

Further change overtook melodrama in the 1850s and 1860s, owing to the dominance of melodramatic innovation by one of its more prolific authors, Dion Boucicault. At first reading Boucicault's melodramas appear removed from the topical stresses of English life and largely concerned with theatrical effect. More than any other English-language dramatist, Boucicault is identified with "sensation" melodrama. His plays are remembered for a burning tenement, a last-minute rescue of the heroine from under the wheels of an oncoming London Underground train, the relief of a garrison from the revenge of India-mutineers, an Oxford–Cambridge rowing regatta, horse-racing with live animals, racing and exploding Mississippi side-wheelers, an escape from a British military prison with a precarious ascent on vines to the sea-cliffs above, and near-murder-by-drowning.[18]

Boucicault is not altogether disengaged from English life, but his melodramas, often first performed for American audiences and invariably shared between audiences in New York, London, the English provinces, and the empire beyond, reflect different interests. Not only is Boucicault the first international melodramatist, but his "sensation scenes" reveal him as obsessed with modernity and current technology as, repeatedly, he instigates the scene-painter, the model-builder, and the full-effects machinery of the Victorian stage – because the Victorian stage itself becomes a machine with which to exhibit and deceive – to create illusions of fire, height, water, and, above all, speed and machine-power.[19] Boucicault's plays, five-act dramas with the sensation episode closing the fourth act and a fifth act necessary to resolve the plot, establish a general length for subsequent melodramas until the century's end. However, with some dramatists and managements the four-act melodrama is not unusual, nor are melodramas of six or seven acts a rarity.

Boucicault, writing roles for his actress-wife Agnes Robertson and for the other actresses with whom he had liaisons as well as professional associations, created a second generation of "she-melodramas", dramas in which the heroine, even more than the villain and certainly more than the hero, is the principal instigator of action. These dramas test the resourcefulness, intelligence, and courage of his heroine.

From the 1870s, a further development appeared. While villainy remains the propelling force in melodrama, a new generation of dramatists, leagued with a handful of leading actors, devise a conflicted protagonist who, though criminal and frequently dissolute, longs desperately to perform good actions.

This role might be called the "divided hero-villain." The protagonist's chief struggle is within his divided or double-self to master his evil nature and to recover in himself some evidence of decency and good, a role reprising the earlier temperance melodrama, but now the stakes are higher because there is more at risk than domestic stability and health. Moreover, these plays are fueled by a growing scientific and lay interest in human psychology and awareness that there are deep fissures between outward behavior and inner lives. The hospital theatre and the public variety house – and even the family parlour where "mesmerism" was an occasional diversion – were venues where slippage between the outer and inner selves might be observed. Whether they were aware of Charcot's experiments with hypnosis or witnessed mesmerism as a variety-turn or party-trick, audiences knew that the inner being might be lured into the open to confront the outer self.

Henry Irving was among the first to bring inner division to the stage. As Mathias in Leopold Lewis's *The Bells* (1871),[20] he played an Alsatian burgomaster and loving parent whose apparent goodness conceals his murder of a helpless traveler. Mathias's crime is brought to light when dreams of a fairground mesmerist cause him to re-live and re-enact his crime. Irving continued his career with similar roles: Sir Edward Mortimer in George Colman the Younger's *The Iron Chest* (1879), Synorix in Alfred Tennyson's *The Cup* (1881), Mephistopheles in W. G. Wills's *Faust* (1885), and the joint roles of Lesurques and Dubosq in Charles Reade's *The Lyons Mail* (1877). Lesurques, a virtuous and innocent man, is mistaken for Dubosq, a murderer, and is tried and condemned for Dubosq's crimes; Mortimer and Synorix are lustful and murderous; Mephistopheles instigates criminal acts in others. Irving's characters were manipulative, cynical – the great Victorian moral failing – and ironic, but they had appealing public personae which misled their victims. Aware of the disturbing resonances between evil acts and hidden guilt, Irving made such roles deeply troubled, nursing longings for innocence and absolution.

Other melodramatists worked variations on the divided hero-villain. Henry Herman and Henry Arthur Jones's *The Silver King* (1882) gave Wilson Barrett the first of several roles in which he played a hero reclaimed from debauchery. "Toga" melodrama, melodramas set in the declining Roman Empire, pitting imperial Romans against early Christians, was an ideal milieu for Barrett to perform the sensual Roman patrician transformed and elevated by the Christian heroine and to confront topical issues relating to the British Empire, the "female question," and subversion of the state. Herman's *Claudian* (1883) and Barrett's *The Sign of the Cross* (1895) were two such toga-plays in which the villain became the hero.[21] T. Russell Sullivan adapted Robert Louis Stevenson's novelette *The Strange Case of*

Dr. Jekyll and Mr. Hyde for the American actor Richard Mansfield. Another novel with the divided hero-villain was George Du Maurier's *Trilby*, which Paul Potter dramatized and sold to the actor-manager Herbert Beerbohm Tree in 1895. Tree undertook the role of Svengali, a protagonist at once repellent and fascinating, dangerous, beguiling, and bestial, who possesses and dominates the soul, talent, and body of the artist's model and heroine. In such late-Victorian melodramas, moral legibility is complicated by the interest and pleasure which such disturbing hero-villains generate. Justice and equilibrium are eventually restored, virtue triumphs, but the processes of negotiating the "happy" ending exposes the spectator to his willingness to tolerate, and even relish, evil and the suffering of the innocent.

Concurrently, the single author manufacturing his or her own plays gave way to collaboration between pairs of dramatists in which each of the partners brought particular skills. The very act of writing hit after hit resembled an assembly-line where each worker bolts on prefabricated parts. A lengthy collaboration between George R. Sims and Henry Pettitt is a case in point. Sims, beginning with *The Lights o' London* (1881), was known for realistically depicting the seamy side of urban life. Pettitt, who had begun as a house-dramatist for the Conquest family and the Grecian Theatre, began a partnership with Sims with *In the Ranks* (1883), Sims devising the characters and basic narrative, Pettit the "strong situations" and more sensational effects. Late-Victorian melodrama was often the result of such collaborations, most notably those of Augustus Harris and Henry Hamilton, Harris and Pettit, Hamilton and Cecil Raleigh, and Raleigh and Seymour Hicks.

These collaborations were responsible for what became known as "autumn drama," the most elaborate melodramas of the late-nineteenth century and early decades of the twentieth. Autumn dramas were the creation of Augustus Harris, lessee of Drury Lane Theatre, who began in 1880 to offer melodramas notable for elaborate settings, large casts, and remarkable sensation effects.[22] Perhaps the best-known of these melodramas and the only one to survive to the present day in a silent motion picture is Hamilton and Raleigh's *The Whip* (1909).[23] In four acts *The Whip* – the title is a racehorse's name – has episodes depicting a horse show, the Chamber of Horrors at Tussaud's waxworks, pursuit of a train by automobile and the wrecking of that train as it ploughs into a railway horse-van supposedly carrying the horse, and a climactic derby at Newmarket.[24] Autumn dramas – the term melodrama is never employed in Drury Lane publicity – were introduced in September when London theatres reopened for the winter season and remained the theatre's principal attraction until late December, when the pantomime appeared. In April the current autumn drama was restaged and remained while the box office was favorable. Scenery and effects for the autumn drama were then reproduced in diminished sizes to fit smaller theatres for touring, casts were rehearsed, and "A," "B," "C," and "D" versions were sent on tour through Britain, the Empire, and America.

I close with the works of a family, the Melvilles, which appeared in the last decade of the nineteenth century and continued to be performed well into the twentieth century, perhaps into the 1930s. What is significant about the work of Frederick and Walter Melville is, first, that their plays continued to speak to current anxieties, especially the "new" or emancipated woman who competed in the workplace with men, sought and won suffrage, and determined her choice of sexual partners. Secondly, the Melville plays are important because they testify to the force of melodrama as a theatrical genre beyond the period traditionally associated with melodrama. Their popularity also identifies a new audience for melodrama: inhabitants of expanding suburbs surrounding British cities. Melville melodramas are "backlash" pieces expressing many of the lower-middle and working-class fears of unruly New Women and a patriarchal society in consequent disarray. Melville titles tell us as much: Walter's *The Worst Woman in London* (1899), *That Wretch of a Woman* (1901), *A Disgrace to Her Sex* (1904), *The Girl Who Wrecked His Home* (1907), and *The Shop-Soiled Girl* (1910), and Frederick's *In a Woman's Grip* (1901), *The Ugliest Woman on Earth* (1903), and *The Bad Girl of the Family* (1909). Some titles are teasers to attract audiences who, expecting the worst, are relieved to discover that Melville heroines – caught, on one hand, between a factual world of dead-end jobs, low pay, marriages to unsympathetic husbands, and too many children and, on the other hand, a mirage of unlimited freedom – cease their delinquency, preserve their virtue, and subsume into solid marriages with agreeable partners. That is how melodrama works.

The Melvilles have not been the subject of a significant study, and this oversight is still typical in many areas of melodrama. Much scholarship remains to be done – or to be done better than we have managed to date. I cannot but hope that readers are encouraged to explore further, to dig deeper, to regard melodrama with respect and enthusiasm and increasing understanding.

NOTES

1. John Fletcher, "To the Reader," one of the several prefaces to the published edition of *The Faithful Shepherdess* (London, 1611).
2. Martha Vicinus, " 'Helpless and Unfriended': Nineteenth Century Domestic Melodrama," in Judith L. Fisher and Stephen Watt (eds.), *When They Weren't Doing Shakespeare: Essays on Nineteenth Century British and American Theatre* (Athens: University of Georgia Press, 1989), pp. 174–86.

3. One of our better sources for the study of melodrama is Jerome K. Jerome's *Stage-Land: Curious Habits and Customs of Its Inhabitants*, illustrated by J. Bernard Partridge (London: Chatto & Windus, 1889), a role-by-role parody of the conventions and necessarily recurrent characters who inhabit Victorian melodrama.

4. David Mayer, *"The Ticket-of-Leave Man* in Context," *Essays in Theatre*, 6 (1987), 31–40.

5. In engravings, oil and watercolor paintings, and lithographic advertising posters and sheet-music covers as well as portrait photographs of actors posed as if performing melodramatic roles. Although, beginning from the 1860s, there are many thousands of photographs of actors costumed for roles, there are *no* photographs which actually show performance. Almost without exception, these were made in photographers' studios and were posed. Photographic technology had not progressed to the point where "action photography" could arrest motion.

6. See Michael Pisani's chapter on nineteenth-century theatre music above.

7. Henry Irving's assistant at the Lyceum Theatre, an astute observer of the late-Victorian theatre.

8. Percy Fitzgerald, *The Art of Acting in Connection with the Study of Character, the Spirit of Comedy and Stage Illusion* (London: Sonnenschein, 1892), pp. 50–57.

9. Peter Brooks, *The Melodramatic Imagination: Balzac, Henry James. Melodrama, and the Mode of Excess* (New York: Columbia University Press, 1985).

10. *Ibid.*, p. 43.

11. Sir Walter Scott, "Essay on the Drama," *Supplement to the Encyclopaedia Britannica*, 1819.

12. Simon Shepherd and Peter Womack, "Melodrama," in *English Drama, A Cultural History* (Oxford: Blackwell, 1996), pp. 188–218.

13. Daniel Gerould, "Melodrama and Revolution," in J. S. Bratton, Jim Cook, and Christine Gledhill (eds.), *Melodrama: Stage, Picture, Screen* (London: British Film Institute, 1994), pp. 185–98.

14. Michael R. Booth, *English Melodrama* (London: Jenkins, 1965), p. 14.

15. Thomas Postlewait, "From Melodrama to Realism: The Suspect History of American Drama," in Michael Hays and Anastasia Nikolopoulou (eds.), *Melodrama: The Cultural Emergence of a Genre* (New York: St. Martin's Press, 1996), pp. 39–60.

16. Katherine Newey, "Melodrama, Legitimacy, and 'The Condition-of-England Question,'" in Joanna Innes and Arthur Burns (eds.), *Rethinking the Age of Reform* (Cambridge: Cambridge University Press, 2002).

17. The plays mentioned are reproduced in microfiche facsimiles.

18. *The Streets of London* (1857), *Jessie Brown; or, the Relief of Lucknow* (1858), *The Flying Scud; or, Four-Legged Fortune* (1866), *Formosa; or, The Railroad to Ruin* (1869), *The Octoroon; or, Life in Louisiana* (1861), *The Shaughraun* (1874), *The Colleen Bawn* (1860).

19. The aesthetic principles and mechanisms for these effects are described in Percy Fitzgerald, *The World Behind the Scenes* (London: Chatto & Windus, 1881), pp. 1–112.

20. David Mayer, *Henry Irving and "The Bells": Henry Irving's Personal Text and Score* (Manchester: Manchester University Press, 1980).

21. David Mayer, *Playing Out the Empire: Ben-Hur and other Toga-Plays and Films, 1883–1908: A Critical Anthology* (Oxford: Clarendon Press, 1994).

22. Michael R. Booth, *Victorian Spectacular Theatre, 1850–1910* (London: Routledge, 1981).

23. The script to *The Whip* will appear in David Mayer and Stephen Johnson (eds.), *Spectacles of Themselves: Significant Melodramas Which Became Important Silent Films* (Westport, CT: Greenwood Press, forthcoming). Maurice Tourneur's 1916 silent film *The Whip* and Fred "Pimple" Evans's parody *Pimple's Whip* are being restored and reissued. Play and film are described in David Mayer, "Changing Horses in Mid-Ocean: *The Whip* in Britain and America," in Michael R. Booth and Joel H. Kaplan (eds.), *The Edwardian Theatre: Essays in Performance and the Stage* (Cambridge: Cambridge University Press, 1996), pp. 220–35.

24. Dennis Castle, *Sensation Smith of Drury Lane: The Biography of a Scenic Artist Extraordinary, Engineer and Inventor of Stage "Disasters," Soldier, Comedian, and Chelsea Casanova* (London: Skilton, 1984).

9

The music hall

The music hall is a specially Victorian institution. It came into existence as the queen was crowned, flowered with her reign, and entered the twentieth century ready to decline. Its heyday was roughly from 1890 to 1910. The first purpose-built halls for this kind of entertainment began to be erected in numbers in the early 1840s, with forerunners such as the Star at Bolton which opened in 1832. Signs of the end were the 1907 performers' strike and the 1912 Royal Command performance. During this period huge success attended the transformation of a multitude of small-scale entertainments presided over by pub proprietors and semi-professional chairmen into seriously capitalized big business that operated according to increasingly strictly enforced and eventually overdetermining rules. At first the growth of the halls provided a leisure service to growing urban populations, and enabled talented individuals to develop star careers and fortunes. Cultural change and aspiration, the broadening of the audience to include more segments of late-Victorian society, and concomitant moves to increase discipline and market control shifted power into the hands of business managers and investors. They spent venture capital on very large and sumptuously appointed auditoria laid out as theatres rather than "halls," transforming the audience/performer relationship; and they protected their investments, via the censorship of material and the contractual disciplining of performers to strict time limits on stage, and bound them to work more or less on demand for the contracting syndicate, while forbidding appearances elsewhere. The transformation resulted not only in the shifting character of the large halls themselves, as they developed into "variety theatres," but also the suppression of small independent halls; it eventually deracinated an institution which then failed to meet the challenge of further developments in the leisure industries.

The usual interpretations of this phenomenon range from the Whiggish popularism of "from pot-house to palace," celebrating the "good old days" of sing-songs and class solidarity, through wry recognition of the halls as a "culture of consolation" that kept the Victorian working man happy in his subservience, and beyond that to their wholesale condemnation as the seedbed of the jingoism, racism, and misogyny of yob culture.[1] My intention here is to replace the halls in the context of the dynamics of British performance during a crucial period in the formation of modern theatre and of attitudes toward its history. In this frame, the music hall has unique features – certain architectural and institutional innovations and formal, esthetic developments – but it is also to be understood in terms of larger cultural and institutional politics.

The music hall was the primary, but by no means the only, Victorian home of professional entertainment: singing and dancing, especially comic and sentimental songs sung by costumed performers "in character," overlapped with opera and operetta in upper-class venues; freaks and novelties, feats of strength and agility and technical mastery, whose exhibitors and practitioners also appeared in circuses, fairs and pleasure-gardens; and verbal and physical clowning, which it shared with farce and pantomime in popular theatres. After the 1843 Theatre Licensing Act any performance containing narrative, whether expressed in dialogue, song or dance, was supposed to be the preserve of the theatres, and throughout the century charges were brought against individual halls for encroachments on this right in the form of *ballets d'action*, spectacular and melodramatic scenas or comic sketches. These were essentially proprietorial turf wars: performers continued to sell their services to whoever wanted them, and audiences chose where to see them in terms of the price, the company, and the other amenities on offer at various venues. In London, where the potential audiences and profits were greatest but the licensing situation most complex, the struggle for audience share conducted through the prosecution of rivals transferred itself seamlessly from the major/minor battles of the previous half-century to attempts to forbid drama in the halls. Elsewhere the opponents of the growth of the halls might similarly be theatrical vested interests, as was the case for example in Sheffield, or rival publicans, as they were in Bolton. After the large halls became established institutions, in the 1860s, they were also assailed by successive waves of moral reform, whose target was drink or sexual immorality. As Dagmar Kift has shown, these largely ineffectual ideological attempts to suppress or discipline entertainment did not always differ as much as they claimed from the commercially driven rivalry of other public caterers: often personal and financial interests attempted to appropriate the developing powers of local government, ostensibly in the name of morality.[2] Nevertheless the cultural politics of pleasure and leisure was a multi-layered and important discourse, then as now, touching upon many significant beliefs and practices; a concentration of financial, class and gender issues made the halls a prime focus of Victorian identity-formation.

The halls were an extraordinary, and aberrant, development in the provision of entertainment. They may be seen as an unintentional consequence of the anti-theatrical prejudice as it was manifest in the early nineteenth century. In previous centuries in Britain professional clowns, tumblers, musicians, actors, and dancers were all part of the same professional group, all liable to legal and social stigmatization, and all competing for audience attention. The players and their writers sought to please educated and, they hoped, wealthy patrons; the managers resorted to the appeal of less intellectual performances when they found it paid better. Patrons and moralists argued the good and evil effects of acting, music, and bodily display, with the drama always easier to defend, but never, in practice, possible to sever from the less easily appropriated pleasures of song and dance. This is an enduring dynamic, and manifested itself across the whole range of performance style and venue, from opera house or patent theatre to barn, inn or fairground booth. From around 1790, however, the concentration of populations in an industrializing society led to the growth of large, often cheap performance venues and hence of competition which challenged established hierarchies, and favored the "lower" entertainment forms, available to all classes, if spurned by some. Dominant opinion was that dramatic performance was losing ground to mindless, lascivious and degrading spectacle. In an attempt to repel the encroachment of low entertainment and to convince moralists of the innocence and utility of the drama, campaigns were mounted to reform theatrical licensing and thus to enable modern, middle-class taste to reform the stage itself, and so "restore" the privileged position of the written play over all other performance forms. The 1843 Act intended to abstract the serious play from its place within the matrix of entertainment, free it from pollution and defend it from competition, and render it answerable to a modern, respectable idea of Art. The rest was rejected, and left to be simply policed by the magistracy, through music and dancing licensing. The division did not and could not work in artistic terms, and just as music halls staged kinds of drama, non-dramatic performances continued to take place in many theatres alongside or as part of plays, and many entertainers moved across the barriers thus created, developing their skills as they always had in collaboration with the whole theatrical world. But the unanticipated result was that the music hall, already in process of formation in response to growing demand from expanding urban audiences, received a license to develop separately from the legitimate stage, which in holding itself aloof from contamination ceased to influence the taste of those who chose to go elsewhere. The distinction between the theatrical and the popular audience was not of course absolute, and many people were part of both; but the distinction was significant in shaping the core activity of the halls. They addressed themselves to an audience of working and lower-middle-class men and women, especially those under thirty-five with disposable income, and middle- and upper-class men who rejected or were evading dominant conventional morality, accompanied by prostitutes rather than by women of their own class.[3] The music-hall audience excluded the respectable, aspirant middle class altogether, until the managerial changes at the end of the century sought to include them, and undercut the extraordinary culture of unalloyed entertainment that had developed in the absence of straight plays and puritans.

A number of existing kinds and institutions of entertainment fed into the early music hall. Everyone from street ballad-singers to the boy choristers hired by gentlemen's supper clubs provided models, materials and personnel for the increasingly voracious new venues. They drew on leisure practices like informal tavern sing-songs, which had modulated in town public houses into "free and easy" nights where a group of local people, more or less known to each other, gathered to sing, increasingly aided by a paid pianist and a chairman. The new music-hall venue also drew on professional musical entertainments staged in concert halls or in pleasure grounds such as the venerable Vauxhall Gardens, augmented by many new sites of that kind in the expanding areas of housing; on dance halls; on the novelties and excitements offered in saloon theatres built onto pubs – often illegally, in London, but with official local support elsewhere; and, most obviously of all, but most often overlooked, on the established theatres, the stage. When the inspectors from the Metropolitan Board of Works began to be alarmed at the sudden building boom in London in the 1840s, where publicans were throwing up in haste what seemed huge and unsafe structures to house their expanding entertainments, the step change they registered was from the (amateur) singing room to the (professional) theatrical space, marked by the provision of a room – often no more than the space under the stage, but still a room – in which performers could change into *costume*.[4] As the new licensing laws strove to discriminate between dramatic venues and the rest, professional performers flooded out into amateur spaces, and a new mix began to crystallize.

The earliest halls showed this mix very clearly. It began with the imperative that a hall should serve its local community: the caterer had little hope of drawing an audience from beyond the surrounding neighborhood, and so the successful pioneers were men and women who could take a leading place in that society, and generate goodwill, credit and social esteem for themselves and their enterprise. This meant that in the packed, shallowly balconied auditorium, where admission was often free or paid for by buying drinks, many kinds of social and performative interactions took place. The chairman, who might well be the proprietor in person, conducted proceedings from a table set across the hall below the platform; his welcome included guests who sat with him, rambled in and out, made up parties at other tables, leant on the bar, or stood craning to see from the back of the gallery. Many patrons liked to feel they were personal guests: the local tradesmen or their sons who had business dealings with the hall expected free entrance, even a "face pass" – recognition by the doorkeeper, a coveted mark of distinction.[5]

> The audience is unique. Everybody seems to know everybody. The gentlemen shake hands heartily, all round, the ladies embrace and kiss each other, and on all sides may be heard affectionate enquiries after the little ones at home, or other friends and acquaintances . . . the audience . . . appear to constitute quite a happy family.[6]

The elevated but not necessarily very large space of the stage itself was only differentially lit by the addition of a few footlights, although it could be made a focus by decorative effects – there was a rising, competitive tide of splendor in the statements made by the décor of the hall, and the stage was naturally dressed up. So, however, were the room, and the patrons: mirrors added glitter and excitement to performance both on stage and off. There were sparkling stages, like the mirrored apse behind the platform at Wilton's in Wellclose Square, London; but also much light and mirroring in the body of the hall. In Manchester the old Folly was mirrored throughout when it was renamed the Tivoli in 1897; as early as 1872 the Middlesex in London was thus lined to give the young men and women dressed up for a night out "abundant opportunities for self-admiration."[7] The stage space itself was not always exclusively appropriated to the professional entertainers, and could be used to elevate local heroes who received benefits when they were struck by calamities, or when, on happier holidays, they took part in competitions, and went forward to say their piece or receive their winnings. But the pressure was in the direction of professionalization, and the bar-room or street performers of previous decades made the transition to full professional status in the new halls, and removed themselves from the community to mix with incoming theatricals in the sub-stage dressing room before making their appearance. On stage, of course, the link to the audience had to be remade. The first moment relied on the chairman in his introduction, which was calculated in the interests of the house; on the good will of the bandsmen, which probably depended on the performer's ability to tip; and on the visual impact of the entry, in immaculate or outrageous clothing.[8] Thereafter the audience-participation chorus song, the exchange of banter, and ultimately the ability to sing or dance or stand on your head so well as to win attention from the competing claims of food and drink, noise, friends and interruptions were the professional tools of the trade – and these came out of the theatrical kit.

Local variations in successful entertainment were quite distinctive: in the north of England the plebeian but complex skill of clogdancing, for example, at a highly polished, competitive level which supported large wagers, was a staple music-hall turn that never found a place in the south, where the audience had no clogs of their own. The sucking-in of street performance styles meant the transfer to the stage of songs from tradition, whether oral or broadside, and some visiting commentators remarked on what seemed to them the incongruous juxtapositions of scantily clad women doing step-dances and singing protracted, ancient, tragic ballads in a rustic style; but others at the time and more recently have seen the music-hall song style as rapidly extinguishing an ancient tradition of folk song.[9] But such appropriations and exchanges were nothing new in the web of performance; ideological discriminations seek to divide up the creative processes, but professional performers will use anything that works. The ballads and morris steps joined "nigger minstrel" images from America and song styles, skills and "novelties" from centuries of stage practice, part of the endless continuum which developed into a distinctive music-hall style under the creative pressure of new conditions and audiences. A very similar voraciousness, and disregard for purity of origin or authenticity of traditions high or low, attends the bricolage culture of the new media today.

From the 1860s the distinctive performance space and style of the music halls was thus established as one point within a network of professional entertainments. In provincial cities and the various districts of London the older, smaller free and easies, the singing saloons and the dance halls licensed for music, still throve alongside and fed into the larger, more highly developed and professionalized halls. The single public auditorium in smaller provincial centres could still be used for classical concerts as well as popular ones; traveling music-hall entertainers could find a booking, or bring their own concert party to town hall or music room. And dramatically licensed popular theatres, in London as well as beyond, continued to use singers, dancers and novelty acts as part of their mixed bill of entertainment, within and alongside the drama, as a matter of course. In Sheffield, Thomas Youdan fought attempts to suppress full-scale drama within his Surrey Music Hall, and eventually continued the same mix under a full theatre license. The Britannia at Hoxton was forced to apply to the Lord Chamberlain in the 1840s, but continued to stage a mixed bill throughout its life. Sadler's Wells, one of London's oldest entertainment houses, which had been appropriated by Samuel Phelps for Shakespeare and drama after the 1843 Act, was rescued from decline by the music-hall showman George Belmont in 1893.[10] Some small, unfashionable halls continued with the mixed bill unmolested until they were effectively destroyed by the syndicate barring clauses (see p. 164 above). In the West End of London, on the other hand, the much larger and more differentiated audience pool made for a long spectrum of venues, but even so many of them booked performers who on other occasions appeared in the halls, before other audiences. The minstrel shows at the St. James's Hall, Piccadilly, on whose programs music-hall black-face stars like E. W. Mackney appeared as guests, prided themselves on an audience that included many moral people who would not enter a music hall,[11] while Drury Lane enabled middle-class families to take their children to see comic stars of the halls such as Dan Leno, booked annually from 1888 to 1903 to play the dame in the pantomime.

The Gaiety, the upper-class burlesque house founded on cross-dressed musical entertainment, catering for the unregenerate male audience who rejected or escaped from the grip of educational Shakespeare, often sought to recruit its stars from those discovered by the music halls. And there were big West-End music halls, charging high prices and in some cases giving an individual style of program – the Alhambra in Leicester Square is the most obvious instance, where a variety bill was always coupled with one or more in-house music-and-dance spectaculars – which were show business at its most commercialized. They nevertheless had their own sectional, even "local" audience, occupying the auditorium in their own way, and finding a mixture of entertainments there. These famously included excessive drinking and prostitution, but their apologists, like the racing-paper journalist J. B. Booth, claimed that the notorious Empire promenade was chiefly a gentleman's club, a place where "men went not so much for the entertainment as for companionship . . . of other men. . . . When one said good-bye to a friend on his way to India, China or Singapore . . . his last words were: 'So long, old man, see you in London again. Sure to run across you in the Empire.' "[12] Booth claims that the West-End halls, during what seemed to him the great days, the 1880s and 90s, were as much a community resource as were those in the working-class districts, for the

> last idea with which one turned into a hall – whether it was the Pavilion, or the Empire, the Tivoli, or the Alhambra – somewhere about nine, was the idea of sitting penned in one's stall amongst total strangers. Each hall had its habitués . . . and there were subtle distinctions. The black-coated, white-shirted, silk-hatted crowd of young "bloods" who filled the promenades of the great Leicester Square houses in the "intervals" differed vastly from those found in the Strand or Piccadilly Circus; but in each crowd there was an intimacy, the intimacy born of coteries which frequently met and whose aim is to enjoy life.[13]

This intimacy was fostered by participatory rituals, in themselves an exercise of power relations across the footlights. The gallery "boys" were supposedly kept in check by the chairman's authority, but had a right to their fun – so a dancer, especially a woman, could be forced to respond to cries of "over!" by turning cartwheels, and even star performers like George Chirgwin might find themselves saddled with the demand always to repeat a song the gallery had fixed upon. House customs developed, like that at the suburban, lower-class South London Palace, where whenever the chairman, Bob or "Baron" Courtney, sang his only song, a patriotic number called "Britannia's Voice of Thunder," they chanted "Good Old Bob! Bob! Bob!" incessantly throughout.[14] Audience scripts existed in the West-End halls too: the Pavilion favorite G. H. Macdermott in the 1870s had a song whose chorus ended "I'll stand glasses round; how much can you drink?" to which the gleefully mendacious audience response was "Not much!"[15]

Performance in the halls

In such a situation of known and expected performance and participation, a distinctive style was fostered. Commentators on the politics of the halls have focused on the song lyrics, using printed texts as evidence; but while comic singing was perhaps the backbone of music-hall entertainment, it was not its sole resource, and the songs should be considered in their setting of clowning, spectacle and parodic cross-readings. The sheet music, often fronted with wonderfully evocative colored engravings of the singer in costume, was an expensive artifact – a single song could cost four shillings, sixteen times the cost of admission to a cheap hall – and one aimed at a different group, the drawing-room singer. The songs deemed suitable, and no doubt often cleaned up, for this market, do not form a representative cross-section of what was actually sung in the halls. To redress the analytical imbalance, what follows describes the major ingredients of the typical music-hall bill during the 1870s, 80s and 90s under three headings: drama, comic song, and "speciality" acts, which I assume, for convenience, to include dance and clowning as well as all sorts of physical feats. It must be understood that a single bill interleaved all these, and often a single turn used more than one such skill.

Drama in the music halls

The enactment of narratives was always entangled with demarcation disputes between the halls and other, often less successful, theatrical enterprises. Many plays were nevertheless seen on the music-hall stage, and their surviving songs, and reviewers' descriptions – often the only available evidence, since they were not required to supply copies for licensing to the Lord Chamberlain's office until 1912[16] – suggest a dramatic style both traditional and innovative. Arguably, these little plays had something not found in the protected legitimate theatre: a vigor that stemmed from synergy with the rest of the entertainment spectrum. The dramas carry antique formal elements forward into the halls – there is a discernible continuum from the *lazzi* of the ancient improvised farce into the comic ballet or song-sketch – but they are also in some sense at the political cutting edge, where current attitudes are revealed and even challenged by their parodic music-hall incarnation.

The basic form was the two or three-handed domestic farce, which could be conducted entirely in song and dance, and which explored the old comedy of relations between the sexes and between classes, that is masters and servants.[17]

The music-hall representation of sexual relationships was material rather than romantic, and concerned itself with marriage, mastery and money rather than just wooing and winning. Male/female duos danced or sang or merely burlesqued the battle of the sexes, moving rapidly on from lovebirds to warring husband and wife to suffragette and policeman; and whatever the ostensible coupling, it was tipped into farce and often violence by its physical extremity: "Les Leons, duettists and comiques . . . introduced the gigantic gentleman in petticoats and the petite lady in the garb of a masher . . . the sight of the very small male making love to the very large female excited much laughter"[18] Real boxers sometimes did exhibition matches as turns, but the dramatized battle was a longer-lasting attraction: a choreographed knock-down fight, framed as fiction, became a beloved music-hall act in it is own right. The apache dance, a lurid enactment of sexuality, jealousy and violence, was danced, straight or in knockabout burlesque, by many duos, the man representing a knife-wielding petty criminal and the woman his unfaithful partner, both supposedly the dregs of the slums of Paris. The famous fight scene from the melodrama *Humanity* required an elaborate set of a collapsing staircase on which a betrayed husband and his wife's lover, in evening dress, fought themselves to a standstill and the set to shreds.[19]

Drama was accorded no special treatment in the halls; its narrative excitement and perhaps its realism could be relished, but audiences did not expect carefully preserved illusion, especially at the expense of other pleasures. Boucicault's racing drama *The Flying Scud* was condensed for the halls with a girl, Nellie Wilson, playing a stableboy; the *Era* reviewer suggests that the audience took her oddly nautical costume in their stride, but were disappointed when she declined to halt the action and perform her speciality top-boot dance. Similarly star turns would act, but saw no reason to compromise their personal image for the sake of the role: Jennie Hill, playing against an impressive revolving scene of Irish landscape in a potted version of *The Shaughraun*, chose to wear a smart "red hunting coat, velvet cap, knee breeches and riding boots" to impersonate Conn.[20] Such motley performances, which class-hostile critics derided as crude incongruity and failure of realism in music-hall plays, actually demanded a sophisticated response, what Peter Davison calls the "multiconscious apprehension" of popular theatre, to their rapidly alternating perspectives, demanding that the audience switch between emotional involvement, technical appreciation, and knowing disengagement.[21] The result is most obvious in music-hall versions of patriotic melodrama:

> in the third scene – Rorke's Drift . . . he is seen potting Kaffirs by the half-dozen, and he is very nearly assegaied by one of them, but is saved by his mortally wounded comrade Tom Green, who is fortunately able to exert sufficient strength to fire his rifle. The savages calm down while Private Travers breaks the monotony of the desert campaign by a song in praise of the British flag . . . Mr G. H. Macdermott [as Travers] . . . is really very funny.

The villain in this piece is "a rich scoundrel in possession of the lands" of his "honest ne'er-do-well" half-brother Travers, and of course he happens to be an officer in the same campaign. At the end, against a "splendid revolving set," "The howls of the gods as he stands cursing over the prostrate form of Mr. Macdermott set the seal on Mr. Day's success" in this role.[22] When the sketch-deviser tells an imperialist story for performers with established personae unlike Macdermott's patriotic heroism, an extraordinary critique of jingoist self-justifications may suddenly emerge. Athol Mayhew devised *In Darkie's Africa* for the brothers Mac, "Irish comedians and knockabouts," with the assistance of the Avolo boys as monkeys doing their gymnastic act on a grove of huge bamboo.

> Brother Mike Mac is the intrepid explorer, who enters upon his duties in Equatorial Africa with all his impedimenta in a child's mail-cart. Brother Joe is the noble "brown" savage, grown fat and scant of breath, with a black wig and a face soiled apparently with the unburnished livery of soot. The latter disguises himself as an alligator, and then, appearing as the untutored savage, indulges in a parley with the explorer, who, rifle in hand, is apparently prepared to shoot at anything. The comic business really commences when the two brothers affect to recognize each other, and start some of their well-known knockabout business. (*The Era*, April 1893)

This clowning is richly suggestive of the music-hall intervention in imperialist discourse: it burlesques triumphalist versions of the invasion of Africa, the heroic tales of explorers pitted against alligators and savages, and also the contradictory nineteenth-century visions of black races as noble and as savage. It is founded upon the parodic expedient of *reductio ad absurdum* – the child's cart, the little comedian as noble explorer, the fat one as a (Hamletesque) savage in a minstrel wig and exaggerated cheap make-up – but also upon the play of ideas around the known brotherhood of the performers; and it resolves into their "well-known" act, satisfying the demand for the expected entertainment (as Nellie Wilson in the example above failed to do) as well as the novelty of the sketch and its new, pointed jokes.

In the period from the South African War to the First World War commentators have stressed the mindless jingoism of music-hall displays of patriotism; Laurence Senelick suggests that the Toryism of the big business and brewing interests that controlled the halls economically imposed a view of imperial politics that alienated the lower-class patrons, and that this contributed to the decline of the halls. Others have asserted that jingoistic songs shared a bill with surviving parodies that express exactly the opposite sentiments, apparently to the approval of the self-same audiences that applauded the patriotic claptraps.[23] This may perhaps be explicable in terms of a distinction that should be made between material presented in West-End halls patronized by "society" men and that acceptable to audiences elsewhere; but in any case such contradictions are often part of communal response. One of the discursive functions of entertainment is to hold the common opinion together by containing contradictions without forcing them into conflict. The Irish brothers Mac in their dramatic sketch were able to send up the empire – as long as they did their knockabout clowning too. No such formally generated complexity of meaning was available to the legitimate stage.

Music-hall songs

Thus, gradually the Sol's Arms melts into the shadowy night, and then flares out of it strong in gas. The harmonic meeting hour arriving, the gentleman of professional celebrity takes the chair; is faced (red-faced) by Little Swills; their friends rally round them, and support first-rate talent. . . . The landlord . . . finding Little Swills so popular, commends him highly to the Jurymen and the public; observing that, for a song in character, he don't know his equal, and that that man's character-wardrobe would fill a cart. . . . In the zenith of the evening, Little Swills says, Gentlemen, if you'll permit me, I'll attempt a short description of the scene of real life that came off here today. Is much applauded and encouraged; goes out of the room as Swills; comes as the Coroner (not the least in the world like him); describes the Inquest, with recreative intervals of piano-forte accompaniment to the refrain – With his (the Coroner's) tippy tol li doll, tippy tol lo doll, tippy tol li doll, Dee![24]

Thus Dickens in chapter 11 of *Bleak House,* 1852–53, capturing the moment of transition, as it occurred in hundreds of public houses, from a group of friends singing to the appearance within the (virtual and material) ritual space of the community – the advertised harmonic meeting, the public room also used for such business as coroner's inquests – of the professional singer, with a "character-wardrobe would fill a cart."[25] The step-change pinpointed by the Metropolitan Buildings Inspectors, the erection of accommodation for a larger audience with a place for the celebrity to don his character dress, followed inevitably upon this professionalizing, theatricalizing shift. To get a closer view of the unique artistic creation of the halls, it may therefore be more fruitful, instead of entering into the more usual ideological debates about its relation to a putative "folk" music, to look at the comic character song's theatrical origins.

Dickens, despite working his own comic/grotesque transformations on the inquest in the paragraphs leading up to this description, suggests that the music-hall representation of "the scene of real life" is ludicrously unrealistic, with a crude attempt at impersonation, in a stereotypical costume presumably drawn from stock – a judge's robe? – and a topical song provided with a traditional participatory refrain. Stage entertainers had been offering such impersonation time out of mind, and the art had been very popular throughout the century. Its best known exponent was Charles Mathews the elder, a friend of Dickens's. At a time when it was death to the highest ambitions of a performer to appear outside the "legitimate," Mathews strained against the limiting roles for which he could be cast in five-act comedy. In 1817 the dramatist Colman wrote for him a short play called *The Actor of All Work* in which he enacted six different parts in quick succession, a feat which developed into the "protean" music-hall quick-change act. Mathews then side-stepped into solo shows, doing impressions of famous judges, politicians and other public figures, and of his legitimate colleagues, past and present, and developing new characters in song and patter from observation of everyday life on the streets. He had a discriminating eye for the absurdities of the developing range of middle-class self-presentation, and his variations upon the ordinary Englishman as well as Scotch fishwives, Irish coachees and Frenchmen with fractured English and, most famously, his pioneering impersonation of a poor African-American, were great fashionable hits. Sixty years on, the work of middle-class self-definition was continued by the music-hall singers. Successors to Mathews's contrasting types were presented by humbler performers like Fred Wilson, whose 1877 act offered a song and a dance in each of four characters: "a deserted Irish wife," "a Chinaman," "a German" and "an aged Negro," as well as stars like Alfred

Vance whose provincial solo show transferred into London music hall. In 1880 his usual finish of style, elegance of dress and "power of illustrating character" were deployed first on "two old girls that were anything but beautiful," then on "a swell of the toothpick and crutch order," then "a jolly old joker" and finally "a Margate bathing woman."[26]

Mathews's status worries did not afflict the performers brought up in the minor theatres before 1843. Those performers who had the talent to stretch and play with the theatrical frame exploited their stage personae and developed songs and character impersonations freely. The Adelphi stars John Reeve and James Wilkinson, for example, accumulated favorite characters from successive plays so that they could invoke them, at their own whim or that of the audience, in any evening's entertainment thereafter. Reeve reached stardom via his frame-breaking, ad-libbing stage persona in 1823 in a topical adaptation called *The Quadrupeds* that allowed him to parody Kean, poke fun at horse dramas and sing comic songs. Wilkinson had an array of topical songs in the role of Logic in the hit dramatisation of Pierce Egan's *Tom and Jerry; or, Life in London* in 1821, including a hymn to various London haunts, to the air "Carnival of Venice," which is very obviously an ancestor of the music-hall topical song:

> Tis fashions lounge, Tis beauties bower
> Tis art's selected depot;
> Tis fancy's mart, industry's bower,
> Tis London's raree show.
> The Opera cannot with it vie
> Despite its colonnade,
> Then let's to Piccadilly hie,
> to Burlington Arcade.
>
> (W. T. Moncrieff, *Tom and Jerry; or,
> Life in London*, 2nd edn (London:
> Thomas Richardson, n.d. [1828],
> p. 20))

In this play even the minor player Chapman had a cameo role of the kind that was to transfer to the halls. As Jack the gaslight man he had a song in character, beginning "I'm saucy Jack the gaslight man, I put the prigs to rout." Such performances simply spilled from the confines of the theatres into the growing network of song rooms and harmonic meetings, and fueled the growth of the characteristic music-hall turn.

Typically a turn would include two or three "characters." In February 1880 the humble first turn Marie Beecher was singing as Rose the parlormaid and as a Jolly Jack Tar; in the summer of 1895 the three sisters

Oliver presented "the girls of the new brigade" as New Women in "rational" costume, changed to appear as chorus girls from the Gaiety, and finished as "coons," i.e., blacked up, with "a smart dance."[27] The origin of such material, drawn by stage writers and composers from all kinds of roots, is less important than its formal suitability as a vehicle for a kaleidoscopic, participatory, intensely personalized picture of contemporary life, which had a powerful role in the structure of feeling of the Victorian period. The character song is more supple than the narrative ballad: it comments on current events of greater and lesser importance – the latest hairstyle, the ticket of leave, the Boer war, the lady cricketer – or on eternal themes of love and power, in a known but malleable structure. Its heart is the chorus, in the early decades set up for participation by the audience, and therefore often in an easier key or time signature than the verses. These tend to be self-contained, and while each of them may tell a little story, none of them has necessarily to be included. So a song not going well can be cut off short; a hit chorus can be exploited afresh by the addition of new and topical verses. The ubiquitous, infuriating popular chorus manifested itself as early as T. D. Rice's "Jim Crow," whose refrain was sung and danced in the London theatres and streets in 1836, and by the time Kipling arrived in London in the 1880s could inspire his story in which the House of Commons sing "The village that voted the *Earth* was flat" until they drop exhausted, because they cannot stop.[28]

Recent cultural studies approaches to the content of these music-hall songs have focused upon a conspicuous concern with class impersonation, the real or fake "swell" whose life story and style presented the dreams, the swagger and the uncertainty of the Victorian clerk or shopman for his own delectation, whether to imitate or deride. The sometimes complex performance dynamic generated by such parodic and at the same time attractive visions as Leybourne's Champagne Charlie and Vesta Tilley's "Piccadilly Johnnie with the little glass eye" has begun to be explored.[29] Character song is also rich in self-conscious presentations of people by local or national type, as if community identities, especially those within the British Isles, needed endlessly to be re-presented, defined and approved or laughed away: transforming regional dialects and song styles by the hegemonic music-hall model, the stage Irishman, the Scot, the northerner, the Welsh girl, and, in many variations and guises, the cockney, became roles rehearsed on stage and accepted or modified by the audience, in a laboratory of style, sentiment and self-confidence. The mixed metropolitan audience, thus interpellated, saw itself reflected and perhaps coerced into conformity to what we might take to be an early version of the consumerist illusion of individuality through choice.

The speciality acts

If the character song was about "us," the self-definition of the audience, the music-hall bill always also contained representations of the other; and just as the self-presentation might sometimes be critical, and set down some too self-satisfied members of the audience, so the spin given to difference and otherness was by no means always derogatory: the amazing and the peculiar were sought after and admired. The fairground sideshow and the circus act became music-hall turns, and ancient subjects of wonder – so-called "freaks" such as dwarfs and Siamese twins – appeared there alongside monkey parachutists, reptile conquerors, globe runners, shadowgraphists, roller skaters, electric frogs, feet equilibrists or white kangaroos.

It could be said that the "coon" acts were the particular music-hall development of the exploitation of otherness. They were certainly among the most regularly appearing staple acts, to be found on almost every bill at halls great and small throughout the period. Modern scholarship has begun to explore the complex meanings attaching to these racial impersonations; the most comprehensive work has been in placing the minstrel show in the crucible of American identity-formation.[30] In Britain the meanings were inevitably different, as the situation on the streets and in the imaginary of Britain differed from that of America. The freedom of the mask, in which identity was figuratively subsumed and literally disguised, and the constraints of Victorian Britishness were set aside, allowed many tyro entertainers their first steps on the halls, and also built up an extravagant repertoire of jokes, sentiments and suggestions tacitly available to both audience and performer that, it has been suggested, offered a valuable free space for the play of the unspeakable.[31] The act described above, in which two Irish knockabout clowns burlesqued African exploration, perhaps suggests some of the extraordinary mix of implications of blackface. Jokes about the imperialist discourse, that nevertheless confirm white superiority, mingled with slapstick clowning and an admired physical skill honed by the brothers act and well known to the audience.

Physical skills carried to a high level of polish were some of the most important elements of music hall, as they were of the circus; and, as had been the case for centuries, a large international pool of artistes was available to offer such non-verbal acts. The halls took in the ancient arts of acrobatics and gymnastics, from contortionists to living statues, trapeze artists to weightlifters; and they housed dance and music-making of all kinds, whether the operatic prima donna, the salterino player or the organophoniconium. If the music hall drew in the showman and his novelties (including the seeds of change in the form of the cinematograph), it also provided audiences for deep-rooted traditional families of entertainers, whose skills were honed and hoarded down many generations of exhibitors. The Lupino family, for example, supplied a "screaming comic ballet" to London halls in the 1880s, but their ancestors had been theatre pantomimists and acrobats in the previous century and their descendants were dancers and film-makers in the next. The music-hall transformation was usually in the direction of speed, "smartness," an added professionalism and a sharpening up, especially as the organization and investment developed, and a standardized product for the market was required. The world-famous clown Grock and his partner, already at the height of circus fame, auditioned for a fat contract with a German music-hall syndicate in 1911, only to be told "You're too broad . . . Tone it down and suit your stuff to variety." To save their careers they developed a whole new act in a hurry, "altogether on a smaller scale, much more sharply defined" with no ad libs, "everything cut and dried," involving an aria from *Traviata*, a fiddle that chirruped, a *jodel* and dance.[32]

Conclusion

Grock gives this anecdote an upbeat outcome: his engagement at a huge salary to perform exclusively for the powerful syndicate. George Belmont, the inventor of two-houses-a-night, was equally sanguine when he told a reporter profiling him in 1894 that

> the bar will play an ever-lessening part in the future of the music hall. For his own part he is absolutely opposed to the man who drops in for a drink or a chat with the proprietor or a manager. Such a person generally wants to come in "on the nod" and his custom is more trouble than it is worth. The tendency of the public is to visit a music hall in search of a variety entertainment, and for no other object.[33]

But however rewarding the evolving variety system was to the most successful performers and proprietors, the new contractual and performance relationships marked the death of the Victorian music hall. Small independent owners were squeezed out; minor performers were progressively bound into contracts that trapped them in low-paid subordination; even the stars were forced to adjust their performances to a code that rendered them up, prompt and innocuous. The chairman and his convivial guests gave way to a printed program of numbered and timed turns. The aspiration of the large syndicates and expensive new London halls was to serve a wider audience. J. B. Booth describes Sir Alfred Butt, the successor to the "father of the halls" Charles Morton at the Palace Theatre, bringing there Pavlova and the Russian ballet, and potted dramas starring Beerbohm Tree or George

Alexander, to mix with the performing seals. Booth claimed the Palace had artistic, social and musical *cachet*; he regarded it as a wonder worthy of remark that Sir Harry Lauder, about to depart on an Australian tour, persuaded "the smartest and most fastidious audience in London" at the Palace to join in a chorus of "Auld Lang Syne."[34] The hall was the site of the first Royal Command Variety performance, in 1912. Booth alludes vaguely to the jealousy and heartache that was generated; he does not specify what caused it, but two stories have passed into legend – the undoubted fact that Marie Lloyd was deemed too unreliable and vulgar to appear, and the rumor that when Vesta Tilley appeared in her usual immaculate male costume, the ladies of the royal party were instructed by the queen to avert their eyes. The real life of the music hall was over.

Its memory, of course, has lived on, one of the highly charged myths of British theatre history. As the institution came to its apogee, and its inevitable onrushing decline caught the attention of *fin-de-siècle* writers and artists such as Kipling, F. Anstey, Max Beerbohm, Arthur Symons, Arnold Bennett, and Walter Sickert, it entered into the British imaginary as a lost golden age of simple good cheer and sentiment. As such it can still be invoked by a litany of names: Our Marie, Little Tich, the George Robey – or by the remembered lilt of a few of the songs and their catchphrase choruses – "It's a great big shame, but if she belonged to me . . . ," or "A little of what you fancy does you good!" The halls have come to be a glittering, warm, tinkling projection of "the world we have lost," and as such are an outstanding instance of the discourse of the popular: a site of national nostalgia probably more powerful, certainly more widely cherished and mourned, than folk song, on the one hand, or the rest of the theatre of the nineteenth century, on the other. A fuller understanding of their material life depends on the re-situating of this mythical topos within the wider context of performance and cultural history.

NOTES

1. For a survey of music-hall scholarship past and present, see Dagmar Kift, *The Victorian Music Hall: Culture, Class and Conflict* (Cambridge: Cambridge University Press, 1996), pp. 17–35.
2. *Ibid.*, pp. 77–134.
3. *Ibid.*, pp. 62–68, 136.
4. See John Earl, "The Metropolitan Buildings Office and the First Music Halls," *Nineteenth Century Theatre* 28, 1 (Summer 2000), 5–25.
5. Peter Bailey, "Business and Good Fellowship in the London Music Hall," revised version in Peter Bailey, *Popular Culture and Performance in the Victorian City* (Cambridge: Cambridge University Press, 1998), pp. 80–100.
6. *The Era*, 18 February 1877, review of Deacon's in Islington, which was further praised for the low price of its drinks.

7. G. J. Mellor, *The Northern Music Hall* (Newcastle upon Tyne: Frank Graham, 1970), p. 25; Bailey, "Business," p. 116, quoting *The Era*, 6 June 1872.

8. Only marginally on the material – almost anything would serve, if it was put across well. Kipling's story about writing a music-hall song captures the crucial moment admirably, though he, in the persona of an anxious songwriter, attributes it to the success of the number itself: "Then came the chorus and the borrowed refrain. It took – it went home with a crisp click" as the guardsmen in the gallery joined in and sang. ("My Great and Only," January 1890, see *The Sussex Edition of the Complete Works in Prose and Verse of Rudyard Kipling*, 35 vols. (London: Macmillan & Co., 1937–39), XXIX: 259–67.)

9. For the oral ballad and scantily clad singers, see Philaster, "Low Singing Rooms" – MS held at Manchester Public Library; Thomas Hardy lamented the extinction of folk singing in Dorset by the coming of music-hall songs via the railway, in the 1840s; see Florence Emily Hardy, *The Early Life of Thomas Hardy 1840–1891* (London: Macmillan, 1928), pp. 25–26; Dave Harker angrily echoes that regret in "Joe Wilson: 'Comic Dialectal Singer' or Class Traitor?," in J. S. Bratton (ed.), *Music Hall: Performance and Style* (Milton Keynes: Open University Press, 1986), pp. 111–30. Kift, *Victorian Music Hall*, pp. 53–54 and *passim*, makes the opposite assumption, that "folk songs" were simply sung in the halls alongside more modern song forms.

10. Kift, *Victorian Music Hall*, pp. 89–96; Dennis Arundell, *The Story of Sadler's Wells 1683–1877* (Newton Abbot: David & Charles, 1965), p. 173.

11. "Strait-laced people who even barred the ordinary theatre patronised St. James's Hall", Frederick Reynolds, *Minstrel Memories* (London, 1928), p. 104.

12. J. B. Booth, *Old Pink'un Days* (London: Richards Press, 1924), pp. 317–18.

13. *Ibid.*, pp. 335–36.

14. J. B. Booth, *Pink Parade* (London: Thornton Butterworth Ltd., 1933), p. 133.

15. *Ibid.*, p. 130.

16. David Cheshire, *Music Hall in Britain* (Newton Abbott: David & Charles, 1974), p. 94; Cheshire also quotes Henry Arthur Jones complaining in a letter to the press in 1910 that "150,000 illegal performances of stage-plays" (p. 92), took place annually in music halls. John Russell Stephens in *The Censorship of English Drama 1824–1901* (Cambridge: Cambridge University Press, 1980), p. 188, n. 2, notes that the music hall was outside the Lord Chamberlain's remit as censor, and that both the 1866 and 1892 parliamentary reports recommended that this state of affairs should be ended. There are many short sketches in the Lord Chamberlain's collection from after 1912, but their linkage to performance in the halls is not established; see Lois Rutherford, " 'Harmless Nonsense': The Comic Sketch and The Development of Music Hall Entertainment," in Bratton (ed.), *Music Hall*, p. 134.

17. The first major London confrontation between theatres and halls was in 1860–61 when Benjamin Webster took Charles Morton, the so-called "father of the halls" who had built first the Canterbury Theatre in Lambeth and then the Oxford, in the West End, to court for staging a "pantomimic duologue" in which two performers played ten characters in a tale of young love that ultimately developed into Clown, Pantaloon, Harlequin and Columbine. See Kift, *Victorian Music Hall*, p. 141.

18. *The Era*, review of Alhambra, 21 June 1890, p. 15.

19. Fred Farren and Beatrice Collyer created a sensation at the London Empire with the apache dance, subsequently imitated and burlesqued by innumerable adagio dancers; see W. Macqueen-Pope, *Ivor* (London: Hutchinson, 1954), p. 100. *Humanity* was the speciality of John Lawson, who bought the provincial rights just for the fight scene, out of a Standard Theatre play of 1882 ostensibly about Grace Darling: see A. E. Wilson, *East End Entertainment* (London: Arthur Barker, 1954), p. 132.

20. Boucicault, out of date in the theatre, was a favorite source of music-hall melodrama in the 1890s. *The Era*, 7 June 1890, p. 15; the sketch was called *Wild Rose* and was that night seen at the Temple, Hammersmith; *Conn* was premiered at the South London Palace and reported in *The Era*, 12 April 1890, p. 15.

21. See Peter Davison, *Contemporary Drama and the Popular Dramatic Tradition in England* (London: Macmillan, 1982), p. 13.

22. *The Era*, 12 April, review of *Our Lads in Red*, devised by Fred Bowyer of the Canterbury Theatre.

23. Laurence Senelick, "Politics as Entertainment: Victorian Music-Hall Songs," *Victorian Studies* 19 (1975–76), 180; Kift, *Victorian Music Hall*, p. 42.

24. Charles Dickens, *Bleak House* (London: Everyman edition, 1907), p. 142.

25. See *Tavern Singing in Early Victorian London: the Diaries of Charles Rice*, ed. Laurence Senelick (London: Society for Theatre Research, 1997) for the experiences of a semi-professional singer on this cusp.

26. Fred Wilson, *The Era*, 4 February 1877, review of Collins's Theatre; Alfred Vance, *The Era*, 18 January 1880, review of the Cambridge Theatre.

27. *The Era*, 8 February 1880, review of the Bedford Theatre; 29 June 1895, review of Collins's Theatre.

28. See Anthony Bennett, "Music in the Halls," in Bratton (ed.), *Music Hall*, pp. 1–22, for an analysis of the chorus and its uses, especially pp. 11–12.

29. See especially Peter Bailey, "Champagne Charlie and the Music-Hall Swell Song," revised version in *Popular Culture*, pp. 101–27.

30. See for example Eric Lott, *Love and Theft: Blackface Minstrelsy and the American Working Class* (Oxford: Oxford University Press, 1993).

31. See Michael Pickering. "White Skin, Black Masks: 'Nigger' Minstrelsy in Victorian Britain," in Bratton (ed.), *Music Hall*, pp. 70–91.

32. Grock, *Life's a Lark*, trans. Madge Pemberton, ed. Eduard Behrens (London: Heinemann, 1931), pp. 45–46.

33. *The Era*, 13 October 1894.

34. Booth, *Pink Parade*, pp. 160, 177–78.

10

PETER RABY

Theatre of the 1890s: breaking down the barriers

Anyone skimming the columns of the *Pall Mall Gazette* in the 1890s might assume that English drama was flourishing, and that theatrical topics were on everyone's lips. New plays and productions are given long reviews; actor-managers' plans for future offerings and seasons are trailed in some detail; and a European dimension is assured by the frequent references to Ibsen and the close attention paid to the visits of the Comédie-Française, or of Eleanora Duse. On 17 February 1893, for example, there is an article by Henry James on *The Master Builder*, with Elizabeth Robins as Hilda Wangel, followed four days later by an edition of the *Gazette* that includes both an interview with George Moore on his forthcoming *The Strike at Arlingford*, and another review – a hostile one – of *The Master Builder*. At the end of February, Wilde's *Salomé*, published in French, is savaged, but the reviewer at least discusses it in a theatrical context. In March comes a revival of *A Doll's House*, in April, the premiere of Wilde's *A Woman of No Importance*, in May the enthusiastic reception of Pinero's *The Second Mrs. Tanqueray*, in June reviews of performances of *Rosmersholm* at the Opéra Comique, of Duse as Nora Helmer, and of the publication of Shaw's *Widowers' Houses*.[1] These are all names or works that retain their resonance a century or more later. Theatre, and theatrical form, was alive.

At the same time, there was a sustained idea prevalent in the magazines and newspapers that all was not well with English dramatic art, if one defined that as the drama performed or published in London. One symptom to cause anxiety, perhaps, was the fact that only one of the people named above, Pinero, was English. The cutting edge of new dramatic writing came from Ireland, the model for a modern, serious theatre from France, in the shape of André Antoine's Théâtre Libre, and the bedrock of modern repertory from Norway. Sandwiched between the columns about Wilde, Ibsen and Shaw come articles on "The Decay of the Stage" or speculations as to why the London theatres are half-empty (defective heating). The year before, the *Pall Mall Gazette* had encouraged a series of statements from novelists such as Thomas Hardy, George Gissing, and George Moore called "Why I Don't Write Plays." The implication of the invitation was that the novel was a "high," serious, and literary form, and characteristically a context in which ideas could be explored; if only the best novelists could be persuaded to write plays, then presumably the whole status of the theatre would be transformed and legitimized, just as Sir Henry Irving's production of Lord Tennyson's *Becket* gave a transfusion of high-quality poetry and middle of the road ethics to the Lyceum, an English counterbalance to *Faust*. Whatever would have happened had Hardy taken up the challenge, and offered a dramatic version of, for example, *Tess of the D'Urbervilles* to Sir Herbert Beerbohm Tree? Presumably, a swift rejection, along the lines of J. T. Grein's judgment that *Mrs. Warren's Profession* was unfit "for women's ears,"[2] or Mrs. Theodore Wright's horror when Shaw read her his play, hoping that she might be interested in the title role after playing Mrs. Alving in *Ghosts*.[3] Hardy, however, was convinced that the theatre's traditions and conditions made it an impossibly constricting place to work, claiming that the characters' parts had to be "moulded to actors," not "actors to parts"; and that the "exigencies of scene-building" were dominant, so that scenes had to be "arranged in a constrained and arbitrary fashion": "The reason for the arbitrary arrangement would seem to be that the presentation of human passions is subordinated to the presentation of mountains, cities, clothes, furniture, plate, jewels, and the other real and sham real appurtenances, to the neglect that the material stage should be a conventional or figurative area."[4] As Hardy makes no reference to specific plays, it is not clear what kind of theatre he has in mind, though his list of settings suggests something historical, rather than contemporary. But his general criticism fits with some of the arguments deployed by Edward Gordon Craig in *On The Art of the Theatre*.[5] George Moore did respond, taking up a wager to provide a new English play for the Independent Theatre, *The Strike at Arlingford*, proving that success as a novelist was not necessarily a qualification for writing effective dramatic dialogue.

Nevertheless, the campaign continued. William Archer, in his role of omniscient critic rather than translator and champion of Ibsen, bemoaned the lack of good writing in the drama of the time. Having praised Wilde for *Lady Windermere's Fan* by calling it "one of the two thoroughly well-written, or really written, plays of our time" – the second was the bizarre choice of *Beau Austin*, a collaboration between Robert Louis Stevenson and W. E. Henley – he went on to give some well-meant but patronizing advice, to the effect that Mr. Wilde would have to conquer his "no less fatal fastidiousness, not to say indolence": on present evidence, Wilde was an artist first, and a playwright by afterthought.[6] In August 1893, he condemned the native output of the

English stage, in a review of "Plays and Acting of the Season": "Were it not for *The Second Mrs. Tanqueray*, the season, however delightful, must have left behind it a certain sense of humiliation. Against a whole regiment of foreign masterpieces, we should have had nothing of our own worth bringing into the field except one single scene in *A Woman of no Importance*."[7] In a further scathing article, "Some Recent Plays," in May 1894, he formulated his charge: "*During the past six months not a single serious play has been produced with success.* Under the term 'serious play' I include everything that is not farce, burlesque, or Adelphi melodrama; so that, in other words, every play of the smallest artistic pretension produced between October 1st 1893, and April 15th, 1894, has been a more or less flagrant failure."[8] The only two "serious" home-grown plays he could dredge up since May 1893 were *The Second Mrs. Tanqueray*, a play "of European" merit, and Sydney Grundy's *Sowing the Wind*, pretty and sympathetic, but comparatively trivial. He laid the blame for this state of affairs on the critics, and specifically their reaction to *Hedda Gabler* and *The Second Mrs. Tanqueray*. "*Hedda Gabler* has made the older men tetchy and suspicious; *The Second Mrs. Tanqueray* has made the younger men intolerant and exacting."[9] This is a strange but revealing analysis. Pinero's play is picked out as a benchmark, a judgment that seems slightly mystifying now, but which demonstrates the perspective that Pinero was exploiting the forms and conventions of the theatre of the day to their fullest extent. The critics, Archer argued, were at fault, for being too quick to take offence or too demanding. The dramatic writers, such as Wilde or J. M. Barrie, were too playful, and did not properly embrace the art of the stage, while the public had become all of a sudden "ferociously frivolous."

Archer's analysis fits in with the declarations of Grein's Independent Theatre, to search out plays that were "artistic," "interesting," and "literary";[10] apart from serving to galvanize Shaw into completing *Widowers' Houses*, Grein's program was unsuccessful, and the theatre's main achievement was in staging Ibsen, and in hosting Aurélien Lugné-Poë's Théâtre de l'Oeuvre. But to expect writers unfamiliar with the conventions of theatre to produce innovative and successful work without a period of apprenticeship was unrealistic, even in a non-commercial venture. (The English Stage Society's first major impact, in its search for new work at the Royal Court in 1956, was achieved with a play by an actor.)[11] It took Shaw most of the decade to find his way as a dramatist, and his "serious," or unpleasant, plays were a false start in terms of his career. Wilde was cut short by the events of his not-so-private life in 1895. He had included Shaw as the second dramatist of the "great Celtic School" – opus 1, *Lady Windermere's Fan*, opus 2, *Widowers' Houses*, opus 3, *A Woman of no Importance*, opus 4, *The Philanderer*.[12] Wilde had set out to write his first modern play not as a result of an artistic challenge but of a straightforward advance from that reviled and supposedly reactionary creature, a male actor-manager. He reportedly asked Frank Harris if it would take one week or three to beat the Pineros and the Joneses, as representing the established English school of dramatic writing.[13] Neither man was, essentially, "literary." Henry Arthur Jones, brought up as a non-conformist forbidden even to attend a theatre, served his apprenticeship with the old style actor-manager Wilson Barrett as a writer of melodramas, the most famous of which was *The Silver King*. Arthur Wing Pinero was an actor in Henry Irving's company, and specialized initially in farce. Both, in the 1890s, turned their attention to "society" drama.

Pinero's first effort in this genre was *The Profligate*, a radical switch from his successes in farce such as *The Magistrate* and *Dandy Dick*, or in sentimental comedy such as *Sweet Lavender*.[14] He wrote *The Profligate* in 1887, effectively pre-Ibsen so far as London theatregoers were concerned, but had to wait two years before John Hare produced it at the Garrick Theatre, with a heavyweight cast that included himself as the wicked Lord Dangars, Johnston Forbes-Robertson as "the profligate," Dunstan Renshaw, and Lewis Waller as the Scottish lawyer with a moral conscience, Hugh Murray. Hare persuaded Pinero to alter the conclusion, to achieve a "happy" ending. Instead of Renshaw swallowing a phial of poison before his pure, young wife returns to announce mercy instead of judgment – "We are one and will make atonement for the past together" – Pinero has him dash the glass to the ground. "This is the deepest sin of all my life – blacker than that sin for which I suffer!", so that Leslie Renshaw finds him kneeling in prayer, a penitent wretch whom she can reform. English audiences were deprived of the unusual spectacle of a man with a past committing suicide. When the play was performed in Melbourne, the original ending was substituted, to the critics' satisfaction, but the public found it too painful, and the "Garrick version" was restored.[15] When the play was published, however, Pinero reverted to his first strong ending. The English problem play was launched. The problem, in short, was sexual fidelity, and the double standard whereby it was apparently acceptable, or even desirable, for a man to sow his "wild oats," a term Pinero employs in an exhaustingly extended way, and then settle down to married life with a good woman. A woman, or certainly a woman from the upper or upper-middle classes, is assumed to be sexually inexperienced, and any doubts about the bargain she is entering into through marriage are quashed by the man's social position or wealth, or ideally both.

The play has, as its title suggests, an uncompromising moral focus, with relatively little comedy to alleviate its serious message. Each act has an epigraph: "This Man and this Woman"; "The Sword of Damocles"; "The End of the Honeymoon"; "The Beginning of a New Life." In fact, it functions much like a morality play, exploiting three stereotypes of Man's Desire – the hardened Dangars, the weak Renshaw, the innocent young Wilfred Brudenell – and three variations of Fleeting Beauty. Lord Dangars is a very wicked lord, well-acquainted with the divorce court. Dunstan Renshaw is, in the words of his ruined and abandoned mistress, eighteen-year-old Janet Preece, "a town gentleman who does ill in the country." Leslie Brudenell, the virginal and impressionable schoolgirl, is married off to Renshaw by her guardian – we are deep in orphan country.

The plot is contrived, the moral decisions inconsistent, the dialogue often labored and flat. Yet the play does contain a power, in its uncompromising concentration on sexual behavior and the social rituals surrounding marriage. There is an honesty about it, even in its reduction of the social spectrum to a few primary colors. The sanctity of marriage in Victorian society, for example, is revealed as a sham. The offstage ceremony in act I is carried out in a rush at a registry office, even though Leslie longed for a church wedding; and she is hustled away to catch a train as though she has been purchased. There is, too, an interesting physical pattern to the play, as it opens out from the gloomy lawyer's office in the Inns of Court to the light and air of Italy, land of romance where emotions are heightened and raw, before a return to the sober, autumnal atmosphere of a dull Holborn hotel. The contrast between the English in London or the home counties and the English abroad is one which Henry James and E. M. Forster would explore in greater subtlety, but is theatrically effective, and was one reason for the play's comparative popularity on the European stage.

The Second Mrs. Tanqueray (1893) marks a huge advance in Pinero's dramaturgy. Ostensibly, the play has the same subject, sexual *mores* within the English upper and upper-middle classes, and the distinction between what is acceptable for a man and for a woman. But here the main focus rests not on a man, or men, with a past, but on Paula Tanqueray, previously "Mrs. Jarman" and a number of other names of convenience, a woman with an impressive series of pasts. At one level, the action is a little too reliant on well-worn and transparent stage conventions, on coincidence, on the regular delivery – or non-delivery – of letters and notes; while the conclusion, the suicide of the "sinful" woman, is only too familiar: all these features seem to place the play within the tradition of the French *drame* as modified for the English stage. (Pinero is not, of course, alone in his exploitation of the genre: Aubrey Tanqueray writing notes at one end of the room while his dinner guests whisper about his *mésalliance* – "the naive machinery of the exposition," in Shaw's phrase – echoes Wilde's handling of the scene in Lord Darlington's rooms in *Lady Windermere's Fan*.) But Pinero rises above these self-imposed limitations in a number of ways.

First, he conveys the stultifying barrenness of English social life, both in the awful male clubbiness of Tanqueray's circle of London friends, and in the dreary routine of months in the country among the Surrey hills, shunned by the neighbors, and in the awkward company of Ellean, the strictly brought up daughter of Tanqueray's first marriage. "What is my existence, Sunday to Saturday?" Paula asks her husband in accusation. "In the morning, a drive down to the village, with the groom, to give my orders to the tradespeople. At lunch, you and Ellean. In the afternoon, a novel, the newspapers; if fine, another drive – *if* fine! Tea – you and Ellean. Then two hours of dusk; then dinner – you and Ellean. Then a game of bezique, you and I, while Ellean reads a religious book in a dull corner."[16] Matters scarcely improve when Paula has her way and invites married house-guests, the bovine Sir George Orreyed and his pretty "actress" gold-digging wife, who provide a comic counterpoint to the Tanquerays: extensive meals, billiards, and copious drafts of whiskey to numb Orreyed into docile semi-consciousness. Everything at Highercoombe is described as "charming and graceful," or as betokening "taste and luxury"; and Paula and Lady Orreyed are in "sumptuous dinner-gowns."[17] Servants hover, cigars are smoked in relays. The contrast between the ostentatious wealth and taste, the surface elegance, and the intellectual and spiritual sterility is powerfully conveyed.

Secondly, the characters, and some of the relationships, function at a greater degree of complexity than might be predicted from the slightly clumsy opening act. Aubrey Tanqueray is presented as a fundamentally decent man, who is genuinely in love with Paula and wishes to marry her because he does not want to treat her "like the rest"; he knows about her past affairs, and is prepared to face the world's contempt. But he is also shown as a man of middle-age, whose first wife is described as frigid, who can be seen – would be seen, perhaps, by Shaw – as buying Paula's youth and sexuality knowing that she will be made to suffer. His loyalties to his former life, and wife, are explored through his friend and neighbor, Mrs. Cortelyon, and more probingly through his relationship with his daughter, who comes back to live with him and Paula. Ellean steps back from the brink of becoming a nun – "I believe my mother in Heaven has spoken to me, and counselled me to turn to you in my loneliness" – in a letter Aubrey Tanqueray reads aloud to the audience just before Paula makes a well-timed entrance on the eve of her wedding: the mechanism creaks, but the triangular relationship that it sets up is disturbingly effective.[18] Aubrey is torn between Ellean and Paula, and between their conflicting sets of values. Paula both resents Ellean and wishes to love her, and be loved by her. The emotional tension, full of uncertainties and ambiguities, is finely handled, especially in the roles of the two young women, Ellean, nineteen, with "a face somewhat resembling a Madonna,"

Paula, at twenty-seven, "beautiful, fresh, innocent-looking." When Ellean returns from her visit to Paris, she introduces the man she has fallen in love with, Captain Ardale, to her stepmother; Ardale has confessed his wild, rackety, bachelor past to Ellean, but has not associated the Paula Jarman he once lived with in Ethelbert Street with his prospective mother-in-law. The world of English society, "our little parish of St James," is uncomfortably small. The incestuous overtones contribute to the portrait of a sick society, in which the external rituals of the wealthy only emphasize the emotional pain within.

Shaw, distancing himself from Pinero to define his own skills as a drama-tist the more sharply, credits him for giving the minor characters "a pass-able air of being human beings," even going so far as to call Cayley Drummle, the convenient and ubiquitous *raisonneur*, a "Thackerayan flaneur."[19] Drummle, gossip, confidant, adviser, meddler, would slip un-obtrusively into an eighteenth-century sentimental comedy, or even, with his claws sharpened, into a Farquhar or Etherege comedy of manners. He comes across not just as a familiar dramatic device, but as a spokesman for his age: suave, worldly, smug, effete, a sexless Judge Brack. His kind inhabits the country houses of Saki's Edwardian stories, and his world will end on the battlefields of the Somme. Hugh Ardale, Ellean's military lover, fulfills a more symbolic function. Ardale has proved himself in India, checking a mutiny in a remote Residency and winning a company and a Victoria Cross for his selfless heroism. For Ellean, the puritan, this week in India "when he deliberately offered his life back to God" has redeemed his earlier sinful life.[20] Within the wider patterns of the play's values, there is an implication that such deeds in India (or Africa, in H. A. Jones's *The Liars*) justify the cushioned, inactive life of London and Surrey.

In Paula Tanqueray, Pinero goes beyond urbane sympathy, and indicates a character of unsettling ambiguity and complexity. He presents her at one level as a woman who has been stereotyped, by society as well as by stage convention, and who is unfairly made to suffer as a result. But she is neither a passive victim, nor someone who has precipitated her fate, like Hedda Gabler. She is trapped, partly by the absurd customs of English society, partly by her sexuality, and partly by her nature. Pinero extends his investigation of the idea of marriage which he began in *The Profligate*, and will continue in *The Notorious Mrs. Ebbsmith*. Paula's analysis about the world – 'The only great distances it contains are those we carry within ourselves – the distances that separate husbands and wives, for instance' – echoes Nora Helmer.[21] Like Nora, Paula is conscious that her prettiness will not last, and that she will then be only a ghost, a wreck, a caricature, and will appear to Aubrey as she appears now to "wholesome folks": a "loose woman," if not quite a whore. No wonder she is not thought suitable to introduce Ellean to "society"; and no wonder, given this set of values, that she kills herself. But parallel to this moral equation are moments of rebellion, malice and devilry, for example when Paula intercepts Ellean's letters to her father – "I felt simply fiendish when I saw them," she informs Drummle, and Pinero's stage directions indicate her internal energy – "fiercely," "with an hysterical laugh," "recklessly."[22] She also has a waspish sense of humor, mocking Drummle in particular – "Why do you hop about like a monkey?" The unmarried, hedonistic days of freedom are contrasted with the dog's life that defines a "happy" marriage. Drummle is the catalyst for a revealing memory of the unmarried past – "Oh, Cayley, do you remember those jolly times on board Peter Jarman's yacht when we lay off – ?" – days in the Mediterranean with vine-leaves in her hair.[23]

The extra factors which helped to transform Pinero's probing but essentially conservative play – although John Hare judged it too radical for his audience at the Garrick Theatre – were the production values of George Alexander at the St. James's Theatre, and the eventual casting of Paula Tanqueray. Archer's suggestion for a production by Grein's Independent Theatre was testily rejected by Pinero. He wanted the kind of refined luxury that Alexander had provided for *Lady Windermere's Fan*, convincingly fashionable settings and sumptuous *haute couture* for the women. As Paula, Pinero initially suggested Olga Nethersole, a standard melodramatic actress who played Janet Preece in *The Profligate* and then toured with it in Australia. But she was a little old to be ideal for the part and Marion Terry – Wilde's Mrs. Erlynne – was too fat. Winifred Emery and Julia Neilson (who was Hester in *A Woman of No Importance*) were considered. Janet Achurch, Nora Helmer in the groundbreaking London production of *A Doll's House*, had the right credentials, but was growing difficult under the influence of alcohol and morphine. Elizabeth Robins – another powerful actress with a strong Ibsen track-record as Hedda Gabler, Hilda Wangel and Rebecca West – was actually contracted, in spite of Pinero's misgivings that she was too "robust," and looked too American.[24] She would convey Paula's intelligence, but not perhaps her sexual energy. Pinero embarked on a tour of London theatres, as did Mrs. Alexander and the designer Graham Robertson. Playing opposite Evelyn Millard, the heroine – "very beautiful, very gentle, very sweet," and suitable for the part of Ellean – was the wicked woman of the play, *The Black Domino*. "She did not look wicked – a startling innovation. She was almost painfully thin, with great eyes and slow haunting utterance; she was not exactly beautiful, but intensely interesting and arresting." She also had a wonderful laugh "low and sweet, yet utterly mocking and heartless."[25] Mrs. Patrick Campbell was released by her management, and joined the St. James's company. She did not take direction, or instruction, easily, and would later complain that playing to Alexander as Aubrey was like acting opposite a walking-stick. She resisted Pinero's emphatic, over-explicit stage directions, refusing to go along with the more melodramatic actions, and subtly indicating a refinement of sensibility and upbringing that conflicted with the rather lurid courtesan's past Pinero seems to have been indicating. Shaw seized on one particular moment to demonstrate the weakness of Pinero's concept of Paula. In act III, Aubrey is interrogating Paula about her past, suggesting that there was a time, only a few years back, when she "hadn't a thought that wasn't a wholesome one," "hadn't an impulse that didn't tend towards good" – that she was, in short, innocent before she "fell," and became corrupted by life's cruelty, and as coarse as a man. Shaw complained about her reply "A few years ago! O God! A few years ago!" (accompanied by *a paroxysm of weeping*").[26] Shaw clearly wanted Pinero to write a different play, one in which Paula would have opened Tanqueray's foolish eyes to the fact that "a woman of that sort is already the same at three as she is at thirty-three": he wanted Paula to assert that she was perfectly "valid" to herself. Not given the words by the author, the actress suggested her own background in the way she played the piano. Pinero's original stage direction had Paula strumming a valse in act III. Mrs. Campbell, asked by Alexander at rehearsal to improvise, responded by playing a piece of Bach with her left hand, enabling her, as Joel Kaplan and Sheila Stowell comment, "to complete for Paula the genteel past Pinero had failed to suggest in his text."[27]

In their chapter "Dressing Mrs. Pat," Kaplan and Stowell chart the meanings of the gowns and dresses deployed on stage. Paula Tanqueray's image, or succession of images, is crucial to the play. In act I, she appears in a "superb" "*décolleté* evening dress of flame-colored satin" contrasted to the subdued walking-dress of her dull married state in act II. But when she re-enters to confront Mrs. Cortelyon, she has changed into an elegantly cut double-breasted coat and over-ornamented hat, and is clearly making a statement.[28] For act III, she makes another kind of statement, her gray dinner gown striking a note of restraint beside the ostentatious flamboyance of Lady Orreyed. This is the act of the mirror: twice the audience's attention is directed towards Paula's reflection in the large mirror over the mantelpiece, and twice she stares into her image in a hand-mirror, the second occasion being the moment that completes the act. Mrs. Campbell's disturbingly thin elegance, and her acute awareness of her own appearance, suggested her character's inner drive towards death, an aspect that Aubrey Beardsley captured in his portrait of her for the first number of *The Yellow Book*. Beardsley was castigated for the image, reviewers implying that he had somehow imposed his own corrupt concept of a New Woman on a classic type of English beauty. Arguably, Beardsley was responding to the extraordinary dimension that Mrs. Campbell's acting had added to the role, and to the play, further confirmation of its capacity to disturb in performance.

Mrs. Campbell's image may have prompted Pinero into creating an explicit New Woman role for her in *The Notorious Mrs. Ebbsmith*, produced by John Hare at the Garrick Theatre on 13 March 1895.[29] The London stage had already featured unsympathetic or comic treatments of more-or-less emancipated women, the quartet in Sidney Grundy's *The New Woman* (1894) and Elaine Shrimpton in Jones's *The Case of Rebellious Susan* (1894) being the most conspicuous recent models. Pinero created a compelling if realistically improbable character in Agnes Ebbsmith, who has suffered from both an alcoholic mother and an abusive husband, embraced the atheism of her demagog father, had a career as a fervent socialist campaigner during which she became known as "mad Agnes," and then become a nurse, having saved the life of her patient, a married English member of parliament called Lucas Cleeve. She has accompanied him to Venice, where they intend to live fearlessly and openly, and write together, principally on the destructive power of marriage. The idea of marriage, and especially the role of marriage within the English social value-system, provides one clear focus within the play. The slight distancing created by the Venetian setting is especially effective, offering an apparent sanctuary from the stifling, introverted network of English convention: in the beauty of Italy, free spirits from England have historically taken refuge. The English, however, appear to have successfully colonized Venice for Easter, and are either holidaying there, or passing through on their way home from India, or have been summoned by train to persuade Cleeve to return to his wife, simply for form's sake, and more importantly for the sake of his glittering career. The overall impact is to present a spectrum of English "influential" society at its worst, a depressing catalog of abusive or sham marriages, the males predatory, the women denying their sexuality, the children unhappy or unhealthy. The amoral Duke of St. Olpherts is suffering from gout, and the protagonists seem to have been made ill by their struggles. Lucas Cleeve is attended by two doctors, who pronounce that there is nothing wrong with him; however, he appears increasingly listless as the action unfolds, unable to make up his mind about anything. Agnes, pale and gaunt, talks about hanging a new dress "on my bones," and the closing image of the play has her lifting her "maimed hand" in response to the Duke. No comforts here for the carriage trade of a West-End theatre.

Max Beerbohm, reviewing a 1901 revival, commented that the play belonged to that period when "Mr. Pinero was respectfully begging to call your attention to his latest assortment of Spring Problemings (Scandinavian Gents' own materials made up. West End style and fit guaranteed)."[30] The role of Agnes was not a guaranteed fit for Mrs. Campbell, who wrote that the first three acts of the play filled her with ecstasy, but that the last act "broke my heart." Once again, but more overtly, she played the part "against the grain." One of Pinero's most arresting stage metaphors was to present Agnes initially in a plain dress, matching the simplicity and honesty of her ideals. To Cleeve this is "slovenliness," or, as he corrects, "shabbiness," and he has ordered for her a handsome *décolleté* dress, which leaves her throat and arms bare, to transform her into a beautiful and sexually desirable woman, in other words his mistress rather than his soul companion. He wants her to be Nora in her tarantella outfit. For the third act, Agnes toys with this role, drinking wine, smoking a cigarette, listening to the love music of mandolin and guitar. The alternative that Pinero places before her is offered by Gertrude Thorpe, in the shape of a remote Yorkshire parsonage, wild moorland, and the music of church bells and organ; and, more concretely, by her parson brother Amos Winterfield's gift of a Bible. At the act's close, Agnes hurls the book into the flames, like Hedda Gabler, but then, horror struck, thrusts her arm into the fire to retrieve it. Act IV reveals her as penitent, clothed "in a rusty, ill-fitting, black, stuff dress," her face haggard, her eyes red and sunken with weeping. Her hour of fulfillment is over, and she is to be healed, we presume, by the bracing northern winds and the teaching of the Church. At least she is spared either suicide, or the "moral" hypocrisy of the Cleeve solution which would relegate her to kept mistress. But Pinero's Yorkshire parsonage seems an unconvincing construction of "home." As Mrs. Campbell explained, she wanted Agnes to preach the doctrine of selfless, unexacting love, not creep back into "the shell of a narrow morality." Deprived of the harangue, or of the opportunity to shut the door on the whole lot of them, she fought against the restrictions of the role, inviting Archer's complaint that she wore the erotic, rustling silk dress like a hair shirt.[31]

Pinero was the favorite in the Archer stakes for an English-language dramatist of European stature, his qualities emphasized by Shaw's swiftness to denigrate *The Second Mrs. Tanqueray* when it appeared in print (another sign of the growing interest in the English stage). Henry Arthur Jones was more of an outsider, solid, too often stolid, but with patches of class and sparkle, particularly evident in the plays he wrote for Charles Wyndham and the Criterion Theatre.[32] *The Case of Rebellious Susan* was Jones's attempt to put some teeth into the form of a society comedy – or, as he described it in a letter to Mrs. Grundy, fictional but all too real keeper of the country's morals, "a tragedy dressed up as a comedy."[33] Jones was almost as keen on a preface as Shaw, but in this instance the preface was provoked by Wyndham, who had persuaded him to soften Lady Susan's conduct, by blurring the nature of her rebellion. Wyndham, speaking not as a moralist but simply "voicing the public instinct," confessed himself bewildered that the author, "a clean-living, clear-minded man," might hope to extract laughter from an audience "on the score of a woman's impurity."[34] Jones, stung, assured Mrs. Grundy that he had no warrant for placing "an instance of English conjugal infidelity" on the English stage, since immorality was known to be confined to the Continent, and especially to France. The immorality in this case is, first, that of James Harabin, Lady Susan's husband, and the rebellion her refusal to accept it like a good English upper-class wife. Instead, she decides to go to Egypt with a woman friend to find a little romance, which she does in the shape of Lucien Edensor. Edensor travels east to India before returning to England, Lady Susan returns to England but not to her husband, and the problem of resolving this delicate situation is placed in the hands of her uncle and *raisonneur*, Sir Richard Kato (significantly played by Wyndham).

At this point Wyndham's intervention blurred the issue. Although Jones extracts considerable comedy from what happened in Cairo when Lady Susan and Edensor were ostensibly attending a very long sermon at the Anglican church (like Venice, Cairo is presented as a colonial extension of Mayfair), and although the text can be played to imply clearly that there was physical passion, Mrs. Grundy, in the shape of Kato, takes over. Edensor, en route now for New Zealand, swears undying love, exchanges rings, and begs Susan to fly with him to the Continent. Kato intervenes, and browbeats Susan into returning, if not to her husband, then to the safety of his house in Harley Street. Edensor gets married on the long voyage out, a piece of male infidelity conveyed comically, and Susan is inevitably, if uneasily, reconciled to her husband: the only victory is her refusal to tell him whether there has been anything physical on her part to confess. Morality has been shaken, and the tragedy of a strictly business marriage of appearances at least hinted at. Kato's original suggestion to the erring husband was to offer his wife a villa at Cannes for the summer and a diamond ring and bracelet from Hunt and Roskell's. At the reconciliation, Harabin promises to buy her the whole of Bond Street.

Jones, apprenticed as a young man in the drapery business, knew well the significance of smart clothes and luxurious trappings. In this world of consumption, the women are priced by their costumes, champagne and anchovy sandwiches fill the gap before luncheon, and half-a-dozen bottles of priceless Madeira are despatched out to New Zealand to reward Edensor (who has already been rewarded by a government job found for him by Kato). The play features a satirical underplot in which a New Woman, Elaine Shrimpton, is mocked, and ends with a mature love agreement between Kato and Inez Quesnel, both experienced in the ways of the world. "Let us leave these problems," says Kato, kissing Inez's hand "very tenderly," "and go in to dinner" – a characteristically English consummation.[35] In spite of this cloak of sentiment, Jones has removed one or two veils from the problem of marriage, and specifically from marriage as encapsulating the codes and values of a distinctly fragile society. He has anatomized the double standard, and Lady Susan's reply to the well-meant platitudes of her women friends – "we poor women cannot retaliate" – is a laconic and unconvincing "I see." Hers is, after all, just a "respectable average case."[36]

In *The Liars*, Jones continues his dissection of English upper-class morality, from his outsider's perspective as the self-educated child of a strict nonconformist farming background followed by first-hand knowledge of provincial trade. Here the main plot concerns the indiscreet flirtation between a beautiful, witty but superficial married woman, Lady Jessica Nepean (played by Wyndham's glamorous leading lady, Mary Moore) and Edward Falkner, national hero, and the only man in England who can negotiate with the East African tribal chiefs and put an end to the slave-dealing. Falkner, a serious character, is genuinely in love, and wishes Lady Jessica to accompany him to Africa. Wyndham played the *raisonneur* and fixer, Colonel Sir Christopher Deering, in love with a beautiful widow, Beatrice Ebernoe: they provide a model of mature, serious courtship. The settings and costumes convey much of the meaning. The play opens in an ostentatious tent on the lawns of a Thames-side house where a house party for, presumably, Henley regatta is in progress, and features heavy cigar smoking and pompous posturing from the men, and bare shoulders and sharp gossip from pretty society women. Act IV takes place in Deering's serious Victoria Street house; Deering is busy packing, and "articles which an officer going to Central Africa might want are lying about."[37]

The action, slight enough, concerns Lady Jessica and a visit she pays to Falkner at the Star and Garter hotel on the Thames, a rendezvous for a *tête-à-tête* dinner which is clearly a metaphor for, or at least a preliminary to, a sexual encounter. In contrast to Cairo, nothing happens, and the comedy of the play's central section is preoccupied with the series of lies that are concocted in an attempt to preserve Jessica's "honor" and satisfy her puffing ass of a husband. Appearances must be maintained, and the process is handled adroitly by Jones in the spirit of near farce, with much overhearing and popping out from behind curtains. Jessica is persuaded by Deering, as Susan was persuaded by Kato, that there can be no future for a woman of her status who abandons her husband: the implication, too, is that she is unfitted for the demands life in Africa would make. The frivolous, and morally worthless, remain in England, to act out their charades and dine at the Savoy, while the serious set off for the unknown trials to come. Deering exclaims, his arms round Falkner and Mrs. Ebernoe, "Tomorrow! My wife! My friend! My two comrades!"[38] However problematic this invocation of Africa may seem today, the rejection of the prevailing values of "best circles" society in the England of *The Liars* is uncompromising and conclusive.

Lying, or the creative art of fiction, is one of Wilde's central concerns and themes, pursued through a range of forms to its high point in the glittering surfaces of *The Importance of Being Earnest*. After two false or unfulfilled starts as a dramatist with the period pastiche *The Duchess of Padua* and a potentially more interesting play about nihilism, *Vera*, Wilde sauntered on to the London stage with a society drama commissioned by Alexander.[39] The title of *Lady Windermere's Fan* scarcely suggests a close engagement with contemporary issues, or a close acquaintance with Ibsen's agenda. The play seems in part closer to a conventional English comedy of manners, transmitted from Congreve via Sheridan, a resemblance strengthened by the clear echo of the screen scene from *The School for Scandal* in act III; in part, as many contemporary critics delighted in pointing out, a skillful imitation of the school of French dramatic art, as practiced by Scribe, Sardou and Dumas *fils*. Traces of drama, if not melodrama, survive Wilde's redrafting, notably in Lady Windermere's soliloquies, and in the blustering of Lord Windermere at the end of act III: "By God!" he exclaims to Lord Darlington, "I'll search your rooms, and if my wife's here, I'll – "[40] An earlier typescript completes the line: "shoot you like a dog."

Wilde followed Jones and Pinero in taking a close interest in the rehearsal process, and in the physical realization of his plays – too close, for some of his producers. The collaboration with Alexander, strained at times, was especially fruitful, and resulted not only in an overall refinement of the text, but in one crucial shift. The fact that Mrs. Erlynne, the alluring, mysterious woman with a number of pasts, is Lady Windermere's mother was originally to have been revealed towards the close of the play, a "dramatic" surprise that would unlock the story for an audience. Alexander's suggestion that it was far more interesting to indicate the relationship gradually through the course of the play – a change that was made with Wilde's agreement after the first night – demonstrates how old forms of theatre could be adjusted to achieve more complex and ironic effects.

The lies, the masquerades, the masks that conceal the truth, like a fan, permeate the play; and the fan is Windermere's present to his wife on her twenty-first birthday, twenty-four hours crowded with incident during which she moves from innocence to experience. The lies cluster around "Mrs.

Erlynne," who abandoned her daughter – and first husband – for a love affair that drove her into exile. She has now returned, surprisingly disguised by her assumed name, and wishes to be accepted into English society, not as a prodigal daughter, but to enable her to acquire a wealthy husband. She extracts money from Windermere to finance her London stay, and everyone from the Duchess of Berwick, spokeswoman of the contemporary school for scandal, to the witty dandy Lord Darlington, believes that Mrs. Erlynne is Windermere's mistress. This fiction drives Lady Windermere to fly to Darlington's bachelor rooms, from which she is rescued by a selfless act on the part of Mrs. Erlynne, who risks her own recently acquired reputation to save her daughter from repeating her own pattern of action. Wilde creates ironic complexity because the truth of the relationship is never revealed to Lady Windermere, who has constructed a false image of her "dead" mother. Similarly, Lord Windermere neither learns of Mrs. Erlynne's moment of goodness, nor that his apparently puritan wife was temporarily prepared to leave him and infant son for a life in exile with Darlington. Fiction, the fiction of satisfactory appearances, triumphs; but the meaning of "good" has been lightly, and wittily, questioned. The subtitle is "A Play about a Good Woman," and the good woman is the female dandy and woman with a past, Mrs. Erlynne.

At the most pragmatic level, the play was, and remains, an undoubted success: it works in the theatre. Wilde created a wonderful language for his characters, a kind of imitation, or extension, of upper-class dialogue, ranging from the polished wit of the dandies, Darlington, Mrs. Erlynne, Cecil Graham, to the magisterial non-sequiturs of the Duchess of Berwick, the restricted vocabulary of her daughter, Lady Agatha, and the inbred fatuities of Dumby and Lord Augustus Lorton. He was not so adept at finding a convincing tone for the more serious moments, a problem with which he continued to experiment until he solved it in *The Importance of Being Earnest* by dispensing with the serious altogether. He also maximized the opportunities provided by the high standards of setting and costume at the St. James's Theatre, notably for the act II drawing-room opening into a ballroom, with an illuminated terrace, a band playing, and "Palms, flowers, and brilliant lights."[41] This was the playground, or stage, of the wealthy and well-connected, the power structure of English society well-known at firsthand to Alexander's audiences, and through the newspapers and popular literature to everyone else; and on to it step the portentous men and the brilliantly dressed women, at whose center stands the "good" Lady Windermere and the "wicked" but by association socially acceptable Mrs. Erlynne: the world will now apply its double standard, and pretend to overlook the "fact" that she is, was, Windermere's supposed mistress.

Wilde presents a society that is as false as fiction, and founded on fictions, a construct that he will develop further in *A Woman of No Importance*, about a good woman with an "immoral" past, and *An Ideal Husband*, about a man whose fortune and career is founded on deceit and who is rewarded with a seat in the cabinet. Within these smart portraits of contemporary and fashionable society – time, the present; place, London or 'The Shires' – few individual characters emerge of the complexity and individuality achieved by Ibsen, or even, perhaps, Pinero. But Wilde is supremely successful in delineating the rituals of a decadent and dying class, and in suggesting the hollowness and inadequacy of prevailing morality and ideals. There is no place in England for Mrs. Erlynne, who finds it too full of fogs and serious people, but equally no place for the serious woman of no importance Mrs. Arbuthnot, or for her illegitimate son Gerald or for the wealthy American orphan Hester.

Wilde's three society comedies were all written for the commercial theatre. In contrast, his more radical experiment in symbolist form, *Salome*, featuring an oriental Hedda Gabler, was banned from the English stage by the censor, even if it was to be acted in French, and had to make its way in the 1890s, in England at least, in printed form, although Aubrey Beardsley's irreverent and brilliant pictures gave the text a distinctive theatricality.[42] A different kind of radicalism infused *The Importance of Being Earnest*, which passed to Alexander from Wyndham and which achieved its effect by embracing the trivial, and mocking English life by subjecting it to the formal discipline of farce. Shaw's marked coolness is an indication of his Celtic rival's triumph, and the effortlessly musical elegance of Wilde's holiday writing provides a display of fireworks that celebrates the end of an era: a kind of theatrical last-night party.[43] It is to this work and style that the English playwrights of the twentieth century variously returned, pervasively (Noël Coward), explicitly (Joe Orton and Tom Stoppard and Mark Ravenhill), but also with discernible traces in writers as contrasting as Edward Bond and Harold Pinter.

If the stage was a natural medium for Wilde, whose entire social existence was a series of performances, it was no less suited to Shaw, whose public life unfolded on soap-box and lecture platform. His writing fingers itched to find the right form, and formula, and by the end of the 1890s he was ready to succeed, and to dominate the English stage for the next three decades. As early as 1884 he began collaborating on a play with Archer, with a plot lifted from a "twaddling cup-and-saucer comedy" by Emile Augier, with dialogue supplied by Shaw, originally called *The Way to a Woman's Heart*, and later *Rheingold* or *Rhinegold*[44]; and in 1886 he sketched a plan for a "St. James's Piece" for John Hare, with the commercial theatre clearly in his sights. Ditching Archer, Shaw returned from time to time to the unfinished play, spurred and inspired by the impact of Archer's translation of *A Doll's House* and Janet Achurch's Nora. When Grein confessed his disappointment at the lack of new British playwrights, Shaw volunteered himself, and the transformed *Rhinegold*, now entitled *Widowers' Houses*. It played for two performances at the Royalty Theatre in December 1892. Shaw, making a speech on the first night in his Jaeger suit, was met with hisses, in marked contrast to Wilde's insouciant appearance, cigarette in hand, after *Lady Windermere's Fan*. Shaw later and provocatively labeled the work "An Original Didactic Realistic Play in Three Acts," and its thesis, that the English middle classes were totally dependent on tainted money stemming from the ruthless exploitation of the poor through slum landlordism, suggests that he was deliberately working out a theory in dramatic form. Cheap housing was a subject Shaw knew about at first hand, having collected slum rentals as a young man in Dublin, and now from his increasingly close involvement in London local politics, and his passion infuses the play. His probing of the fierce demands of money, lust and social respectability is painful, and Archer's complaint that every character "is ill-conditioned, quarrelsome, fractious" entirely justifiable.[45] As Shaw's preface states, he has shown "middle-class respectability and younger son gentility fattening on the poverty of the slum as flies fatten on filth. That is not a pleasant theme."[46]

What Shaw does achieve is an extraordinary and disconcerting energy, especially in the character of Blanche Sartorius, the entrepreneur's daughter. He conceives her as "vital and energetic" rather than "delicate and refined," and she takes the initiative in the love-making with the young doctor Harry Trench. Shaw's indicators litter her speeches – "impatiently," "sharply," "moodily," "impatiently," "desperately." She is infused with anger, like Katherina in *The Taming of the Shrew*, and in one extraordinary scene rages at the parlormaid, and half strangles her. Fiona Shaw's controversial 1999 production for the Royal National Theatre introduced a number of bizarre elements – notably, an unscripted and illogical pregnancy – but captured brilliantly the raw emotions, the sense of activity and violence, that surge below the surface of Shaw's first play. "I admire the horrible flesh and blood of your creatures," wrote Wilde, on receiving the published text, opus 2 of the great Celtic school, in return for a copy of *Salome* in purple raiment.[47] Opus 2 buzzes with energy, physical, emotional and intellectual, even if – perhaps because – Shaw was not in complete control of his material.

Shaw, convincing himself if not everyone else that *Widowers' Houses* had put him on the theatrical map, wrote *The Philanderer*, rewrote it at the suggestion of Lady Colin Campbell, and had it rejected by Grein: Shaw later described the piece to Ellen Terry as a "combination of mechanical farce with realistic filth which quite disgusted me."[48] He decided to tackle another social issue, prostitution, undertook some rapid research, borrowed a copy of *The Second Mrs. Tanqueray* from Archer, listened to Janet Achurch recount the plot of the play she was writing based on Maupassant's story "Yvette," and prepared *Mrs. Warren's Profession* for Grein and the Independent Theatre. Grein rejected it, as "unfit for women's ears," and would not even organize a private production. The Stage Society provided this service in 1902, and the 1905 world premiere in America resulted in prosecution. The play was not performed publicly in Britain until 1925. The Lord Chamberlain refused *Salome* a license on the spurious grounds that its subject matter was biblical, and so unperformable, and *Mrs. Warren's Profession* would have been refused because it was immoral and otherwise improper for our stage; but in the case of Shaw's second "unpleasant" play, Mrs. Grundy added her powerful voice. All this furore provoked Shaw into writing one of his most spirited prefaces when the play was published in 1902, although the controversy may also have contributed to his own later unease about its worth.

As with *Widowers' Houses*, Shaw addresses a social problem, organized prostitution, and dramatizes it through its impact on the lives and sensibilities of the individuals affected by it, and centrally through Vivie Warren, the daughter whose upbringing and education have been paid for by her mother's career, first as a prostitute and later as the manager of a string of upmarket European brothels. Vivie Warren begins and closes the play, and Shaw reverses expectation and conventional pattern by placing the reconciliation and understanding between mother and daughter in act II, and concluding with the child's rejection of her parent – a rejection marked by Mrs. Warren slamming the door behind her. Vivie at the same time refuses the traditional alternative of love's young dream in the shape of Frank Gardner, and embraces instead the world of work as one of two women partners in a firm of actuaries. Shaw incriminates the whole of society in the business of prostitution; he also fails to condemn Mrs. Warren or her (off-stage) sister Liz for escaping from penury and exploitation by taking control of their only assets, their bodies. Liz ends up as a respected county lady, living in Winchester next to the cathedral, while Kitty Warren continues her profitable career – it is this "unnecessary" continuation that prompts Vivie's rejection. The two major scenes between mother and daughter are raw and vivid, but Shaw also sketches with deft economy a society that both permits, even promotes, prostitution and yet claims that it does not exist. The three older male characters represent, embody, contemporary respectability: Praed, aesthete, "artist," refined man of education and leisure; the Reverend Samuel Gardner, country parson, humbug, hypocrite; Sir George Crofts, sensualist, capitalist, man of the world. Their stories are presented against a backdrop of conventional English tranquility, a Surrey country cottage and a rectory garden, on

Figure 10 Harley Granville Barker as Frank Gardner, Madge Macintosh as
Vivie Warren, and Julius Knight as Praed in the Stage Society's production of Shaw's
Mrs. Warren's Profession, 1902.

cloudless summer days and starlit nights. Shaw prods and probes: both Crofts
and Gardner are old clients of Mrs. Warren, and either, it is suggested, may be
Vivie's father. In an early draft, Shaw makes Vivie and Frank half brother and
sister. The final text draws back from that explicitness, but nevertheless the
theme of incest that Shaw echoed from *The Cenci* and from Ibsen remains.

He portrays a corrupt, sick society, unredeemable even by a younger generation. Frank wants to play babes in the wood with Vivie in earnest: he holds out his arms to her, and invites her: "Come and be covered up with leaves again."[49] Vivie rejects this with a cry of disgust: "You make all my flesh creep," and the fourth act, after the melodrama of Crofts's violent proposal and Frank's appearance with a rifle, offers a sharp, analytical justification of the world of work, a world now dominated by serious women. If the partnership between Mrs. Warren and Crofts represents the aggressive aspects of natural selection and the survival of the fittest, Vivie's response is, first, refusal to be nurtured any longer by such a system, and, secondly, refusal to breed. In its implications, this play remains one of Shaw's bleakest condemnations of the century's values, for all the comedy he extracts from his moral odyssey.

Shaw's playwriting took a new direction in 1893. Florence Farr, one of his muses, was presenting a season at the Avenue Theatre, and asked both Yeats and Shaw to write plays for her. Yeats's *The Land of Heart's Desire* materialized, but as Shaw's effort was not ready, John Todhunter's *A Comedy of Sighs* made up the bill. This proved disastrous, so Shaw was persuaded to complete *Arms and the Man*, which was hastily rehearsed as a replacement, with Alma Murray as the "romantic heroine" Raina and Farr as the pragmatic servant Louka. Aubrey Beardsley designed the poster, perhaps the first theatre poster to receive its own reviews, featuring an unmistakable "Japanesey" New Woman, an appropriate image for Shaw's previous play, but not especially relevant to his witty demolition of heroism. The first-night audience was a roll-call of the new drama: Archer, Jones, Wilde, George Moore, Yeats, Charles Charrington, and Janet Achurch, and Yeats referred to the event as "the first contest between the old commercial school of theatrical folk and the new artistic school." Yeats reacted to Shaw's play "with admiration and hatred," finding it too mechanical.[50] Shaw, like Wilde, was skillful at selecting elements of play-construction, and using them for his own ends – in this case, the device of the borrowed overcoat, which provides the evidence for the chocolate-cream soldier Bluntschli's night visit to the Petkoff house. Was the play serious, or trivial? Shaw changed the subtitle to "An Anti-Romantic Comedy," in an attempt to shift the balance. The lightness is deceptive. Although Charles Wyndham decided not to give the play a West-End run, it had a provincial tour and a successful production in America.

Shaw became a theatre critic, and learned to write plays that would work on the commercial stage without compromising his originality and intelligence. Wilde's *The Importance of Being Earnest*, "A Trivial Comedy for Serious People," can be seen in part as Wilde's response to the new Shaw of carpet-bags and creatively lying servants – just as Shaw's *You Never Can Tell* reflected his own reception of Wilde's "heartless" comedy. Each dramatist found ways to puncture the hypocrisy and false idealisms of the age, including the idealism of the Victorian happy family. Wounded families and isolated orphans inhabit their scenes, serious and trivial, unpleasant and pleasant, alike. This was not, perhaps, the "frankly doctrinal theatre" that Shaw advocated in *The Quintessence of Ibsenism*, his impassioned argument for the right of drama to take scriptural rank, and for Ibsen's own right to canonical rank "as one of the major prophets of the modern Bible."[51] Act IV of *Mrs. Warren's Profession* fits Shaw's advocacy of one major Ibsen innovation, the introduction of the discussion. But the second, more crucial, shift, was to make "the spectators themselves the persons of the drama."[52]

The focus on marriage, and on the surrounding context of social status and property, may seem simply the traditional stuff of drama. Shaw's preamble to his interpretation of Ibsen's individual plays explored "Ideals and Idealists" and "The Womanly Woman," and his base line involved the organization of society "for the perpetuation of the British family as we know it at present."[53] The "happy English home"[54] is what the modern post-Ibsen drama of the 1890s scrutinized, while the imperial stages on which the British, or English, appeared – India, Australia, New Zealand, Africa, Ireland – remained as a shadowy but significant background, yet one more ideal waiting to be exploded. Pinero and Jones stretched existing dramatic form to make way for contemporary issues. But it was the more drastic and playful handling of Wilde and Shaw, with their verbal fireworks and love of paradox, their cunning exploitation of reversal and surprise, that shook the drama into life. Disarmingly, they trapped the audience within the action by their unsettling use of comedy, and their polished and misleadingly innocent technique formed a collective bequest, gift-wrapped for the playwrights of the next century.

NOTES

1. See the *Pall Mall Gazette*, LVI new series, 17 February 1893, pp. 1–2; 21 February 1893, pp. 2 and 3; 27 February 1893, p. 3; 13 March 1893, p. 2; 20 April 1893, p. 2; 29 May 1893, p. 2; 1 June 1893, p. 4 (with further reviews of Elizabeth Robins in *Hedda Gabler*, *The Master Builder*, and *Brand*); 10 June 1893, p. 4 (Eleanora Duse); and 19 June 1893, p. 4 (*Widowers' Houses*).
2. Quoted in Michael Holroyd, *Bernard Shaw, 1: 1856–1898, "The Search for Love"* (London: Chatto & Windus, 1988), p. 296.
3. *Ibid.*, p. 296
4. *Pall Mall Gazette*, 31 August 1892.
5. Edward Gordon Craig, *On The Art of the Theatre* (London: Heinemann, 1911).

6. William Archer, "The Drama in the Doldrums," *The Fortnightly Review*, July 1892, p. 160.
7. William Archer, "Plays and Acting of the Season," *The Fortnightly Review*, August 1893, p. 255.
8. William Archer, "Some Recent Plays," *The Fortnightly Review*, May 1894, p. 600.
9. *Ibid.*, p. 604.
10. Holroyd, *Shaw*, p. 280. For the Independent Theatre and its context, see John Stokes, *Resistible Theatres: Enterprise and Experiment in the Late Nineteenth Century* (London: Paul Elek Books Ltd., 1972), especially part IV, "A Literary Theatre: The Lessons of the Independent Theatre."
11. The raw theatricality of the unknown John Osborne's *Look Back in Anger* succeeded in contrast to, for example, the well-known novelist Angus Wilson's *The Mulberry Bush*.
12. See Wilde's letter to Bernard Shaw, 9 May 1893, and Hesketh Pearson's interpretation, in *The Complete Letters of Oscar Wilde*, edited by Merlin Holland and Rupert Hart-Davis (London: Fourth Estate, 2000), p. 563.
13. Frank Harris, *Oscar Wilde, His Life and Confessions* (Garden City, NY: Garden City Publishing Co., 1932), p. 388.
14. See John Dawick, *Pinero: A Theatrical Life* (Boulder: University Press of Colorado, 1993), and the introductions in J. S. Bratton (ed.), *"Trelawny of the 'Wells'" and Other Plays* (Oxford: Oxford University Press, 1995), and George Rowell (ed.), *Plays by A. W. Pinero* (Cambridge: Cambridge University Press, 1986), and Stephen Wyatt (ed.), *Pinero, Three Plays* (London: Methuen, 1985).
15. See introductory note by Malcolm C. Salaman to Arthur W. Pinero, *The Profligate* (London: William Heinemann, 1891).
16. Bratton (ed.), *"Trelawny of the 'Wells,' "* p. 163.
17. Pinero took the name of Highercoombe from a Surrey house he himself had rented.
18. Bratton (ed.), *"Trelawny of the 'Wells,' "* p. 160.
19. Bernard Shaw reviewed the published text of *The Second Mrs. Tanqueray* in February 1895 in *The Saturday Review*, under the title "An Old New Play and a New Old One" – the "Old New Play" was *The Importance of Being Earnest. Dramatic Opinions and Essays*, 1 (New York: Brentano's, 1928), pp. 36–40.
20. Bratton (ed.), *"Trelawny of the 'Wells,' "* p. 205.
21. *Ibid.*, p. 209.
22. *Ibid.*, p. 183.
23. *Ibid.*, p. 168.
24. See Angela V. John, *Elizabeth Robins: Staging A Life, 1862–1952* (London: Routledge, 1995), p. 66, and Margot Peters, *Mrs. Pat: The Life of Mrs. Patrick Campbell* (London: Bodley Head, 1984), pp. 69–79.
25. See "Of the St. James's Theatre and Mrs. Patrick Campbell" in Graham Robertson, *Time Was* (London: Quartet Books, 1981) (originally published by Hamish Hamilton, 1931), pp. 247–60, and A. E. W. Mason, *Sir George Alexander and the St. James's Theatre* (London: Macmillan, 1935), pp. 45–55.
26. Shaw, *Dramatic Opinions and Essays*, p. 39.

27. Joel H. Kaplan and Sheila Stowell, *Theatre and Fashion: Oscar Wilde to the Suffragettes* (Cambridge: Cambridge University Press, 1994), p. 55. The whole of chap. 2, "Dressing Mrs. Pat," is illuminating.

28. *Ibid.*, p. 51.

29. See Jean Chothia (ed.), *"The New Woman" and Other Emancipated Woman Plays* (Oxford: Oxford University Press, 1998), for an introduction to *The Notorious Mrs. Ebbsmith*, and for a modern text.

30. Max Beerbohm, "Mrs. Ebbsmith and the Bensonians," *The Saturday Review*, 9 March 1901, reprinted in Max Beerbohm, *Around Theatres* (London: Rupert Hart-Davis, 1953), pp. 131–35. Beerbohm offers an astute analysis of the play's faults, and strengths, emphasizing that the play's two essential characters are "remarkably abnormal," and arguing that Pinero did not dare allow his creation, Mrs. Ebbsmith, to act for herself.

31. William Archer, *The World*, 27 March 1895.

32. Henry Arthur Jones's preface, in the form of a letter to Mrs. Grundy, was dated 28 August, 1894. Jones was in Dieppe, across the channel from Worthing where Wilde was writing *The Importance of Being Earnest*. See Russell Jackson (ed.), *Three Plays by Henry Arthur Jones* (Cambridge: Cambridge University Press, 1982), for the text, and a critical introduction. See also Penny Griffin, *Arthur Wing Pinero and Henry Arthur Jones* (New York: St. Martin's Press, 1991).

33. Jackson (ed.), *Three Plays by Henry Arthur Jones*, p. 117.

34. Doris Arthur Jones, *The Life and Letters of Henry Arthur Jones* (London: Victor Gollancz Ltd., 1930), pp. 164–5.

35. Jackson (ed.), *Three Plays by Henry Arthur Jones*, p. 161.

36. *Ibid.*

37. *Ibid.*, p. 209.

38. *Ibid.*, p. 219.

39. The textual references are keyed to Peter Raby (ed.), *Oscar Wilde, "The Importance of Being Earnest" and Other Plays* (Oxford: Oxford University Press, Oxford, 1995). See, for other commentary, Sos Eltis, *Revising Wilde: Society and Subversion in the Plays of Oscar Wilde* (Oxford: Oxford University Press, 1996); Kerry Powell, *Oscar Wilde and the Theatre of the 1890s* (Cambridge: Cambridge University Press, 1990), and Peter Raby (ed.), *The Cambridge Companion to Oscar Wilde* (Cambridge: Cambridge University Press, 1997).

40. Raby (ed.), *"The Importance of Being Earnest,"* p. 47.

41. *Ibid.*, p. 21. See also Kaplan and Stowell, *Theatre and Fashion*, pp. 13–20, for commentary on the dress codes of the play.

42. See Peter Raby, *Aubrey Beardsley and the 1890s* (London: Collins and Brown, 1998), p. 112.

43. Shaw's coolness is all too apparent in his *Saturday Review* piece, *Dramatic Opinions and Essays*, pp. 32–35.

44. On Shaw and the Archer collaboration, see Holroyd, *Shaw*, pp. 274–76 and 280–81, and Peter Whitebrook, *William Archer: A Biography* (London: Methuen, 1993), p. 72. Shaw's reading of his first efforts sent Archer to sleep. When Shaw asked Henry Arthur Jones what this might mean, Jones replied "Sleep is a criticism."

45. William Archer, *The World*, 14 December 1892.

46. Shaw's preface to *Plays Unpleasant* (1898, reprinted by Penguin Books, Harmondsworth, 1946) (in commemoration of Shaw's ninetieth birthday), p. xxiv.
47. Wilde to Shaw, *Complete Letters of Oscar Wilde*, p. 563.
48. See Shaw's preface, *Plays Unpleasant*, pp. xii–xiv, and Holroyd, *Shaw*, pp. 296–97.
49. Shaw, *Plays Unpleasant*, p. 264.
50. See Holroyd, *Shaw*, pp. 302–06, and R. F. Foster, *W. B. Yeats: A Life* (Oxford: Oxford University Press, 1997), 1: 140–42. Also W. B. Yeats, *Autobiographies* (London: Macmillan, 1955), pp. 282–87.
51. Bernard Shaw, *The Quintessence of Ibsenism* (London: Constable, 1922) (first edition 1891), p. 209.
52. *Ibid.*
53. *Ibid.*, p. 205
54. Mrs. Allonby makes this deprecating comment as she surveys Mrs. Arbuthnot's pretty sitting-room through her lorgnette in Act IV of *A Woman of No Importance*, in Raby (ed.), *"The Importance of Being Earnest,"* p. 144.

11

CARY M. MAZER

New theatres for a new drama

In 1904, the Court Theatre was a shabby, late-Victorian playhouse seating barely more than 600 patrons, a few underground stops away from the fashionable "theatreland" of the West End. That spring, H. Granville Barker, twenty-seven, an actor, director, and playwright, hired to direct and to play a supporting role in a production of *The Two Gentlemen of Verona*, booked the theatre for a series of matinees of *Candida*, by George Bernard Shaw. By the following fall, Barker, in partnership with J. E. Vedrenne, the business manager for the theatre's previous principal lessee, embarked on his own management of the theatre. Every second week a new staging would be given three matinee performances; if public attention or artistic merit warranted, the production would be moved into the evening bill for a limited run. Over the next three seasons, the Vedrenne–Barker management produced 988 performances of thirty-two plays, including the first commercial London stagings of Shaw's *Candida*, *The Philanderer*, *Man and Superman*, *How He Lied to Her Husband*, and *Captain Brassbound's Conversion*, and a revival of *You Never Can Tell*; and premieres of *John Bull's Other Island*, *Major Barbara*, and *The Doctor's Dilemma*; Barker's own *The Voysey Inheritance* and (with Laurence Housman) *Prunella*; *The Silver Box* by John Galsworthy; *The Return of the Prodigal* and *The Charity That Began at Home* by St. John Hankin; *The Camden Wonder* by first-time playwright John Masefield; *Votes for Women!* by Elizabeth Robins; other new plays by Frederick Fenn, Robert Vernon Harcourt, Maurice Hewlitt, and Cyril Harcourt; one-act plays by Arthur Schnitzler and William Butler Yeats; plays by Henrik Ibsen (*The Wild Duck* and *Hedda Gabler*), Gerhart Hauptmann (*The Thieves' Comedy*), and Maurice Maeterlinck (*Agalvaine and Selysette*); and stagings of Gilbert Murray's translations of *Hippolytus*, *The Trojan Women*, and *Electra* by Euripides. Audiences at the Court were unconventional, self-defined as intellectuals ("I prefer addressing minorities," Barker wrote; "one can make them hear better"); and they were, in significant numbers, women.[1] Both Prime Minister Arthur Balfour and the future prime ministers, Henry Campbell-Bannerman and H. W. Asquith, came to see *John Bull's Other Island*; and, at a special performance, the rotund King Edward VII, it was reported, laughed so hard he broke his chair.

I begin with the Vedrenne–Barker management of the Court because it produced what theatregoers and critics would recognize – even if they couldn't define it – as "The New Drama." The plays examined social and political issues – class inequities, "the woman question" (the marriage market, the sexual "double standard," and women's suffrage), workers' rights, and the class system – using the tools of politically progressive, often socialist, political economics; they were dramaturgically unconventional, eschewing many if not all of the plot devices and formulae of more conventional contemporary drama, and were often structured around extended discussion and debate; with only a few exceptions, the plays were contextually and scenically realistic; and virtually all of the plays were already, or would soon be, available in print, and aspired to be experienced, not only in the theatre, but as written texts by readers of serious modern literature.

In addition to producing a recognizable New Drama, the Court Theatre exemplified what was already known as "The New Theatre." Plays were presented in rotating bills (if not in daily alternating repertory, which was the ultimate goal of the movement) and not in unlimited long runs. The management was designed to serve the repertoire, rather than to enrich the bank accounts of the theatre's "principal lessee" and his or her silent investors; and the theatre was explicitly designed to appeal to a sector of the theatregoing public who thought of themselves as intellectuals, and who felt that they could see plays and stagings that could not otherwise be presented by commercial London theatrical managements.

I am defining – or at least describing – the New Drama and the New Theatre as distinct phenomena, but the key here is their connection. Supporters of the New Drama were invariably supporters of the New Theatre and vice versa, seized with the conviction that only a New Theatre could provide a theatrical home for the New Drama and would encourage a new generation of playwrights to write for the theatre. Many of the supporters of the New Drama and New Theatre fought for the abolition of the censorship – the system of new-play licensing, through the office of the Lord Chamberlain and his appointed "Examiner of Plays," which had been in place since the Theatre Licensing Act of 1737.[2] And, despite their skepticism about state control, they lobbied indefatigably for the creation of a national theatre: a theatre officially recognized by the state and operating under an endowment, which would be freed from the pressures of the marketplace to preserve and develop dramatic and theatrical art.

The Court under Barker became the flagship of the New Drama and New Theatre movements, and served as the inspiration and example for a wide range of theatrical activity in the remaining years before the First World War. Aside from Barker's subsequent seasons at the Savoy, the St. James's, and the Duke of York's Theatres (which we will look at later), progressive theatres were managed by Barker's wife Lillah McCarthy (whose production of Shaw's Pirandellian satire on the New Drama and its befuddled critics, *Fanny's First Play*, ironically, and counter to New Theatre goals, received the longest run of any Shaw play of the period), Gertrude Kingston, Dennis Eadie, and others. The Court example proved most compelling for a generation of New Drama and New Theatre advocates who established theatres in Manchester, Liverpool, Glasgow, and Birmingham, which turned to the Court Theatre for much of their repertoire and a significant percentage of their actors.[3]

It is tempting to view the Court years, for the dramatic movement that it helped to spark and the theatres that it inspired, as a triumph. And, in its own terms, so it was. If, as is often said, history is written by the victors, in this case victory was declared by the writers. Many of the principals in the battle for a New Drama and a New Theatre were working journalists; as Shaw boasted, in his theatre column in *The Saturday Review* in 1896, "The twentieth century, if it concerns itself about either of us, will see you as I see you."[4] With the self-applied label "New," the advocates of the New Drama and New Theatre had declared the war; and, without even waiting for the battle to be over, they claimed victory; and then wrote the histories themselves. Moreover, one of the goals of the New Drama was to create a drama that could rank as literature. For the literary scholars and anthologists of the next several decades, the history of the theatre was the history of the drama it produced; and the dramatic histories and anthologies of the first half of the twentieth century cared above all about "Modern Drama," an open-ended canon beginning with Zola and Ibsen and stretching to the present day. In this schema, the New Drama was the British branch of a worldwide movement toward Modernity; the British advocates of the New Drama and New Theatre had had the wisdom to champion Ibsen, and the gumption to create a canon of British playwrights, major (Shaw, and his Irish contemporaries Yeats and Synge) and minor (Barker, Galsworthy, Hankin, Robins), as well as some equivocal precursors and fellow travelers (Henry Arthur Jones, Arthur Wing Pinero), and some *sui generis* masters who might still be claimed for the movement (Oscar Wilde, J. M. Barrie).

But the pioneering theatre historians of the last third of the twentieth century – Michael R. Booth, George Rowell, David Mayer, and others – have

radically changed the way we view the theatre activity of the century before the First World War, as the present volume testifies. Theatre activity is
no longer valid solely on the basis of having created a body of drama; and
that drama is no longer valid solely on the basis of its canonical value as
"literature." Rather, theatre activity is most culturally and socially meaningful at its most popular. And in the nineteenth century, theatre was – despite
the prevailing antitheatricalism of official high culture – perhaps the most
widespread arena of popular culture

How, then, do we appraise the significance of a theatrical movement that
defined high art as something counter to popular culture, that set itself up as
an alternative to the commercial mainstream and the dramatic status quo,
and that defined its worth as a theatrical movement on the basis of the literary
value of the dramatic scripts it produced? The answer might be to appropriate
the analytical tools of the movement, and to use these tools to dismantle the
movement itself. With the tools of (largely socialist) political economy, the
New Drama and the New Theatre saw how theatrical activity is inevitably
implicated in the material conditions of its own manufacture, that theatrical
production is a form of industrial production. But although they wished to
create a theatre that could be freed from such material considerations, their
own activities were inescapably tied to them. It is more useful, then, to see the
Court seasons – and the entire New Drama and New Theatre movements,
along with the performances, scripts, and institutions, they created – as the
product of the inevitable tension between what the theatre was and what
theatre activists wanted it to be.

In this context, the story of the Court seasons – indeed, of virtually all
Edwardian and Georgian New Theatres – is not the success story that its
early chroniclers and canon-formers claimed it to be. Born out of a dream of
a national theatre, the Court and the managements that followed were not
exemplary cases but provisional experiments, compromised at every level
by the very material conditions that the movement was designed to transcend. Despite all of the theatres and managements in London and in the
provinces that the Court inspired, the theatre failed to sustain itself. Despite
the testimony and lobbying of many New Drama and New Theatre activists
in 1908, Parliament declined to abolish the censorship. After several tem-
porary homes, Barker and his collaborators ultimately failed in their one
last attempt to create a working repertory theatre in the West End. And the
movement's repeated attempts to create a functioning National Theatre, a
dream that seemed near to being realized by 1916, ended in failure, not only
because of the onset of the war, but because of repeated compromises in
the institution's mission and structure. If the advocates of the New Drama
and the New Theatre were right in viewing dramatic writing as enmeshed

in the theatres that could produce them, and the theatres as needing to be exempt from the material demands of a capital-driven entertainment and leisure industry; if, as Matthew Arnold wrote, in a much quoted call for a national theatre in 1879, "The theatre is irresistible; organise the theatre!"; then, by their own standards, the advocates of the New Drama and the New Theatre failed, both in reorganizing the structure of the theatre industry and in creating a theatre that could co-exist with the existing structures.

It is instructive, then, to trace the history of the movement, from the events that led to the seasons at the Court to the experiments and managements that followed, concluding with the two institutions – the repertory season at the Duke of York's Theatre in 1910, and the ill-fated Shakespeare Memorial National Theatre – in the context of the material conditions the movement was forced to grapple with, and that it attempted, and failed, to supplant.

The movement began a generation before Barker; and a convenient date for its origins can be set at 7 June 1889. The cast of characters: George Moore (1852–1933), the francophile Anglo-Irish novelist who had embraced Naturalism – a literary movement that advocated quasi-scientific attention to material conditions and their effect on social behaviors – and who, like that movement's founder, Emile Zola, believed that Naturalism must come to the theatre as well; J. T. Grein (1862–1935), a Dutch-born theatre editor and journalist; William Archer (1856–1924), Scottish, fluent in Norwegian, a prolific theatre polemicist and critic; Charles Charrington (?–1926) and Janet Achurch (1864–1916), actors and spouses; actress Florence Farr (1860–1917); Elizabeth Robins (1862–1952), American-born actress, friend and protégée of Henry James and Oscar Wilde, just beginning to make a career in Drury Lane melodrama; and her friend Marion Lea (1861–1944), another American-born actress. These artists, managers, and critics turned to several models for their inspiration: Continental European "official" state-, court-, and municipal-supported theatres, such as the theatre troupe supported and directed by Georg II, the Duke of Saxe-Meiningen, and the Comédie-Française, which appeared at Drury Lane in 1879, inspiring Arnold's article in *The Nineteenth Century* calling upon the British theatre to organize; the new avant-garde theatres on the Continent, particularly André Antoine's Théâtre Libre, which had been founded as a small members-only theatre dedicated to creating a Naturalist theatre, and which toured to the Royalty Theatre in London in 1889; and, most of all, the published plays of Ibsen.

As Thomas Postlewait has observed, Ibsen was known to readers and theatre activists, well before the plays could have been seen by them in performance, through Archer's own essays and books, and from over a dozen different editions of translations, including what would become Archer's own authorized English translations.[5] Ibsen became a focal point of the movement, not only because he was being read in translation, but because he *could* be read in translation, i.e., because his work was accessible to serious readers unfamiliar with stage practice, who would consider the plays, for better or for worse, as the peers of other literary genres and other forms of serious polemical prose writing.

That Ibsen could also be, as Archer argued as early as 1882, a vehicle for actors to create psychologically complex characters, and a means of examining serious social ideas, was made clear when Charrington and Achurch, in consultation with Archer, staged *A Doll's House* at the Novelty Theatre on 7 June 1889. Moore and Grein, in the meantime, were forming a committee to oversee the creation of what was originally to be called the British Théâtre Libre. On 13 March 1891, what was now called the Independent Theatre presented *Ghosts* at the Royalty Theatre, before an audience of members (as the play would not have been able to obtain a license from the Examiner of Plays in the Lord Chamberlain's Office). Within the next few years, there were special matinees, single performances, or fully mounted stagings of *Pillars of Society*, *A Doll's House*, *An Enemy of the People*, *Rosmersholm* (with Florence Farr), and, most notably, *Hedda Gabler*, produced by Robins and Lea (who played Hedda and Thea) in association with Archer. The Independent Theatre produced *The Wild Duck* in 1894. Then, after a production of *Little Eyolf* (and José Echegaray's *Mariana*) in 1896, which they financed by selling subscriptions in advance, Robins and Lea joined Archer in establishing the New Century Theatre in London, presenting *John Gabriel Borkman* as their first production.

Though the Independent Theatre tried to remain true to its Parisian counterpart and to Moore's naturalist agenda (staging Zola's own adaptation of his novel *Thérèse Raquin*, and Moore's own *The Strike at Arlingford*), its production of *Ghosts*, along with the flurry of other productions of Ibsen, established the New Drama and New Theatre movement as an Ibsen movement, rather than a Naturalist movement. This had several implications for the shape the advanced drama and the theatre would take over the next decade. In part because of the limited budgets, the productions did not emphasize slavishly detailed scenic contexts; and the favored milieus for the plays were middle-class drawing rooms, rather than the lower-class tenements and hovels common to Naturalism. This was a theatre of progressive – and specifically feminist – political ideas, rather than of scientific sociology. Moreover, the New Drama and New Theatre movement in this era became a theatre of actors – and, significantly, actresses – rather than of institutions.

What the New Theatre movement did not succeed in doing, despite its best efforts, was to provide a home for serious new British dramatic writing. The Independent Theatre and the New Century Theatre let it be known that they were interested in new plays by like-minded new playwrights, and several saw performance (for example, the Independent Theatre staged *Alan's Wife* by Robins and Mrs. Hugh Bell). But with one notable exception (about which more later), no plays these theatres commissioned generated a playwright with a future. Perhaps this was the result of the movement's momentary focus on Ibsen. It may, ironically, have also been a product of an explosion of serious dramatic writing in the mainstream theatre. Henry Arthur Jones, who launched his career in the 1880s with a series of melodramas, and Arthur Wing Pinero, known mostly for farces and sentimental comedies, were now inspired to write serious realistic plays about social problems. The influence of Ibsen here is uncertain; as Archer later wrote, Pinero and Jones "knew their business too well to despise him, but loved him not at all."[6] What is clear is that the shift in emphasis in the New Drama movement from Naturalism to social problem plays about middle-class families had served as an invitation to mainstream playwrights to revisit the issues that had already permeated mid-century British drama: the woman-with-a-past (familiar from 1860s sensation melodramas such as *East Lynne* and *Lady Audley's Secret*), and the intersections of courtship and class (familiar from the "cup-and-saucer realism" plays from the 1860s by Pinero's mentor, Tom Robertson). The mainstream playwrights of the nineties were also the beneficiaries of the new American copyright law in 1891, which enabled playwrights to publish their works without sacrificing overseas performance rights;[7] and so the New Drama's demand that drama be read as serious literature was answered, not by new playwrights of the avant-gard, but by the newly Ibsenized playwrights of the West End. The social plays of the nineties, beginning with Pinero's *The Second Mrs. Tanqueray* (1893) and *The Notorious Mrs. Ebbsmith* (1895) – were not politically progressive in the resolutions they offered to the social questions they raised (though they were not as retrograde as Jones's earlier satiric comedies from the late eighties, which parodied aestheticism and feminism); but they were embraced by the progressive theatre critics, among them William Archer. The advocates of the New Drama, who had spent the better part of the decade trying to invent a New Theatre to accommodate it, surrendered the banner to the dramatists of the mainstream. And the pioneering feminist actresses who fueled the movement – Achurch, Farr, Robins, and Lea – yielded the limelight to actresses such as Mrs. Patrick Campbell: catapulted to success as Paula Tanqueray and Agnes Ebbsmith, "Mrs. Pat" flirted with the New Women of the New Drama (Magda in Sudermann's *Heimat*, the Rat Wife and then Rita

Allmers in the New Century Theatre *Little Eyolf*, and much later Hedda for Barker at the Court in 1907), but directed her career instead toward trying to succeed Ellen Terry in the Shakespearean repertoire (as Ophelia, Juliet, and Lady Macbeth in partnership with Johnston Forbes Robertson), and in a series of roles recapitulating the neurasthenic heroines she had created for Pinero.

The one significant playwright to have come out of the New Drama and New Theatre movement of the nineties was Bernard Shaw, who, as theatre critic for *The Saturday Review* from 1895 to 1898, did not join Archer's enthusiasm for what he called the "Pinerotics" of the new West-End problem plays. Shaw (1856–1950) was a music critic, socialist pamphleteer, lecturer, and author of books on Wagner and Ibsen and five published (if largely unnoticed) novels when, in 1892, Grein invited him to collaborate with Archer on a new play for the Independent Theatre, which became Shaw's first solo effort, *Widowers' Houses* (Shaw took Archer's initial scenario and drafted an entire play without Archer's further participation). The case of Shaw's plays of the nineties is instructive, not solely because of Shaw's subsequent status in the canon of modern drama, but because it illustrates the precarious relationship of the New Drama of the nineties to the viability of New Theatre institutions that could support it. Shaw's plays struggled to find their audiences in the nineties, not only because the Independent Theatre and the New Century Theatre couldn't stage them, and not only because one of them, *Mrs Warren's Profession* (1893) was refused a license, but because Shaw, like Pinero, Jones, and Wilde, designed most of them for the West End, consciously shaping them to conform to the formulae of popular theatrical genres (farce, melodrama, society comedy, costume history play, etc.), and creating roles specifically for the star actor-managers who might perform in them. The melodrama *The Devil's Disciple* (1896), for example, was written for William Terriss, the farce *You Never Can Tell* (1896) for Charles Wyndham; and *The Man of Destiny* (1895) for Henry Irving and Ellen Terry. But the mainstream theatre could not make room for these plays' political messages; nor could the mainstream theatre comprehend the formalist games Shaw was playing with their generic formulae. And the mainstream theatre certainly could not handle the dream fantasy, political vituperation, and philosophical oratory of *Man and Superman* (1900), however much its relatively lightweight plot resembled a more traditional courtship comedy. The only way Shaw could reach an audience in the nineties was to bring out his plays in print.

There was one exception: in 1894, Shaw's Ruritanian comedy satirizing warfare and heroism, *Arms and the Man*, was produced by Florence Farr at the Avenue Theatre, on a double-bill with W. B. Yeats's *The Land of Heart's*

Desire, and ran for fifty performances. Not recorded on the program was the identity of the person who had financed the production, fully expecting that she would not see a return on her investment: tea-heiress Annie E. Horniman, who would later underwrite the transformation of Yeats's Irish Literary Theatre into the Irish National Theatre Society at the Abbey Theatre in Dublin, and who became a key figure in the creation of the regional repertory theatre movement in Britain. What to the average theatregoer appeared to be a traditional commercial West-End management was, in fact, an early experiment in theatrical subsidy. Though the Independent Theatre had provided an institutional home for advanced plays, and had begun to mobilize a community of like-minded artists and audiences, it did not yet provide a model for a theatre that could, structurally and institutionally, serve as a viable ongoing home for new work, or a model structure for a new industry. The development of a New Drama would perforce await the existence of a New Theatre, or at least the working model for one.

Barker (1876–1946) was the first of a generation of intellectual and politically progressive artists to have come of theatrical age in the New Drama and New Theatre movements. As a young actor he had toured with Ben Greet and with Mrs. Patrick Campbell, but he quickly saw that his creative and professional future lay with the alternative theatres and managements. He had first corresponded with Archer when he tried to get the New Century Theatre interested in producing his play, *The Weather-Hen* (written in collaboration with fellow actor Berte Thomas). He had twice acted in Elizabethan revival productions with William Poel, playing Shakespeare's Richard II and Marlowe's Edward II. And he was an active participant, as an actor, director, and playwright, with a new theatrical institution that proved to be the incubator for the New Theatre movement of the new century: the Stage Society.

The Stage Society had been founded in 1899 by Frederick Whelan, Charrington, Achurch, and others, in part to carry on the work of the Independent Theatre. Plays were presented for a single performance in rented or borrowed theatres on Sundays, the day that actors otherwise engaged in commercial long runs would be available. Audiences consisted of members (at first 300 members) and, after the membership was raised to 500, the press. As a members-only society, the theatre could, like the Independent Theatre, present plays that had been refused licenses by the Examiner of Plays, including Shaw's *Mrs. Warren's Profession* in 1902 (with Barker as Frank Gardner). The Stage Society was able to do something that the Independent Theatre and the New Century Theatre had not: it created an ongoing laboratory for new dramatic writing, both for new plays and for plays (such as Shaw's) that had not yet received a commercial production. Between 1899 and 1903, the Stage Society had presented, among other plays, Shaw's *You Never Can Tell, Man and Superman, The Admirable Bashville* (1901), *Candida* (1894) with Barker as Marchbanks, *Captain Brassbound's Conversion* (1899) with Barker as Captain Kearney, and Barker's first solo dramatic effort, *The Marrying of Ann Leete* (1899).

The Stage Society was serving the New Drama, but it was not helping to create a viable New Theatre; and so its most vociferous advocates continued to call for a theatre, insulated from the pressure of the marketplace, which could exist outside of, and alongside of, the existing structures of the commercial industry. Barker's management of the Court had come out of both of these impulses. On 21 April 1903, Barker wrote to Archer with a proposal: "To take the Court Theatre for six months or a year and to run a stock season of uncommercial drama: Hauptmann – Sudermann – Ibsen – Maeterlinck – Schnitzler – Shaw – Brieux, etc."[8] Barker's scheme called for many elements already advocated by Archer and others who, in the 1890s, had proposed a national theatre:[9] changing programs (if not alternating repertory, then at least a change of new production every second week); relatively low prices; tickets sold primarily by subscription; an audience drawn from intellectual members of the working class as well as from the relatively leisured classes; and, if not a subsidy, at least an initial reserve fund of £5,000 serving as a "guarantee." "It seems to me," Barker put it to Archer, "that we may wait a very long time for our National Theatre, and that when it comes we may have no modern National Drama to put in it. We must get vital drama from somewhere, and if we can't create it we must import it first."[10]

Barker would have to wait a year until a theatre (quite coincidentally the Court) came available for his scheme. But in the interim he was also involved in a significant step toward the creation of a National Theatre. In response to rumors circulating that the Scottish-born American millionaire Andrew Carnegie was willing to endow a National Theatre if viable plans for the theatre's operations were to exist, Barker and Archer drafted and privately printed a "blue book" entitled *Scheme and Estimates for a National Theatre*, laying out in detail the structure, finances, and repertoire for such a theatre.

The launching of the Vedrenne–Barker seasons at the Court and the initial private publication of *Scheme and Estimates* represent the last convergence of the New Drama and New Theatre movements and, ironically, also mark their first significant, and irreconcilable, parting of the ways. The Court seasons proved that there were indeed a sufficient backlog of New Drama waiting to be performed, a large enough body of new playwrights who would benefit from the opportunity, and on top of it all, in Shaw, one extremely prolific playwright with a seemingly endless supply of new and old plays ready for production. But it was also a Trojan Horse: even with its precarious financial underpinnings, it tantalized the New Drama advocates into believing that it could thrive without a fully endowed New Theatre as its home, that a New Theatre could exist within, and not apart from, the commercial theatre industry – a dream that, as we shall see, proved illusory. At the same time, the dream that the National Theatre could serve the New Drama was being sacrificed to coalition-building with the establishment. In writing *Scheme and Estimates*, Archer and Barker sought the endorsement of mainstream theatre artists who had supported the idea of a national theatre but were, to varying degrees, opponents of the New Drama. "There is a misconception to be guarded against," they wrote in their preface: "It is not an 'Advanced Theatre' that we are designing."[11] The great national and civic theatres of the Continent, they argued, follow the advances of the progressive theatres, as an army follows the advanced outposts; "Outposts are necessary to the army of progress; but no army can be all outposts." And so, while the proposed repertory included nine plays by Shakespeare (along with plays by Jonson, Molière, Congreve, Sheridan, Bulwer Lytton, Labiche, Dumas *fils*, Gilbert, and Stevenson), the only modern Continental plays were by Sudermann, Brieux, and Maeterlinck; and, aside from five hypothetical new plays by unnamed authors, the only modern British plays were *The Benefit of the Doubt* and *Trelawny of the "Wells"* by Pinero, *The Liars* by Jones, and *The Importance of Being Earnest* by Wilde. This effort to dissociate the National Theatre movement from the New Drama movement had the effect the authors evidently desired – *Scheme and Estimates* appeared with an endorsement on its first page from Henry Irving, Squire Bancroft, J. M. Barrie, Helen D'Oyly Carte, John Hare, Henry Arthur Jones, and A. W. Pinero. But, as we shall, see, the National Theatre – the ultimate goal of the New Theatre movement – was forever severed from the dramatic movement it had been designed to serve.

Just how difficult it was to sustain a progressive theatre management in London dedicated to the New Drama became apparent to Barker and Vedrenne when, for the 1907–08 season, they moved their operations to the Savoy Theatre, a fashionable theatre in the center of the West End, seating close to a thousand. The venture was thwarted artistically and financially. Barker had wanted to stage Ibsen's fantastic verse play, *Peer Gynt*. Instead, the repertoire proved more artistically conservative. *Medea* continued the Court's association with Murray's Euripides translations; but Galsworthy's new play, *Joy*, proved to be less politically acute than *The Silver Box* at the Court; Barker's new play, *Waste*, was denied a license by the Examiner of Plays; and in comparison to the Shaw plays at the Court, *The Devil's Disciple* (in its first London production) and an open-ended revival of *Arms and the Man* revealed how desperate the management was to attract the audiences they needed to keep the doors open. But not even emergency loans from Shaw (which, according to Dennis Kennedy, eventually totaled £5,250) could keep the management afloat. "The important thing to consider is this," Barker told the press at the end of the season, "that if they want anything in the shape of a theatre like this they cannot have it under the present conditions that obtain in London of enormous rents. If they want even so much as a repertoire theatre as we have been running, the building must be kept rent free."[12]

Before the launch of the Savoy season, Archer and Barker published their blue book, now titled *A National Theatre: Scheme and Estimates*, for the general public, with a new preface by Barker (in the form of a letter to Archer) which, in part, served as an advertisement for the Savoy season. Acknowledging the lengths that he and Archer had gone to in 1904 to renounce the New Drama in their prospectus for a national theatre, Barker now wrote: "Helping you with the book to-day, I should unhesitatingly, both from motives of good policy and personal taste, advocate the inclusion of every author whom we so carefully excluded four years ago – Ibsen, Hauptmann, d'Annunzio, Shaw, and the rest."[13] Barker also suggests that pioneering subsidized repertory theatres might be more likely to arise not in London but in provincial cities such as Manchester and Birmingham, where civic pride might generate subsidies, where theatres were available and less expensive to rent and operate, and where theatregoing habits were less entrenched.[14]

Barker's suggestion proved prophetic. Annie Horniman, who had begun to quarrel with Yeats at the Abbey, began to look for other cities and theatres on which to bestow her financial largesse. Alfred Wareing, the booking manager for the tour of the Irish National Players in 1906, hoped that she would underwrite his plans to open a repertory theatre in Glasgow. But B. Iden Payne, resident stage director at the Abbey, suggested Manchester instead, where Horniman financed a preliminary season in 1907 before she took over the Gaiety Theatre and transformed it into what is generally regarded as the first full-scale modern repertory theatre the next year. Wareing launched his theatre in Glasgow in 1909, with backing from a committee of citizens, until it collapsed under repeated losses (one season after Wareing's health collapsed) in 1914. And, after an experimental repertory season in 1911, the somewhat more conservative Liverpool Repertory was established, financed by a committee of 900 shareholders.

The regional repertory theatres succeeded in part because of the presence of a benefactor, or a network of smaller benefactors and patrons, willing to cushion the theatre from the financial risks that had brought down the Barker–Vedrenne Savoy management. But the next time Barker and his associates attempted to create an ongoing repertory theatre venture in London – at the Duke of York's Theatre in 1910 – they chose instead to protect themselves from the considerably higher expenses of the West End by forming a partnership with a commercial theatre producer, the American Charles Frohman, whose principal London successes had been plays by Pinero and Barrie, directed by Dion Boucicault and starring Boucicault's wife, Irene Vanbrugh. The original prospectus called for new plays by Court playwrights such as Shaw, Barker, Galsworthy, and Masefield, along with new plays by Henry James, another Murray translation of Euripides, and significant revivals of half-a-dozen Court plays. The initial repertory (with a changing bill each night) ended up including premieres of Galsworthy's indictment of the criminal justice system, *Justice*; a triple bill of two Barrie one-acts paired with a Barker staging of a dramatic fragment by George Meredith; Elizabeth Baker's *Chains*; and Shaw's *Misalliance* and Barker's *The Madras House*, two interlocking plays about sex, courtship, and the fashion industry. But with so many plays receiving their premieres in the evening bill, none of them had the chance to build an audience such as the plays at the Court had, with their two or three weeks of matinees. As at the Savoy, the management replaced these new plays, with their diminishing receipts, with revivals: Barker and Housman's *Prunella* and Pinero's *Trelawny of the "Wells,"* an 1890s play that nostalgically looked backward to the Robertsonian dramatic watershed of the 1860s. When Frohman terminated the management on the death of King Edward in May, ten plays had been given 128 performances. "All we have succeeded in doing," Shaw wrote to Barker, "is to prove the impossibility of a high art theatre under a commercial management."[15]

The fortunes of the National Theatre in the years before the First World War are even more indicative of the difficulties of establishing an alternative structure within an existing industry. In 1903 and 1904, Richard Badger, a wealthy Shakespeare enthusiast, had written to *The Times* offering to endow a memorial in London to Shakespeare. A committee was formed in 1905, including several prominent West-End actor-managers, charged with determining an appropriate form for the memorial. The committee considered the idea that Badger's bequest might be used as the nucleus for the endowment of a National Theatre, but the idea was quashed, in the privacy of the committee room, by the actor-manager Beerbohm Tree, who was that year beginning the annual practice of reviving his own elaborately staged Shakespeare productions in a spring festival. But when the Shakespeare Memorial Committee recommendation (for a statue in Leicester Square) was finally made public in 1908, a year after the publication of *Scheme and Estimates*, the announcement became a rallying point for a renewed call for a national theatre. Despite his earlier (and secret) role in scotching the national theatre plans, Tree now stepped forward as peacemaker, and brokered a "Shakespeare Concordat," creating a Shakespeare Memorial National Theatre (SMNT) Committee, charged with the goal of creating a National Theatre that would begin operations by the 1916 tercentenary celebrations of Shakespeare's death.

If *Scheme and Estimates* had already distanced the National Theatre movement from the New Drama, the Shakespeare Concordat further embroiled the movement in the cultural politics of Shakespeare, and in the theatrical battles being waged between the West-End producers of elaborate pictorially realistic "Modern" stagings of the plays, "Elizabethan revivalists" such as William Poel, and practitioners (such as Edward Gordon Craig) of the "New Stagecraft." Moreover, the SMNT proved to be a disastrous linkage between progressive New Theatre advocates (many of whom, like Barker, favored a hybrid Elizabethanism in staging Shakespeare) and commercial theatre managers. Tree, along with other actor-managers on the SMNT executive committee, attempted to divert the funds to existing managements, and packaged his own Shakespeare Festival as an industry-wide showcase that could prove a National Theatre unnecessary.

Just as the death of Edward VII had given Frohman the excuse to terminate the Duke of York's repertory venture, the outbreak of war in August 1914 provided ample reason for the SMNT to miss its 1916 deadline. And, like the Duke of York's repertory, the tribulations of the SMNT illustrate the paradoxes facing the New Drama and New Theatre movements. The movements defined themselves by their status on the margin; and yet they sought radically to recreate the structure of the center. They recognized the connection of theatrical art to the material conditions under which theatre is created; and yet they sought to create new art even while the existing material conditions prevailed. The experimental managements of the first decade of the twentieth century, and the regional repertory movement they spawned, created a home for a new drama and a new, less structured, more didactic dramaturgy; and they gave new life to the plays and careers that had not found an artistic home in the last decades of the preceding centuries. But the dream of a new theatre remained very much a dream.

NOTES

1. *The New Quarterly* 2 (1909), 491, quoted in Dennis Kennedy, "The New Drama and the New Audience," in Michael R. Booth and Joel H. Kaplan (eds.), *The Edwardian Theatre: Essays on Performance and the Stage* (Cambridge: Cambridge University Press, 1996), p. 142.

2. See Samuel Hynes, *The Edwardian Turn of Mind* (Princeton, NJ: Princeton University Press, 1968), pp. 212–53, and Dennis Kennedy, *Granville Barker and the Dream of Theatre* (Cambridge: Cambridge University Press, 1985), pp. 91–98.

3. See George Rowell and Anthony Jackson, *The Repertory Movement: A History of Regional Theatre in Britain* (Cambridge: Cambridge University Press, 1984) p. 26.

4. George Bernard Shaw, *Our Theatres in the Nineties* (London: Constable, 1932), II: 161.

5. Thomas Postlewait, *Prophet of the New Drama: William Archer and the Ibsen Campaign* (Westport, CT: Greenwood, 1986), pp. 50–51.

6. William Archer, *The Old Drama and the New* (Boston: Small, Maynard, 1923), p. 307.

7. *Ibid.*, pp. 309–10, and John Russell Stephens, *The Profession of the Playwright: British Theatre, 1800–1900* (Cambridge: Cambridge University Press, 1992), p. 132.

8. Eric Salmon, *Granville Barker and His Correspondents* (Detroit: Wayne State University Press, 1986), p. 42.

9. See William Archer: "A Plea for an Endowed Theatre," *The Fortnightly Review* 51 (May 1889), 610–26; and "On the Need for an Endowed Theatre," *The Theatrical "World" of 1896* (London: Scott, 1897).

10. Salmon (ed.), *Granville Barker.*

11. William Archer and H. Granville Barker, *A National Theatre*: *Scheme and Estimates* (London: Duckworth, 1907), p. 36.

12. *Pall Mall Gazette*, 14 March 1908, quoted in Rowell and Jackson, *Repertory Movement*, pp. 27–28.

13. Archer and Granville Barker, *Scheme and Estimates*, p. xi.

14. *Ibid.*, pp. xi–xiv.

15. C. B. Purdom (ed.), *Bernard Shaw's Letters to Granville Barker* (New York: Theatre Arts, 1957), p. 165.

12

SOS ELTIS

The fallen woman on stage: maidens, magdalens, and the emancipated female

Having dominated French theatre for over two decades, at the end of the nineteenth century the fallen woman became an ever-present figure on the English stage. In 1873 Henry James declared in disgust, "Just as the light drama in France is a tissue of fantastic indecencies, the serious drama is an agglomeration of horrors." Confronted by a string of plays by Alexandre Dumas *fils*, Sardou and Augier, which variously enjoined husbands to chastize, forgive, banish or shoot their unfaithful wives, James concluded of the French drama that "adultery is their only theme."[1] A decade later, adulterous heroines still dominated the Parisian stage and threatened to extend their influence across the channel. The intellectual sterility of the British stage was such, warned George Bernard Shaw in 1885, that "we look on French dramatists as bold grapplers with social problems because their heroines sometimes commit adultery. Some of our own critics and playwrights, when lauding the French drama, occasionally express themselves in a manner that indicates their conviction that a little adultery would purify and ennoble the British stage." But, he hastened to add, "Our drama is sinking for want, not of an Augier, but of an Ibsen."[2] His warnings were in vain. Dramas centring on adultery, seduction, and the issue of the sexual double standard became a staple of the London stage, so that by 1905 J. M. Barrie could write a comedy, *Alice Sit-by-the-Fire*, in which the inevitable affect of theatregoing on a young girl's imagination is to make her believe that her mother must have a lover. As Shaw has his heroine Fanny complain, fashionable plays were

> Always the same – what they call oversexed:
> You always know just what is coming next:
> The husband and the lover and the wife,
> Not one of them a bit like real life.[3]

Despite these protests at the late-Victorian and Edwardian theatre's obsession with errant wives, the fallen woman in her many manifestations had been a familiar figure on stage throughout the nineteenth century. Her progress

222

reflected both contemporary debates on the role and position of women, and the changing styles and concerns of the British stage through the century.

The epithet "fallen" could be applied to any woman who had indulged in sex outside the legal and moral bonds of marriage, whether as a seduced virgin, adulterous wife or professional prostitute. Her novelistic manifestations ranged from the child-mother whose seduction and redemption are narrated in Elizabeth Gaskell's *Ruth* (1853), to the scheming bigamist of Mary Elizabeth Braddon's sensational *Lady Audley's Secret* (1862), and the "pure woman" of Hardy's *Tess of the D'Urbervilles* (1891). Whereas novelists like Gaskell, Braddon, and Hardy were concerned with the psychology of the sexually delinquent woman, melodrama's forte was exterior action not internal motivation, so the fallen woman on stage was predominantly a convenient plot-mechanism rather than the focus of sympathetic analysis. The discarded mistress, seduced maiden, and unmarried mother crop up again and again as the motivation behind untold acts of villainy and familial disruption. In Edward Fitzball's *The Inchcape Bell, or the Dumb Sailor Boy* (1828), for example, Guy Ruthven, illegitimate son of Sir John Trevanly, kidnaps the rightful heir to avenge his abandoned and heartbroken mother.[4] Clara Talboys, heroine of *The Adventuress* (1871), is forced to make a living by tricking money out of her admirers, but is finally revealed to be the long-lost daughter of Major Clifford, stolen from her nurse by a vengeful fallen woman.[5] In *Cast Aside, or Loving Not Wisely But Too Well* (1871), the wicked Edgar Clifden seduces the trusting governess and tries to abandon her. Forced by friends and family to fulfill his promises of marriage, he spends the remaining acts unsuccessfully attempting to have her murdered, until he falls victim to his own hired assassin.[6]

The fallen woman on stage had three essential manifestations: the seduced maiden, the wicked seductress, and the repentant magdalen. Given sufficient stage time, a fallen woman could run through all of these incarnations in the course of a play. Dion Boucicault's *Formosa, or The Rail Road to Ruin* (1869) introduces us to Jenny, a country-bred girl who is working as a lady's companion in London, and whose earnings have helped to support her worthy parents. Jenny, however, is soon revealed to be none other than "Formosa . . . The most celebrated of those tawny sirens of Hyde Park! The High Priestess of Ruin!"[7] Having conspired to cheat the aristocrat of his fortune, she repents, hands over her jewels to buy him out of prison, and throws herself into the arms of her bewildered parents, crying, "I can never be to you what I was; but don't leave me to become what I shall be. I don't ask you to forgive me the past – but, oh, save me from the future!"[8] In Sims and Buchanan's Adelphi melodrama *The Black Domino* (1893), the country-girl Clarice Barton leads a similar double-life as the renowned courtesan Belle Hamilton. She finally sees the error of her ways, takes poison, and dies begging forgiveness for her sins.[9]

As these examples make clear, one of the primary functions of these melodramas was didactic: a warning of the dangers and disgrace that were the inevitable wages of sexual sin. Sex outside the bonds of marriage posed a threat to more wholesome relationships, broke up families, and generated all manner of villainy and vice. These extravagant scenarios reflected widespread social concern in the mid-nineteenth century over the number of women working as prostitutes and their possible effects on the moral fibre of society. Religious, social, and medical tracts on the subject proliferated, warning of the dire consequences of female sexual incontinence. Edward Tilt, for example, declared in 1852 that the influence of degenerate women could "by the subversion of all public morals, lead to sixty years of revolution," while another social commentator declared that the "pestiferous influence exercised on society by the single, fallen woman" could be found "in the dissolution of domestic ties, in the sacrifice of family peace, in the cold desolation of promising homes; but, above all, in the growth of practical Atheism."[10]

Serious treatises and melodramatic plays narrated the same highly colored tales to underline the same moral conclusion, constructing identical stories of the prostitute's inevitable decline and death. So in 1850 W. R. Greg wrote of the plight of the streetwalker:

> If the extremity of human wretchedness . . . is a passport to our compassion, every heart should bleed for the position of the English prostitute, as it never bled at any form of woe before . . . the agonies of grief and terror she must have endured before she reached her present degradation; the vain struggles to retrieve the first, false, fatal step; the feeling of her inevitable future pressing her down with all the hopeless weight of destiny; the dreams of a happy past that haunt her in the night-watches and keep her ever trembling on the verge of madness . . . the career of these women is a brief one; their downward path is a marked and inevitable one . . . they are almost never rescued; escape themselves they cannot.[11]

In an 1858 melodrama by William Travers, a mistress berates her aristocratic seducer in remarkably similar terms:

> I see the downward path step by step, the slow but certain approach of degraded feeling sweeping the finer feelings from the heart. I see the cheek wan and pale with inward agony, lighted up by the artificial bloom that smiles as if in mockery at the very blush of health. I hear the reckless laugh of the degraded midnight reveller dying away in the tears of the morning sun. I see the emaciated frame, the shroud, and the lonely death bed, the winding sheet, the coffin and the grave.[12]

Sure enough, she dies on the streets, having taken poison, using her last breath to beg any women present to "Shun I implore you the guilty draught of sinful pleasures, though the cup be crowned with glittering gems. Lest you find too late, as I have done, it is the path to ruin, misery and death."[13] The tale of the tortured and doomed prostitute was pervasive, and could be found in paintings, plays, novels, newspaper articles, and treatises on medicine, religion, and social regulation, achieving a shift in status from melodramatic warning to accepted social fact.[14]

While the depiction of the fallen woman on stage remained remarkably stable until the last decade of the century, debate over the status and suitable treatment of prostitutes became fiercely contentious in the 1860s. The Contagious Diseases Act, passed in 1864, and followed by further Acts in 1868 and 1869, provided for the medical and police inspection of prostitutes in garrison towns and ports. The high level of venereal disease in the armed forces was to be tackled by enforcing genital examination of suspected prostitutes, and the incarceration of any infected women in "lock hospitals" until they were cured. These Acts provoked widespread opposition among middle-class reformers and feminists on two main fronts: that respectable women would be placed in danger of undergoing humiliating examination if mistaken for streetwalkers; and that women alone were to be examined while the men who consorted with them were left free not only from examination but of any implied criticism. The Acts enshrined the sexual double standard and gave license to male debauchery, for, as a Royal Commission report into the Acts concluded: "With the one sex the offence is a matter of gain; with the other it is an irregular indulgence of a natural impulse."[15] The vigorous campaign against the Acts, which resulted in their repeal in 1886, provoked wide-spread discussion in Parliament and the press over the sexual double standard, the profitability of prostitution, and whether such women could be unambiguously differentiated from their more respectable sisters by a policeman walking down the street. The image of the fallen woman, marked out by her painted face and condemned to an early grave, began to be challenged in public debate by more complex and pluralistic versions of her life.

While critics of the Contagious Diseases Acts questioned the sexual double standard, often depicting the prostitute not as a moral degenerate but as a victim of social and economic forces, on stage the fallen woman remained uninfected by such pluralism. She continued to fulfill her inevitable doom, repent and die an untimely death – or, in occasional more fortunate cases, had her sentence commuted to incarceration in a nunnery. It was not until the end of the century that this convention became the butt of jokes. Remarking the high mortality rate among wicked women, Jerome K. Jerome advised them in his 1889 satire on stage conventions, "Never repent. If you value your life, don't repent. It always means sudden death!"[16] When Henry Arthur Jones killed off his wicked woman Drusilla Ives, heroine of *The Dancing Girl* (1891), who dies on a Wednesday morning for no more discernible reason than having danced on the previous Sunday evening, his moral conclusion was quickly parodied. London audiences were soon being treated to *The Prancing Girl: A Travesty on the Modern Drama up to Date*, in which the actress playing "Priscilla" objected to being so summarily dispatched, and stubbornly continued to dance till the end of the play in unwavering good health.[17]

While opponents of the Contagious Diseases Acts questioned the police's ability to immediately identify a "common prostitute," the physical appearance of the theatrical fallen woman continued to declare her sexual status in no uncertain terms. Whether dripping with jewels or disguised as an innocent country maiden, her sexual status was unmistakable. The fallen heroine of *Formosa* may pretend to be the pure maiden, Jenny, but an admirer can still tell the difference between her and the genuinely innocent Nelly, declaring that "Nelly is an angel – and as such I love her – but I love Jenny like the devil."[18] The visible taint upon the sexually impure woman emphasized the permanent and disastrous consequences of her fall. On stage, good and bad women were worlds apart, and contact between them had to be carefully policed. Indeed, the potentially corrupting influence of the fallen woman was so great that her mere touch could pollute a maiden's purity. Precautions were taken; when the famous courtesan La Faneuse embraces her pure daughter in Pierre Leclerq's *Illusion* (1890) she not only wears gloves but "pulls down her veil which completely covers her face and almost falls to her feet."[19]

The reason for such conservatism was easy to see; any deviation from the conventional could raise the hackles of the Lord Chamberlain, and result in the refusal of a license for performance. One of the most famous fallen woman plays of the nineteenth century, and one of the first to center on the psychology and character of the courtesan, rather than using her merely as a plot device, was Alexandre Dumas's *La Dame aux Camélias*. Written in 1849, the play follows the fate of Marguerite Gautier, a beautiful adventuress who falls in love with a virtuous young man and sacrifices her fortune, health and happiness for the sake of him and his innocent sister. Marguerite obeys all the conventions: regretting her lost purity, admitting her unworthiness to marry a good man, and dying of consumption at the end of the play. Despite this, the play was refused a license for performance in England until 1879, simply because the courtesan was presented as capable of true love and noble self-sacrifice. As George Henry Lewes commented: "The very skill with which the young Dumas has treated it, makes his crime all the greater, because it tends to confuse the moral sense, by exciting the sympathy of an audience."[20]

In France *La Dame aux Camélias* set a trend, and numerous playwrights followed suit, so that, as Henry James and Bernard Shaw noted, illicit sex became virtually the only topic for dramatic treatment. These plays centered on the psyche and motivation of the fallen woman, and began to question settled conventions by raising questions about how such women should be judged, whether they could be rehabilitated, whether men should be similarly judged, and so forth. The answers offered to such questions were, however, mostly conservative. For example, both Émile Augier's *Le Mariage d'Olympe* (1855) and Dumas's *La Femme de Claude* (1873) ask what an honest man should do if married to an adulterous woman. In both cases the answer is the same: shoot her! In England, although a number of these French plays were presented on the London stage, either during visits by the Comédie-Française or in translation, the fallen woman "problem play" only really took root in the 1890s.[21] Plays centering on the issue of women's sexuality, adultery, and the double standard then became so popular that some of the most successful late-Victorian playwrights seemed to write almost exclusively within this genre. Henry Arthur Jones's fallen woman plays include *The Masqueraders* (1894), *The Case of Rebellious Susan* (1894), *Michael and His Lost Angel* (1896), *The Liars* (1897), *Mrs. Dane's Defence* (1900) and *Whitewashing Julia* (1903). Arthur Wing Pinero wrote one of the most successful plays in the genre, *The Second Mrs. Tanqueray* (1893), which he then followed up with *The Notorious Mrs. Ebbsmith* (1895), *The Benefit of the Doubt* (1895), *Iris* (1901), *His House in Order* (1906), and *Mid-Channel* (1909). No playwright's oeuvre was complete without their contribution to the genre: *Lady Windermere's Fan* (1892) and *A Woman of No Importance* (1893) in the case of Oscar Wilde; *Mrs. Warren's Profession* (1893) and *Candida* (1895) in case of George Bernard Shaw.[22]

This phenomenal upsurge in fallen woman plays accompanied the widespread debate over marriage and women's legal rights following such significant legislation as the Divorce Act of 1857, the Contagious Diseases Acts of the 1860s, and the Married Women's Property Acts of 1870, 1882, 1886, and 1893. Women's incursion into previously male preserves such as higher education, journalism, and medicine, and the growing agitation for female suffrage, raised debate on women's role in society. Henrik Ibsen's plays further fueled debate. English critics tended to concentrate on the challenges to conventional ideas of femininity offered by Ibsen's heroines: Nora Helmer's abandoning of husband and child to pursue her higher duty to herself; Mrs. Alving's regret at having played the dutiful role of wife and concealed her husband's debaucheries; Hedda Gabler's restless ambition and ruthless manipulation of those around her.[23] However, Ibsen's plays never became major box-office successes in England, but they did serve to make the sentimental drama and melodrama look increasingly old fashioned, and set a new standard for intellectually demanding and socially challenging theatre. The fallen woman plays of the 1890s attempted to combine elements of the Ibsenite modern problem play with a familiar and crowd-pleasing genre.

Pinero's *The Second Mrs. Tanqueray* proved that this combination could pay, finding a lucrative middle-ground between Ibsenite radicalism and conventional melodrama. It opened in 1893 and ran for 223 performances, taking over £36,000 at the box office. The central role of Paula Tanqueray made Mrs. Patrick Campbell famous, and provided a staple part for her for over twenty years – a part which was also taken on by leading actresses such as Sarah Bernhardt and Eleanora Duse. Mixed critical reactions attested to Pinero's balancing act: the heroine's "Ibsenitish tendencies" raised the ire of the conservative critic Clement Scott; Shaw accused Pinero of disguising a "conventional Adelphi piece" as "intellectual drama"; while William Archer declared that it "satisfies the intelligence more than any other modern English play."[24] Following the fate of Paula Tanqueray, a high-class courtesan married to a respectable member of society, the play examines the possibility of rehabilitating the fallen woman. Her husband Aubrey wishes simply to bury her past life, but when one of her former lovers reappears engaged to her innocent stepdaughter Ellean, Paula despairingly concludes that, "the future is only the past again, entered through another gate," and shoots herself.[25]

Pinero took considerable trouble to cast a previously unknown actress as Paula, in order to avoid introducing echoes of previous fallen-woman roles. Though Shaw attributed all the novelty of the play to Mrs. Pat's performance, Pinero was at pains to differentiate Paula from common courtesans, endowing her with a warm heart, impulses of affection toward her stepdaughter, and a desire to be accepted by polite society.[26] Pinero even went so far as to challenge the sexual double standard; the husband condemns himself and Paula's former lover for having led "a man's life."[27] But the play also preserved the traditional iconography of the prostitute. Paula's temper, her coarsened mind and instinctive cynicism make her an unfit companion for her pure stepdaughter. Though convent-educated, Ellean is able to read the degradation written on Paula's face, declaring that, "From the first moment I saw you I knew you were altogether unlike the good women I'd left; directly I saw you I knew what my father had done."[28] The inevitable downward trajectory of the fallen woman is also maintained in Paula's vision of her future as a "poor worn-out creature . . . a ghost, a wreck, a caricature."[29] Her repentance and self-inflicted death fulfil traditional expectations, though the conclusion lies ambiguously between tragic waste and the only possible solution to an insuperable problem. Ultimately her demise leaves the audience free to indulge whatever degree of pity she has inspired without being challenged to find a place for her in their social and moral scheme.

Bernard Shaw was particularly disgusted by Paula's acquiescence in the conventions which condemned her, declaring that "in a play by a master-hand" she would have rejected the hypocrisy of society and celebrated her own personal morality.[30] In *Mrs. Warren's Profession* Shaw declared himself just such a master-hand by writing a play that deliberately reversed every convention of the fallen-woman drama. His fallen woman is not a glamorous courtesan who wears silks and jewels for three acts and then dies of consumption, but a vulgar matron who wears gay blouses and brilliant hats and ends the play in robust good health. When her daughter Vivie, a self-sufficient Cambridge graduate, learns that her mother made her living through prostitution, Mrs. Warren responds not with shame and repentance, but with vigorous self-justification. It is not, she explains, a question of sexual morality but of simple economics; society left her with the immoral choice between starvation and slow death working in a white-lead factory, or prostitution, the only profession which paid enough to maintain one's self-respect. Vivie spends the next act with her arm around her mother's shoulders, until she learns to her horror that what was once a matter of necessity is now a matter of profit; her mother's fortune derives from running a chain of international brothels. Despite Mrs. Warren's tearful offers of balls, clothes and the best of everything, Vivie calmly turns away and ends the play quietly pursuing the career in accountancy for which her education (ironically funded by prostitution's ill-gotten gains) has prepared her.

Shaw eschews the dichotomy between innocent and fallen women. Not only do mother and daughter embrace without the precaution of gloves and a veil, there is also a strong family resemblance between them. Both women are independent, energetic, determined and in possession of an excellent head for business. The very same qualities that made Mrs. Warren a "bad" woman make Vivie a "good" one. Vivie refuses her mother's traditional bribe of jewels and silks because the life of a kept woman would bore her; her appetite for work must find an outlet, just as her mother's energies took her first onto the streets and then into the brothel business. It is circumstance not character which determines their individual fates.

This was Shaw's most important challenge to the genre, shifting the burden of guilt from the individual to society. As he roundly declared, he wrote the play "to draw attention to the truth that prostitution is caused, not by female depravity and male licentiousness, but by simply underpaying, undervaluing, and overworking women so shamefully that the poorest of them are forced to resort to prostitution to keep body and soul together."[31] Shaw turns the focus onto working conditions, wage levels, and the exploitation of women within the capitalist system. Factory owners who pay starvation wages, restaurant and bar owners who exploit their waitresses' sexual attraction to further their own profits, and the dukes, bishops and MPs who invest their money in such businesses and live off the unearned interest, are all part of this corrupt system. Where audiences of conventional fallen woman plays were free to condemn or pity their protagonists from a position of detached superiority, Shaw points the finger at his own audience, denying them any resolution or catharsis. Instead of shedding tears for the conveniently expired courtesan, Shaw's audience is left uncomfortable and dissatisfied. Vivie washes her hands of her mother but does nothing to alleviate the plight of other women not privileged with her education; no vicarious solution is provided on stage, leaving resolution firmly in the hands of the audience and their future actions.

Vivie Warren with her firm handshake, mathematics degree and cigarette-smoking, whisky-drinking habits, is one of a new breed of women, dubbed by 1890s journalists "The New Woman."[32] Often caricatured as a plain, bespectacled spinster, clutching a latchkey and a copy of Ibsen's plays, the new woman presented a direct challenge to the traditional limitations of women's sphere, venturing beyond the confines of the home to seek access to higher education, suffrage, and male professions. The threat she posed to conventional sexual morality was considerable, for, where the repentant fallen woman internalized society's judgment and sighed nostalgically for her abandoned place at the domestic hearth, the new woman challenged society's judgment itself, seeking a place neither at the hearth nor on the streets.

From the 1890s onwards, the new woman often featured prominently in fallen-woman plays as a contributory source of disruption and misguided rebellion against the "natural" order. In Dorothy Leighton's *Thyrza Fleming* (1894), a newly married bride, Pamela, leaves her husband under the mistaken suspicion that he is having an affair. Her inability to trust her husband is traced to the unhealthy influence of her feminist cousin, Theophilia, a woman with "close-cropped hair, manly attire, [and] divided skirt," whose new method of securing happy marriages is to hire private detectives to investigate all prospective husbands. Pamela's high-minded desertion of her husband is greeted by Theophilia as "helping your sex to emancipate themselves," but Pamela is eventually taught the error of her ways by Thyrza Fleming, who convinces her instead that "It is a sign of strength rather than of weakness to understand a man's nature sufficiently to put away one's own preconceived ideas and love him 'for better, for worse.'"[33]

Henry Arthur Jones also introduced the new woman as a background character in his comedy on the sexual double standard, *The Case of Rebellious*

Susan (1894), which centers on Lady Susan's desire to teach her adulterous husband a lesson by paying him tit for tat. In Jones's original version, Susan has a brief affair but then returns to her husband, desperately afraid of losing her reputation and willing to accept her husband's flaws. Charles Wyndham, however, who first produced the play, unequivocally condemned such acceptance of female incontinence, writing to Jones that he was "astounded at a practical long-experienced dramatic author believing that he will induce married men to bring their wives to a theatre to learn the lesson that their wives can descend to such nastiness, as giving themselves up for one evening of adulterous pleasure and then return safely to their husband's arms, provided they are clever enough, low enough, and dishonest enough to avoid being found out."[34] Jones was forced to excise Susan's adulterous guilt from the performed version, but the message of both versions remained the same: the man she fell in love with humiliates her by rapidly forgetting her, and she accepts marriage to an adulterous husband as the only practical solution.

Running parallel to Susan's story is that of the new woman Elaine, whose marriage founders because she devotes her energies to political agitation instead of her husband's dinners. Elaine and her Boadicean Society accidentally incite some Clapham post-office girls not only to strike but also to destroy the post office, for which Elaine's hen-pecked husband is delighted to hear that she is likely to receive a long jail sentence. The moral drawn from both these tales is that "There is an immense future for women as wives and mothers, and a very limited future for them in any other capacity . . . Nature's darling is a stay-at-home woman, a woman who wants to be a good wife and a good mother, and cares for very little else."[35]

When Sidney Grundy wrote a comedy ridiculing the new woman, he implied that her motives and desires were no different from those of the fallen woman. Mrs. Sylvester is collaborating with Gerald on a book on the ethics of marriage "viewed from the standpoint of the higher morality," but it soon transpires that her real interest is in conducting an adulterous affair with her co-author.[36] Grundy's new women write books entitled variously *Man, the Betrayer*, *Foolish Virgins*, and *Naked and Unashamed!*, but their challenge to the sexual double standard adds up to nothing more than a recipe for female depravity, as two of his feminists argue:

> ENID: And *I* say that a man, reeking with infamy, ought not to be allowed to marry a pure girl –
> VICTORIA: Certainly not! *She* ought to reek with infamy as well.[37]

Grundy's traditional good woman and faithful wife rejects an invitation to a retaliatory affair with Mrs. Sylvester's husband and finally wins the day, publicly denouncing the new woman as "not New at all," but "just as old as Eve, and just as hungry for the fruit she plucked."[38]

In *The Notorious Mrs. Ebbsmith* (1895), Pinero proffered a similar argument in more serious form. Agnes Ebbsmith, a radical platform speaker and a bitter critic of marriage, expounds her new-woman ideal of a free relationship between man and woman, bound only by mutual trust and defiant of society and church. Agnes's ideology is, however, revealed by Pinero to be self-deceiving and misguided. When her lover Lucas proves dissatisfied with their pure and sexless, ideal union, she gives into her womanly instincts and exchanges her severely plain dress for a minimal and expensive confection, described by Shaw in the first production as "cut rather lower in the pectoral region than I expected."[39] At last, faced with Lucas's long-suffering wife, she realizes her own guilt and makes the final traditional costume change of a repentant magdalen, retiring to live in a parsonage in a "rusty, ill-fitting, black, stuff dress."[40] Despite his sympathetic focus on Agnes's suffering, Pinero depicts her attempts to defy the conventions of marriage as contrary to woman's instinctive nature, and ultimately portrays the new woman as the fallen woman in a different frock.

Pinero, Grundy, and Jones undermined the rhetoric of new womanhood by linking it to age-old sexual motives, thereby reducing feminist principles to purely personal gripes and aberrations. The real challenge to the conventions and ideology of the fallen-woman play was offered by playwrights who, like Shaw, reversed this process, linking individual lives to larger social and economic forces. The conventional formula portrayed the fallen woman's destiny as dictated by her character, a character which declared itself publicly not only in her face but her dress, which unavoidably signaled her true nature. Plays by St. John Hankin, Harley Granville Barker and Elizabeth Robins undermined such essentialist notions by showing how actions and clothes were assigned values and meanings within man-made systems of economy, law, and fashion.

In *Mrs. Warren's Profession* Shaw suggested that there was no difference between prostitution and marriage where both saw women using their sexual attractions to buy their way out of poverty. In *The Madras House* (1909), Shaw's friend and protégé, Harley Granville Barker, widened such associations, suggesting that social and economic structures reduced all women to little more than inhabitants of a harem. Each act has a different setting, thematically linked by the situation of the women within them. In the first act we meet Mr. Huxtable's six unmarried daughters, condemned to frustrated and useless spinsterhood as family respectability denies them access to "unsuitable" professions and husbands. In the business offices of the drapery firm Roberts and Huxtable we meet the Brigstocks, employees who have been forced to keep their marriage secret because they cannot afford to leave the living-in system, whereby workers live in the firm's dormitories, receiving board, lodging and meager wages. Another worker, Miss Yates, is unmarried and pregnant, but defies the firm's right to condemn her or to control her sexuality. The third act shows a business meeting in which the heads of the firm are treated to a fashion display, and the final act takes us back to the home of Philip Huxtable, and his elegant, beautiful, and highly fashionable wife, Jessica.

The play reveals the fashion business as one in which women are dressed for display in a sexual market; the women modeling the clothes are treated as animated mannequins, dressed in revealing garments which prevent them even sitting down. Granville Barker's point is further emphasized by a straw-hat, whose design is derived from La Belle Hélène, "a well-known Parisian cocotte . . . who sets many of the fashions our wives and daughters afterwards assume." As Philip cynically observes, "what could be more natural and right than for the professional charmer to set the pace for the amateur?"[41] The ornamental elegance of women such as Jessica Huxtable is presented as parallel to that of the Parisian courtesan, and is paid for by the bonded slavery of women workers, confined within the firm's living-in system so that their sexual freedom is surrendered to economic necessity. Constantine Huxtable, who has abandoned Philip's mother and advocates eastern-style polygamy as the only civilized way of treating women, defends his views by arguing that English society has already reduced its women to inhabitants of a harem, whether the home-bound trophies of the rich or workers in "an industrial seraglio."[42] The only woman to renounce such sexual bondage is Miss Yates, the unmarried woman who is revealed to be carrying Constantine Huxtable's child, but who spurns his money and is determined to support herself and her offspring. Ironically, the fallen woman is the only exception to society's prostituting of women's sexuality to its own ends.

Janet, heroine of St. John Hankin's *Last of the De Mullins* (1908), is a similarly defiant unmarried mother. Free-spirited and self-reliant, she meets her lover in the style of the new woman when riding her bicycle, and avoids the traditional fate of the fallen woman by learning to play society at its own games. She makes her fortune as a fashionable milliner by suing the aristocrats who refuse to pay their bills, and by selling hats for ready cash to the middle classes. Financially independent and proud of her maternity, she is able to scorn the shocked respectability of her lover and her father's demands for penitent submission. Unlike her doomed predecessors whose sexual guilt was to be read by every observer, Janet expertly adapts her appearance to suit the demands of circumstance; her elegant dress guarantees her respectability, while the assumed French label of "Claude et

Cie" gives her hats that fashionably risqué air which commands a higher price.

Elizabeth Robins perhaps went furthest in breaking the conventions of the fallen-woman play in her 1907 suffrage drama, *Votes for Women!*, in which Vida Levering, the elegantly dressed women's suffrage campaigner, is revealed to be the former lover of MP Geoffrey Stonor. Although guilty not only of non-marital sex but also of aborting the resultant child, Vida has all but forgotten the existence of her former lover, shows no desire to marry him, and has instead learnt through her own sufferings a clearer understanding of women's place in the social system. She campaigns for hostels for destitute women in order to give them an economic alternative to the streets. She tells a suffrage rally about a young girl condemned for abandoning her baby while the wealthy father got off scot-free. This sexual double standard is, she implies, perpetuated by a legal system under which the girl was not tried by her peers, but "brought before a man judge, tried by a jury of men, condemned by men, taken to prison by a man, and by a man she's hanged!"[43] Robins traces the social responsibility for individual fates. The private grief of the fallen woman transmutes into political conviction. The time has come, as Vida declares, for women to ask, "What general significance has my secret pain? Does it 'join on' to anything?"[44] The secret pain of the fallen woman joins on to the limited choices available to women, their social vulnerability, economic dependence, and the man-made laws that condemn them. In the hands of a new-woman playwright the fallen woman ends the play not drinking poison, or retiring in shame to a nunnery, but proudly banding with other women to demand greater civil rights.

Changing sexual attitudes finally put paid to the fallen-woman play. It is impossible to put a precise date to its demise, but in 1924, when Noel Coward wrote *Easy Virtue*, the genre was seen to be defunct. Coward wrote his drawing-room drama as a deliberate nostalgic tribute to Pinero, but sexual *mores* had changed, and in order to explain the rejection of his sexually experienced heroine, he had to introduce her into a family of Freudianly repressed prudes. As Coward concluded, "Those high-toned drawing-room histrionics are over and done with. Women with pasts to-day receive far more enthusiastic recognition than women without pasts."[45] The morality which had condemned so many disgraced heroines to untimely and morally instructive deaths was itself finally defunct. After appearing in so many different forms – seduced maiden, repentant magdalen, scheming vixen, problematic heroine, new woman – the fallen woman was nearly indistinguishable from the rest of womankind. In the flapper generation of the 1920s a woman's sexual activity no longer constituted a "fall," and Noël Coward's heroine was free to find her natural reward not in the confines of convent walls but in the elegant salons of Paris.

NOTES

1. "The Parisian Stage," *Nation* 16 (9 January 1873). Reprinted in Peter Rawlings (ed.), *Henry James: Essays on Art and Drama* (Aldershot: Scolar Press, 1996), pp. 41–42.
2. Letter to the Editor, *The Dramatic Review*, 27 June 1885. Reprinted in Bernard F. Dukore (ed.), *The Drama Observed*, 1: *1880–1895* (Pennsylvania: Penn State University Press, 1993), pp. 33–34.
3. Shaw, *Fanny's First Play*. This rhymed prologue was first performed at the Theatre Royal, Birmingham, on 18 September 1916. *Bernard Shaw Collected Plays*, IV (London: Bodley Head, 1972), p. 348.
4. *The Inchcape Bell*. Reprinted in Michael R. Booth (ed.), *"The Lights o' London" and Other Victorian Plays* (Oxford: Oxford University Press, 1995).
5. *The Adventuress* by unknown author. British Library, Lord Chamberlain's Plays (hereafter abbreviated to LCP) 53092.
6. *Cast Aside*, by C. H. Hazlewood, LCP 63100.
7. *Formosa*, LCP 53078, act I, p. 10.
8. *Ibid.*, act III, pp. 52–53.
9. *The Black Domino*, George R. Sims and Robert Buchanan, LCP 53523.
10. Edward Tilt, *Elements of Health* (London, 1852), pp. 13, 52. "Popular Objections Considered," *The Magdalen's Friend and Female Homes' Intelligencer* 2 (1861), 134. Quoted in Lynda Nead, *Myths of Sexuality: Representations of Women in Victorian Britain* (Oxford: Basil Blackwell, 1990), pp. 92 and 110.
11. W. R. Greg, "Prostitution," *Westminster Review*, 53 (1850), 451 and 454. Quoted in Nead, *Myths* p. 138.
12. *A Poor Girl's Temptations; or A Voice from the Streets* (1858), LCP 52972, act I, p. 9.
13. *Ibid.*, act III, p. 24.
14. See for example Augustus Egg's triptych *Past and Present* (1858); William Acton, *Prostitution* (London, 1870); William Tait, *Magdalenism*, 2nd edn. (Edinburgh, 1840); W. E. H. Lecky, *The History of European Morals*, II (London, 1869).
15. Report of the Royal Commission on the Administration and Operation of the Contagious Diseases Acts 1868–69, *Parliamentary Papers* (1871). Quoted in Judith R. Walkowitz, *City of Dreadful Delight: Narratives of Danger in Late-Victorian London* (Virago: London, 1992), p. 23. For detailed discussion of the Acts and the campaign for their repeal, see Judith R. Walkowitz, *Prostitution and Victorian Society: Women, Class and the State* (Cambridge: Cambridge University Press, 1980).
16. Jerome K. Jerome, *Stage-Land: Curious Habits and Customs of its Inhabitants* (London: Chatto & Windus, 1889), p. 37.
17. Campbell Rae Brown, *The Prancing Girl* (1891), LCP 53485, p. 25.
18. *Formosa*, act I, p. 7.
19. *Illusion*, LCP 53453, act III, p. 63.

20. William Archer and R. W. Lowe (eds.), *Dramatic Essays: John Forster, George Henry Lewes. Reprinted from the Examiner and the Leader* (London: Scott, 1896), pp. 141–42.

21. For example, *L'Étrangère* and *Le Demi-Monde* by Dumas *fils* were performed by the Comédie-Française in London in June 1879, and Clement Scott's translations of *Odette* and *Dora* by Victorien Sardou were performed in 1882 and 1878 respectively.

22. *Mrs. Warren's Profession* was written in 1893, but was not performed until 1902.

23. *A Doll's House* (1879); *Ghosts* (1881); *Hedda Gabler* (1890).

24. *Illustrated London News* (22 July 1893); *The Saturday Review* (16 March 1895); *World* (31 May 1893).

25. *The Second Mrs. Tanqueray* (London: Heinemann, 1898), act IV, p. 188.

26. See *The Saturday Review*, 23 February and 16 March 1895.

27. *The Second Mrs. Tanqueray*, p. 193.

28. *Ibid.*, p. 182.

29. *Ibid.*, pp. 189–90.

30. "An Old Play and a New One," *The Saturday Review*, 23 February 1895.

31. Preface to *"Mrs. Warren's Profession," Bernard Shaw Collected Plays*, I (London: Bodley Head, 1970), p. 231.

32. The term was first coined by Sarah Grand in her article "The New Aspect of the Woman Question," *North American Review* 158 (1894), 271–73, but was soon widely adopted. See, for example, *Life*, 13 June 1895, p. 395; and *Punch*, 10 April 1894, p. 194.

33. *Thyrza Fleming*, LCP 53565, act III, p. 56.

34. Quoted in Doris Jones, *The Life and Letters of Henry Arthur Jones* (London: Victor Gollancz, 1930), pp. 164–65.

35. *The Case of Rebellious Susan* (London: Chiswick Press, 1894), act III, p. 76.

36. Sidney Grundy, *The New Woman* (London: Chiswick Press, 1894), act I, p. 24.

37. *Ibid.*, p. 28.

38. *Ibid.*, act III, p. 90.

39. "Mr. Pinero's New Play," *The Saturday Review*, 16 March 1895.

40. *The Notorious Mrs. Ebbsmith* (London: Heinemann, 1895), act IV, p. 206.

41. *The Madras House* (London: Sidgwick and Jackson, 1911), act III, pp. 79–80.

42. *Ibid.*, p. 105.

43. *Votes for Women*, act II, p. 77.

44. *Ibid.*, act III, p. 114.

45. Introduction, *Coward: Plays*, I (London: Methuen, 1979).

13

SUSAN CARLSON AND KERRY POWELL

Reimagining the theatre: women playwrights of the Victorian and Edwardian period

Virginia Woolf declared as late as 1929 that bookshelves contained "no plays by women" and noted the common assumption that "women cannot write the plays of Shakespeare."[1] But actually there was a significant and growing number of women writing for the English theatre by the latter part of the Victorian period, and women dramatists became both more numerous and vigorously political in the early twentieth century. Not only were the denials of their existence greatly exaggerated, but the contributions of women playwrights to the Victorian and Edwardian theatre were momentous, although still not as widely recognized as they deserve to be.

As Virginia Woolf's comment in *A Room of One's Own* illustrates, women playwrights worked under a cultural assumption that they did not and could not write drama – although they were doing just that. William Archer, the leading proponent of Ibsen and Shaw, omitted any notice of women playwrights in his canon-fixing book on the development of modern drama, *The Old Drama and the New* (1923), although he knew several notable women dramatists personally.[2] By saying nothing at all on the subject, Archer and many other male critics who should have known better were able to perpetuate the widespread belief that women were unequipped to become playwrights. Nevertheless, by the end of our period women dramatists were increasingly difficult to ignore, and for those with eyes to see were breaking out of the myth of their own invisibility.

Victorian women and the theory and practice of playwriting

Cicely Hamilton, who would become a leading playwright of the early twentieth century, wanted more than anything else at the outset of her career in the 1890s "to write a good play." When her first one-act piece was about to be produced, however, Hamilton learned from a manager that "it was advisable to conceal the sex of its author until after the notices were out, as plays which were known to be written by women were apt to get a bad press."[3] That is the reason why the heroine of *Our Flat* (1889), written by a woman playwright known only as "Mrs. Musgrave" *about* a woman playwright, signs her first play with her husband's name, withholding her own identity as author "till the agreement is signed."[4] A few years after *Our Flat* was staged, Elizabeth Robins and Florence Bell disguised their authorship of *Alan's Wife* from Beerbohm Tree, who they hoped would produce it at the prestigious Haymarket Theatre, being well aware of Tree's view that "women can't write" and that he had never read a good play from a woman's hand.[5] By the 1890s there was an increasing number of successful women playwrights – including Clotilde Graves, Pearl Craigie, Mrs. Musgrave, Mrs. Pacheco, and Madeline Ryley – who wrote plays that achieved the status of hits by running for 100 performances or more.[6] One popular magazine drew attention to what it regarded as the surprising fact that two plays by women had been staged at major London theatres during the theatrical season of 1894, Constance Fletcher's *Mrs. Lessingham* and Lady Violet Greville's *An Aristocratic Alliance*. The anonymous critic explained that "though we can count women novelists by the score, the number of women dramatists is extremely limited, and can easily be told off on the fingers."[7]

Men usually came to playwriting from other male-dominated careers – for example, stage-managing (like Ben Webster and George Conquest), or journalism and dramatic criticism (J. M. Barrie, John Oxenford, Bernard Shaw, George R. Sims, Tom Taylor, Edmund Yates). Men's clubs like the Arundel and Garrick brought together members of the varied professions from whose ranks writers for the stage typically emerged.[8] Actresses, who often had connections with powerful men in the theatre, were prominent among the women who became dramatists. Among them were Elizabeth Robins, Cicely Hamilton, Harriett Jay, and perhaps the two most commercially successful women playwrights of the age – Madeline Lucette Ryley and Clotilde Graves. Indeed, when asked once by an interviewer how she came to write plays, Clo Graves accounted for her seemingly anomalous position as a woman playwright by virtue of having been an actress first.[9] The plight of the heroine in Constance Woolson's story "Miss Grief" could stand as representative of women playwrights who were less well-connected in the theatre than Clo Graves. The title character, a would-be woman playwright, has written a drama that is thrilling in its "earnestness, passion, and power," but is never performed because Miss Grief lacks any entrée to the theatre managers who could assist her with getting it produced.[10]

The theory and practice of playwriting combined, therefore, to exclude women purely on the grounds of gender. Yet it was obvious to anyone who thought about the matter that women had achieved distinction as playwrights before the Victorian period, if not during it – women like Hannah More, for example, and Joanna Baillie. When the Victorians took these women into account in theoretical discussions of playwriting, their success could be explained by the "power of influence" and "good offices" exerted on their behalf by male friends – David Garrick in the case of Hannah More, or Sir Walter Scott for Joanna Baillie.[11] Masculinity, by contrast, was counted as a qualification for writing plays in itself, and as an attribute of the theatre as an institution. The author of *The Stage of 1871*, for example, identifies playwrights as *men*, specifically those with wide experience of the world – "men who, in addition to literary ability, have mixed much with all classes, and experienced the ups and downs of life."[12] Another reviewer expressed the view that a good dramatist "must be everything else" – a man, yes, but with the kind of wide experience no Victorian woman could know. "He must be a politician, a historian . . . and an orator . . . a man of action and of thought . . . above all, he must directly and publicly impress a crowd of other men."[13] The best plays would therefore be written for, as well as by, men – the ideal audience being, in the words of no less advanced a critic than William Archer, "principally masculine of course."[14]

Imagine the surprise of male critics, therefore, when Clo Graves's *A Mother of Three* scored a box-office success at the Comedy Theatre in 1896, at the same time as another play of hers was being performed at a major theatre in London. *The Sketch* observed that "probably it has never before occurred in the theatrical annals of London that two plays by the same woman have been running at the same time" – the other being *A Matchmaker*, which Graves co-authored with Gertrude Kingston for the Shaftesbury Theatre. Madeline Ryley's hugely popular *Jedbury Junior* came out the same year, as well as several plays in which women authors collaborated with male playwrights, such as *The Strange Adventures of Miss Brown* by Harriett Jay and Robert Buchanan. Suddenly women playwrights were an irresistible subject of interest, even among drama critics. *The Era*, for example, launched "an inquiry into the subject of female playwrights, not many of whom have achieved any lasting success or fame up to the present period." Despite good reviews and large audiences, *A Mother of Three* by Clo Graves was portrayed by the reviewer as a curiosity – "an example of what can be achieved by industry" rather than a cause to re-examine the assumption that women were constitutionally unfit for playwriting. Typically, the critic for *The Era* found in the supposed nature of women a handy explanation for their under-representation as dramatists. Their use of language is undisciplined, he argues, lacking the architectural rigor believed necessary for good playwriting; and their personalities generally lack the comic sense that most plays require:

Chiefly, perhaps, because most women are devoid of deep and mirthful humour, and on account of their prolixity of diction and their tendency to introduce an abundance of small irresponsible details into their writings, as witness the lady novelist and her methods, female dramatists have been few and far between, though quite a large number of authoresses have essayed to write for the stage.[15]

Women fail as playwrights, therefore, for the same reasons that they succeed as novelists.

But Olive Logan, in her mid-Victorian book on stagecraft, argues that women could contribute to dramatic literature something that is missing from the plays of men. "It is not too much to believe that if women wrote more frequently for the theatre," Logan says, "they would impart to its exhibitions something of their own grace, purity, and elegance." Her objection to the "licentious" women among the characters in many plays by male playwrights is in its own way typically Victorian. But Olive Logan acutely realizes that male-authored plays define women from a male perspective and provide a means of control over actresses. The woman as playwright would, or could, she believes, raise the horizon of actresses and liberate them from the dictation of men. She would help bring into existence something like a women's theatre, and with it a different kind of drama and an improved outlook for actresses. "By dignifying the drama," writes Logan, "she would dignify that vocation which so many of her sisters follow, and would rescue from the indignation of the censor and the sneer of the scandalous those who are sometimes causelessly blamed."[16]

The invisible theatre: Victorian plays by women

Although there were more Victorian women playwrights than Olive Logan's comments would suggest, it is certainly true that they were outnumbered by men and less successful in their careers as professional dramatists. Given the widespread prejudice against women dramatists, much of it institutionalized in the theatre itself, we believe that Victorian women who wrote plays competed on an equal basis against male dramatists very rarely. Two of those occasions were open playwriting competitions – one near the beginning of the Victorian period and the other at the end – and both were won by untried women playwrights. In 1844 Catherine Gore won the £500 prize for best new play in a competition sponsored by the leading actor-manager Ben Webster for her play entitled *Quid Pro Quo: or, The Day of Dupes*, one of ninety-seven dramas sent in anonymously, as the contest required, and judged by a special committee.[17] At the close of the Victorian period, in 1902, the Playgoers' Club, with George Alexander and Beerbohm Tree leading the way, staged another open playwriting contest in response to grumblings that the cozy association of actor-managers and "certain well-known dramatists" made it difficult for new playwrights to get a fair hearing. After a special committee had read hundreds of new plays in manuscript, the winner was *The Finding of Nancy* by Netta Syrett, a woman novelist who by her own account was, like most professional women writers, "absolutely ignorant of the stage."[18] The play by Netta Syrett, like Catherine Gore's prize-winning play almost sixty years earlier, failed miserably with critics.

Catherine Gore attributed the initial flop of her play in 1844 – it enjoyed some success in revivals – to the "vast expectations" arising from her £500 prize and the organized resentment of rival playwrights at opening night. She also pointed out that in *Quid Pro Quo* she had attempted a "broader style" than she employed as a novelist, influenced by the notion that plays were a "very different species of entertainment" from fictions and demanded from the author a different kind of writing. In her comedy, in fact, Gore was inadvertently following the prescription of what William Archer would call, decades later in his manual for playwrights, the "conventionally dramatic" prescription for crises and shocks in the action of a play and "disproportion" in the drawing of character. Dramatic critics, mostly male and playwrights themselves, would not allow a woman to succeed in playwriting, Gore believed, and thus influenced popular opinion against her even though she had written a play to their own recipe. Gore was convinced that her play failed because it was written by a woman, and that the animosity of the theatrical establishment, which, Gore observes, had "succeeded in condemning the very superior plays of Joanna Baillie, Lady Dacree, and Lady Emmeline Wortley, could scarcely fail to crush any attempt of mine."[19]

Although *Quid Pro Quo* was a satirical comedy of manners, the plots of many plays by Victorian women centered on heroines or female villains who were violent or mad, or who performed strong and unconventional reinterpretations of their roles as mothers, daughters, and wives. These subversive and passionate characters are not explicitly feminist or even political, but like many heroines of Victorian fiction they rebel against the gendered role imposed upon them as women – for example, Lisa Selby in Clara Cavendish's *The Woman of the World*, staged at the Queen's Theatre in 1858, who resorts to forgery, theft, and attempted murder to satisfy her desire for power and pleasure.

This association of women and violence in earlier Victorian plays by women was carried on into the New Drama by women playwrights in the

1890s, where it tended to be presented within the context of a social problem and, as such, more thoughtfully rationalized. Although the heroines of these late-Victorian plays display on many occasions the power and aggression of female characters in earlier dramas by women, they often resonate with a psychological complexity rarely to be found in their precursors. They also confront more straightforwardly the social codes which women's plays of an earlier date called into question by implication more than direct challenge. In *The Mirkwater*, for example, written by Elizabeth Robins in the early 1890s, Felicia Vincent assists her sister, incurably ill with breast cancer, in committing suicide by drowning. "I did all I could to dissuade her – and then – all that love could do to help," Felicia Vincent says just before policemen arrive at the final curtain to arrest her for murder.[20] The love that comes closest to the "perfect thing" that Felicia Vincent imagines in *The Mirkwater* exists only between women, a bond too powerful to be constrained by the law or by the opinions of those who judge them as outcasts from "decent society." Thus abandoning erotic love for a concern with breast cancer and assisted suicide, *The Mirkwater* unsurprisingly found no producer – although George Alexander, before declining, considered staging it in exchange for total rights to the play. It remains unproduced and unpublished, a monument to the difficulties that beset women playwrights when they placed unconventional heroines at the center of their work. Had it gone into production, *The Mirkwater* could well have occasioned the same kind of disturbance in the London theatre that was caused by Robins's first play, *Alan's Wife* (co-authored by Florence Bell) with its story of a mother who kills her own child.

Estelle Burney's *Settled Out of Court*, produced at the Globe in 1897, takes for its main character a woman who in the first act leaves the husband who "never loved me, his heart is on his work." Eventually she becomes the wife of the man she elopes with, only to be overcome within a short time by her daughter's death and her new husband's unfaithfulness. "They don't think of these things in our Courts," reflects Moyra Delacourt, who takes matters into her own hands, appoints herself God's executioner, and with a mad but "almost happy" laugh attacks her husband with a knife at the final curtain.[21] Legal but unscrupulous behavior by men forms the background also for *Mrs. Lessingham*, Constance Fletcher's play of 1894 in which the title character turns her violent impulses against herself. Gladys Lessingham has left her abusive husband to live with another man whom she eventually marries. When she learns of her new husband's attachment to someone else – a "good woman" – Gladys Lessingham takes poison and dies, perceiving that in her world women receive no "second chance."[22] Although a suicide at last, Mrs. Lessingham, like other violent heroines in Victorian plays by women, provided an actress with a rare opportunity to represent a character of depth and power. The play ran for thirty-three performances at the Garrick Theatre, making it one of the more successful productions of a woman's play in the West End in the *fin de siècle*.

A few women won distinction as writers of comedy in the late Victorian period, most notably Clo Graves, whose title character in *A Mother of Three* (1896) puts on men's clothing in order to masquerade as her own husband. From the opening scene, wrote the critic for *The Sketch*, the question was whether a woman playwright could do justice to a story in which a mother takes on the identity of her vanished husband in order to advance the fortunes of herself and the three daughters he left behind. When actress Fanny Brough, as the crossdressing mother, first appeared in trousers, the critic wondered: "Is the rest of the play merely to be a 'Charley's Aunt' with sexes reversed . . . [or] has Miss Clo Graves the constructive skill to build up a plot on the well-worn theme of the troubles of a human being disguised in the clothes of the other sex?" Although this critic ultimately answered his own question in the negative, the press in general was enthusiastic about the "clever and well-written play" which drew large crowds to the Comedy Theatre night after night.[23] The scenes which drew the loudest laughter were those in which Fanny Brough wore wig and trousers to pass herself off as the father of her three marriageable daughters – thus providing them a "certificate of respectability." The return of the real father in the final act, however, not only throws matters into confusion, but awakens him belatedly to his own "neglected responsibilities." Recognizing his duty to assist his wife at last "in the discharge of her domestic duties," the absent father takes on a feminized aspect just as his wife had earlier put on the clothing as well as the responsibilities of a man.[24] Clo Graves's farcical comedy thus concludes with a collaboration of masculine and feminine worked out in the masculinized dress and behavior of Mrs. Murgatroyd and, in the final scenes, the feminization of her long-absent spouse. Almost totally forgotten since its successful run at the Comedy Theatre in London in 1896, *A Mother of Three* is a funny and good-naturedly subversive play which deserves to be read and revived today.

The Victorian period ended as it began, as we have pointed out, with a playwriting competition "open to the whole of Great Britain."[25] Sponsored by the Playgoers' Club, some of whose members had complained that actor-managers invariably went to established dramatists for their plays, this contest ended with the same result as its predecessor almost sixty years earlier – it was won by a woman. Like Catherine Gore when she wrote the prize play of 1844, Netta Syrett had never before written a full-length play, but was an experienced novelist. Like Gore's, moreover, Syrett's play was given a production with an all-star cast in a distinguished theatre – the St. James's in this case – but with results that were dismaying to the playwright. Her play, *The Finding of Nancy* (1902), concerns the cramped life of Nancy Thistleton, a lonely single woman who works as a secretary in a business office. "Or do we and thousands of women like us live at all?" the title character asks a friend, who answers "you are right; it isn't life . . . nothing happens . . . nothing ever *will* happen." Wanting to live, wanting "anything but just *nothing* – blankness," Nancy Thistleton becomes involved with a married man who is separated from his alcoholic wife. Although, as she says, "I haven't kept the rules of the game," the final curtain finds the heroine in the arms of her ineligible lover, looking forward to a lifetime of happiness.[26]

As for the critics, with the exception of Max Beerbohm they found the play to be offensive and flawed as drama by virtue of its female perspective. Beerbohm, writing in *The Saturday Review*, called *The Finding of Nancy* one of those rare plays that "really matters" and one of the impressive achievements of the drama "in my time."[27] But Clement Scott, the influential critic of *The Daily Telegraph*, wrote in hysterical terms of the play's so-called immorality and the culpability of the woman who wrote it. Other reviewers perceived that Syrett's play failed to observe the prescribed formulae, above all by adopting a woman's point of view. "The play is written not only by a lady – Miss Netta Syrett – but for ladies," *The Times* complained. "That is to say, it assumes as a matter of course that the great interest for all of us in life, the thing we want most to hear about, and that we go the play to see, is the career of woman."[28] Such an approach to narrative, the critic adds, sounding a prominent theme in Victorian dramatic criticism, has all the usual characteristics of "feminine fiction." *The Finding of Nancy* proved to *The Era*, if nothing else, that actor-managers were the best judges of "dramatic effect," and that there were not, in fact, any significant number of unacted masterpieces or unproduced dramatists of genius, female or male, whose merits no manager had yet recognized.[29]

The Finding of Nancy was never published and apparently never produced after its staging in 1902 at the St. James's Theatre as the prize-winning play in a national competition. Although buried in oblivion under the scorn of male critics, this play about characters in whose lives "nothing happens . . . nothing ever *will* happen" anticipates the plays of Samuel Beckett a half-century later and opposes the prevailing Victorian assumption that strong action marked by shocks and crises is the basis of good drama. *The Finding of Nancy* was a different kind of play structurally, and its focus on working women and questioning of social codes of sexual morality disrupted the commercial

West-End theatre of the *fin de siècle*. As a young actor who played a small role in the play said to the author, Netta Syrett: "You women have courage. You say things we men wouldn't dare to say."[30]

Into the new century

An encyclopedia entry and an annual report, both from 1911, suggest the ways in which politics must stand at the center of our shift to Edwardian women playwrights. In the eleventh edition of the *Encyclopaedia Britannica*, published in 1911, the entry on "Women" equates the history of women with a progressive drive for women's rights; it conflates the high profile, enlightened politics of women's equality (including the campaign for the vote) with women's very existence in the early twentieth century.[31] At publication, the initial approval of women's vote was still eight years off, so the entry cannot record women's enfranchisement, but the forward-looking account offers a telling intellectual background for the study of women playwrights in the new century, for in the theatrical realm too, an understanding of women's very presence is inextricably tied up in gender politics, most centrally women's drive for the vote. The records of Edy Craig's Pioneer Players also suggest the ubiquitous nature of suffrage politics. In its first annual report, the female-dominated Pioneer Players took exception to their being characterized solely as a suffrage theatre, noting that *any* thoughtful playwright could not help but offer dramatic commentary on women's rights: "It is obviously quite impossible nowadays to produce thoughtful plays written by thoughtful people which do not bear some traces of the influence of the feminist movement – an influence which no modern writer, however much he may wish it, can entirely escape."[32] As we move out of the Victorian era and into the new century, we will see how the increased visibility of women's stage writing can only be understood with a focus on such political forces.

In their recent collection of essays, *The Edwardian Theatre*, editors Michael R. Booth and Joel Kaplan have compiled compelling proof of women's politicized and central presence in the Edwardian theatre. As scholars in the collection analyze a variety of theatrical components, from musical comedy and music hall to theatre management, from audience to reviewers, they repeatedly find that the era's reconfiguring of women's social and political roles swayed artistic and economic decision-making. As several of the scholars note, feminist politics were lampooned and feared as often as they were valorized; we will see also in our focus on women's playwriting that the politics of the Edwardian woman playwright are not transparent, not automatically pro-suffrage, but are varying responses to the cultural and political forces shaping these women's era.

Suffrage theatre

On 9 November 1909, the Actresses' Franchise League (AFL) hosted a memorable evening of theatre and politics at the Scala Theatre. The AFL had been formed just a year earlier to provide actresses a venue for their participation in the suffrage campaign and had quickly become an essential part of high-profile suffrage activities in London. The program outlines an ambitious plan; plays included Cicely Hamilton and Christopher St. John's "The Pot and the Kettle," Gertrude Mouillot's "Master," Beatrice Harraden and Bessie Hatton's "The Outcast" and the spectacular *The Pageant of Famous Women*, written by Cicely Hamilton, arranged by Edy Craig, and boasting the stage's biggest star, Ellen Terry, in the cast. The event established a pattern to be followed in many league-sponsored events by bringing together the efforts of actresses and writers, in mixing artistic performance and political speech, and in joining theatre with the commitment to women's franchise. As many commentators have noted, the forces allied in the fight for the vote made the campaign theatrical and conversely made the theatre political. We owe a great debt to Julie Holledge's *Innocent Flowers* and Sheila Stowell's *A Theatre of Their Own*, both of which establish convincingly that it is impossible to analyze Edwardian women's playwriting without understanding the context of suffrage activism.

Most notably, the link between theatre and suffrage activism allowed women, in unprecedented numbers (Holledge cites over 400),[33] to think of themselves as playwrights. While one can trace in the early years of the century a steady output of plays by women writers, including the notable work of writers like Edith Lyttleton, Lucy Clifford, Clotilde Graves, Netta Syrett, and Madeline Lucette Ryley, once Elizabeth Robins's *Votes for Women!* established the aesthetic compatibility of suffrage politics and theatre in 1907, stages all over London became home to the outpouring of plays by women. Actresses became playwrights, costume designers became producers (two notable examples are Edy Craig and Annie Horniman), and working-class women wrote dramas about their lives. As noted by Israel Zangwill, himself both a playwright and a suffragist, the pairing of women and a theatre about women's rights was a natural: "The stage is the sphere which women adorn equally with men, if not indeed with superior lustre, and in which women have worked – when all of scandal is said – on those terms of sexless camaraderie which the new social development demands."[34]

Elizabeth Robins's *Votes for Women!*, the only female-authored play put on by the Barker–Vedrenne management, announces its politics in its title and single-handedly established the "suffrage theatre" at an accomplished level. As many scholars have established, Robins is adept in the familiar genre

Figure 11 Trafalgar Square in *Votes for Women!* Court Theatre, 1907.

of society comedy and offers the story of a woman-with-a-past who turns personal turmoil into triumphant politics. While few other suffrage writers adopted the three-act format (due both to the need for short plays and to the inexperience of the writers), Robins established key dramatic qualities which other suffrage playwrights developed and refined: the "conversion" narrative, the political expediency of comedy, and the centrality of community in suffrage plays.

It is this final quality, perhaps, which most sets this theatrical/political phenomenon of suffrage theatre apart. Robins's second act, with its recreation of a suffrage rally (Harley Granville Barker directed the famous staging of the act), offered a meta-political moment during which suffrage activists in the audience could see themselves campaign on stage. The rallying, communal nature of such staging marked several other major works of suffrage theatre, notably *The Pageant of Famous Women* and "The First Actress."

The Pageant of Famous Women, initially staged at the Scala extravaganza of 1909, developed around the array of accomplished historical women characters majestically parading across the stage (the number varied from fifty to ninety). This created a stately community on stage which glorified the work of the committed women making up most of the audiences. Edy Craig, the mastermind behind the execution of the pageant, took this event to venues all over England, from London to Bristol, from Liverpool to Cambridge, and in each new location recreated the play to suit the local community of activists who took the silent roles of the famous women. According to Kathleen Cockin, Craig directed the play at least thirteen times from 1909 to 1912.[35]

Craig's partner Christopher St. John also expanded Robins's staging of community, in her "The First Actress," written in 1911 for Craig's Pioneer Players. The play offers a portrait of the power and ideas that accrue when a large group of women collects, in this case a group of famous English actresses. On a smaller scale, this focus on group can be seen in plays as diverse as Margaret Wynne Nevinson's grim "In the Workhouse"(where women sequestered in the workhouse become a community as they bemoan a range of handicaps which prevent their controlling their own lives) and Cicely Hamilton and St. John's comic "How the Vote was Won" (where a group of female relatives hound their nearest male relative to his political conversion). In all of the genres through which women practiced their suffrage politics – one-acts, pageants, comedies, and even monologues – the creation of a double community, both on and off the stage, allowed these writers to burst out of the claustrophobic, isolating interiors of Ibsen and John Galsworthy. The demoralized groups of women in Harley Granville Barker's plays are replaced with women of independent thought and initiative. Women's space in these plays becomes any public space big enough to hold them, marking the most compelling development in women's writing of this era.

In reimagining the theatre, these activist playwrights also sought out new venues for publication. Victorian women rarely saw their plays brought to print, but the suffragists took corrective action. At their own press, they published many of the plays with direct political content and sold copies at their shops. Additionally, journalists in the movement made prime space for plays in their four weekly suffrage newspapers.

As astounding as the accomplishments of suffrage theatre were, it is reductive to label the women writing suffrage-inspired drama merely "suffrage playwrights." Many of the plays most closely associated with the movement include suffragist characters or suffrage events and politics, including *Votes for Women!*, "How the Vote was Won," "The Pot and the Kettle," "The Apple," and "At the Gates." Many plays by women writing during the suffrage agitation, however, focus not on the vote, but on other issues of special concern to women. Beatrice Harraden and Bessie Hatton's "The Outcast," Hamilton's "Jack and Jill and a Friend," and Gertrude Vaughan's "The Woman with a Pack" serve as important examples. Indeed a list of "suffrage playwrights" would tell only part of the story, for the work "inspired" by the suffrage cause and its foment spread far beyond suffragist platforms and onto almost all Edwardian stages. Christopher St. John complained in 1909 that the West End had not taken up any play dealing "with the vital question of Votes for Women"[36] since Robins's 1907 play and that *Votes for Women!* "had no successors." Ironically, St. John's own career shows that the label of "suffrage playwright" is restrictive and misleading.

St. John was, of course, a central figure in suffrage theatre, making her impact as a journalist and activist as well as a playwright. While some of her plays were clearly written for the suffrage rally, other plays suggest how she extended the blatant campaigning of those plays into other work. For example, "The Coronation" (1911) refines suffrage pageantry for other venues. Co-written with Charles Thursby, it is a political fantasy which uses a nearly all-male cast to reimagine political rights. During the coronation procession of King Henricus, he and his advisers in the country of Omnisterre are shaken by a woman protestor who demands his recognition of the poverty in his country. The play traces his political conversion and ends with the king and the woman in league against starvation and social inequality. St. John and Thursby's play was performed by Edy Craig's Pioneer Players at the Savoy, though the Lord Chamberlain's copy in the British Library shows alarm over its king and his politics as well as over the critique of capitalism. St. John's 1914 play, "Her Will," best exemplifies her mainstreaming of the suffrage agenda. At the center of the play is Miss Loring-Parke, an assured woman with effective, graceful ways of bending the recalcitrant characters around her. The comedy traces her efforts to convince Helen Wilton's heirs that accepting Wilton's progressive politics is, indeed, a happy ending. In another comedy, "In Clover. Or Just a Wife or Two," which St. John wrote with Anthony Ellis after the war (1919), the focus is the revolutionary assumption that marriage should simply be considered a tool through which thinking, caring people can subvert laws and customs.

Suffrage politics inspired both activist and non-activist women to write plays, and proponents for the cause set up organizations and structures to support this theatre work. As a result theatre became the location of women's (usually politicized) communities for the first time.[37]

Beyond suffrage, beyond London

Women's participation in the pre-First World War theatre also had narratives other than those plotted by suffrage politics. While all of these alternate narratives are in some telling way connected to the women creating and sustaining suffrage theatre, they remind us that the theatre of the day offered women a variety of ways to take up playwrighting and allowed for multiple ideological stances.

Notably, for example, the women playwrights of the Edwardian stage were not solely English. American theatre, in particular, fed into the strengthening of English women's theatre work. American-born Elizabeth Robins spent most of her professional life in English theatre, first bringing Ibsen to London and later playing a major role in subscription theatres. Her collaboration with Florence Bell on *Alan's Wife* rocked the theatre in the 1890s just as her *Votes for Women!* established suffrage theatre. While American Madeline Lucette Ryley is less critically known, her many successful productions in West-End theatres established her as perhaps the most successful woman playwright at the turn of the century. In the early Edwardian years, she had a series of plays produced in the West End, several of them starring the prominent husband and wife team of Johnston Forbes-Robertson and Gertrude Elliott (also an American). Plays like *Realism* (1900), *Mice and Men* (1902), *The Altar of Friendship* (1903), *Mrs. Grundy* (1905), *An American Citizen* (1906), and *The Sugar Bowl* (1907) made her a popular and well-known writer. Her forte was light comedy, and while plays like *Jedbury Junior* are predictable and slight, they are also cleverly plotted and deftly dialogued. Other American cross-over was less sustained, but still important. For example, Charlotte Perkins Gilman's play "Three Women" was one of the most innovative suffrage plays circulating in the day as Gilman cleverly lays out the various consequences of women's conflicting roles in career and family. Edy Craig, not surprisingly, chose to produce the play in London.

It is finally an American, Henry James, whose influence on Edwardian women playwrights was perhaps most widespread. While his own playwriting career was a series of frustrating starts and stops, and while he was irritated by suffragists' aggressive strategies, his example and advice shaped the work of many women, most notably Florence Bell, Elizabeth Robins, and Lucy Clifford. Among those people who joined in celebrating James's seventieth birthday were these and other women playwrights: Beatrice Harraden and Edith Lyttleton. While the suffrage commitment accounts for the highly politicized theatre of women writing in these years, the omnipresence of James may account for the subtlety and nuance to which so many of these writers aspired.

This trans-Atlantic component of Edwardian women's playwriting was complemented by an influential group of women – both in London and elsewhere – who ran theatres and/or theatre companies in the first two decades of the century. Crucially, their record of supporting women's playwriting is unmatched by men in similar positions. Annie Horniman's career offers an astounding case in point. First at the Abbey Theatre in Dublin and more significantly at the Gaiety in Manchester, Horniman took the principles of repertory theatre (particularly those of Granville Barker at the Court) and sustained them for the long term, showing how they could encourage both a diverse theatre audience and women's writing. Sheila Gooddie describes the bustling audience on the Gaiety's opening night in September 1908: "Jew greeted Gentile, Church of England acknowledged Nonconformist, German accent blended with Lancashire, in a harmonious mingling of the city's cultures."[38] The list of women's plays Horniman produced is impressive, including Emily Symonds's "Clothes and the Woman," Antonia Williams's *The Street*, Gertrude Robins's "Makeshifts," Margaret Mack's "Unemployed," and Elizabeth Baker's *Chains*. The most famous of these, Baker's *Chains*, offered a brutally honest portrait of the compromises and sacrifices both men and women make in marriage. The play's challenge to conventional morality was common in many of the plays Horniman produced and its picture of women's indenture to marriage was complemented by the work of Robins, Williams, and others.

While her Pioneer Players (as a subscription theatre with Sunday performances) worked on a more modest scale than Horniman's Gaiety, Edy Craig was an equally powerful force in Edwardian theatre. In the years from 1911 to 1920, her group offered writers an important space for experimenting with innovative work, as George Bernard Shaw noted: "by singleness of artistic direction and unflagging activity [they] did more for the theatrical vanguard than any of the other coterie theatres."[39] Craig, like Horniman, produced significant plays by women, including Susan Glaspell's "Trifles" and *The Verge*, Gwen John's *The Luck of War*, St. John's "The First Actress," and her translation of Hrostwitha, Charlotte Perkins Gilman's "Three Women," Cicely Hamilton's "Jack, Jill, and A Friend," Margaret Mack's "In the Work-house," and Edith Lyttleton's "The Thumbscrew" in addition to many others. While Craig's group is certainly the most significant venue for women's writing, other repertory theatre groups joined her and Horniman in bringing women's writing to the stage. The Abbey Theatre of Dublin brought the work of Lady Gregory to London on several occasions. In addition, the Pioneers produced work by Diana Cholmondely and George Paston; the Incorporated Stage Society produced Margaret Mack; the Play Actors produced Paston, Inez Bensusan, Elizabeth Baker, and Mrs. Havelock Ellis; and the Dramatic Debaters produced Priscilla Craven and Edith A. Browne. Not coincidentally, the society-sponsored productions listed above ran from 1907 to 1909, the years in which women's playwriting increased exponentially. Clearly women's new positions running theatre managements and the independent theatre movement, as well as suffrage activism, all demonstrated at the same moment how important women's voice had become.

This importance was notable also among women managers working in more commercial theatres. A remarkable group of women managers – Lena Ashwell at the Kingsway, Gertrude Kingston at the Little, Lilian Bayliss at the Old Vic, and Lillah McCarthy at the Savoy, Little and Kingsway Theatres – promoted an aesthetic that welcomed women's work. Ashwell notes of her effort, "Everything that could make a theatre original, attractive, and full of well thought out individuality was done."[40] These women's vision and efforts account for several key works by women, including Githa Sowerby's *Rutherford and Son*, Lucy Clifford's *A Woman Alone*, and Cicely Hamilton's *Diana of Dobson's*.

It is fitting to end with a look at two of these influential plays, Clifford's *A Woman Alone*, and Hamilton's *Diana of Dobson's*, for they measure out the range of women's work at the end of our period. Clifford's *A Woman Alone* is a compelling portrait of a woman torn between need for independence and need for love. Originally produced in 1903, the play was revived by Gertrude Kingston at her Little Theatre in 1914. Though it thoughtfully takes on the issues of women's independence and has the main character Blanche saying to her husband after one year of marriage, "it was glorious to be free [before marriage]," the play stages her decline in the four years she is separated from him. In the end, Blanche gives up her autonomy and returns to marriage, saying that women want "to be loved . . . more than anything in the world."[41] Blanche's dilemma is a telling recreation of the era's push and pull between the progressive politics of equality and conventional women's choices; as Clifford herself put it, "in Blanche Bowden I wanted to draw a woman full of intellectual energy and ideals who, since she was not strong enough to carry them to achievement alone, longed to see them take shape in the life that was dearest to her."[42] The play's dilemma remained real even in the heat of suffrage campaigning and even to those fully invested in the cause.

Hamilton's *Diana of Dobson's* is a more inventive work, noted even in its day for its shocking first act and its grim final setting on the Thames Embankment. Lena Ashwell produced the play at her Kingsway Theatre with great success in 1908 and 1909. Like Elizabeth Baker's "Miss Tassey" and Edith Lyttleton's *Warp and Woof*, this play stages the constricted lives of working women. In the dormitory of act I, outspoken Diana bristles at the humiliations of her job; in act II she displays a gusto for leisured life which is charming to those bored by its sameness; and in act III she – like Blanche – weighs her options and makes her best deal, also marriage. While recent commentators on the play find subversion in her acceptance, the ending seems to offer both a gesture toward romance and a resigned recognition of women's economic dependence on men.

Both Clifford's and Hamilton's plays show how, on stages run by women at the opening of the twentieth century, marriage continued to be a main site for women writers' exploration of conventional cultural assumptions. While playwrights like Christopher St. John were finding ways to decenter the role of marriage in women's lives, most of the plays we have noted as significant in the era – from *Votes for Women!* to *Chains*, from *The Street* to *Rutherford and Sons* – take women's entanglements with men as a central subject matter. This conventional focus is why the suffrage playwrighting of the Edwardian years is so crucial to the theatre, for it produced a remarkable body of plays *not* only or centrally about marriage, but about women's work, women's politics, and women's friendships with one another. This novel subject matter as well as the optimism of this politicized era indeed mark a memorable stage in women's playwriting.

When Edy Craig's Pioneer Players produced Susan Glaspell's *The Verge* in 1925, one reviewer valorized Glaspell as the first woman playwright of note: "Up to now we have had no women dramatists who could be ranked with the big men . . . But now here is Susan Glaspell, hailed as a pioneer. Will she, with no axe to grind for feminism, and with all the detachment of the artist, show us in what direction the theatre of to-morrow will be influenced by the new feminine mind."[43] Curiously, he overlooks decades full of strong writing by his own countrywomen. Perhaps it is no coincidence that Glaspell's more abstract (and American) politics in *The Verge* could be safely praised, while the work of Cicely Hamilton, Christopher St. John, Githa Sowerby, Bessie Hatton, George Paston, Margaret Wynne Nevinson, Gwen John, Madeline Lucette Ryley, Lucy Clifford, Elizabeth Baker, and others might be discarded as dated, formulaic, or propagandistic. But such comments, while they reflect the persistent prejudice women faced in writing for the stage, cannot erase either the quality or the quantity of plays by Victorian and Edwardian women.

There is in this era a marked advance in the number of women's plays written and staged, a proliferation of professional opportunities for women who saw the theatre as their career, and both increases were indeed fueled by the ongoing cultural upheavals of feminism and suffragism. We must remember, of course, that the theatre is not run by "blind" competitions in which the name and gender of any aspiring playwright is concealed in the interest of Fairness. If it were – and as our examples of Gore and Syrett suggest – the history of women's playwriting might be very different. But with the odds stacked against them by a patriarchal theatre, women still brought new paradigms of plot, of character, and of theatrical event to the Victorian and Edwardian stage. When Netta Syrett awarded the happy ending to a single secretary and her already married lover; when Clo Graves let a mother, Mrs. Murgatroyd, romp through her world as a trousered man; when Edy Craig organized theatre pageants for female audiences; and when suffragists turned to comedy for an efficient political weapon, they forced a genuine tussle over what would continue to be "theatrical." In the era of the "New Woman," New Theatre was never easy.

NOTES

1. Virginia Woolf, *"A Room of One's Own" and "Three Guineas"* (London: Hogarth, 1984), pp. 43–47.
2. William Archer, *The Old Drama and the New* (Boston: Small, Maynard, 1923).
3. Cicely Hamilton, *Life Errant* (London: Dent, 1935), p. 60.
4. Mrs. Musgrave, *Our Flat: Farcical Comedy in Three Acts*, is quoted from the licensing MS in the Lord Chamberlain's Collection. The play was first performed in London at the Prince of Wales's Theatre and was apparently never published.
5. Letter from Bell to Robins, possibly from November or December 1892, MS in the Elizabeth Robins collection at the Fales Library, New York University.
6. These figures are derived from J. P. Wearing, *The London Stage, 1890–99: A Calendar of Plays and Players* (Metuchen, NJ: Scarecrow, 1976).
7. "Women as Dramatists," *All the Year Round*, 29 September 1894, p. 299.
8. John Russell Stephens, in *The Profession of the Playwright: British Theatre, 1800–1900* (Cambridge: Cambridge University Press, 1991), provides an excellent and detailed survey of the professional environments of playwriting in the Victorian period.
9. "A Chat with Miss Clo Graves," *Sketch*, 21 February 1900, p. 218.

10. Constance Fenimore Woolson, "Miss Grief," in Joan Myers Weimer (ed.), *Women Artists, Women Exiles: "Miss Grief" and Other Stories* (New Brunswick, NJ: Rutgers University Press, 1988), p. 256. Woolson's friendship with Henry James potentially puts her, like him, in a wide circle of theatre practitioners.

11. See Frank Archer, *How To Write a Good Play* (London: French, 1892), pp. 18, 20.

12. *The Stage of 1871: A Review of Plays and Players*, by "Hawk's Eye" (London: Bickers [1871]), p. 15.

13. Quoted by Olive Logan, *Before the Footlights and Behind the Scenes: A Book about the "Show Business" in All Its Branches* (Philadelphia: Parmelee, 1870), p. 391.

14. William Archer, *English Dramatists of To-Day* (London: Low, Marston, 1882), p. 76.

15. "Female Dramatists of the Past," *The Era*, 23 May 1896, p. 18.

16. Logan, *Before the Footlights and Behind the Scenes*, pp. 412–13.

17. This is the account given by Catherine Gore in the preface to *Quid Pro Quo* (London: National Acting Drama Office, n.d.), p. iii.

18. For accounts of the 1902 contest, see *The Times*, 9 May 1902, p. 8, and (quoted here) Netta Syrett's memoir *The Sheltering Tree* (London: Bles, 1939), p. 118.

19. Gore, preface to *Quid Pro Quo*, p. v.

20. *Mirkwater* is quoted from a typescript in the Elizabeth Robins collection of mansucripts and papers at the Fales Library, New York University.

21. *Settled Out of Court* is quoted from the licensing manuscript in the Lord Chamberlain's Collection of the British Library.

22. Constance Fletcher ["George Fleming"], *Mrs. Lessingham* (London: Miles, 1894), pp. 41, 55.

23. *The Sketch*, 15 August 1896.

24. Quoted from *A Mother of Three: An Original Farce in Three Acts* (London: French, n.d.), which is apparently the only published text of the play.

25. Syrett, *The Sheltering Tree*, p. 116.

26. Netta Syrett, *The Finding of Nancy*, never published, is quoted from the licensing manuscript in the Lord Chamberlain's Collection of the British Library.

27. Max Beerbohm, review of *The Finding of Nancy*, in *The Saturday Review*, 17 May 1902, pp. 633–34.

28. *The Times*, 9 May 1902, p. 8.

29. *The Era*, 10 May 1902, p. 19.

30. Syrett, *The Sheltering Tree*, p. 126.

31. "Women," *Encyclopaedia Britannica*, 11th edition (Cambridge: Cambridge University Press, 1911), vol. 28, pp. 782–88.

32. "First Annual Report. 1911–12," *The Pioneer Player Reports, 1911–1915*, Ellen Terry Memorial Museum at Smallhythe, p. 7.

33. Julie Holledge, *Innocent Flowers* (London: Virago, 1981), p, 3.

34. Israel Zangwill, "Actress versus Suffragette," *The Vote*, 18 November 1909, p. 44.

35. Kathleen Cockin, *Edith Craig (1869–1947)* (London: Cassell, 1998), p. 230.

36. Christopher St. John, "The World We Live In," *Votes for Women*, 12 November 1909, p. 103 (the reference is to the feminist periodical, not the play by Elizabeth Robins).

37. While it remains difficult to trace the power of suffrage theatre in succeeding years, Maggie Gale has adeptly shown that the war did not constitute a complete break in women's theatre, but rather signaled the end to women's highly politicized theatre. See both Maggie Gale's book *West End Women: Women and the London Stage, 1918–1962* (London: Routledge, 1996), and her essay "Women Playwrights of the 1920s and 1930s."

38. Sheila Gooddie, *Annie Horniman: A Pioneer in the Theatre* (London: Methuen, 1990), p. 122.

39. As quoted by Christopher St. John in *Ellen Terry and Bernard Shaw: A Correspondence* (1931) (rpt. London: Reinhardt and Evans, 1949), p. 85.

40. Lena Ashwell, *Myself a Player* (London: Michael Joseph, 1936), p. 149.

41. Lucy Clifford, *A Woman Alone* (London: Duckworth, 1915), pp. 24, 76.

42. *Ibid.*, p. vii.

43. "A London Letter: Situation Unchanged," *Yorkshire Post*, 3 April 1925, in scrapbooks at Ellen Terry Memorial Museum.

14

HEIDI J. HOLDER

The East-End theatre

The inherited view of the East-End, largely working-class, theatres of Victorian and Edwardian London, is all too often that of someone firmly planted in the West End. Many of the contemporary reports on East-End entertainments come to us via critics and commentators who are ostentatiously "visitors": explorers who will report back to an audience of middle- and upper-class readers on the amusements of the denizens of "darkest London." The problem, for historians and students of the nineteenth-century theatres of London, is to discern the ways in which the East-End theatres were both like and unlike their better-known and much commented-on counterparts to the west.

Certainly the East-End theatres merit analysis, if only for the sake of the sheer number of theatregoers they entertained.[1] Even before the Theatre Regulation Act of 1843 broke the patent system restricting the performance of spoken drama to Drury Lane and Covent Garden, "illegitimate" theatres such as the Pavilion in Whitechapel were catering to a booming population. The area encompassed by the East End was remarkably diverse, and changing. Hackney, for instance, was considered, in the 1860s, to be "one of the handsomest suburbs in London" (although this district would suffer economic decline in later decades); while Stepney in the 1850s had "no public drainage, but a name for cholera."[2] In mid-century London, more than half of the population was "working class." The rise in population was the result of the building boom of the first half of the century, particularly the development of the London Docks.[3] As the population grew, theatres appeared, despite pre-1843 restrictions on spoken drama outside the patent theatres. The Pavilion opened in 1828 (and would remain an active theatre until 1928), as did the ill-fated Brunswick Theatre (which collapsed shortly after opening). In the next fifteen years, no fewer than six theatres would appear: the Garrick (on Leman Street in Whitechapel) in 1831, the Grecian (on City Road in Shoreditch) in 1832, the Effingham (later the East London Theatre, on Whitechapel Road in Stepney) in 1834; the National

Standard Theatre (on Shoreditch High Street) in 1835, the City of London (Norton Folgate, in Bishopsgate) in 1837, and the Britannia (on High Street in Hoxton) in 1841. Several of these began life as "saloons" – a lower caste of venue, attached to a public house.[4]

After the patent system, which essentially limited the spoken drama to Drury Lane and Covent Garden Theatres, was broken in 1843, the managers of the saloons would fight an extended battle to become full-fledged theatres, a process that involved not only altering a building's physical structure but wheedling permission to use the term "theatre" from the Lord Chamberlain. In January 1847, Thomas Rouse, manager of the Grecian from 1843 to 1851, explained to the Lord Chamberlain his desire to call his business a "theatre": "so long as, with the word 'saloon' are associated, late hours, indiscriminate company, gambling, and excess of various kinds, so long will my property come within the suspected category, and I shall be unable to render it what I should wish it to be; a perfect and unrivaled English opera house."[5] He strikes the same note in correspondence from 1848 to 1849, always emphasizing his desire for "respectability." While the "rise to respectability" has long been a hallmark of the Victorian theatre of the West End, it was a particularly problematic concept for East-End theatres, which faced considerable class-based prejudice. Some managements had considerable success at gaining prestige. Richard Nelson Lee and John Johnson gave polish to the City of London Theatre in the 1850s and 60s, until a troubled economy presented a hopeless obstacle. The managements of the Lanes at the Britannia and the Douglasses at the Standard endured for decades. At the outset, their theatres were often sneered at in the West-End press; however, by the end of their managements in the 1880s and 90s, they presided over what had become venerable institutions.

It should be noted that the theatres of the East End ranged in size from a capacity of 462 – in the Garrick's second building, which opened in 1854 – to 2,000 at the Effingham and City of London theatres, to over 3,000 at the Pavilion, the Standard and the Britannia. In the later decades of the century renovation and increased safety regulations would lead to a drop in seating capacity at some of the larger theatres.[6] The size of the theatregoing population in the East End clearly rivaled, at mid-century, that of the West End of London.

Two images of the East-End theatres are common from contemporary reports, and they are, at times, mirror images. The first is squalid and low, even criminal. One finds in many newspaper accounts of East-End productions the assertion that *these* theatres, which provide entertainment to so many in such unfashionable districts, are inevitably and deeply different from those of London's western neighborhoods. Such accounts are sometimes more anthropological exercises than reviews: the clothing, hygiene, and eating habits of the audience members receive extended discussion. Thomas Erle is typical in this respect when he carefully describes the food consumed by a theatregoer at the Britannia, who

> rashly embark[s] on "am sandwidges" and open tarts, with a glass of gin and treacle imprudently called sherry. It is a misfortune that the cold pease pudding, which used to be offered as an aristocratic delicacy to the occupants of the private boxes and dress circle at the old Britannia, is now, under mistaken notions of progress in refinement, withheld from them.[7]

Theatrical commentators in *Figaro in London* in the 1830s draw firm lines early. A visitor to the Garrick in 1838, for a production of *The Bloody Hatband; or, The Fatal Gossamer*, offers a back-handed salute to the author:

> We have heard that Mr. Somerset's new piece will, technically speaking, "make up a splendid bill" and will enable the manager to insert in red letters the startling line, "REAL MAN KILLED ON THE STAGE." If this does not attract the whole of the East, there is no working upon them at all.[8]

The suggestion here that the play will blur the line between theatrical representation and actual crime points to a central difficulty faced by East-End theatres: the charge that their audiences, credulous and tending towards vice, were easily led, by theatrical performance, into mimicking acts – particularly criminal acts – witnessed on stage. Again and again one comes across this theme of "literalization" in condemnations of East-End plays. Later that same month, *Figaro* would visit the "ill-fated Standard" (a theatre that grew to be eminently respectable), and declare it a hopeless venture, suggesting the natural end of such a low spot: "this place will never do any good as a theatre, and the sooner it is converted into something else the better. From the number of murders committed there, it would make an excellent slaughterhouse."[9]

Even while condemning the theatres as degraded and low, such critics cannot envision any transformation that would lead to a better, more edifying kind of entertainment. Observing the City of London (then the City Theatre), *Figaro* kindly pointed out the limitations the management faced:

> [the] company is good, and the pieces produced just such as to suit the taste of the Shoreditchoions [sic] . . . they cannot understand the classical drama, for it is out of their line, much about in the same ratio as silk-stockings would be to an Irish pig-driver. But everyone to their fancy, and the manager is perfectly right in tickling theirs with the right sort.[10]

The authorities had the same notion. Sir Thomas Henry, Chief Magistrate of the Bow Street Police Court, strongly asserted this difference when testifying before a Joint Select Committee investigating theatrical regulations in 1866. When asked why a single governing authority (the Lord Chamberlain's Office) remained useful, Sir Thomas replied, "great benefit is derived from that, because the licensing authority can then regulate what sorts of amusements should be afforded to the public according to the localities in which they are to be granted . . . The theatre that is suited to the West End would not be suited to Whitechapel."[11]

The second, quite opposing, view of the East-End theatres presents them as bastions of native virtue, uncorrupted by wealth or foreign influence. The Britannia in particular attracted such praise; most notably, Dickens and Shaw acclaimed "the Brit," not so much for its own sake, as to show up the failings of the West End. Dickens, in his account of "A Cheap Theatre," published in *All the Year Round* in 1860, wanders through the neighborhood of Drury Lane and Covent Garden with marked dissatisfaction:

> these streets looked so dull, and, considered as theatrical streets, so broken and bankrupt, that the F O U N D D E A D on the black board at the police station might have announced the decease of the drama, and the pools of water outside the fire-engine makers at the corner of Long-acre might have been occasioned by his having brought out the whole of his stock to play upon its last smoldering ashes. And yet . . . within half an hour I was in an immense theatre capable of holding nearly five thousand people.[12]

After building up the suspense, Dickens reveals the theatre to be the Britannia, and he goes on to praise that theatre as "infinitely superior" to its more fashionable West-End counterparts. It is not so merely because it is comfortable and well-regulated. The Britannia is also more *moral*. Dickens describes the audience as "we" – his use of the plural pronoun is pointed, indicating that he has joined the "none too clean" crowd: "We all agreed (for the time) that honesty was the best policy, and we were as hard as iron upon Vice, and we wouldn't hear of villainy getting on in the world – no, not on any consideration whatsoever."[13]

Shaw would use the Britannia in a similar fashion to castigate the West-End theatres when, in 1898, he visited "the Brit" to see its famous pantomime, which he compared favorably to the "expensively dreary" productions of the West End:

> Who would not rather look at and laugh at four men pretending to be seasick in a wildly comic way than see a row of young women singing a chorus about being "Gaiety Girls" with the deliberate intention of conveying to the audience that a Gaiety chorister's profession – their own profession – is only a mask for the sort of life which is represented in Piccadilly Circus and Leicester Square after midnight?[14]

Blanchard Jerrold in his influential *London: A Pilgrimage*, commented thus on the Garrick: "Virtue is always rewarded in these humble dramatic temples; manly courage gets three times three; and woman is ever treated with respectful tenderness." He notes, "the helper of the 'female in distress' (dismissed from the West End long ago) is sure of his rounds of applause."[15]

It is clear from these reports that when the East End is praised, it is usually not the real subject at hand; the commentators are all concerned with the state of the theatres of the West End. Often, towards the end of the century, working-class audiences might be lauded for shunning the influence of Ibsen, or of the French theatre (especially in their treatment of sexual matters). Note, for example, the manner in which Samuel Smith, MP, dismisses Arthur Wing Pinero's man-with-a-past play *The Gay Lord Quex* (Globe, 1899): "I can only say that if wealth and rank admire such scenes, they are below the breeding of the average costermonger."[16]

Given these opposing images, how to determine the actual differences and similarities between the theatres in these two areas of London?[17] One can take a closer look at the plays. At first glance, it would seem that there was a considerable degree of overlap in the theatrical entertainments of different districts. Staples such as Bulwer Lytton's *The Lady of Lyons*, Mrs. Maria Lovell's *Ingomar the Barbarian*, Isaac Bickerstaffe's *The Padlock*, and J. Sheridan Knowles's *Virginius* appeared frequently across London's theatrical spectrum. Interestingly enough, the movement of plays is not in one direction only. While it would seem natural to critics who see the East End as "low" and in need of edification that the most popular West-End plays might show up in the East End as uplifting imports, how to explain the occasional success of the East-End play in the West End? James Anderson's *Civilization* (an adaptation of Voltaire's *Le Huron*), staged with great success at the City of London Theatre in November 1852, moved shortly thereafter to the Strand. Later in the century several plays produced at the Pavilion (while Isaac Cohen was manager) would move to the Princess's Theatre, including Arthur Shirley and Benjamin Landeck's plays *Tommy Atkins* (1895), *Women and Wine* (1897), and *Going the Pace* (1898).

Despite the very real affinities with the theatres to the west, the East-End drama had some distinctive features. Early on, its audiences displayed what was, to authorities, an alarming taste for dramas centered on criminals: Newgate plays, highwayman dramas, and the like. So alarmed was the Lord Chamberlain at this development that his office restricted performances of such works.[18] Characters including Jack Sheppard, Dick Turpin, Spring-Heel'd Jack and Claude Duval were wildly anti-authoritarian, law-breaking heroes, their exploits often cheered by audiences. The specific representation of crime was only part of the problem. The characters were figured as rebels, of a sort, and it was their success in standing, victorious (at least for a time), outside the existing social order that made them attractive to a working-class audience and feared and detested by authorities.

Looking at the Lord Chamberlain's Day Book, in which the Examiner of Plays records required changes and omissions in play texts, one finds a vigilant eye not simply for the representation of crime, but also for any criticism of authorities and institutions. Representations of court proceedings, especially those showing the imposition of a death sentence, were closely monitored and often subject to cuts. The Britannia's *Lynch Law; or, The Warden of Galway* (1854) had scenes featuring a sentence of death and an execution removed; the Pavilion's *Bound to the Wheel* (1866) received the same treatment. The examiner (William Bodham Donne) notes: "the representation of the proceedings in a court of justice is permitted on the stage; but it should be rather suggestive than complete."[19] Interestingly, stage pictures of justice, as well as crime, are apparently sources of anxiety and contention. Other institutions are carefully protected from criticism. Workhouses and the Poor Laws, perennially hated by anyone who might rely on them, were given a (rather light) nudging in lines cut from the pantomime *The Demon Dwarf* (Grecian 1871):

> I dreamed the Gasmen, for what they didn't like
> Like a band of heroes, went upon the strike;
> The striking effect of which is, that it entails
> Increase of inmates in workhouses and gaols
> I dreamed the poor laws worked as first intended,
> I also dreamed the Tichbourne case was ended.[20]

The reference to the infamous Tichbourne claimant case (which would very likely have been cut at any theatre) is not the only problem here. Pantomimes at all theatres often tried to get away with such topical references and pointed criticisms. But a closer eye was kept on the East End, where negative comments about social institutions appeared across genres. In November 1870 a line critical of the Metropolitan Police was cut from the Grecian's *A Flash of Lightning*. In a melodrama of empire, *The Queen's Colours* (Grecian, 1878) set during the Zulu War, the examiner deemed offensive a line about soldiers being "badly fed, badly clothed, and short of ammunition."[21] The vogue for plays about criminals must be put into the larger context of a persistent desire on the part of East-End audiences to experience, at least in the theatre, some resistance to and criticism of the authorities. Even after the Newgate craze had passed (or been suppressed) that desire was monitored, and to some extent held in check, by the Lord Chamberlain's office.[22]

The subgenre of urban melodrama was a strong presence in the east. While representations of city life were popular in the more fashionable theatres – witness William Moncrieff's *The Scamps of London* (Sadler's Wells, 1843), Andrew Halliday's *The Great City* (Drury Lane, 1867) and G. R. Sims's *The Lights o'London* (Princess's, 1881) – the audiences in the east apparently could not tire of seeing the problems of the London poor resolved on stage. The East End's most popular dramatists mined this subgenre. William Travers, who wrote at one point or other for virtually all the major East-End houses, featured realistic London settings in his plays *A Poor Girl's Temptations; or, A Voice from the Streets* (City of London, 1858), *The Watercress Girl* (City of London, 1865), and *The Dark Side of the Great Metropolis* (Britannia, 1868). Mrs. Henry Young, who wrote numerous successful melodramas for the Effingham at mid-century, featured London scenes in *The Dark Woman* (1861), and *Nobody's Son; or, Half a Loaf Better than None* (1866). Other notable examples include the anonymous *St. James's and St. Giles's* (City of London, 1853), James Elphinstone's *London Labour and London Poor; or, Want and Vice* (Pavilion, 1854), and J. B. Johnstone's *London Highways and Byways* (Pavilion, 1864). Colin Hazlewood, who specialized in depictions of aristocratic vice and working-class woe, made use of the urban scene in *The Wild Tribes of London* (City of London, 1856), *The Workgirls of London* (Britannia, 1864), and *Lizzie Lyle; or, The Flower Makers of Finsbury* (Grecian, 1869).

The vogue for these plays emerged during the heyday of the "social explorer," in the years after Henry Mayhew wrote his influential series of articles for the *Morning Chronicle* (1849–50), later published as *London Labour and the London Poor*. One can hear echoes of Mayhew even in the titles of some of the works, including Travers's highly successful *The Watercress Girl* (such a figure offered one of the most touching and troubling of Mayhew's images of child laborers).

While the plight of "outcast London" was being endlessly analyzed in the West-End press, the East-End theatres were offering up their own versions of their troubles. The plots are generally boilerplate melodrama, with the hero and/or heroine persecuted unjustly, and true identities revealed in the end. But the East End sometimes provided a slightly different interpretation to standard plots. Take the case of the title character in *The Street Arab; or, Adrift on the World* (Garrick, 1871). Clement, the King of the Street Arabs, represents the rootlessness and criminality of London's underclass. Yet, at the end of the play, he is shown to be a long-lost heir to a fortune, he has married a wealthy, upper-class woman, and he is determined to save his wretched half-brother from a vice-ridden life. His final speech points up the lesson:

Figure 12 Playbill from the City of London Theatre.

Behold the moral of a vagrant's life. My early days were clouded with misery and despair – but I never forgot that unerring hand that held the balance – I fought temptation with a youthful heart and learned to wait and hope that the storm had subsided – do you the same – for there is many makings of a great and noble hero in those hunted-down sons of old England if a kind word were only spoken to the poor street Arabs.[23]

Clement calls upon his fellow poor to have heart, to pursue a virtuous life; however, he is also calling upon unspecified others (the wealthy, the powerful, and authorities?) to offer up that crucial "kind word." The responsibility must be shared. The play performs a remarkable transformation of Clement from an embodiment of a social problem into a model of a possible solution. The denouement is, on the one hand, utterly conventional melodrama, but the "moral" relies on context to be understood.

In the case of other plays, the East-End milieu also shapes the characters and stories. It also, again, offers a different picture of London life. From their early days, the East-End theatres featured representations of London's minority communities, including Indians, Africans or African-Americans, and Jews. In a departure from their representation in West-End theatres, such characters are not always comic and minor. Minority characters in the West-End theatres were overwhelmingly low and comic (and marginalized), beginning with those seen in the various adaptations of Pierce Egan's *Tom and Jerry* in the 1820s and continuing through Paul Meritt and George F. Rowe's *New Babylon* (Duke's Theatre, 1879) and Joseph Derrick's *Twins* (Olympic, 1884). But as early as Edward Fitzball's *The Negro of Wapping*, London's minority populations were given central roles. And, as in *The Street Arab*, what could be a negative class- or race-based stereotype is given a twist in the end.

The central character of *The Negro of Wapping*, Black Sam, would certainly seem to be a villain. He robs, and commits murder; although he didn't plan to kill, he doesn't seem terribly remorseful. During the darkened scene of the robbery, when illuminated only by lightning, Sam is deliberately depicted as demonic or "infernal." When, in the end, Black Sam is ready to kill both his partner in the crime and the young woman who witnessed it, he makes some extraordinary speeches that completely change the tone of the play. First he denies that his partner, Jack, is his friend:

Do not say friend. The African, torn by the hand of cruelty from his native home – dragged on board a ship, and doomed to labour till his once-proud limbs become warped and feeble, then left to beg or rob, or die of famine in a strange land, might well be pardoned his disbelief of the white man's sincerity, were it as true as heaven.

He wonders at his own capacity for feeling (something we have not seen hitherto in his character): "Heart – heart! Why rush such melancholy thoughts across thee now? I thought thou had'st become too callous – long, long ago." Sam imagines fleeing back to Africa with his stolen gold, but his fantasy is not to be realized. And when he is facing death, he once again bitterly blames the white man for his fate, but this time we move from Africa to London in his account of his sufferings. Suddenly we hear of an earlier encounter with the man he has killed:

> I begged of him one cold and wintry night, with tears in my eyes, when I was starving, only a morsel of bread; had I been a dog, rather than a man, he could not have spurned me with more fury. 'Till that moment I had been honest – famine made me desperate – I stole for the first time – one crime led to another – he might have saved me from all – by a little charity he might have saved himself – and I – but the negro's story is told – oh! [Music – he falls and dies. Picture].[24]

Sam becomes an entirely new character in the closing scene. We have not previously heard anything about him being a slave, or starving on the streets. In fact, he seems a rather flat character, and his race is not much commented on. Suddenly, the audience gets a back story, one that shifts the condemnation to the cruelty of those more powerful than Sam – those who enslaved him and spurned his pleas for charity. The villains, it seems, are not always in the expected places. This use of non-white characters to voice criticism of the wealthy and powerful would become a recurring feature of working-class melodramas; another notable example would be found in the use of a key Indian character in James Willing and Frank Stainforth's *Glad Tidings*, an enormously successful play at the Standard Theatre in 1883.[25]

The more diverse population of the East End finds further dramatic representation in the Jewish drama. A. E. Wilson, in his conversational history of the East-End theatres, cites several journalists who comment on the "Israelitish-looking people" in the districts of the east. Of the City of London Theatre, one observes that "It was literally a house of Israel, as if all Bishopsgate, St. Mary Axe, Shoreditch, and Finsbury Circus had disgorged their fusty tenantry in one huge mass of Anglo-Jewish capitalists . . . enough to have stormed and retaken old Jerusalem."[26] The Jewish population certainly grew rapidly in the nineteenth century. By the end of the Edwardian era there were approximately 120,000 Jews in London, mostly settled in the East End.[27]

By the second half of the nineteenth century, theatres were catering to this audience, with plays in both English and Yiddish. The Britannia, by the 1870s, was staging a "Jewish Annual," sometimes a play by "E. Manuel"

Figure 13 Playbill from the Britannia Theatre, Hoxton.

(Johnny Gideon). These plays, including *Jewess and Christian; or, The Love that Kills* (1877), *Rachel's Penance; or, A Daughter of Israel* (1878), and *The Rabbi's Son; or, The Last Link in the Chain* (1879), often featured Jewish/gentile romances, and dealt with issues of assimilation. The Yiddish theatre would find a home at the Effingham in the 1880s and after when the rebuilt theatre was known as The Wonderland. Most important, perhaps, to the Jewish community in the east, was the Pavilion, which presented not only English-language plays such as James J. Hewson's *Under the Canopy* (1903) but also performances by Feinman's Jewish Operatic and Dramatic company, with a full repertory of plays in Yiddish.[28] Interestingly enough, the notion that the East-End theatres could have a "civilizing" effect on the people of the east endures in depictions of the Jewish audience. In 1908, writing in the *Pall Mall Gazette*, Anthony Ellis suggests that the Jewish drama is in its infancy, inextricably linked to assimilation. In his account, the Jewish theatre emerges just as the specific "Jewishness" of its audience is being modified or diluted. Note his idea of progress when he looks at the Jewish audience:

> If you observe closely the young men and women of the newer generation, you will see that already the Semitic appearance of their forebears is modified in them, and that in feature and complexion they approximate more to the English physical type.[29]

These distinctive features of East-End plays should not lead us to draw too sharp a line between east and west. The similarities require more comment, particularly in relation to that enduring idea of the theatre's civilizing influence. Even while the Lord Chamberlain's office was attempting to quash the vogue for the so-called Newgate plays in the 1840s and 50s, theatre managers and critics were touting their own attempts to edify audiences, particularly through performances of Shakespeare. In fact, Shakespeare's plays were performed with considerable regularity at East-End venues, from their inception. Jane Moody has observed that the Pavilion, in the late 1820s, put Shakespeare on the stage more frequently than the patent theatres.[30] (To avoid rousing the authorities, "illegitimate" theatres often had to rely heavily on the music and gestures of melodrama, but occasionally they defied the Lord Chamberlain with spoken drama.) In 1847, *The Theatrical Times* takes note of a successful production at the City Theatre: "it was cheering to behold the attention and interest displayed by a densely crowded, and in general, respectful audience to the performance of 'Othello' on Tuesday last."[31] In 1850, *Tallis's Dramatic Magazine* comments:

We are gratified at having it in our power to say that while melodrama does prevail at the 'East-end,' Shakespeare is not forgotten here. During the earlier part of the month *Hamlet, Othello,* &c., have been performed and that too in a very commendable manner. Indeed the fact that such is done at all, would almost prevail upon us to look upon them with a less critical eye than ordinary, and we congratulate the management upon the taste that it displays.[32]

When the Standard Theatre staged *King John* in March of 1856, *The Times* summoned up some praise: "This far-east theatre, perhaps scarcely known, even by name, to the West-end habitués, is one of the few places which afford a retreat to the genius of Shakespeare, while the egotism of the age gives its preference to spectacle and melodrama over the faithful representation of human life and passion."[33]

East-End theatres persisted in staging a rather eclectic mix of plays: "main-stream" melodramas such as *Ingomar the Barbarian* and Bulwer Lytton's *Lady of Lyons* appeared alongside local favorites such as Travers's *The Watercress Girl* and "classic" repertory works such as Shakespeare's *Othello*. A look at playbills for productions at the City of London Theatre in the late 1850s to early 1860s is instructive. There are numerous popular urban or "crime" melodramas considered typical East-End fare, including *The Life of a Beggar* (17 September 1859), *The Slaves of London* (3 October 1859), *Oliver Twist* (10 December 1859), *The Wild Tribes of London* (11 August 1860), *The String of Pearls* (a Sweeney Todd play, 22 July 1861), and *Jerry Abershaw the Highwayman* (14 December 1861). The warhorses of melodrama are well represented: *The Lady of Lyons* (30 April 1860), *Pizarro* (30 April 1860), *Virginius* (3 December 1860), *Miss Eily O'Connor* and *Ingomar the Barbarian* (both in the week of 14 March 1863). And Shakespeare is produced, in visits by tragedians T. C. King and Gustavus Vaughan Brooke: extended visits by King in May and December of 1860 featured performances of *Macbeth, Othello, Hamlet,* and *Richard III*; Brooke's roles (in November 1862) included Macbeth, Richard III, and Julius Caesar.

It is doubtful that Shakespeare would have been staged so commonly in the East End if he did not please the public. While "high-toned" plays might lend credence to managers' claims to be uplifting their audiences, such polish would not keep the theatres in business. Nonetheless, managers rarely seemed to miss an opportunity to draw attention to visits by Shakespearean actors. When J. Johnson and Nelson Lee initially invited Brooke to the City of London Theatre in 1854, the business of arranging the visit itself was very public. Johnson and Lee posted, as a bill, a copy of their invitation to Brooke, claiming that they are "most anxious to provide for the citizens of

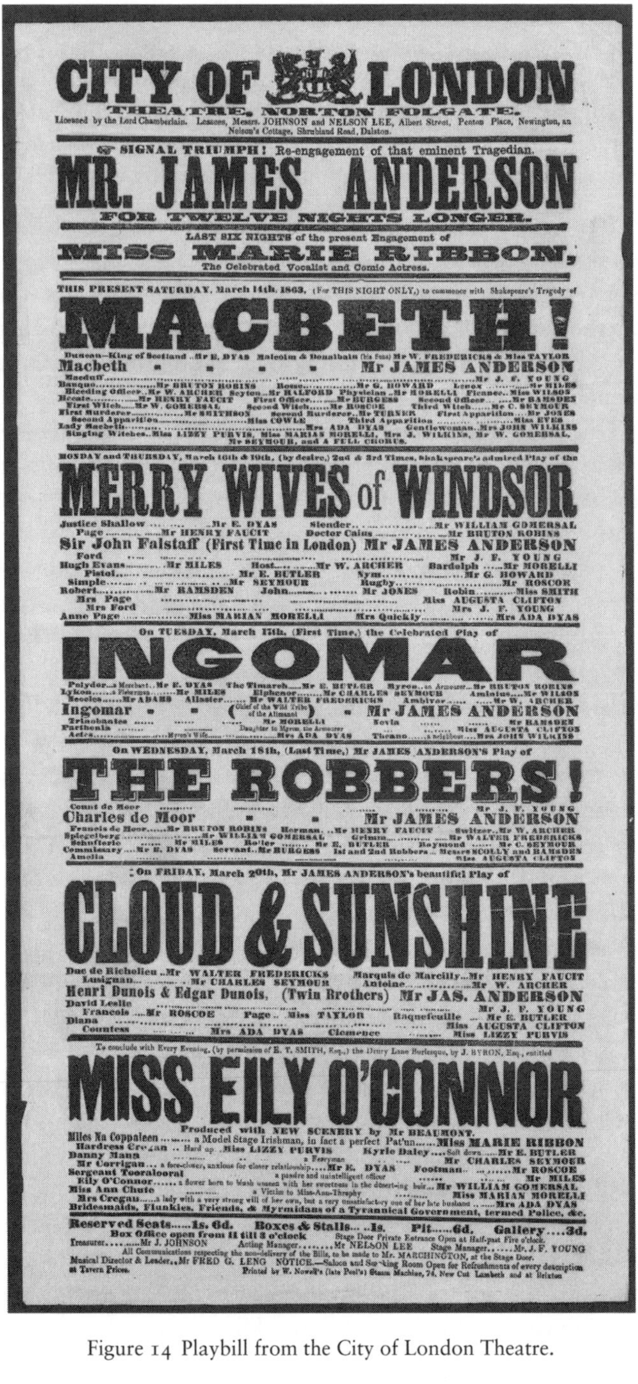

CITY OF LONDON
THEATRE, NORTON FOLGATE.
Licensed by the Lord Chamberlain. Lessees, Messrs. JOHNSON and NELSON LEE, Albert Street, Penton Place, Newington, an Nelson's Cottage, Shrubland Road, Dalston.

SIGNAL TRIUMPH! Re-engagement of that eminent Tragedian.
MR. JAMES ANDERSON
FOR TWELVE NIGHTS LONGER.

LAST SIX NIGHTS of the present Engagement of
MISS MARIE RIBBON,
The Celebrated Vocalist and Comic Actress.

THIS PRESENT SATURDAY, March 14th, 1863, (For THIS NIGHT ONLY,) to commence with Shakespeare's Tragedy of
MACBETH!
Duncan—King of Scotland ..Mr E. DYAS Malcolm & Donalbain (his Sons) Mr W. FREDERICKS & Miss TAYLOR
Macbeth - - - - Mr JAMES ANDERSON
Macduff ... Mr J. F. YOUNG
Banquo ... Mr BRUTON ROBINS Rosse ... Mr G. HOWARD Lenox ... Mr MILES
Bleeding Officer..Mr W. ARCHER Seyton...Mr HALFORD Physician ..Mr MORELLI Fleance..Miss WILSON
Hecate ... Mr HENRY FAUCIT First Officer ... Mr BURGESS Second Officer ... Mr RAMSDEN
First Witch ... Mr W. GOMERSAL Second Witch ... Mr ROSCOE Third Witch ... Mr C. SEYMOUR
First Murderer ... Mr SMITHSON Second Murderer..Mr TURNER First Apparition ... Mr JONES
Second Apparition ... Miss COWLE Third Apparition ... Miss EVES
Lady Macbeth ... Mrs ADA DYAS Gentlewoman..Mrs JOHN WILKINS
Singing Witches..Miss LIZZY PURVIS, Miss MARIAN MORELLI, Mrs J. WILKINS, Mr W. GOMERSAL, Mr SEYMOUR, and A FULL CHORUS.

MONDAY and THURSDAY, March 16th & 19th, (by desire,) 2nd & 3rd Times, Shakspeare's admired Play of the
MERRY WIVES of WINDSOR
Justice Shallow ... Mr E. DYAS Slender ... Mr WILLIAM GOMERSAL
Page ... Mr HENRY FAUCIT Doctor Caius ... Mr BRUTON ROBINS
Sir John Falstaff (First Time in London) Mr JAMES ANDERSON
Ford ... Mr J. F. YOUNG
Hugh Evans ... Mr MILES Host ... Mr W. ARCHER Bardolph ... Mr MORELLI
Pistol ... Mr E. BUTLER Nym ... Mr G. HOWARD
Simple ... Mr SEYMOUR Rugby ... Mr ROSCOE
Robert ... Mr RAMSDEN John ... Mr JONES Robin ... Miss SMITH
Mrs Page ... Miss AUGUSTA CLIFTON
Mrs Ford ... Mrs J. F. YOUNG
Anne Page ... Miss MARIAN MORELLI Mrs Quickly ... Mrs ADA DYAS

On TUESDAY, March 17th, (First Time,) the Celebrated Play of
INGOMAR
Polydor...a Merchant..Mr E. DYAS The Timarch ... Mr E. BUTLER Myron...an Armourer...Mr BRUTON ROBINS
Lykon...a Fisherman ... Mr MILES Elphenor ... Mr CHARLES SEYMOUR Amintus ... Mr WILSON
Neocles ... Mr ADAMS Allastor ... Mr WALTER FREDERICKS Ambivar ... Mr W. ARCHER
Ingomar - - (Chief of the Wild Tribe of the Allmanni) - Mr JAMES ANDERSON
Trinobantes ... Mr MORELLI Novio ... Mr RAMSDEN
Parthenia ... Daughter to Myron, the Armourer ... Miss AUGUSTA CLIFTON
Actea ... Myron's Wife ... Mrs ADA DYAS Theano ... a neighbour ... Mrs JOHN WILKINS

On WEDNESDAY, March 18th, (Last Time,) Mr JAMES ANDERSON'S Play of
THE ROBBERS!
Count de Moor ... Mr J. F. YOUNG
Charles de Moor - - Mr JAMES ANDERSON
Francis de Moor ... Mr BRUTON ROBINS Herman ... Mr HENRY FAUCIT Switzer..Mr W. ARCHER
Spiegelberg ... Mr WILLIAM GOMERSAL Grimm ... Mr WALTER FREDERICKS
Schufterle ... Mr MILES Roller ... Mr E. BUTLER Reymond ... Mr C. SEYMOUR
Commissary ... Mr E. DYAS Servant..Mr BURGESS 1st and 2nd Robbers... Messrs SCOLLY and RAMSDEN
Amelia ... Miss AUGUSTA CLIFTON

On FRIDAY, March 20th, Mr JAMES ANDERSON's beautiful Play of
CLOUD & SUNSHINE
Duc de Richelieu ..Mr WALTER FREDERICKS Marquis de Marcilly...Mr HENRY FAUCIT
Lusignan ... Mr CHARLES SEYMOUR Antoine ... Mr W. ARCHER
Henri Dunois & Edgar Dunois, (Twin Brothers) Mr JAS. ANDERSON
David Leslie ... Mr J. F. YOUNG
Francois ... Mr ROSCOE Page.. Miss TAYLOR Raquefeuille ... Mr E. BUTLER
Diana ... Miss AUGUSTA CLIFTON
Countess ... Mrs ADA DYAS Clemence ... Miss LIZZY PURVIS

To conclude with Every Evening, (by permission of E. T. SMITH, Esq.,) the Drury Lane Burlesque, by J. BYRON, Esq., entitled
MISS EILY O'CONNOR
Produced with NEW SCENERY by Mr BEAUMONT.
Miles Na Coppaleen ... a Model Stage Irishman, in fact a perfect Pat'un ... Miss MARIE RIBBON
Hardress Cregan .. Hard up ..Miss LIZZY PURVIS Kyrle Daley ... Soft down ... Mr E. BUTLER
Danny Mann ... a Ferryman ... Mr CHARLES SEYMOUR
Mr Corrigan ... a fore-closer, anxious for closer relationship ... Mr E. DYAS Footman ... Mr ROSCOE
Sergeant Tooralooral ... a paadre and unintelligent officer ... Mr MILES
Eily O'Connor ... a flower born to blush unseen with her sweetness in the desert-ing hair ... Mr WILLIAM GOMERSAL
Miss Ann Chute ... a Victim to Miss-Ann-Thropy ... Miss MARIAN MORELLI
Mrs Cregan ... a lady with a very strong will of her own, but a very unsatisfactory one of her late husband ... Mrs ADA DYAS
Bridesmaids, Flunkies, Friends, & Myrmidons of a Tyrannical Government, termed Police, &c.

Reserved Seats ... 1s. 6d. Boxes & Stalls ... 1s. Pit ... 6d. Gallery ... 3d.
Box Office open from 11 till 3 o'clock Stage Door Private Entrance Open at Half-past Five o'clock.
Treasurer ... Mr J. JOHNSON Acting Manager ... Mr NELSON LEE Stage Manager ... Mr. J. F. YOUNG
All Communications respecting the non-delivery of the Bills, to be made to Mr. MARCHINGTON, at the Stage Door.
Musical Director & Leader,, Mr FRED G. LENG NOTICE.—Saloon and Smoking Room Open for Refreshments of every description at Tavern Prices.
Printed by W. Nowell's (late Peel's) Steam Machine, 74, New Cut Lambeth and at Brixton

Figure 14 Playbill from the City of London Theatre.

London entertainment of a superior cast."[34] Brooke initially turned down the invitation, claiming to be too busy, whereupon Johnson and Lee circulated a petition among local bankers and tradesmen. These local worthies – over 250 of them – pleaded with Brooke to reconsider:

> Thousands of our fellow citizens, at the east end of this metropolis, having, owing to the distance, business hours, and other circumstances, been debarred the pleasure of witnessing your masterly impersonations – but are most desirous to do so – and learning your contemplated journey to Australia, we, the undersigned, are induced to request that you will favour us with that delight and satisfaction at one of our theatres, if only for a few nights.

Brooke acquiesced in the face of this "most gratifying testimonial," observing that "were I to refuse so marked a token of respect, I should feel myself unworthy of the unparalleled encouragement bestowed upon my humble efforts in this country." This entire exchange appears on the bill, drawing attention to the desire of East-End audiences (here clearly figured as respectable, with a strong middle-class component) for quality performances of classic dramas. There is a rather staged quality to the interplay among manager, performer, and audience: the suitability of Shakespeare for the East End is determinedly made visible.

If the East End could pose itself as "refined," it could also play on its reputation as "low." That playwrights well knew the suspicions and anxieties of the censor (and, by extension, the government and ruling classes) is clear, I think, in the case of James Elphinstone's 1854 play *Rotherhithe in Olden Times; or, The Female Highwayman* (eventually performed, much cut, at the Pavilion). As James Stephens has noted, this play caused great anxiety for the Examiner of Plays, William Bodham Donne.[35] Elphinstone apparently used a checklist of forbidden subjects: criminal activity, lewdness, blasphemy, and more criminal activity. In one scene, in a cemetery, two servants are forced to strip to their underwear by robbers – "and this in a churchyard!" the examiner writes in the margins. The title character, Lily, gives some amazingly fierce speeches, which the Examiner of Plays rejected in their entirety. In one such speech she cheerfully recounts some of the highlights of her career in crime:

> My name is Captain Finch, the notorious highwayman, the nobby housebreaker and aristocratic footpad. I'm so dreaded on the highway that the mail coach takes a different road every night, I run away with heiresses by the dozen; jump over hurdles and haystacks, spit in the faces of toll-gate keepers, and as to breaking into houses, I once forged a check for a million and a half of money, presented it myself, got the cash and by doing so broke the firm of Smith, Brown, Jones, and Robinson the biggest bankers in the city.

One of the listeners responds with awe, "Damme, that's what I call house-breaking with a vengeance!"[36] A version of the play, minus its subtitle, would be licensed for performance later that year. The cemetery scene would be lost, and Lily would now be masquerading as a gentleman rather than a highway-man. Reading Elphinstone's original text, it's hard to believe that he, as both playwright and manager of the Pavilion, expected it to receive a license. He seems to be baiting the censor. Or, perhaps, at least diverting his attention. In his haste to cut the scenes of criminal behavior, Donne did miss some rather questionable bits of dialogue, such as when the disguised Lily taunts her lover, claiming to have slept with his sister; "I and Clara used to sleep together formerly," Lily says slyly.

Theatre managers and playwrights seemed quite capable of working within the "doubleness" of the East-End theatres, wielding the idea of "elevation" while at the same banking, as much as possible, on the popular plays featuring criminals. Even while producing Shakespeare, theatres such as the Effingham would attempt to dodge the censor's suppression of plays lauding such criminals as Jack Sheppard by slight shifts in focus or alterations of names. *The Illustrated Sporting News* wryly notes in 1865 that the Effingham "has produced 'Tom Sheppard,' a drama which illustrates the career of the father of the immortal 'Jack,' who, being banished from the boards, avenges himself on the Lord Chamberlain by raking up his father's ghost as a vehicle for keeping before the public such names as Blueskin, Wild, Quilt Arnold and Darrell."[37] The East-End theatres at times used their association with criminality as a kind of sales pitch. An 1867 performance of *Spring Heel'd Jack* – a play with a notably slippery criminal for a "hero," was advertised by the Effingham in a playbill in the form of a "Wanted for Murder" posting:

> Whereas a notorious robber named SPRING HEEL'D JACK! Who has, for some weeks past, eluded the officers of justice. It has been discovered, on reliable authority, that he will be lurking in the neighbourhood of the Effingham Theatre, on May the 8th next. Though robbing the rich of their gold and Jewellery, it cannot be said that the above Criminal ever committed the heinous crime of MURDER.[38]

In its cheeky parody of a "wanted" poster, an image associated with the officialdom of law and order, the advertisement mocks, to the theatre's own advantage, the very notion of the theatre as a locus of criminality. J. B. Johnstone's *London Highways and Byways* (Pavilion, 1864) actually puts the regulation of theatres on stage in a scene set at a penny gaff. An actor, Patter, enters as a "heavy Baren [sic]," uttering this generic speech: "my vassals, my castles, all my wide domains are valueless, because I have no one to share them with me, if Rose of the Mill would but listen to me, here she comes." When Rose refuses him, and he assaults her, the resulting conflict is interrupted when someone cries "Behold, here comes the spectre!" Rather than that gothic favorite, a police officer enters to arrest the actors.[39] Significantly, the setting is a gaff, a low, illegal theatre, and not one of the legitimate East-End stages. But the mocking of the relationship between the law and working-class venues is evident.

The East-End theatres had their heyday in the middle of the nineteenth century. Despite achieving remarkable stability and grudging respect from the authorities, the economic downturn of the late 1860s hit hard, and most theatres never recovered. The Standard, the Britannia, and the Pavilion were the longest-lived of the lot, but by the Edwardian period only two theatres remained as sites of theatrical performances: the Standard and the Pavilion. The Pavilion, as discussed above, produced plays for a Jewish audience. The Standard, however, found another niche, in sensation dramas centered on female villains.

The East End's apparent fascination with crime would reach an apotheosis of sorts in the sensational melodramas of the Melville brothers, Walter and Frederick, who took over the management of the Standard in 1889. With such plays as *The Worst Woman in London* (1899), *That Wretch of a Woman* (1901), and *The Girl Who Wrecked his Home* (1907), the Melvilles extended the life of the Standard by mining apparently aging stereotypes. Their villainesses embody evil – but also represent the desire for, and corrupting influence of, wealth. The gender politics of these melodramas is strongly contingent upon class. A paradigmatic scene in the Melvilles' *The Girl Who Took the Wrong Turning* (Standard, 1906) shows the villainess, Vesta le Clare, dressing up the innocent Sophie as a lady – as Elaine Ashton and Ian Clarke put it, a "mirror image of Vesta."[40] Sophie's material elevation – the donning of rich clothes, the styling of her hair, and her education in sophisticated movement and gesture – are ultimately degrading. Her dissatisfaction with her lowly status, indicated in her cry "I despise the poverty that surrounds me,"[41] ironically leads her to a much greater debasement.

The internal contradictions here reveal a deep ambivalence. A more reformist writer such as Shaw would, to very different ends, undermine the melodramatic tradition of changing poor people into rich people in plays ranging from *Mrs. Warren's Profession* (1893) to *Pygmalion* (Covent Garden, 1913). Shaw's purpose is to force the audience really to think about intersections of wealth and morality, and about the implications of class affiliation. Like Sophie, his Eliza Doolittle is in danger of being undone by being made into a "lady." It may seem odd to put the Melvilles and Shaw together;

nonetheless, the exaggerations of Melvillian melodrama, its fantastic, even nightmarish violations of class boundaries, do connect it with the work of reformist playwrights such as Shaw, Harley Granville Barker, and the feminist playwright Cecily Hamilton. In the end, as in the beginning, the relationship between the theatres of London's East End and West End would reveal *both* connections and diversions.

NOTES

Research for this essay was supported by the Stanley J. Kahrl Fellowship in Theatre History, Houghton Library, Harvard University; and by a research grant from the faculty research and creative endeavors committee, Central Michigan University.

1. The exact nature and composition of audiences for the East-End theatres remains a difficult subject. It appears that, despite the area's identification as working class, pockets of (relative) wealth were present at mid-century. There was certainly a middle-class presence in many of the early East-End theatres. For information on audiences, see Jim Davis and Tracy C. Davis, "The People of the 'People's Theatre': The Social Demography of the Britannia Theatre (Hoxton)," *Theatre Survey* 32 (1991), 137–65; Clive Barker, "The Audiences of the Britannia Theatre, Hoxton," *New Theatre Quarterly* 12: 45 (1996), 27–41. Jim Davis and Victor Emeljanow's book, *Reflecting the Audience: London Theatregoing, 1840–1880* (Iowa City: University of Iowa Press, 2001) contains the useful chapter " 'Orientalism': London's East End Audiences."

2. Roy Porter, *London: A Social History* (Cambridge, MA: Harvard University Press, 1994), p. 93. The comment on Hackney was made by the journalist George Rose Emerson. For a useful overview of London's population in the nineteenth century, see Porter, *London*, chap. 9, " 'The Contagion of Numbers': The Building of the Victorian Capital 1820–1890." Davis and Emeljanow, *Reflecting the Audience*, also provide much useful information on the neighborhoods of the East End.

3. See Michael R. Booth's analysis of the connection between rise in population and theatre-building in the East End, in "East End Melodrama," *The British Theatre 1800–1900: Essays on the Nineteenth-Century Stage*. Special issue of *Theatre Survey* 17: 1 (May 1976), 58–59.

4. There are some useful studies of two of the largest East-End theatres. On the Standard, see Allan Stuart Jackson, *The Standard Theatre of Victorian England* (Rutherford, NJ: Fairleigh Dickinson University Press, 1993); on the Britannia, see Jim Davis, *The Britannia Diaries of Frederick Wilton* (London: Society for Theatre Research, 1992).

5. For the Rouse correspondence with the Lord Chamberlain, see LC 7, Public Records Office, London.

6. Diana Howard's *London Theatres and Music Halls* (London: Library Association, 1970) provides an invaluable guide to theatre records of the period.

7. Thomas Erle, *Letters from a Theatrical Scene Painter* (London: private printing, 1880), p. 81.

8. *Figaro in London* (comic periodical published from 1831 to 1839), 6 October 1838, p. 158. The play is, presumably, by Charles Somerset, who wrote a number of works for the Garrick at this time. I can, however, find no record of the play in Allardyce Nicoll, *A History of English Drama, 1660–1900* (Cambridge: Cambridge University Press, 1952–59).

9. *Figaro in London*, 27 October 1838, p. 170.

10. *Ibid.*, 6 May 1838, p. 137.

11. *Report from the Select Committee on Theatrical Licences and Regulations: together with the Proceedings of the Committee, Minutes of Evidence, and Appendix* (1866). In *Irish University Press Series of British Parliamentary Papers. Stage and Theatre*, vol. 2. Shannon: 1970, p. 31.

12. Charles Dickens, "A Cheap Theatre," in *The Dickens Theatrical Reader*, edited by Edgar and Eleanor Johnson (Boston: Little, Brown, and Co., 1964), p. 321.

13. *Ibid.*, p. 324.

14. George Bernard Shaw, "The Drama in Hoxton," in *The Saturday Review*, 9 April 1898, pp. 487–88. The scene referred to depicts four seasick men fighting over a bucket.

15. See Blanchard Jerrold, *London: A Pilgrimage*, illustrated by Gustave Doré (London: 1872), p. 46.

16. Samuel Smith, *Plays and their Supervision: A Speech by Samuel Smith, Esq., M.P., in the House of Commons, May 15th 1900 and the Reply of the Home Secretary with an Appendix* (London: Chas. Thynne, *c.* 1900). pp. 7–8.

17. For the purposes of this essay I am restricting my discussion of the working-class theatres to those of the East End. The East/West dichotomy provides, of course, an over-simplified picture. There were theatres on the Surrey-side of the Thames (such as the Victoria, the Surrey, the Bower, and Astley's Amphitheatre) that catered, at least in part, to a working-class audience; so did the Marylebone, to the north.

18. See James Stephens, *The Censorship of English Drama, 1824–1901* (Cambridge: Cambridge University Press, 1980), pp. 62–67.

19. *Register of the Lord Chamberlain's Plays* (LCP). On *Lynch Law*, see ADD MS 53703 (vol. 2, 1852–65), February 1853; On *Bound to the Wheel*, see ADD MS 53704 (vol. 3, 1866–73), March 1866.

20. *Ibid.*, ADD MS 53706 (vol. 4), December 1871.

21. *Ibid.*, vol. 3, November 1870; vol. 4, May 1878.

22. The appetite for transgressive, rule-breaking characters extended, in the East End, to female roles. Often these aggressive heroines and heroic villainesses appeared in plays written by women. See Heidi Holder, "The 'Lady Playwrights' and the 'Wild Tribes of the East': Female Dramatists in the East End Theatres, 1860–1880," in Tracy C. Davis and Ellen Donkin (eds.), *Women and Playwriting in Nineteenth-Century Britain* (Cambridge: Cambridge University Press, 1999), pp. 174–92.

23. *The Street Arab; or, Adrift on the World*. LCP 55032, British Library. P. 58v.

24. Edward Fitzball, *The Negro of Wapping* [1838?]. Prompt Book, Harvard Theatre Collection, pp. 21 and 24.

25. For a more detailed examination of the representation of racial minorities in East-End melodrama, see Heidi Holder, "Other Londoners: Race and Class in

Plays of Nineteenth-Century London Life," in Pamela Gilbert (ed.), *Imagined Londons* (New York: State University of New York Press, 2002), pp. 31–44.

26. Cited in A.E. Wilson, *East End Entertainments* (London: A. Barker, 1954), p. 74, p. 146.

27. See Davis and Emeljanow, *Reflecting the Audience*, part 3, for extended consideration of the development of Jewish audiences in the east.

28. Jim Davis gives an excellent overview of the Pavilion's years as a predominantly Jewish theatre in his essay "The East End," in Michael R. Booth and Joel Kaplan (eds.), *The Edwardian Theatre: Essays on Performance and the Stage* (Cambridge: Cambridge University Press, 1996): pp. 201–19.

29. Anthony L. Ellis, "The East End Jew at his Playhouse," *The Pall Mall Gazette*, new series 41: 78 (February 1908), p. 174.

30. See the chapter on "Illegitimate Shakespeare" in Jane Moody, *Illegitimate Theatre in London, 1770–1840* (Cambridge: Cambridge University Press, 2000), p. 135.

31. *The Theatrical Times*, 20 February 1847, p. 54.

32. *Tallis's Dramatic Magazine*, December 1850, p. 56.

33. Clipping from *The Times*, 1856 (exact date unclear). Clipping in scrapbook, Arnold's Collection, Harvard Theatre Collection TS/999.8.

34. Item in playbill file for the City of London Theatre, Harvard Theatre Collection.

35. Stephens, *Censorship*, p. 74.

36. *Rotherhithe in Olden Times; or, The Female Highwayman*, LCP 52948F; the much-cut text that received a license is LCP 52948L.

37. *The Illustrated Sporting and Theatrical News*, 2 December 1865, p. 614.

38. Playbill, 1 September 1867, Theatre Museum, London.

39. J. B. Johnstone, *London Highways and Byways*, LCP 53032L. Licensed 14 May 1864. The penny gaff scene is act II, scene 1, p. 26.

40. Elaine Ashton and Ian Clarke, "The Dangerous Woman of Melvillean Melodrama," *New Theatre Quarterly* 12: 45 (February, 1996), 39.

41. *Ibid.*

SELECT BIBLIOGRAPHY

The bibliography includes books of general interest in the field of Victorian and Edwardian theatre. Studies of individual playwrights, actors, and managers are cited in the endnotes of individual chapters, as are editions of plays and other specialized resources.

Auerbach, Nina. *Private Theatricals: the Lives of the Victorians*. Cambridge, MA: Harvard University Press, 1990.

Booth, Michael R. *Theatre in the Victorian Age* Cambridge: Cambridge University Press, 1991.

Booth, Michael R. *Victorian Spectacular Theatre, 1850–1910*. London and Boston: Routledge & Kegan Paul, 1981.

Booth, Michael. R. and Joel H. Kaplan, eds. *The Edwardian Theatre: Essays on Performance and the Stage*. Cambridge: Cambridge University Press, 1996.

Bratton, Jacky, ed. *Music Hall: Performance and Style*. Milton Keynes: Open University Press, 1986.

Bratton, Jacky, ed. *Acts of Supremacy : the British Empire and the Stage, 1790–1930*. Manchester: Manchester University Press, 1991.

Brooks, Peter. *The Melodramatic Imagination: Balzac, Henry James. Melodrama, and the Mode of Excess*. New York: Columbia University Press, 1985.

Carlson, Susan. *Women and Comedy: Rewriting the British Theatrical Tradition*. Ann Arbor: University of Michigan Press, 1991.

Corbett, Mary Jean. *Representing Femininity: Middle-Class Subjectivity in Victorian and Edwardian Women's Autobiographies*. Oxford: Oxford University Press, 1992.

Davis, Jim, and Victor Emeljanow, *Reflecting the Audience: London Theatregoing, 1840–1880*. Iowa City: University of Iowa Press, 2001.

Davis, Tracy C. *Actresses as Working Women: Their Social Identity in Victorian Culture*. London: Routledge, 1991.

Davis, Tracy C. *The Economics of the British Stage 1800–1914*. Cambridge: Cambridge University Press, 2000.

Davis, Tracy C., and Ellen Donkin, eds. *Women and Playwriting in Nineteenth-Century Britain*. Cambridge: Cambridge University Press, 1999.

Foulkes, Richard, ed. *British Theatre in the 1890s: Essays on Drama and the Stage*. Cambridge: Cambridge University Press, 1992.

Gardner, Vivien, and Susan Rutherford, eds. *The New Woman and Her Sisters : Feminism and Theatre, 1850–1914*. Ann Arbor: University of Michigan Press, 1992.

Jackson, Russell, ed. *Victorian Theatre: The Theatre in Its Time*. New York: New Amsterdam, 1989.

Kaplan, Joel, and Sheila Stowell. *Theatre and Fashion: Oscar Wilde to the Suffragettes*. Cambridge: Cambridge University Press, 1994.

Kift, Dagmar. *The Victorian Music Hall: Culture, Class and Conflict*. Cambridge: Cambridge University Press, 1996.

Macqueen Pope, W. *Carriages at Eleven: The Story of the Edwardian Theatre*. London: Hutchinson, 1947.

Marshall, Gail. *Actresses on the Victorian Stage: Feminine Performance and the Galatea Myth*. Cambridge: Cambridge University Press, 1998.

Meisel, Martin. *Realizations: Narrative, Pictorial, and Theatrical Arts in Nineenth-Century England*. Princeton: Princeton University Press, 1983.

Meisel, Martin. *Shaw and the Nineteenth Century Theatre*. Princeton: Princeton University Press, 1963.

Mayer, David. *Playing Out the Empire: Ben Hur and Other Toga-Plays and Films, 1883–1908: A Critical Anthology*. Oxford: Clarendon Press, 1994.

Penzel Frederick, *Theatre Lighting Before Electricity*. Middletown: Wesleyan University Press, 1978.

Powell, Kerry. *Oscar Wilde and the Theatre of the 1890s*. Cambridge: Cambridge University Press, 1990.

Powell, Kerry. *Women and Victorian Theatre*. Cambridge: Cambridge University Press, 1997.

Rees, Terence. *Theatre Lighting in the Age of Gas*. London: Society for Theatre Research, 1978.

Rowell, George. *Theatre in the Age of Irving*. Oxford: Basil Blackwell, 1981.

Rowell, George. *The Victorian Theatre, 1792–1914: A Survey*. Cambridge: Cambridge University Press, 1978.

Senelick, Laurence, ed. *Gender in Performance: The Presentation of Difference in the Performing Arts*. Hanover: University Press of New England, 1992.

Stephens, John Russell. *The Censorship of English Drama, 1824–1901*. Cambridge: Cambridge University Press, 1980.

Stephens, John Russell. *The Profession of the Playwright: British Theatre, 1800–1900*. Cambridge: Cambridge University Press, 1991.

Stokes, John. *Bernhardt, Terry, Duse: The Actress in Her Time*. Cambridge: Cambridge University Press, 1988.

Stokes, John. *Resistible Theatres: Enterprise and Experiment in the Late Nineteenth Century*. London: Paul Elek, 1972.

Stowell, Sheila. *A Stage of Their Own: Feminist Playwrights of the Suffrage Era*. Ann Arbor: University of Michigan Press, 1992.

Taylor, George. *Players and Performances in the Victorian Theatre*. Manchester: Manchester University Press, 1989.

Trewin, J. C., *The Edwardian Theatre*. Oxford: Basil Blackwell, 1976.

Vlock, Deborah. *Dickens, Novel Reading and the Victorian Popular Theatre*. Cambridge: Cambridge University Press, 1998.

Wilson, A. E. *Edwardian Theatre*. London: Arthur Barker, 1951.

INDEX

CAMBRIDGE COMPANIONS TO LITERATURE

CAMBRIDGE COMPANIONS TO CULTURE